VOICES OF THE POOR
From Many Lands

VOICES OF THE POOR

From Many Lands

Edited by
Deepa Narayan
Patti Petesch

*A copublication of Oxford University Press
and the World Bank*

Contents

Foreword

This is the final book in a three-part series entitled *Voices of the Poor*. The series is based on an unprecedented effort to gather the views, experiences, and aspirations of more than 60,000 poor men and women from sixty countries. The work was undertaken for the *World Development Report 2000/2001: Attacking Poverty*.

The first volume in the series, *Can Anyone Hear Us?*, draws from studies conducted in the 1990s and brings together the voices of over 40,000 poor people from fifty countries. The second volume, *Crying Out for Change*, is based on comparative fieldwork conducted in 1999 and includes the voices of over 20,000 poor men and women in twenty-three countries. *From Many Lands* presents a selection of these country studies. The Voices of the Poor study is different from all other large-scale poverty studies. Using participatory and qualitative research methods, the study presents directly, through poor people's own voices, the realities of their lives. How do poor people view poverty and wellbeing? What are their problems and priorities? What is their experience with the institutions of the state, markets, and civil society? How are gender relations faring within households and communities? We want to thank the project team led by Deepa Narayan of the Poverty Group in the World Bank, and particularly the country research teams, for undertaking this work.

What poor people share with us is sobering. A majority of them feel they are worse off and more insecure than in the past. Poor people care about many of the same things all of us care about: happiness, family, children, livelihood, peace, security, safety, dignity, and respect. Poor people's descriptions of encounters with a range of institutions call out for all of us to rethink our strategies. From the perspective of poor people, corruption, irrelevance, and abusive behavior often mar the formal institutions of the state. Nongovernmental organizations (NGOs), too, receive mixed ratings from the poor. Poor people would like NGOs to be accountable to them. Poor people's interactions with traders and markets are stamped with their powerlessness to negotiate fair prices. How then do poor people survive? They turn to their informal networks of family, kin, friends, and neighbors. But these are already stretched thin.

We commend to you the authenticity and significance of this work. What can be more important than listening to the poor and working with our partners all over the world to respond to their concerns? Our core mission is to help poor people succeed in their own efforts, and the book raises major challenges to both of our institutions and to all of us concerned about poverty. We are prepared to hold ourselves accountable, to make the effort to try to respond to these voices. Obviously we cannot do this alone. We urge you to read this book, to reflect and respond. Our hope is that the voices in this book will call you to action as they have us.

CLARE SHORT,
Secretary of State for International
Development, U.K.

JAMES D. WOLFENSOHN,
President,
World Bank

Acknowledgments

We are grateful to the poor men and women who participated in the Voices of the Poor study and shared their struggles and dreams with us.

The Voices of the Poor study was based in the Poverty Reduction Group of the World Bank, and we appreciate all of our colleagues' ongoing support. Magüi Moreno Torres conducted background research and analysis and seemingly endless fact checking for all fourteen case studies. Bryan Kurey and Talat Shah also contributed research support. Simone Cecchini, Giovanna Prennushi, and Kalpana Mehra provided guidance on quantitative data, and Simone prepared the tables in annex 2. In addition, we benefited greatly from the contributions of four senior researchers outside the Bank who drafted initial portions of many chapters: Vanessa Gray, Wendy Hammond, Carrie Meyer, and Justine Sass.

Michael Walton, Boniface Essama-Nssah, and Lynn Bennett gave us very useful comments on the opening and closing chapters. We also want to thank World Bank staff and others who provided background materials and feedback on drafts of chapters and country case studies: Nilufar Ahmad, Sabina Alkire, John Blaxall, Alf Ivar Blikberg, Sudarshan Canagarajah, Sandra Cesilini, Nancy Cooke, Aline Coudouel, Boryana Gotcheva, Simon Gray, Stella Ilieva, Polly Jones, Ratna I. Josodipoero, Sanjay Kathuria, Gregory Kisunko, Valerie Kozel, Pilar Larreamendy, William Maloney, Kofi Marrah, Suman Mehra, Stan Peabody, Jeeva Perumalpillai-Essex, Jessica Poppele, Giovanna Prennushi, Jeff Procak, Kinnon Scott, Sandor Sipos, Jim Smith, David Steel, Jorge Uquillas, Joachim von Amsberg, Eduardo Wallentin, Eliza Winters, and Salman Zaidi.

Kristin Rusch worked with us very closely for over a year, providing substantive editorial support. We could not have finished this book without her. We also thank Cathy Sunshine for her copyediting, and the Bank's Office of the Publisher for its assistance in bringing the book to publication.

This third volume was made possible through the generous financial support of the U.K. Department for International Development, the Swedish International Development Cooperation Agency, and the World Bank.

Introduction

Deepa Narayan and Patti Petesch

Living through hunger and physical hardship from infancy to premature old age; living through economic shifts that close factories and strip currency of its value in an instant; living through social turmoil, political upheaval, and war; through it all, poor men and women in communities around the world keep coming back to their deep longing for a better future for their children. *Whatever happens, they say, let the children be all right.*

From Many Lands presents the experiences of people who are worn down by persistent deprivation, and buffeted by severe shocks they feel ill equipped to overcome. Poor people's stories are a testimony to their resilience, their struggle against hopelessness, their determination to accumulate assets, and their will to live for their families—particularly their children. The stories reveal some of the reasons why poor people remain poor, despite working long hours day after day. They document frequently demeaning encounters with state, market, and civic institutions that distort well-intended political, economic, and social policies. Poor people's stories also communicate their growing insecurity in an era of global changes.

Volumes 1 and 2 of the *Voices of the Poor* series explored the striking commonalities in the experiences of poverty across countries.[1] In this final volume, we focus on the diversity of poverty in fourteen countries, highlighting key findings.[2] The countries are presented by region

Africa	South and East Asia	Europe and Central Asia	Latin America and the Caribbean
Ghana	Bangladesh	Bosnia and Herzegovina	Argentina
Malawi	India	Bulgaria	Brazil
Nigeria	Indonesia	Kyrgyz Republic	Ecuador
	Russia		Jamaica

This chapter describes the research framework, a few of the key challenges in writing and editing this book, and the importance of context in understanding poverty and illbeing.

Methodological Framework and Study Process

The methodological framework draws upon epistemological traditions from sociology, anthropology, and participatory research, particularly Participatory Poverty Assessments (PPAs). However, the study is not a conventional sociological or anthropological analysis of poverty, nor is it conventional participatory research undertaken to inform collective action at the community level. The study methodology is discussed in depth in volumes 1 and 2 and is summarized below.

Study Background

The study design was influenced by three factors: the overall objective of informing the World Bank's *World Development Report 2000/2001: Attacking Poverty* (WDR 2000/01) and the tight deadline this implied; participatory research practices; and research traditions in the World Bank.

The methodological framework was developed mainly to ensure that the study would be useful for the WDR 2000/01. The initiating brief, "Voices of the Poor to Inform the WDR 2000," written in July 1998, begins with the premise: "The poor are the true poverty experts. Hence, a policy document on poverty strategies for the 21st century must be based on the experiences, priorities, reflections, and recommendations of poor children, women, and men."[3]

Research funding for Voices of the Poor was confirmed in November 1998, and the WDR team wanted the main results by July 1999. The challenge was thus to complete a very large study in a very short time. The deadline pressures led to the decision to narrow the focus of the study to four sets of issues: poor people's definitions of who is poor and who is not; leading problems and priorities in their communities; the most important institutions in their daily lives; and changes in gender relations over the past decade.

Second, the methodology was influenced greatly by the decision to use participatory research methods. Participatory research tools are usually open-ended and interactive to enable an exploration of issues and shared learning among local people and outsiders. With participatory methods, local people act as partners in problem identification, data collection, analysis, and follow-up action. A range of techniques is used to facilitate participatory research, including small group discussions. Small group sessions often incorporate diagrammatic exercises, such as the wellbeing matrix found in the Russia chapter, or the institutional evaluation in the Brazil chapter. Appendix 3 summarizes the topics and methods used by the research teams for this study.[4]

Third, the study design was influenced by the World Bank's research paradigm, which is quantitative in nature. Quantitative studies typically entail conducting large household surveys that are nationally representative. These research methods are well established, and World Bank poverty statistics are valued worldwide by academics and policymakers. To be taken seriously in this environment, a study based on participatory methods would have to be conducted on a sufficiently large scale to reduce the probability that it would be dismissed as producing merely interesting anecdotes.[5] This concern led to a decision to conduct the new comparative study in at least fifteen to twenty countries, which eventually became the twenty-three-country study on which this book and volume 2 are based.[6]

Research Partnerships

The Voices of the Poor project catalyzed diverse research partnerships across the globe. Researchers came from academia, field-based NGOs, private consulting firms or think tanks, and World Bank staff, or were independent consultants.

The study was announced within the World Bank in January 1999, and staff were invited to submit proposals. In Indonesia, Nigeria, and Vietnam, field-based Bank staff managed the study and were also closely involved in the fieldwork and analysis. In an additional sixteen countries, numerous headquarters-based Bank staff also became involved, identifying matching research funds and local researchers, and reviewing the sample design and draft reports for those countries.

NGOs in Bangladesh, Bolivia, India, and Somaliland managed the study themselves. In the case of Bangladesh, the umbrella NGO Working Group on the World Bank contacted us about participating in the study and funded that entire study themselves. It was felt that field-based NGOs were particularly likely to use the findings to take quick follow-up action at the community level.

Sampling Framework

The sampling framework for the study was purposive. Researchers were asked to select eight to fifteen communities to reflect the most prevalent poverty groups and the diversity of poverty in their particular countries. Community selection was based on existing poverty maps and socioeconomic information, geography, ethnicity, particularities of vulnerable social groups, location of industry, and other factors that define the nature of poverty in a particular context. The sampling methods as applied to particular countries are described in the country chapters. The findings represent primarily the voices of those still in poverty, not those who have escaped poverty.

Within communities, researchers used a variety of techniques to reach poor women, men, elderly people, youths, and occasionally children. Participants in small group discussions were identified with the assistance of key local and external contacts who were familiar with the community. Researchers also identified study participants through the work of the initial discussion groups.[7] Nevertheless, researchers did not always have control over who participated in the groups. It is quite likely that the poorest of the poor are underrepresented in the study because they are extremely marginalized within communities, even among other poor people.

In addition to working with groups, researchers conducted open-ended interviews to gather brief life histories of men and women who had fallen into poverty, been poor their whole lives, or managed to climb out of poverty. Researchers also held interviews with a range of people who were familiar with the communities, including local and district officials, informal and formal leaders, and schoolteachers.

Data Analyses

The evidence or data from qualitative research differs from survey evidence. Qualitative research methods are often viewed with suspicion by those who are used to structured, quantitative surveys. According to their argument, because the units of analysis are text data rather than numbers, researchers can pick and choose what they want to report based on their biases. However, minimizing bias is also an issue for researchers who use numerical data. In both qualitative and quantitative methods of research it is important to use techniques to minimize bias and to disclose data processing methods.[8]

An inductive approach to systematic content analysis was used in this study. At the field level, researchers kept detailed field notes and cross-checked findings. They aggregated findings first within each discussion group and individual interview and then across discussion groups and interviews in preparing a consolidated community report. In several countries, workshops were held with the entire field team to compare and analyze community-level findings. Each country team then prepared a national synthesis report.

To further cross-check data, two data subsets were systematically quantified. In addition, study findings were cross-checked with other quantitative data on growth, poverty trends, human development indicators, and other relevant research, although these are not always cited.

Frequency counts were applied to two topic areas, institutions and gender, whose categories for analysis evolved through a painstaking, iterative process of identifying and sorting common themes and determining the number of times these themes were mentioned across the data sets. This method was first applied to understanding what poor people said about institutions. Within each discussion group, poor people rated institutions as most important, most effective, and most ineffective. The five institutions considered most important by each discussion group in each community were tabulated in two different ways, weighted and unweighted. Two coders then recoded the entire data set to ensure that the ratings were correct. This process alone took two full-time research analysts two months. The patterns of results reported in each national report were generally confirmed, although there were differences in some cases. The analysis contributed, for instance, to the more nuanced findings about NGOs and religious organizations and confirmed the importance of family, kin, and friends in many poor people's survival strategies.[9]

Similarly, the patterns of findings on domestic violence were complex, problematic, and controversial. To cross-check country-specific findings, two researchers went back to the data provided by each discussion group to identify what participants said about trends in physical violence against women in their homes. This research did indeed modify the initial findings, which stressed overall declines in violence. The additional analysis revealed that physical domestic violence was present in 91 percent of the communities. Discussion groups from less than one-third of the study communities reported declines in levels of violence against women in the household in recent years, but even in many of these communities, domestic violence was still seen to be widespread.

To bring consistency to the presentation and analysis across the country chapters, we as editors played a major role in shaping the analytical framework, drafting, integrating other data sources, and incorporating the feedback of reviewers. In addition to the above quality checks, this book required further analysis of the country-level findings and community reports.[10]

The chapter findings were compared with quantitative data on economic and poverty trends, human development indicators, the benefit incidence of public spending, and the size of the informal economy. These statistics proved to be especially valuable because they helped frame, affirm, and add credibility to the economic and social trends that poor people reported.

On two issues the quantitative data were not consistent with our findings. First, there are a few countries where the overall economy was growing, but most study participants reported rising hunger and hardship in their communities. Such was the case in Ghana, for instance, where a closer review of geographic poverty data revealed that large areas of the country are not benefiting from the country's growing economy, and researchers visited some of these areas. Second, official data on unemployment often failed to convey the extent of joblessness and poor people's reliance on temporary and informal work.

Follow-up

Without links to funds, participatory policy research has a low probability of bringing immediate benefits to the lives of poor participants. The methodology guide and field training stressed the importance of not raising expectations in poor communities and of being explicit in not promising any follow-up projects.

Nonetheless, we tried to conduct the study and choose partners in ways that would maximize the probability of action at the community level. Community feedback on results was a part of all research contracts. Once the study was completed, we raised additional funds for study teams either to go back to the communities themselves or to work with others who had field presence. Five research teams took advantage of these funds. In Brazil, a community leader independently distributed the report for his community, including sending it to the state governor and president of the country.

In response to the study, the World Bank has scaled up its investments in community-driven development activities in all regions. In addition, WDR 2000/01 as well as most of the World Bank's major strategy documents for the twenty-three participating countries and for numerous sectors (transport, gender, rural development, urban development, social protection, health, water, energy) draw upon the global or national findings from the Voices of the Poor study.[11]

More generally, the study has helped qualitative and participatory methods to become more widely recognized as a credible research tool for understanding poverty and for informing the design, undertaking, and evaluation of actions to reduce poverty. The study has also reawakened a dialogue among researchers from qualitative and quantitative research traditions, and the debate is moving forward constructively and across disciplines.[12]

Challenges in Writing and Editing this Book

Throughout the study process we follow standard rules and procedures for good qualitative research. We do, however, break with convention in how we present our findings. We decided to forego technical, academic writing in favor of a straightforward, simple style that highlights poor people's own voices. Our use of direct quotes to present findings has been a source of controversy surrounding the first two volumes, with some referring to it as "analysis by quotation."[13] We want to reiterate here that quotations were selected *after* intense content analyses clarified the pattern of findings; quotations by themselves, obviously, are not an analytical device.

We use two other writing devices to communicate the findings. First, although the fieldwork was conducted in 1999, we write in the present tense to try to narrow the gap between the reader and the study participants, whose poverty is not in the past. Second, in the interest of readability and to conform with the two previous volumes in the series, we have chosen not to qualify findings every time we report them. Instead, we urge the reader to keep in mind that the findings cannot be generalized and applied to all poor people of that country.[14]

Throughout our analyses and writing, we were conscious of the tension between presenting specific contexts and presenting overall patterns. One of the greatest contributions of open-ended research is the focus on the differing contexts of social actors. Social differences did emerge based on ethnicity, geography, income, caste, and gender. We discuss these differences where there is sufficient data. While we often use the phrase "poor people," we do not intend to homogenize the poor. We identify speakers by gender, age, ethnicity, and the like, wherever possible.

Several reviewers of draft chapters were upset by the "negative," "exaggerated," or "emotional" tone of poor people's reports. Some of the strongest feedback was expressed by reviewers who work in the Europe and Central Asia region, who reacted to poor people's expressions of hopelessness and to their "distorted nostalgia" for the secure jobs and public services that they had in the past. Reviewers felt that the participants and the researchers had forgotten food and other shortages as well as the old adage, "Your employer pretends to pay you, so you pretend to work."

Regardless of the validity of these reviewers' points, open-ended participatory methodology is designed to elicit people's views. Trained researchers probe without leading, cross-check information with others, and record poor people's interpretations of their own experiences. Hence, to assume that people are remembering incorrectly when their memories do not fit our biases would be a violation of the basic tenet of the open-ended participatory approach.

The Importance of Context Specificity

Poverty—who is poor and why—is complex and context-specific. Understanding poverty fully requires understanding its historical, political, social, cultural, ecological, and economic contexts. This study does not draw extensively on these disciplines to offer an in-depth analysis of poverty's root causes. We nonetheless endeavor to provide enough background to give the reader at least a minimal framework for making sense of patterns that emerge in each country across the communities and social groups visited. The introduction to each chapter offers a brief review of key political, economic, and social trends, and additional context is provided where we felt it particularly important to do so.

As a result of concentrating on specific countries and local realities in specific communities, more distinct patterns emerge from our data here than are available in the first two volumes. To better illustrate, consider the challenge of distinguishing who is rich from who is poor and why. Poor people for this study engaged in lengthy discussions about these differences and provided concrete criteria and reasoning for identifying rich and poor.

In Bosnia, for example, poor people repeatedly cite the war as the main cause of poverty. Those who are poor, estimated to be some 80 to 95 percent of households, are "unemployed" or have "irregular and insecure income . . . poor housing, no health insurance, [and] fear of not being able to pay bills," according to discussion groups in Mostar West, Bosnia. Poor households also included refugees, displaced people, and pensioners. Participants single out war profiteers as among the better-off groups in their communities. For poor people, the war and wrenching recovery have brought a massive displacement of people, extensive joblessness, and the disappearance of state services that are desperately needed. These findings are unique to this country among the fourteen case studies. But Bosnian participants also describe the rich in terms that are commonly used to describe rich people across the region: the rich are those who have secure jobs, a house or an apartment, and health insurance.

The story about who is poor and why in Nigeria is altogether different, although there are also some striking similarities. As in Bosnia, there have been dramatic surges in poverty in the 1990s. In addition, ethnic divisions and corruption tear at the political and social fabric and disrupt basic state operations in a country that might otherwise be quite rich, given its oil wealth. A discussion group of men from Umuoba Road–Aba Waterside, a shantytown in Nigeria's Abia state, say that the wealthy members now comprise 5 percent of their community, down from 10 percent a decade ago. Wealthy people own cars, eat well, educate their children, and have investments, but they are no longer able to help people as they did in the past. At the other end of the scale are the approximately 60 percent of the community who are "jobless" and "survive on alms." Their numbers have nearly doubled in the past decade.

In Bosnia, except for refugees, poor people in urban areas generally have access to basic infrastructure, whereas in Nigeria, in urban areas, access to working toilets and clean water is a distant dream. Life expectancy in Nigeria is 47, in Bosnia 73—a gap of 26 years. The tables in appendix 1 will help give the reader a sense of the vast differences among the countries featured in this book.

Moreover, poverty experienced in a crowded and sewage-flooded urban slum of Nigeria is profoundly different from poverty in a remote Nigerian village that survives on subsistence agriculture. Thus, the case studies distinguish rural from urban findings within countries, although many other dimensions of difference are also explored.

Poverty also may look quite different seen through the eyes of a poor man or a poor woman. Joblessness, hunger, and the shame and stigma that accompany poverty take an enormous toll on households. Men and women are often forced to forsake deeply ingrained gender roles and endure widespread social disapproval as they move into new roles solely in order to survive. While unemployment may strip men of their breadwinner role, poor women out of desperation frequently resort to work outside the home even though only degrading or low-paying work is available to them. In Nurali Pur, Bangladesh, women earn only half of what men earn for the same work—when they get paid in cash at all. In most cases, women work for food or in-kind compensation.

Poor people in very diverse settings report that the stress this situation causes to poor households frequently triggers increasing family conflicts, rising alcohol abuse among men, and heightened domestic violence against women. Yet, men and women may perceive even physical violence very differently, and again context is vital to understanding these differences. In small group discussions about domestic abuse in Ghana, with the exception of one community, both men and women report that physical violence against women is widespread. Married women describe forced sex as abuse, and say that they are beaten if they refuse sex and "even then the men will satisfy themselves." Women feel they should have the right to refuse sex, especially to avoid HIV/AIDS as their husbands refuse to practice safe sex. A man from the same community, in contrast, says, "If a man beats his wife because she has refused to give in to sex the man is justified."

Gender barriers are a critical source of deprivation but by no means the only one. Researchers met with Roma (gypsy) men and women of diverse ethnic, religious, and linguistic backgrounds in Sofia, Dimitrovgrad, Varna, and Razgrad in Bulgaria. In sharing their lives, the participants repeatedly describe experiences with ethnic discrimination when seeking jobs or state services. They also feel keenly disadvantaged by their neighborhood locale, as many Roma reside in segregated quarters that lack services readily available to their better-off neighbors. Moreover, exclusion from social benefits begins early in life: many Roma children attend segregated schools, and dropout rates are extraordinarily high. Other country reports illustrate experiences of poverty unique to specific social groups, such as displaced people in Bosnia, pensioners in Russia, indigenous people and blacks in Ecuador, and lower castes in India.

As with definitions of who is poor and why, the institutional findings are also context-specific. The case studies for Argentina and Brazil illustrate this well. The two countries happen to be very similar with respect to the leading problems identified by men and women in the urban communities visited. Both reports feature sections on deindustrialization, increased unemployment, and the rise of the service and informal economies, as well as sections on high levels of crime and violence in the streets and abuse of women and children in the home. The case studies diverge, however, in the most important institutions identified by study participants.

In the slums of Brazil, community-based organizations emerge overwhelmingly as the most highly rated institutions among discussions groups. Many of these community groups were formed to resist eviction from lands settled illegally; once these legal battles were won, the community groups went on to secure infrastructure and services for the residents. These groups and the local Catholic Church are the ones that Brazilian participants in the study say they routinely turn to when problems arise. In contrast, participants from Argentina display much less enthusiasm when discussing the contributions of community groups and churches, although the work of soup kitchens, neighborhood watches, and the like is mentioned and valued.

The reasons for lower levels of community activism in Argentina are not clear from this study; however, participants do discuss a plethora of public assistance programs that help them cope with hunger and lack of income, although many problems with quality and coverage are reported. Poor people also say that some forms of community activism were once and continue to be a target of police repression.

The institutional landscape in a country like Russia is different still. There, the work of community groups does not even figure in discussions of important local institutions. Nor do discussion groups in this country assign much importance to state institutions of any kind. Rather, poor people across the Russian communities visited report that the once-extensive public supports have all but collapsed in the transition to democracy and competitive markets. In their place, participants say, they can only rely on their personal networks of *blizkie*, literally "close ones"—family, neighbors, and friends. This leaves them deeply insecure because many of these people also have strained resources.

Of course, in every country, the mere fact of being poor is itself cause for being isolated, left out, looked down upon, alienated, pushed aside, and ignored by those who are better off. This ostracism and voicelessness tie together poor people's experiences across very different contexts. The manifestations of this exclusion, however, are endlessly diverse, as poor people's experiences in the country chapters attest.

Organization of the Book

Each country chapter that follows opens with a brief life story. These life stories were chosen because they highlight concerns raised not only by poor women and men living in that particular community, but because the same concerns were echoed in other parts of the country. The chapters then unfold around particular sets of issues that emerged repeatedly in group discussions and individual interviews throughout each country. It is important to stress again that this was primarily a global study, and the purposively selected and small number of communities visited at the country level means that the findings reported in the chapters cannot be generalized to represent poverty conditions for an entire nation. Despite these caveats, the chapters bring to life the peculiarities of what it means to be poor in various communities, in fourteen countries, and from a perspective that is not often featured in development literature: the perspective of poor people.

In the final chapter we look at four major patterns that emerge from these very different regions and contexts. First, because an array of shocks and disadvantages coalesce into formidable barriers to wellbeing and security, poor people need an equally diverse set of assets and capabilities if they are to survive and overcome poverty. Second, although many poor people do not participate in the formal economy, economy-wide policies and shocks have a profound impact on poor people's lives, often depleting their assets and increasing their insecurity. Third, the culture of mediating institutions often negatively distorts the impact of well-intended policies and excludes poor people from gains. Finally, gender inequity within households, which is reflected in broader institutions of society, is persistent, and children are acutely vulnerable as households struggle to survive. We conclude by sketching out a vision of development that focuses on five areas of action to increase poor people's assets and capabilities, empowering them to move out of poverty.

Poverty anywhere is a problem for people everywhere. Economic policy is embedded in political and social realities. The deep problems of inequality, unaccountable governance, and failed states around the world must be addressed with urgency. Poor people's long hours of work for next to nothing, their resilience in the face of setbacks, their determination not to surrender to hopelessness, and their deep longing to better their lives for themselves and their children call us to act now.

Notes

1. For volume 1, see Deepa Narayan, with Raj Patel, Kai Schafft, Anne Rademacher, and Sarah Koch-Schulte, *Voices of the Poor: Can Anyone Hear Us?* (New York: Oxford University Press for the World Bank, 2000). For volume 2, see Deepa Narayan, Robert Chambers, Meera K. Shah, and Patti Petesch, *Voices of the Poor: Crying Out for Change* (New York: Oxford University Press for the World Bank, 2000).

2. The fourteen country profiles in this book are part of the twenty-three-country Voices of the Poor study, undertaken by the World Bank to inform *World Development Report 2000/2001: Attacking Poverty.* The Voices of the Poor study draws from discussions with 60,000 poor men and women from sixty countries, and consists of two parts. Volume 1 in the series, *Can Anyone Hear Us?,* is based on eighty-one Participatory Poverty Assessments carried out in the 1990s with 40,000 poor people. However, these studies, as discussed in detail in volume 1, were conducted using different methods, at different times, and for different purposes. To complement the analyses of existing studies, a new set of studies was launched in 1999, based on a common methodology in twenty-three countries: Argentina, Bangladesh, Bolivia, Bosnia and Herzegovina, Brazil, Bulgaria, Ecuador, Egypt, Ethiopia, Ghana, India, Indonesia, Jamaica, Kyrgyz Republic, Malawi, Nigeria, Russia, Somaliland, Sri Lanka, Thailand, Uzbekistan, Vietnam, and Zambia. The findings from these studies are reported in volume 2, *Crying Out for Change,* and in the present volume.

3. Deepa Narayan, "Voices of the Poor to Inform the *WDR 2000*" (World Bank, Poverty Group, internal memorandum, July 1998).

4. To introduce some comparability across countries, a detailed sixty-seven-page methodological guide was developed in Washington for the research teams. The guide was based on discussion of methods in three workshops and pilot studies to test the methods in four countries: Thailand, India, Bolivia, and Sri Lanka. The methodology guide is available on the Voices of the Poor website at www.worldbank.org/poverty/voices/reports.htm.

5. At the time of the study more than eighty Participatory Poverty Assessments and many more Social Assessments had been completed. There is a long tradition of social analysis within the World Bank; however, the impact of these studies until recently has been very uneven. Recent changes include requiring all projects to specify the kind of social assessments undertaken to inform project design and to specify the extent of participation by a range of stakeholders. The World Bank is also currently developing methods to conduct Poverty and Social Impact Analyses to inform the design, sequencing, and implementation of macroeconomic policy making.

6. Contrasting with desires to do a large-scale study were suggestions for a smaller and more open-ended study from participatory research practitioners outside the Bank who were advising the study. These and other differences of opinion about the study process meant that many compromises had to be made, sometimes with less than satisfying results. For example, agreement could not be reached to include a questionnaire that probed the same institutional and social issues, to integrate random sampling methods, and to quantify the entire data set at a later stage. On other issues, such as whether to develop a standardized methodology guide to be used across countries and whether to conduct the study in a large number of countries, consensus was eventually reached.

7. Some discussion groups created social maps that indicated the location of poor households. Also, many groups conducted a detailed wellbeing exercise that involved identifying specific characteristics of poor and better-off people and households and estimating their percentages in the communities.

8. For a detailed discussion of content analysis see *Voices of the Poor* volume 1, *Can Anyone Hear Us?*, 18–27, and volume 2, *Crying Out for Change*, 13–18.

9. Some researchers have asked why the World Bank was not featured in the institutional analysis. The answer is simple. The World Bank works through governments, and most people at the community level do not know whether particular activities are financed by the World Bank or not.

10. We were supported in this additional analysis by four senior research consultants, a full-time research assistant, and two part-time research assistants.

11. Follow-up has been most systematic in Uganda and Vietnam, where government officials were involved throughout the study process and developed poverty action plans based on the findings.

12. See Ravi Kanbur, ed., "Qual-Quant: Qualitative and Quantitative Poverty Appraisal—Complementarities, Tensions and the Way Forward" (working paper, Cornell University, Department of Applied Economics and Management, Ithaca, N.Y., May 2001).

13. This issue of using poor people's voices to communicate the findings after painstaking content analysis is also discussed in *Voices of the Poor* volume 1, *Can Anyone Hear Us?*, 23–24, and volume 2, *Crying Out for Change*, 18.

14. In both previous volumes we caution against over-generalizing, but have chosen to write without constant qualifiers. See *Voices of the Poor* volume 1, *Can Anyone Hear Us?*, 23–24, and volume 2, *Crying Out for Change*, 18.

Ghana

"Empty Pockets"

Ernest Y. Kunfaa and Tony Dogbe
with Heather J. MacKay and Celia Marshall[1]

Ziem Der lives in Tabe Ere, a settlement of nearly 400 households in the northern savanna zone. It is Ghana's poorest region, where 70 percent of the rural population and 43 percent of the urban population fall below the expenditure poverty line. Bounded by the Black Volta River and the border with Burkina Faso, it is a low-lying area of grasslands, shrubs, and scattered trees; rain falls sporadically between April and September. Clean drinking water is scarce, and there are no sanitation, power, or postal facilities in the village. It is four kilometers from Tabe Ere to the nearest paved road, and the nearest health service is nine kilometers away. The community has one small primary school.

Ziem was born in 1948, the fourth of sixteen children. His father owned land as well as sheep, goats, and cattle. Ziem's father did not view formal education as a priority for his children, and consequently only four of the siblings attended school; Ziem was not one of them. Ziem describes himself as zung *or "blind," a metaphor for illiterate. He explains that because he is unable to read or write, he cannot get a job in town.*

Ziem has two wives and eight children of his own. In addition, when his brother died, he left Ziem his two wives and seven children, bringing the number of people in Ziem's household to twenty. Feeding his large family has become extremely difficult for Ziem. His wives search for firewood, which they then trade for food.

Ziem emphasizes that he was not always poor. When his father died, the father's herd was divided among Ziem and his brothers, so Ziem once had plenty of animals and a productive farm. But in 1997 twelve of his

cattle were stolen in one night; another fourteen were stolen the follow-
ing year. Meanwhile, most of his goat herd has fallen ill with dysentery.
Adding to his hardship, in recent years the rains have been unreliable, and
the soil no longer yields what it used to.

Ziem attributes his downfall primarily to the theft of his cattle, but
he adds that one's fortunes—good or bad—depend on God. He observes
that it is easier for a rich man to fall into poverty than for a poor man to
pull himself up into a state of wellbeing.

Ziem's community is able to provide scant assistance to help him and
his family survive. Social networks, employment opportunities, and gov-
ernment services are strained or simply nonexistent. Like Ziem, many
people in Tabe Ere live in extreme poverty. Residents estimate that 80
percent of them have but one tattered piece of clothing to wear, insuffi-
cient food, no money, no shoes, and no relatives who can help.

While Ghana's economic and poverty trends have been positive overall in the 1990s, there are important regional differences. This
study presents the experiences and perceptions of poor people whose
communities, like Tabe Ere, are very poor and have not participated in
Ghana's growing economy.

Ghana's GDP averaged 4.3 percent growth between 1990 and 1999.
Similar improvements occurred with respect to poverty rates: expenditure
poverty fell from 52 percent of the population in 1991–92 to just under
40 percent in 1998–99. The largest poverty reductions, however, have
been heavily concentrated in two areas: Accra, the nation's capital, where
the population below the expenditure poverty line fell from 23 percent to
4 percent between 1991 and 1999; and the forest zone, where the poverty rate declined from 62 percent to 38 percent of the population in the
same period. Elsewhere in the country, poverty reductions have been very
small, and in the urban centers of the savanna zone, the poverty rate actually worsened. Another feature of poverty in Ghana is that it remains
quite severe despite overall declines. Thirty percent of the country's 18.8
million people could not meet their basic food needs in 1998–99, and this
figure decreased only marginally in the 1990s.[2]

Ghana, now a multiparty democracy, was ruled by the National
Democratic Congress of Jerry Rawlings at the time of the study. He came
to power in a military coup in 1981, and won the elections that ushered
in the 1992 transition from military rule. John Agyekum Kufuor of the

ruling New Patriotic Party was sworn in on January 7, 2001, for a four-year term. The Rawlings administration, with extensive donor support, had steadily guided the country toward a more open economy, but the pace of reforms—which included reducing fiscal deficits and the size of the public sector, as well as improving infrastructure and delivery of basic services—was uneven.

Researchers visited seven rural and two urban communities across Ghana (see table 1, Study Communities in Ghana, at the end of this chapter). The research areas were chosen to reflect the country's diverse geography and poor population.[3] Preference was given to communities where the researchers had previous experience and could recruit local researchers. The nine study communities are distributed among Ghana's four geographic zones. Located in the northern savanna are Tabe Ere, Dobile Yirkpong, and Adaboya. This zone, the poorest, has the worst ecological degradation and least developed services in the country. The Atlantic coastal zone is represented by Teshie, a gritty seaside slum on the fringe of Accra; the village of Doryumu is also located in the coastal zone. In the middle belt, where lush forest used to predominate, are the communities of Atonsu Bokro and Twabidi. The former is an urban neighborhood on the outskirts of Kumasi, Ghana's second largest city, while Twabidi is a remote forest settlement. Finally, Ghana's so-called transition zone is represented by Asukawkaw, a resettlement project associated with the Volta dam, and also by the village of Babatokuma.

Research teams interviewed a wide cross-section of community members. Group discussions were conducted with people who shared common characteristics based on gender, profession, or age. The history of each community was obtained through interviews with chiefs and other community elders. A total of fifty-six discussion groups were conducted, of which forty-three consisted solely of poor people. The teams also conducted in-depth individual case studies in each community, usually of a poor woman, a poor man, a poor youth, and a woman who was previously poor but is now better-off. A total of forty-one such case studies were conducted, covering sixteen poor people, nineteen people who are better-off now but once were poor, and four people who were rich and are now poor.

Experienced researchers from Ghana's Centre for the Development of People conducted the study. Fieldworkers included social workers, professional researchers, civil servants, gender/women's advocates, traditional rulers, and development practitioners. Fieldwork was carried out during March and April 1999.

This chapter first explores the acute nature of illbeing among the poor men and women who participated in this study, focusing on rural and urban hunger and on people's livelihoods and coping strategies. The chapter then turns to a discussion of basic infrastructure missing in poor communities, followed by study participants' views of the public and civic institutions with which they interact. Finally, we hear from poor women and men regarding gender norms and their effects on families' wellbeing.

Hunger and Illbeing

Farmers in Dobile Yirkpong refer to 80 percent of their community as "empty pocket," meaning "a person who has nothing but the body God gave him, is unable to feed his family most of the year, and cannot send his children to school." Similarly, men and women in Doryumu say that 70 percent of the community "owns one piece of clothing, looks pale and hungry, [and] walks barefoot." Older women in Asukawkaw report that 96 percent of their village "does not have enough to eat."

In some rural communities visited, poor men and women point to hunger as the defining characteristic of poverty and illbeing in their communities. A man in Dobile Yirkpong says, "Food is life, and no hungry man can claim to have a good life." In Adaboya a woman states, "Poverty is when you are not getting enough to eat." In Babatokuma poor people say that wellbeing is directly proportional to the quantity of food in one's possession.

Urban study participants also describe extensive and severe illbeing, but more often focus on material deprivations other than food. A discussion group in Teshie reports that 85 to 90 percent of the 200,000 residents "wear tattered clothes and depend on charity for survival." Twenty percent of Atonsu Bokro's inhabitants are said to be "at the dying point" due to lack of jobs, money, and education. Moreover, children from these poor families cannot afford the education necessary to find a good job. Acknowledging that their children will probably not be able to help them financially in their old age, Atonsu Bokro women expect to be even worse off in the future.

The name Twabidi literally means "cut some and eat." The once-dense forests around this farming community used to be a bountiful resource, but an expanding population, deforestation, exhausted soils, and lack of rainfall have brought hunger and illness to the village's 800 residents. Women there report that 60 percent of their community can find work that pays "only for enough food to eat but not enough to save any money." Another 30 percent of the community is said to be so poor that they cannot eat regularly. Figure 1 shows how a discussion group of women in Twabidi identified the multiple causes and impacts of poverty in their village.

Like the women in Twabidi, poor men and women across the communities visited in Ghana identify many causes and impacts of poverty; however, their lists of causes converge around a few key disadvantages. Similar diagrams made in all nine communities show that poor people consider lack of money, unemployment, and having too many children as leading causes of poverty. Other causes mentioned in most communities relate to low crop yields and soil infertility, and to diseases and ill health. In their diagrams on the impacts of poverty, every single community mentions poor health or premature death. Other common impacts include crime, especially stealing, as well as madness and mental stress. In five communities, prostitution is identified as an impact of poverty.

As indicated in figure 1 and in the brief life stories throughout this chapter, poor people often speak of their large households and the added stress this can place on meager resources and social relations. In almost every diagram they create on the causes of poverty, women and men have included "unplanned births," "lack of family planning," or "too many children." According to a discussion group of men in Adaboya, "At first the people were not numerous, but now they have plenty of children, and because the crop yield is not good they cannot care for the children. Hence, both the parents and children become poor." Feelings of being neglected or abandoned by family also emerge in many other discussions about what it means to be poor. A group of young people in Babatokuma says that half the people in their village "have no food, no money, no wife or husband, and no children; live in isolation; and are hopeless and miserable." Women in Tabe Ere speak of giving birth to children who are neglected by their fathers, and they view this as a form of punishment from the men.

While poverty is declining in some areas of the country, with very few exceptions discussion groups in the nine communities visited report that the percentage of poor people in their villages and settlements has increased, and they view overall conditions where they live as more difficult at present than ten years ago. Many discussion groups indicate that there are fewer better-off residents than before. In Tabe Ere drastic declines in the fortunes of the rich are attributed to cattle theft. A discussion group of men in Adaboya says that rich and poor alike are worse off today than

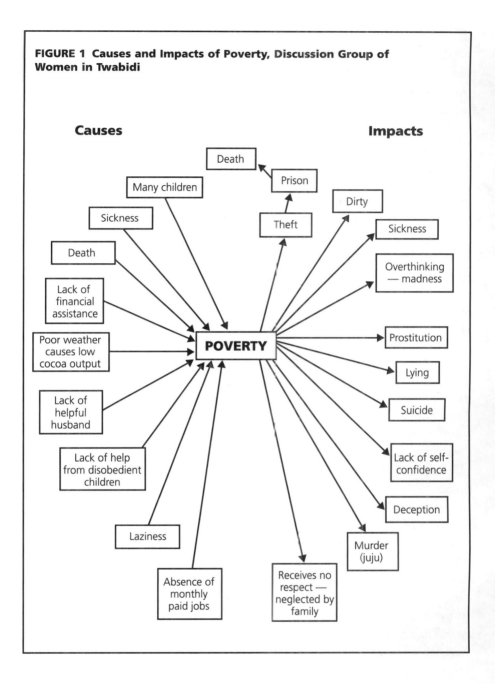

FIGURE 1 Causes and Impacts of Poverty, Discussion Group of Women in Twabidi

Causes

Death

Many children

Prison

Sickness

Dirty

Theft

Death

Sickness

Lack of financial assistance

Overthinking — madness

Poor weather causes low cocoa output

POVERTY

Prostitution

Lying

Lack of helpful husband

Suicide

Lack of help from disobedient children

Lack of self-confidence

Deception

Laziness

Murder (juju)

Absence of monthly paid jobs

Receives no respect — neglected by family

Impacts

ten years ago due to large families and population increases, loss of livestock, poor rains, and poor crop yields. The next sections explore in greater detail poor people's perceptions of the principal causes of these negative trends, as well as their survival strategies.

No Money

In all the communities except urban Teshie, where unemployment is viewed as the leading hardship, participants emphasize that lack of capital is a pressing problem that makes it impossible for them to get enough to eat and improve their livelihoods. Many poor Ghanaians remark that since the economy has become monetized, life is more difficult because one needs money in order to eat, farm, engage in petty trade, go to the hospital, and clothe oneself.

Bayor Dakorah, a 50-year-old man from Babatokuma, began life as a mason but is now a poor farmer. Bayor describes poverty as a person's "inability to get money for farming in order to feed himself, his wife, and his children." He says,

> I started work . . . as a mason, but life was not all that smooth, so I left Tamale to return to Babatokuma to start farming. But I wish I had remained in Tamale as a mason because ever since I became a farmer things have changed from bad to worse. I do not have any friends. Nobody comes to visit me because I have no money.

Bayor's farm does not yield enough food to feed his family, so he never has any surplus produce to sell. "At times I work as a farm laborer for other people to get money for other needs. My wife farms along with me and burns charcoal [to be sold as fuel] for the family's upkeep," he explains.

Similarly, women and middle-aged men in Doryumu say that the main cause of poverty in their rural community is lack of capital for farming. "We are basically farmers like the Ashantis. In Ashanti one can weed with the cutlass because their soil is good. Over here our soil is claylike, therefore we need a tractor to weed the soil. Tractors cost money; we don't have the money so we sit at home." In Doryumu groups of men and women reiterate that money enables one to do everything one needs as well as to gain respect and dignity from all sections of society. "With money we could get a tractor and pay our children's school fees so that they would prosper," a middle-aged woman in Doryumu notes. Women in Twabidi say they could expand their farms if they had money to employ labor and buy other farming inputs that would facilitate their work.

Vendors and would-be entrepreneurs in both urban and rural communities also single out lack of money as a principal hindrance to their trade and to more active markets. Ohemaa Addae, a woman from Aton-su Bokro, says, "My main problem is lack of money." She explains that with capital she wouldn't be poor today, because she could trade more, rent decent housing, pay her children's school fees, and eat well. A 38-year-old woman in Dobile Yirkpong says her main need is for money to launch a small business. Without the initial start-up capital, she believes, she will remain poor forever. Mary Esi Asiedu, a woman who trades yams in Babatokuma, struggles in a slow market. She remarks,

> *Ten years ago was far better than today. I built my house five years ago; if I had wanted to build it today, I could not have built it. Now, customers don't buy my yams, not because people are no longer hungry or because they don't eat yams anymore, but because they don't have the money. Now, even when I sell on credit, it is difficult for me to get the money.*

Diverse Obstacles to Farming

Poverty in Ghana is highest by far among those whose principal livelihood is food crop farming; they account for 58 percent of those identified as poor.[4] Subsistence agriculture is the main livelihood in every rural community in the study, and all are beset by food insecurity and hunger. In addition to lack of capital discussed above, poor people identify bad roads, a range of weather and environmental problems, and livestock theft as the major obstacles to more successful farming and food security in their communities.

Bad or nonexistent roads emerge as problems for six of the seven rural communities visited. Men in Twabidi point out that their road becomes impassable during the rainy season. Also, truck drivers charge very high fees to transport farmers' crops because of the rough road. As a result, the men say, a large share of their harvest remains on the farms, creating post-harvest losses and deterring farmers from improving yields. Likewise, a discussion group of men in Adaboya, a village eight kilometers from the nearest road, says their security would improve greatly if a "direct road would be constructed to Bongo to improve business and trading." All but one of the six discussion groups in Asukawkaw named their poor road as a major problem for the community, and in Babatokuma a "lack of roads to farms" is viewed as a significant cause of poverty.

In addition to widespread transportation difficulties, people in every community report lower rainfall in recent years, and they describe very harmful effects from this change. A group of men in Adaboya indicates that ten years ago they could depend on plentiful rains for their crops, a full river, and abundant vegetation for their livestock. But nowadays, they say, late, irregular, and inadequate rains have put them at great risk of low yields and in imminent danger from hunger and famine. Already, women and youth in Adaboya report that more than half the villagers "beg for grain, are weak, thin, and dirty, their lips and the soles of their feet are cracked, and they have no sleeping place." Harvests are poor, so people have no choice but to consume all the food they collect, leaving no crops from which to obtain seed for the next season's planting. In Tabe Ere women add that "hunger affects the wild animals who roam to destroy our crops because they are not well fed by nature due to lack of rains."

Soil depletion is another problem mentioned frequently by poor farmers. Women in Dobile Yirkpong explain that soil fertility has declined as a result of bush fires and continuous cropping. Men in Tabe Ere also note that lands are less productive, but they identify low rainfall and lack of irrigation facilities as well as bush fires as the causes. Bush fires also worry the older men in Asukawkaw, where such fires destroy large tracts of land and food crops. Discussion groups in Adaboya, Babatokuma, and Tabe Ere mention fertilizer and other farm inputs as pressing needs and link worsening soil conditions to the lack of credit for inputs.

Deforestation—the result of clearing land for farms, gathering wood for fuel, and commercial logging—also creates hardships for rural communities. Youths in Adaboya remark that farming constraints have pushed many people into burning charcoal and gathering wood to sell as fuel. These activities, they say, are in turn intensifying the rate of soil degradation and desertification, creating a destructive cycle. In Twabidi agricultural livelihoods are said to be endangered by soil depletion from overuse and lack of farm inputs, combined with commercial logging activities (box 1).

Some people, such as Ziem, whose story opened this chapter, emphasize the risks of livestock theft. Whatever farmers have can be taken by others. Loss of livestock to thieves, a new phenomenon that is considered both a cause and a result of poverty, is prevalent in Adaboya, Dobile Yirkpong, and Tabe Ere. A group of men in Adaboya says that rearing poultry, pigs, goats, and sheep could provide a valuable form of security, but because most of these animals are left on open range, they are subject to theft; the men believe the number of thieves in the area has increased. In Tabe Ere a group of women indicates that fear of theft keeps them from raising livestock. In communities that have police, poor people widely remark that the police are ineffective at protecting them from theft or apprehending the culprits.

For those with fertile land and know-how, farming can bring well-being. Mohammed Bukari was born and raised in Dobile Yirkpong. He has three wives and seven children. Other dependents include his mother, his sister and her two children, a stepchild, the two wives of his younger brother, and the child of his brother-in-law, who stays with them to attend school, for a total of nineteen people in the household. Following his father's death, Mohammed inherited his father's farm and profitably reinvested proceeds from the farm in goats, sheep, and poultry. He explains that keeping livestock is an important contribution to his success because he can sell them as needed for clothing, health needs, or even to buy food during lean times. As cattle theft is a serious problem in Dobile Yirkpong, Mohammed quickly sells any cows that he manages to purchase.

Mohammed has two farms. The farm just within the community lies on low, fecund land that does not require fertilizer. The second farm, some distance from the village, has lost virtually all its fertility over the past couple of years because the fields were never allowed to remain fallow. An experienced farmer, Mohammed changed his crops to groundnuts and cowpeas, which require fewer inputs, but he is unable to procure a tractor or even bullocks to plant more lucrative crops. He says he is limited because of *kpiangaa* or *nanga*, lack of funds. Thus Mohammed primarily plows his land manually.

Joblessness

Unemployment is the primary concern among poor people in both urban settlements visited, and rural villagers identify it as one of their communities' leading problems. Many in Atonsu Bokro lost their jobs when the nearby jute and shoe factories closed, and they have experienced a significant decline in wellbeing since then. In Teshie local jobs are so hard to find that scores of young men are said to migrate to neighboring Accra, the capital of Ghana, or even abroad, to Nigeria.

Work opportunities are described everywhere as extremely scarce. Baah Inkoom, a 22-year-old man from Atonsu Bokro, dropped out of primary school after five years to help his family survive by selling uncooked rice and salt. "I later started selling ice water," says Baah, "but it was not any more profitable." Attempting to find a viable livelihood, Baah took steps to become a truck driver. He paid an apprentice fee of 30,000 cedis (about US$11 in 1999), but his trainer refused to take Baah on his daily trips and teach him how to drive. Soon after finding a new trainer, Baah fell sick for a long period and was unable to work. Still unemployed and discouraged, he says he now hates to be around the truck depot because he doesn't want to pick up the bad habits of the drivers, such as smoking. "I do not envision myself coming out of this situation easily. I can only come out if I have a truck to drive, but currently there are few such opportunities in the system. I will keep on searching for one in the hope that I can improve my situation," says Baah.

Many urban and rural young people feel they have no choice but to leave home in search of work, and migration is seen as both a cause of and a response to poverty. A recent survey finds that 52 percent of all Ghanaians are migrants, having previously lived somewhere else. An additional 16 percent had moved away from their birthplace but subsequently returned. Women migrate at almost the same rate as men.[5]

Young villagers often go no farther than a "chop bar" (local restaurant) in a nearby urban area. A group of young men in Adaboya reports that many of them must travel to find work in wealthier farming communities so that their remittances will buy food and basic necessities for parents and younger siblings back home. At the same time, once young people leave the community, there are fewer hands left to assist with farming. Indeed, the noticeable absence of able-bodied youths in all the rural communities in this study is another disturbing indicator of the effects of food insecurity.

There is evidence, moreover, that many migrants do not fare well. According to one young Teshie man, the little money these workers are able to save is immediately spent again in the continued search for other employment, which they rarely find. Participants also gave examples of migrants who returned to their home villages and towns infected with HIV/AIDS and died. In both Twabidi and Tabe Ere, groups of older men speak of the spread of AIDS and say that one of their greatest fears is the imminent extinction of their ethnic group.

Researchers met with a few individuals who have managed to climb out of poverty, some by getting the resources necessary to start their own businesses. One such woman, Ayorkor, 40 years old and raising three children in Teshie, says,

> *I managed to save a little and feed my children at the same time. When I managed to save enough, I started selling cooked yam, and here I made more money and managed to save. I was lucky to meet a friend who gave me secondhand clothes on credit to sell. This I did very well and started building my capital. Now I am trading with my own money. My first two children are in the secondary school and my last child, who is 18 months old, is in a crèche [day-care center]. I managed to get out of poverty because I was not ready to give up, and so I fought hard and with the help of a friend I succeeded. I believe with hard work and luck one could get out of poverty and be self-sufficient.*

Coping

Across Ghana poor people survive by diversifying their livelihoods. In Babatokuma, where conditions for farming have become increasingly difficult, men in a discussion group provide a list of coping strategies used in their village:

- ▸ Selling their cows in times of need
- ▸ Letting all the children work in farming activities
- ▸ Gathering and selling firewood
- ▸ Burning and selling charcoal

- Using deceit and fraud to cheat others
- Supplying sand and gravel to masons
- Making and selling kitchen fans
- Offering labor to other farmers
- Accepting support from wives
- Depending on well-off friends
- Living on loans until food comes

People say they undertake several coping activities simultaneously and shoulder a very heavy work burden. Jemilatu, a 38-year-old woman in Dobile Yirkpong, is married to a town council member and has nine other people in her household: her aged mother, her husband, her four children, and three of the eight children left behind by her older sister who died three years ago. To make ends meet, Jemilatu farms on a subsistence basis, breaks stones and sells them to people for construction projects, and engages in petty trade. Despite several income-generating activities, she says her diet, health, and housing are precarious (she sometimes eats only once a day so that the children can eat twice). She is unable to send the children to school or to a hospital when they are sick.

Some coping strategies deplete productive resources, adding to the risks that poor people and their children will face in the future, but they say that in the face of hunger they have no other choice. For example, farmers in Adaboya may plant a crop early to obtain food sooner and then try for a second harvest despite the added pressure on the soil. Men in that community report that poor people 'continue to till the infertile land with the hope of getting some food." They also gather firewood for sale, sell off livestock or other family belongings, and even beg in the marketplace.

In Atonsu Bokro discussion groups of men identify four ways they cope with desperate times: borrow money; tell lies and deceive or defraud people; depend on someone else (friend or family member); and collect remittances from those who have migrated, money from friends, or outstanding debts. The women's discussion group identified quite different means of coping. For instance, the women say they may look for boyfriends who have money, or they may spend the night with men to ease overcrowding at home. They also say that they take advantage of traditional norms of hospitality by visiting friends and staying until meal times so that they have to be fed, too. They might also use witchcraft to obtain money, but they point out that this is risky, and many are too afraid. Finally, they may take a job as a domestic or simply "pray and have faith."

Government Is Important, but Its Help Falls Short

Poor people in Ghana named institutions that are important in their daily lives and rated them against many criteria, but focused particularly on effectiveness. In Teshie discussion groups define effectiveness as the ability to have things that have been planned come to fruition. Accordingly, study participants acknowledge and express appreciation for public and civic institutions that deliver, and they give low scores to those that fail to carry out their responsibilities or do not keep their promises.

Participants generally report that the most effective institutions are assemblymen, chiefs, and churches. In communities where assemblymen or chiefs are not viewed as serving the people's interests, people express strong concerns that their community's development is thwarted. Although not widely present, community-based trade and self-help groups are also valued. NGOs receive sharply negative reviews and private-sector entities rarely appear on poor people's lists of important institutions in their lives.

Over the last decade, Ghana decentralized its public administrative apparatus, creating a five-tiered system consisting of the central government; regional councils; district assemblies; sub-metropolitan, subdistrict, and town councils; and finally a network of committees at the neighborhood and village level. It is noteworthy that the study participants made little or no mention of the new community-level committees. Parliamentarians also do not figure in discussions of institutions helpful to poor people.

The elected assemblyman, who represents local communities in the district assembly, provides a key channel to government support and receives strong reviews by both men's and women's discussion groups in most communities visited. Community grievances and other administrative cases are also channeled through the assemblyman to the district assembly. Tabe Ere's assemblyman is considered an effective liaison between villagers and the government because he calls them to meetings to share ideas and information about what goes on in the assembly. Whenever one of the villagers runs into trouble, such as losing all his crops to bush fires, a report is made to the assemblyman, who is said to organize some form of assistance for the victim.

Adaboya stands out among the communities visited because people are very hopeful about their development prospects. In recent years, Adaboya has received sustained assistance from a number of external agencies, which they credit for helping them eat through the dry season. According to villagers, the assemblyman has played a pivotal role by organizing residents for development projects and serving as the intermediary to outside agencies. They say, "He is very good to us." Villagers feel they can call on their assemblyman even in the middle of the night, though no one recalls having had to do so.

Favorable reports of assemblymen emerge in other communities as well. Although they have been waiting fifty years for a health clinic, residents of Twabidi still hope that one might soon be built because the "dynamism of the assemblyman and the high self-help spirit is likely to pay off." In Asukawkaw participants say, "The only point of unity is the assemblyman." Men in Babatokuma say they can always go to their chief or assemblyman for help in times of crisis because that is his responsibility.

In a few poor communities, however, the presence of the assemblyman and government is weak, and poor people express feelings of abandonment. In the very remote village of Dobile Yirkpong, the only local institution that people there could identify was a new women's group; a poor woman reports that the assemblyman does not live near them and is therefore ignorant of their needs. In the urban communities, only women mention the assemblyman; men did not consider or rank the assemblyman, which suggests some disconnection with this otherwise key channel of governance. In urban Teshie the assemblyman is not ranked highly because, according to residents, he listens only to his family and not to the general public. A resident of Teshie, where people have been waiting since colonial times for a health post or clinic, asks, "What have we done? When development starts in Accra it ends at La. When it starts at Tema, it ends at Nungua. We are always left stuck in between."

Missing Basic Services

In most of the rural communities visited, basic services—wells, toilets, roads, schools, and clinics—are either inadequate, inaccessible, unaffordable, or altogether absent. Services are only slightly better in the two urban neighborhoods. People say they have no means to influence service providers. While the lack of drinking water is a long-standing problem, many poor people view the lack of other services, such as sanitation, as new problems that have only recently emerged because expanding populations and the encroachment of developments surrounding the communities have made the services necessary (box 2). Access to health care is especially difficult.

Dissatisfaction with missing infrastructure is most intense in Asukawkaw, a settlement created thirty-seven years ago when the community of Akosombo was displaced for construction of the Volta hydroelectric dam. Residents blame the Volta River Authority for the high level of illbeing in their community and say that successive governments have done little or nothing to improve their lot. The new houses were never completed and are too small for their families. And while their community was uprooted for the construction of a power facility, they remain without power, although neighboring villages are electrified. Moreover, their water source, the Asukawkaw River, afflicts them with bilharzia and river blindness; it also overflows seasonally, causing great loss of livestock and other property.

Scarce Water and Sanitation

At the national level, access to water improved in the 1990s, with statistics indicating that nearly all urban and two-thirds of rural households in Ghana had access to potable water in 1998–99. However, many Ghanaians must rely on high-cost vendors, neighbors, or other private sources because government systems are not accessible or are plagued with seasonal, quality, or operational problems. With the exception of

---

BOX 2 New Needs in a Changing World

Tabe Ere women note that some of their community's priorities, such as obtaining a school, are quite new. In the past they did not see a need for a school and so they did not consider the lack of one to be a problem. Similarly, in other rural areas the demand for sanitation and electricity is recent. Women in Dobile Yirkpong explain that open-range defecation was not a problem until the village ceased to be surrounded by natural expanses. Now, without sanitation infrastructure, the town would be extremely unhygienic and hazardous to health if it were not for the women who regularly clear away and burn the local refuse. Men in Tabe Ere point out that ten years ago they had never heard of electric power and therefore did not desire it. Nowadays, almost all nearby villages have been connected to the national grid except theirs, and this irritates them.

Doryumu, participants in every community in this study report difficulties obtaining water. While sanitation services have also expanded in this period, access rates are far lower than for water.[6]

Men in Adaboya report that the government provided three wells to the village, but two are not working and so the water shortage is getting worse. They also indicate that they are unable to make the required contributions toward maintaining the remaining borehole because most of them have no money. Women in the village say that they waste a great deal of time and energy fetching water for their families. In Dobile Yirkpong, Twabidi, and Adaboya, water taken from boreholes is said to be infested with guinea worm.

In the two urban communities, Atonsu Bokro and Teshie, piped water does not reach all the homes, and residents report that the supply is irregular. Three discussion groups in Teshie say that ten years ago, the taps, although there were few, were running all the time. To meet their requirements now, however, Teshie residents must purchase water from reservoirs built by private entrepreneurs who fill them with treated water imported from Accra, Nungua, or La. The entire community also relies on two poorly functioning public toilets and a single bathhouse. Sometimes a toilet explodes, burning people in the process. In Babatokuma there are only three public toilets for 4,000 residents—and two of these are out of order—so children relieve themselves in the river, where people also wash.

Health at Risk

The importance of good health to poor people cannot be overstated. "It is when we have good health that we can work for the money we need so much," remarks a woman in a Twabidi discussion group. Physical health is vital for the types of livelihoods on which poor people depend, and they worry immensely about the prospect of illness or injury, which are costly in terms of both lost earnings and medical care. All communities visited except Dobile Yirkpong identify the lack of local health care facilities as an important problem. Indeed, when illness strikes, poor people across the communities report that getting medical care is out of the question due to the cost of treatment, the distance to health care facilities, and the exorbitant transportation fees.

Women in Twabidi say, "Because of the distance, money, and other inconveniences involved [in obtaining health care currently], we consider the need for a clinic as the first priority." Vehicles to take a sick person out of the village for medical attention are few and irregular. There have been many instances when strong men from Twabidi have had to walk the eighteen kilometers to Tepa carrying a sick person on their backs.

Likewise, when people in Adaboya fall ill, they must walk eight kilometers to Bongo, the district capital. A group of men in Adaboya says that to meet expenses, "the family may sell some property or livestock to enable the sick person to be sent to the hospital." To ease the difficulty of travel for health care, people in the village hope that a road might soon be built to replace the footpath to Bongo.

Poor people in urban settlements do not necessarily have better access to health services. No public facility serves Teshie's 200,000 people. A doctor runs a private clinic there, but residents say he charges fees too high for them to afford.

A recent national poll confirms poor people's reports for this study on access to medical care. The survey indicates that the number of people seeking public health care decreased by about 25 percent between 1992 and 1998, reflecting both problems of access and dissatisfaction with services available. Underpinning this trend are patterns of public spending on health care that favor wealthier groups in urban areas and higher-level health services, such as hospitals, over primary care clinics.[7]

Education Hurdles

Like health care, education is often out of reach for poor families, who face formidable barriers of access and cost in trying to send children to school. Attendance at primary and junior secondary schools is supposed to be compulsory and free, but in practice all schools collect required "contributions" from students to supplement their budgets. Public spending on education is more equitably invested across consumption groups than health care spending, but there are concerns with quality. Levels of achievement are extremely low, with only 6 percent of public school children meeting the English standards on criterion-referenced tests (compared with about 70 percent doing so in private schools).[8]

Three villages report that they have no primary school for their children. In Adaboya men say that their children must walk about four kilometers to attend school, which they consider too far. While there is a school building in the village, it sits in disrepair and cannot be used in the rainy season. Poor people in Tabe Ere also say it is very difficult for their children to make the daily trek to the closest school. In Twabidi women indicate that their village is too remote to attract teachers, but they have plans to convert an abandoned school building into a teacher's bungalow in an effort to get a teacher.

Incidental school fees are identified as a pressing problem in seven communities, and poor households with numerous children are said to be most affected. Some people sell their assets, such as livestock, to pay fees. Occasionally they try to borrow money to cover the fees and pay it back after the harvest. Often children must simply be withdrawn from school until money becomes available. Yao Quaye Foli, from Asukawkaw, is 23 years old and determined to finish his education, but says he has been turned away by a school for having unpaid fees of just 1,000 cedi (38 cents). Tabe Ere youths express resentment toward their parents for not sending them to school, saying that now they are not qualified to find employment that requires any level of education.

Faith in Chiefs and Churches

In the absence of effective public services, poor men and women rely heavily on local leaders and groups. Chiefs are held in the highest esteem by rural communities, followed by other individuals or organizations over which the communities exercise a degree of control, including assemblymen (discussed above) and churches. In a few places, community groups are also important resources.

In six of the seven rural communities, chiefs are highly regarded. Many people remark on their important role in settling community and household disputes, organizing communal development activities, and seeking external aid. They also are valued for enabling people to take part in local decision making. Adaboya men say of their chief,

> *He is our leader and he settles disputes. He calls us whenever there is something that needs to be discussed. With some issues, he will call the whole community together and give each person a chance to express his or her view. He also takes advice from the elders, but they are a small group.*

In Twabidi the chief is well regarded by discussion groups of men and women, and women say he meets regularly with the villagers and includes them in decision making. They indicate that he is educated, unlike earlier chiefs, and can seek assistance for Twabidi from external agencies. He also organizes villagers for communal labor every Tuesday.

In places where chiefs do not play an active role, which include the two urban communities and the village of Doryumu, their absence is strongly felt. In Atonsu Bokro discussion groups express strong dissatisfaction with their chief, explaining that he has been selling off community land, leaving nothing for future development, while neglecting to organize communal labor activities or initiate projects. They also have little regard for their assemblyman and thus say they count heavily on their church in times of need. In Teshie discussion groups report that there is a chieftaincy dispute, and so their fetish priest now commands highest authority. People in Doryumu say the chief and elders are "bedeviled with disputes" and this is slowing down development in the community, although they acknowledge that the chief has helped to resolve family and marital conflicts.

While the authority of women is slowly growing at the household level in Ghana (see below), community meetings remain largely the responsibility of men in both urban and rural areas. In Atonsu Bokro a discussion group of women observes that women are largely denied power and influence over community affairs, but a woman with money may sometimes be able to express her views.

The work of churches is valued in every community where they are present. Catholics in Tabe Ere say, "Even though the Father does not hold power, he leads us in prayer as a means of protection." The priest is said to provide help when needed, especially food to feed children, and the Muslims also agree with this. In Twabidi a discussion group of men and women explains that they rank the Christian priests highest among institutions "because the priests in their various churches give us both moral and material support when needed." The Catholic mission in the village provided a well and sometimes offers food aid during the lean season. In Atonsu Bokro, where the church is the institution rated most highly by both women and men, women say, "If someone is in need, the church and the congregation will never turn them away." But in Asukawkaw older women say that "the church has been helpful to members of its congregation," implying that it is not helpful to non-members. This sentiment is echoed in Doryumu.

A few communities mention local institutions that have evolved to help fill a variety of needs. Women in Twabidi rate very highly several local groups to which they turn for livelihood support and health care. These include professional associations of traditional midwives, of plantain buyers and sellers, and of dressmakers and tailors. In Teshie two discussion groups of men rank the Classmates Union as the most important in their community because it has successfully implemented local development projects. The 1964 Classmates Union dredged a local lagoon and restored fish stocks with support from the Ghanaian government, the United Nations Development Programme, and the multilateral Global Environment Facility. The only institution identified as present in Dobile Yirkpong is a year-old women's group whose name means "Love One Another, Help One Another, and Cover Each Other's Shame." They hope that by pulling together, the organization can help rebuild the town and perhaps gain access to the services of a bank outside the village.

Little Regard for NGOs

Nongovernmental organizations have done some work in half of the communities visited, but views of their activities are quite mixed due to unfulfilled promises and poorly performing projects. Also, study participants feel they have little influence over NGO programs. World Vision in Adaboya is ranked highly by discussion groups for providing food for schoolchildren, small loan programs for women, and other development activities. Yet even this highly regarded international NGO is found lacking by a discussion group of men, who say they wish to have more control over the development organization so that they could obtain more assistance to improve the education of their children.

In the other communities where NGOs are present, people generally think little of their contributions. Adaboya youths name the Salvation Army as the lowest-performing institution because the community did not benefit much from its work. The organization installed a grinding mill, which worked for only a short time and then broke down and has never been repaired. Furthermore, nobody in the community was consulted before the decision was made to provide them with the mill. Some participants even added that the mill had never benefited them at all, since it was purely commercial and charged the same rates as other mills; and in addition, preferential treatment was given to community members who were members of the Salvation Army Church. Sight Savers received the lowest institutional ranking given by Asukawkaw villagers because the organization used to be there but left, abandoning the villagers.

Growing Responsibilities for Women, but Few Rights

Ghanaian women manage traditional household tasks, and many must shoulder the additional responsibility of earning income and giving out "chop money" for household expenses and school fees when men are unable or unwilling to do so. Moreover, many women in the study report that they are single, widowed, separated, or divorced, and are forced by circumstances to cover their household's budget single-handedly, often through petty trade. Despite a growing role in earning income, however, women still have low social status and face continuing disadvantages. A woman typically owns little or no property of her own and may be one of several wives. Violence against women is widespread.

Women in a discussion group from Dobile Yirkpong argue that inequality and physical abuse of women start in childhood. While girls and women are busy doing household chores, boys and men are playing or relaxing. Women in Tabe Ere explain that men make decisions about educating children, and preference always goes to educating boys. The women also explain that without any schooling, girls often become pregnant and may marry as young as 14 or 15.

Women in Adaboya consider discrimination and violence against girls to be the biggest problem in their community. They report that rape and forced sex are common experiences for girls, and the girls become worn down by it. In such situations, girls may be compelled to marry their attackers; some women consider the measure of security this brings as the lesser of two evils, even if the girls are forced into marriage against their wishes and those of their mother. There are also a few reports of girls being sold into marriage to cover a family's debt.

Once married, women find their status and security are greatly diminished by the common practice of polygamy. Many of the study participants say their households have two wives, and some have three. The most extreme case mentioned was a prosperous Babatokuma farmer who has six wives and thirty children. Men in Adaboya view having multiple wives, many children, and several farm animals as a form of security. In Dobile such "possessions" are considered to indicate wellbeing.

For women, however, the presence of multiple wives often means reduced support from the husband, and it sometimes results in wives being abandoned altogether. A woman from Babatokuma explains, "I have to struggle to pay my children's school fees because my husband uses his money to marry more women and for his pleasure only!" When asked why her husband is not contributing to the education of their children, Mary Esi Asiedu, a 43-year-old woman from Babatokuma, says, "How can he contribute with seven or more concubines with him over there in Tamale?" Some women in the study express the opinion that it is abusive when a husband takes an additional wife without consulting the first wife. In Doryumu a group of literate women includes polygamy in their list of poverty's causes.

Women in Ghana are legally their husband's property, and this naturally affects their legal status in other areas related to family life. In Adaboya, for example, the male lover of an adulterous woman is obliged to pay restitution to her husband, but the wife of an unfaithful husband has no recourse.

Women lose even more status after their husbands die, and since many cannot inherit their husband's property, they often plummet into poverty after his death.[9] Daughters also have few inheritance rights, and their security is tied to their husbands' fortunes, as Rose Yaa Ansah's experience illustrates in box 3.

Economic Gains?

More and more women in poor communities in Ghana are directing impressive entrepreneurial energies toward feeding their families, clothing and schooling their children, and supporting themselves. While the extra

---

BOX 3 The Helplessness of Widows

Rose Yaa Ansah, a 65-year-old woman from Babatokuma, married and had ten children, eight of whom survived. Her husband died young, and Rose Yaa was left alone to care for the children. Even though her father owned land, Rose Yaa didn't inherit any of it because she is female. She had to beg for a portion on which to farm in order to feed her children. Seven of her surviving children are now all married with children of their own, but "they didn't get responsible husbands and so are living in poverty like me," she says. Her last child, a boy, cannot go to school because she cannot afford the fees. She doesn't get any help from her family relations. They even insult her if she goes to them to borrow money. "My only problem now," she says, "is money. If I had money I could employ people to farm for me to feed my household and repair my roof, which leaves me at the mercy of rain whenever it falls." She has no hope for the future and believes she will be in poverty until she dies.

household income raised by women has relieved some of the financial pressure on men, it does not necessarily bring greater security to poor households.

According to Ohemaa Addae, a 34-year-old woman from Atonsu Bokro,

> *A woman I befriended near my house started giving me pineapple to sell on commission. This gave me enough money to fend for myself. I became attached to a cobbler with whom I had three children. He later lost his job and life became very unbearable. The little I got from the pineapple was not enough to feed five of us. After a month in this condition he deserted me. Now I don't know his whereabouts, but I feed the children and my parents and three siblings out of the little I get.*

Abena Mansah Sarpong, a 45-year-old mother of five in Teshie, works tirelessly smoking fish and peddling dry goods. She is convinced she can rise out of poverty if she never marries again. Each of her three former husbands had a drinking problem and she has decided that the most practical path is to live on her own. Some women struggle with supporting an alcoholic husband and entrust their security to their children instead. This is the case for a poor woman from Tabe Ere:

> *My husband is not working and has taken to heavy drinking, especially* akpeteshie *[a strong alcoholic drink brewed locally]. I have to feed and clothe him in addition to my children. All this makes life very hard since my income is not much anymore. At times I find it very difficult to pay for my children's school fees. My hope and future are in their education . . . for when I am old and can't work any longer. My children have seen how I've suffered to educate them so they won't end up like their father and me. I am doing my best so that in the future they will let me enjoy the benefits of my hard work.*

Unfortunately, despite their earnings, most Ghanaian women in both urban and rural communities conclude that overall they are worse off than in the past because men are less responsible toward their families and are drinking more, and because it is more difficult for everyone to earn a living.

Widespread Gender Violence

Discussion groups in this study report that there is a great deal of conflict in gender relations at the household level. Women describe a variety of abuses against them by their husbands, from being denied food or permission to visit health practitioners to being robbed, raped, and beaten. With the exception of Asukawkaw, where violence against women is said to be uncommon, men and women in the communities visited portray wife battering as both pervasive and accepted. In the words of a teacher in Babatokuma, "This happens a lot. We men assault them and also abuse them psychologically." Men pay for their brides in Ghana, and many believe that this entitles them to rule over their wives.

As described above, forced sex is widely reported as an abuse facing married as well as single women and girls. In Tabe Ere a group of adult women says that if they refuse sex, they are beaten, and "even then the men still satisfy themselves." They say they get pregnant unwillingly and give birth to children whom men in most cases do not provide for. "The men even decide when we should go to the clinic when we are pregnant," one woman adds. Some women in Tabe Ere say they would like to avoid sex because their husbands refuse to practice birth control or because they fear being infected with HIV/AIDS.

A man in Adaboya explains that "If a man beats his wife because she has refused to give in to sex the man is justified." He reasons that when a man has married a woman and has fully completed all the customary marriage rites, the woman becomes the property of the man and has no right to resist any demands for sex by her husband. He added that beating her for this reason is justified, particularly "if you have provided food for the woman to eat throughout the day as well as provided for all her other needs, such as clothing and health care." Adaboya women, however, refer to husbands forcing them to have sex "even on an empty stomach." They also indicate that men increasingly return from the market drunk and force them into sex, and they say that protests against violence may result in more beatings or divorce.

Men's increased difficulties earning a living are also said to cause turmoil and violence in gender relations. Women in Dobile Yirkpong explain that tension in the family arises when men cannot provide for household needs, and this may lead to "dissatisfaction, quarrels, and beatings." A young man from Teshie asserts, "It's because of unemployment and poverty that most men in this community beat their wives. We have no money to look after them."

Finally, several discussion groups say women's expanded economic role is itself a source of stress on couples. In Babatokuma, where women have taken up trading fish and yams, the men's group reports that violence has increased against women because women no longer obey and respect men; the men cannot tolerate this dissent and so become angry and aggressive. The discussion group of women disagrees, however, and concludes that domestic violence is on the decline because they now have their own money. Men in Dobile Yirkpong say that women's growing earning capacity is of no benefit to women and may even cause them harm. They explain that in the past conflicts were fewer because women obeyed their husbands more and shared their incomes with them. But now, in response to the financial independence of the wives, these men explain, the husbands beat them, divorce them, refuse to eat the food they prepare, and marry other women.

Conclusion

Ten years ago, people living in the communities visited in Ghana were poor by almost any standard. Yet most now say that life was better then. According to a discussion group of women in Dobile Yirkpong, there was no serious need for money a decade ago because food crops were abundant. Today, growing populations, less fertile lands, infrequent rains, and theft have undermined subsistence farming and deepened poverty in the village. Indeed, women in Dobile Yirkpong say the very definition of what it takes to have a good life has changed: money has now become important and food alone is not enough. Having "deep pockets" means having clothing, modern housing, property, a car, and the means to educate children.

Even in the context of the country's overall economic growth, poor people visited for this study say they feel farther away from having deep pockets than a decade ago. The benefits of a growing economy do not seem to be reaching the communities in this study. Rural livelihoods are portrayed as increasingly precarious, and young Ghanaians are on the move in very large numbers in search of better opportunities, often in towns and cities. Yet prospects in the two cities visited also appear limited. Every single Teshie group spoke of worsening economic conditions, with many participants describing the country's economy as in crisis. They emphasize that if the economy does not turn around, even the *shikatse* (rich people) will disappear. "The rich are getting poorer because we the poor borrow from them and never pay back," quips a middle-aged Teshie woman.

In addition to more secure livelihoods, basic services are priorities for all the communities in the study. Most lack adequate roads, struggle with broken or polluted wells or, in urban areas, unreliable piped water, and cannot reach or afford health care or schools. Study participants also call for help with credit and savings. Although they say most government services are ineffective and unaccountable, assemblymen are prized by people in many communities for the connections and occasional good works they bring. The recent moves toward a more decentralized government provide a potentially powerful resource for improving services and markets for poor people in Ghana, but the institutional advances are not yet felt in the communities visited for this study. In addition, the dismal track record of NGOs and the private sector in poor communities requires policy attention, as these resources also need to be marshaled if such sweeping local needs are going to be addressed more systematically.

While it is often essential that women earn income, their earning power is identified not as a source of greater security but as a cause of turmoil in the home and violence against them by their husbands. Both married and unmarried women report being "worn down" by rape. Polygamy is widespread, and women view it as a cause of poverty. Legal action and awareness campaigns to empower women will be vital to strengthening the capacity of poor women to feed and educate their children.

For poor women, children are their greatest security as well as their hope for a better future. One woman explains, "At times I find it very difficult to feed my children and pay their school fees but my hope and future are in their education to help me enjoy life when I become old and cannot work any longer." With so few signs that poverty is abating, however, others see few prospects even for their children. A woman from Atonsu Bokro remarks, "If things should continue in this condition then I don't have any hope because my children are going to be worse off than me."

TABLE 2 Study Communities in Ghana

RURAL COMMUNITIES

Adaboya, Bongo District, Upper East Region Pop. 1,500	The village is located about eight kilometers from the nearest road and about an hour's walk from the nearest telephone. The men are mainly farmers, with a minority also involved in raising cattle. A few others weave baskets and other items, burn charcoal, and trade or sell firewood. The women are also heavily involved in farming (about 75 percent); some do petty trading and raise animals. Infertile soils coupled with lack of social services have led to excessive out-migration of youth to larger communities to sell their unskilled labor. Their remittances help keep their aged parents and younger siblings alive back home. There is no health facility or post office, and visits by an agricultural extension worker are irregular. The majority of the population practice traditional religions; approximately 20 percent are Christian and 5 percent Muslim.
Asukawkaw, Kete Krachi District, Volta Region Pop. 2,710	This village was chosen as a settlement for the people of Akroso who were moved from their original location so that construction could begin on the Volta hydroelectric dam at Akosombo. The settlement consists mostly of unfinished cement block buildings. A majority of people live in overcrowded households. Farming is the main source of livelihood for men and women; about 90 percent of the people cultivate yam, cassava, and maize. There are also a few petty traders and teachers. There are two primary schools, one nursery school, one junior secondary school, and one agricultural senior secondary school. There is also a small health facility. The incidence of waterborne diseases, including river blindness and bilharzia, is high. The river overflows its banks during the rainy season, causing extensive property damage.

RURAL COMMUNITIES (continued)

Babatokuma, Kintampo District, Brong Ahafo Region Pop. 4,400

Babatokuma is known in the district for its yam production. Almost 98 percent of the men engage in farming, while about 80 percent of the women trade agricultural products. Most of the houses in the community have thatched roofs, and the risk of fire is an important concern for the villagers. The community has one primary and one junior secondary school but no clinic or post office. However, Babatokuma is only about ten minutes' drive from the district capital and the road that links the Northern Region to the southern part of Ghana passes through the settlement. The population includes about twelve ethnic groups.

Dobile Yirkpong, Upper West Region Pop. 330

Although this village is a suburb of Wa, the regional capital of the Upper West Region, it does not display typical urban characteristics. Seventy-five percent of adult men are farmers and each farmer owns some livestock, usually goats, sheep, cattle, and guinea fowl. Men also engage in masonry, petty trade, and carpentry, and work as guards. The women are predominantly traders of vegetables and firewood. They also help their husbands farm and some rear animals. Dobile Yirkpong has no school, no electricity, and no sewerage. Pipe-borne water is not readily available, so the community obtains water from hand-dug wells, although they are believed to be infested with guinea worm. The people are predominantly Wala; 25 percent are Muslims, and the rest are Christians.

Doryumu, Dangbe West District, Greater Accra Region Pop. 2,500

A rural farming community, Doryumu is seventeen kilometers from the district capital, Dodowa. About 60 percent of the working population is engaged in farming, 15 percent in trading, 10 percent in stone cracking (breaking stones and selling them for use as construction material), 10 percent in artisanship, and the remaining 5 percent in salaried jobs like teaching and road construction. There is a Methodist primary school and a public junior secondary school. The settlement has piped water, electricity, and access roads, but it lacks a health facility and post office. Eighty percent of the villagers are Dangbe-speaking people, indigenous to the area, who adhere to traditional religions. The rest, mostly Ewe, Akan, and Fulani people, immigrated from elsewhere.

Tabe Ere,
Lawra District,
Upper West Region
Pop. 1,162

This settlement's inhabitants actually come from four distinct communities; however, they have one meeting place, share facilities, and all recognize one chief. Ninety percent of men and 60 percent of women are farmers; others fish or engage in petty trade. The only school, a primary school, is located in the geographic center of the four settlements, which are about one and a half kilometers from each other. The communities are located about four kilometers from the nearest permanent road. There is neither a health clinic nor a post office, and only two of the settlements, Kuowob and Tabe Ere, have boreholes (water wells, provided in this case by the Catholic Church). The nearest health services are about nine kilometers away. Many people are immigrants from Burkina Faso or other parts of the Lawra District. The majority are Christians (70 percent) and the rest are Muslims.

Twabidi,
Ahafo-Ano
North District,
Ashanti Region
Pop. 800

Because farming has flourished here, people from many communities, including Asotwe, Bogyawe, Mampong, Dwaben, as well as some northerners, settled in the village. The majority of men are crop and cocoa farmers, while some are involved in livestock rearing, trading, and growing vegetables. The women are housewives, and a small proportion of them farm crops and cocoa, raise animals, and grow vegetables. The settlement has no basic services or infrastructure such as electricity, a post office, or a health facility.

Atonsu Bokro, Kumasi Metropolis, Ashanti Region Pop. 10,000

This suburb of Kumasi, the second largest city in Ghana, is surrounded by industrial activity: lumber yards and sawmills, breweries, and bottling plants. Atonsu Bokro serves as a densely crowded dormitory town for workers in these industries, and for this reason the community has very mixed ethnicity. Almost 50 percent of the population is currently unemployed because two large industries have been closed down for quite some time. A significant proportion live on irregular incomes or work as civil servants. Ninety-five percent of the community has electricity, but there is no post office in the area. There are no permanent roads and the drainage system functions poorly.

Teshie, Greater Accra Region Pop. 200,000

This suburb of Accra, the national capital, is located on the Atlantic coast. Though originally a fishing community, its proximity to the capital has allowed residents to pursue diverse occupations. The men are mostly fishermen and the women fishmongers, but there are also petty traders, artisans, carpenters, masons, drivers, and tailors. Whereas Teshie is well endowed with basic educational facilities (ten public primary and junior secondary schools, one senior secondary school, and a host of private educational facilities), health facilities are not well developed. There is no public hospital and only one private clinic. However, a heavily used major road connecting Accra and Tema (the industrial city) bisects Teshie, which is only nine kilometers from Accra. Although the community has been connected to the Accra water supply system, residents rarely get water from the taps. Similarly, public toilets are few, and there is one public bathhouse. The community has a post office and access to telephone lines.

Notes

1. Ernest Y. Kunfaa, Tony Dogbe, Heather J. Mackay, and Celia Marshall led the study team. Other members included Harriet Adjapong Avle, Bright Asare Boadi, Philip Acheampong, Michael Tsike, Godfred Fosu Agyem, Adjapong Avele, Nana Awuku, Richard Basadi, Solomon Yaw Fordjour, Victoria Kumi-Wood, Joe Lambongang Aba Oppong, Prudence Seeninyin, and Victoria Tuffour.

2. Poverty data from W. K. Asenso-Okyere with D. A. Twum-Baah, A. Kasanga, et al., "Poverty Trends in Ghana in the 1990s" (Ghana Statistical Service, Accra, October 2000), 7–9. GDP and population data from World Bank, *World Development Indicators 2001* (Report 22099, April 2001), 194, 44.

3. Ethnically, Ghana includes many small groups speaking more than fifty languages and dialects. Among the more important linguistic groups are the Akan (44 percent), who include the Fanti along the coast and the Ashanti in the forest area north of the coast; the Guan, on the plains of the Volta River (19 percent); the Ga-speaking and Ewe-speaking peoples of the south and southeast (8 percent and 13 percent respectively); and the Moshi-Dagomba–speaking ethnic groups of the northern and upper regions (16 percent). See U.S. Department of State, "Background Notes: Ghana, February 1998" (Office of West African Affairs, Bureau of African Affairs, 1998).

4. Another nearly 25 percent of poor people are self-employed in nonfarm activities. Asenso-Okyere et al., "Poverty Trends," 13–14.

5. Ibid., 41.

6. Ibid., 21.

7. S. Canagarajah and Xiao Ye, "Public Health and Education Spending in Ghana in 1992–1998: Issues of Equity and Efficiency" (World Bank Policy Research Working Paper 2579, Development Research Group, April 2001).

8. Ibid., 4. Between 1994 and 1998, education accounted for roughly 4 percent of the GDP. Education budgets grew during this period, but not nearly as fast as other areas of public expenditures. The share of education spending relative to total government expenditures fell from 22.2 percent of the budget in 1990 to 11.4 percent in 1999.

9. Most land in Ghana is held in trust for the people by the local chiefs, land (fetish) priests, and clan heads, who allocate (or lease) land to people who want to use it to farm, build houses, open shops and so forth. This has often resulted in discrimination against women. In the patrilineal system that operates widely in northern Ghana and the Volta Region, the man owns the children as well as landed property. In most parts of southern Ghana, by contrast, a matrilineal system permits women to own children and a significant amount of property—houses, land, vehicles, businesses, and the like.

The process of individualization of land tenure institutions in Ghana was strengthened by the passing of the Intestate Succession Law in 1985, which allows children and wives to gain access to land that they were previously denied under traditional law. Husbands can also give their wives strong property rights to land in return for the wives helping them establish cocoa plots. Thus, contrary to expectations, individualization of land rights in a situation where there has been increased demand for women's labor has actually strengthened women's rights to land. Interestingly enough, this change began even before the promulgation of the Intestate Succession Act. Ibis, "NYT LAND—GHANA" (Copenhagen, 1998).

Malawi

Tangled Web

John M. Kadzandira, Stanley W. Khaila, and Peter M. Mvula[1]

Nyuma Munthali, 51, lives with her eight children in Khwalala, a village beside the shore of Lake Malawi in the country's northern region. Nyuma's father died just before she was born, and as a child she worked to pay her own school fees to grade three. "I am grateful for the availability of casual labor at that time," she says. "Without it I wouldn't have managed to get any education."

Nyuma married and had her first child at 16. Seven more children followed. To support her family, Nyuma grows cassava and rice. In the early years she was able to produce enough food for the household and have some left over to sell in order to raise money for school fees, clothes, and other necessities:

> *In those days, farming was profitable because soils were fertile and rains were reliable. But today rains are unpredictable. They can be too heavy and wash away our crop. . . . Soil fertility has been lost due to heavy rains and over-cultivation. This has increased the problem of hunger.*

The rains also have made roads difficult to navigate and have caused many of Khwalala's fragile thatched houses to collapse. Nyuma says that the heavy rains and poor yields have been reported to authorities, "but the government is silent. This has made me think that there is no remedy and our situation will not in any way improve. And this year it's even worse, floods are just everywhere." Villagers who participated in the study are confident that they can fix the roads and the houses once the rains end. The hunger, though, seems here to stay.

Until recently, farming in Khwalala was done largely by women, while many men migrated to South Africa for work and sent their earnings home. When the cassava, Khwalala's principal crop, became infested with mealybugs in 1987, men turned to farming to help their families survive. The harvests have not fully recovered, and South Africa's migrant labor program ended in 1989.

Nyuma's oldest son is employed in the city of Mzuzu and helps by sending money. The other children, including a daughter now divorced, are unemployed and depend on her for support. "I hardly make it. I don't know what to do," says Nyuma. "If there were any job opportunities in this village, I would send my children to the better-off people to work so as to get some money for upkeep. But with all these dependents, I don't see how I will ever get out of poverty."

Nyuma's life in Khwalala illustrates some of the disadvantages and vulnerabilities commonly faced by poor people in Malawi, one of the world's poorest countries. There has been little development progress in Malawi for generations, not even in recent years when both its economy and political system have become much more open. The average yearly per capita income in 1999, US$180, or about 49 cents a day, was lower than it was in 1990, when it stood at US$190.[2] The country's economy has in fact grown steadily in the 1990s, with 3.6 percent GDP growth between 1990 and 1998, and 4.0 percent in 1999.[3] But a rapidly increasing population, an agriculture-based economy dependent on the weather, and a host of other factors explored in this study have left no margin for improvements in living standards.

Sixty-five percent of the country's population lived in extreme expenditure poverty in 1998.[4] While comparable data on earlier poverty rates are not available, there is strong evidence to suggest that poverty has not declined in the 1990s.[5] Nine-tenths of Malawi's population lives in the countryside and survives largely on subsistence agriculture, although engagement with markets is a growing necessity due to land scarcity and the need to purchase food and other basic goods. The country's population, about 11 million, is expanding rapidly due to a fertility rate that reached 6.3 births per woman in 1999.[6] Life expectancy at birth, however, is just 39. Children under 5 years of age are about 20 percent of the population, and one in five will not make it to their fifth birthday. With the HIV/AIDS infection rate at 16 percent of the working-age population and with 31 percent of women in pre-natal clinics HIV-positive, many of these children are, or will become, orphans.[7]

After three decades of authoritarian rule under Hastings Kamuzu Banda, Malawi held its first post-independence competitive elections in 1994; elections were held again in 1999. Bakili Muluzi of the United Democratic Front (UDF) won both elections narrowly. Party loyalties in the country largely follow regional lines, with UDF maintaining control in the most heavily populated southern region. While the Muluzi cabinet has been able to advance many free-market policies and oversee a period of growth, it has confronted high inflation (28 percent at the end of 1999) and continued problems with misappropriation of and weak controls on public spending. With major support from international aid agencies, the Muluzi administration introduced a wide range of reforms, including free universal primary education; agricultural liberalization ending restrictions on small farmers' production and trade of cash crops; and the lifting of public subsidies, state-provided credit, and trade barriers.[8] However, there is little evidence that poor people are benefiting yet from the policy changes.

The conditions that lock so many Malawians into poverty are numerous and intertwined. Most study participants report that the share of people in their communities without enough to eat has grown in the past decade. Some participants, particularly those in the south where the ruling party is based, find signs of progress in the new government and more open economy but say that, so far, the changes have improved only the lives of people who are better off. Poor men and women feel especially disadvantaged by the reforms affecting agricultural markets.

The study is based on discussions with poor people in seven villages and three urban settlements scattered throughout the northern, central, and southern regions of this narrow country in southern Africa (see table 2, Study Communities in Malawi, at the end of this chapter). Five of the communities visited are in the southern region, home to about half the country's total population and half of those who live below the expenditure poverty line. There are also extremely poor districts in the central and northern regions, as well as very high levels of poverty in many urban areas, such as in Blantyre, which has a 61 percent poverty rate at the district level.[9] Districts were selected for the study based on their agricultural history and livelihood sources using data from previous studies.

Within each district, the communities were chosen with the assistance of district development officers, district commissioners, and agricultural officers. Participants for the various discussion groups and case studies were selected with the assistance of local leaders (chiefs or their assistants), fieldworkers from the Ministry of Agriculture, and local development committees. Local residents (poor and non-poor) were convened randomly for the first discussion group, which assisted the research team in identifying study participants from poor areas and households in the community. A total of seventy discussion groups were completed, including sixty with poor people and ten with poor and better-off people. Fewer discussion groups were held than planned in urban communities because the research team, despite repeated attempts, had difficulty recruiting men for discussions during the work-day. Researchers completed fifty-five case studies of poor people, including fifteen men, thirty women, and ten youths. The study was conducted by the Center for Social Research at the University of Malawi.

This chapter explores the complex tangle of persistent disadvantages that keep people from escaping poverty, such as infertile land, weak markets, unemployment, and scarce drinking water. It also looks at intermittent shocks such as death, divorce, and theft, which can initiate a life-threatening downward spiral in the lives of individuals and house-holds barely getting by. It concludes with the experiences of a few poor Malawians who have managed to improve their wellbeing.

Doing Well and Doing Poorly: No Plate-Drying Rack

In Malawi the gap between doing poorly and doing well is often narrow. The standards of a good life are modest. According to study participants, someone who is doing well has a house that doesn't leak, bedding, shoes, fishing nets, and a plate-drying rack, and "drinks tea with milk."

In both urban and rural areas, wellbeing comes from possessing the resources needed to earn a living and meet basic needs.[10] In a fishing community, this means having fishing equipment; in other rural areas it means being able to grow tobacco and other cash crops. In urban settlements, employment status is the yardstick, according to study participants. Households with assets can protect themselves from disasters because they have adequate food for the entire year, secure shelter, access to decent medical care, and enough steady income to withstand crises such as famine, price hikes, and diseases. These assets, say people in the study, allow individuals with wellbeing to have peace of mind.

Poor people in squatter settlements have the most luxurious descriptions of wellbeing. One group of women from Phwetekere says that 20 percent of the population is doing well, and describes this group as having cars, groceries, electricity, and sofa sets, in addition to jobs and education. Others in Phwetekere say that about 10 percent of the population has cellular phones, videos, refrigerators, and expensive clothes.

In contrast, illbeing comes from the constant deprivation of life's basic necessities, such as food, medical care, and shelter. In general, illbeing is characterized by hunger for extended periods of the year, poor health and stunted growth, unemployment or irregular income, lack of access to livelihood resources such as fishing equipment and agricultural materials, and dilapidated housing.

Rudeness, delinquent behavior, witchcraft, jealousy, excessive beer drinking, quarrels, and, at the household level, fighting and unstable families are also reported to be aspects of illbeing. Women from the village of Mbwadzulu describe poor people as "those who sit on the floor. . . . They go to the garden without eating first; they cook under the sun; they have no pit latrine or bathing area, and no plate-drying rack."

Many discussion groups describe a category of the "most poor" that includes orphans, the aged, people with physical handicaps, and the mentally ill. These are people without gardens to grow their food, who may be casual laborers or beggars, and who may have nowhere to sleep. Study participants also say the poorest of the poor are excluded or exclude themselves from most community affairs. A group of women in Nampeya refers to those who are the worst off as 'those with stunted growth . . . They do not have any food . . . they fall sick frequently . . . they are thin . . . their hair is not strong . . . their bodies do not shine even after taking a bath." The women estimate that 30 percent of the population of the village falls in this bottom category.

Although there are variations, most discussion groups in the study report that the number of poor people has grown over the last decade, particularly over the past few years. Ongoing or periodic hunger affects about 80 to 90 percent of households in their communities, according to discussion groups, while a decade ago hunger affected an estimated 30 to 40 percent.

Caught in a Web of Misery

Poor people worked in small discussion groups to identify and rank the leading problems facing their communities and priorities for action. With very high frequency in villages as well as urban settlements, men and women report a large set of interrelated problems, including hunger, land shortages due to population growth, unemployment, lack of loan facilities, high commodity prices, poor roads, unsafe water, diseases and poor access to medical care, and rising crime and theft. In addition, poor people in Malawi face unexpected shocks that may include the destruction of homes and crops, deaths, and orphanhood. Farming communities have been severely disadvantaged in recent years by erratic weather (drought, floods, high winds) leading to unreliable agricultural production. Urban communities report that they confront child abductions, armed robberies, and murder. Women indicate that in addition to the problems named above, they are vulnerable to divorce and rape. Malawi stands out not only for the number of severe problems that emerge from the discussions with poor people, but for the extent to which a confluence of these problems entangles every community visited. These are described below.

Empty Stomachs

Hunger is reported to be the most critical problem across all ten study communities. Participants report that they sometimes go days without food. Chaundumuka Chiphiko, a youth from Khwalala with seven siblings, says,

> We have a small garden because the area is densely populated by migrant fishermen. We lack clothes and food. We usually have one meal a day, and sometimes we go without food for two or three days. When there are food shortages, we normally beg maize from Mr. Jere, a rich man who owns a grocery. Sometimes, the government distributes maize to the villages.

A participant in a group of men and women in Chitambi reports, "Food consumption is erratic; even children sleep on empty stomachs on most days." Indeed, some people indicate that children may be especially vulnerable to hunger and to the many diseases that may accompany malnutrition. States Patuma Jali, a mother of seven in Nampeya,

Whenever I have a child, the child is found to be malnourished. Some of my children suffer from malnutrition due to lack of food, as you can see. This child of mine is 17 months old, but he still does not walk. He has many diseases because he lacks food, mainly the three food groups.

Fifty percent of children under 5 years of age in Malawi are stunted, and half of these are severely stunted.[11]

Early Marriage, High Fertility, and Less Land

Several communities in the study are faced with a decreasing availability of land, which they attribute in part to early marriages and large families. A young man from Mtamba comments, "My sister failed [to advance to secondary school] just because of school fees. As I am talking, she is married because she had nothing to do." Poor women throughout the study mention frequently that they married and began having children at a very young age. Nambwewe of Madana village, for instance, dropped out of school after grade three because her family could not afford school fees.[12] Nambwewe recounts, "Soon after reaching puberty, I got married to a man from my village. We had eleven children, but six of them died." Nambwewe's first husband died, and she remarried a man whose wife had died. Nambwewe says of her current marriage. "We do not have any children together yet, but he also has some eight children by his late wife. The good thing is that my husband is not worried that I haven't given him any children; he has accepted me as I am."

Except in the southern village of Nampeya, poor men and women identify their communities' rapidly growing populations as a key cause of food shortages. There is simply less land for crops and home gardens to go around. The average size of landholdings among poor people is about half a hectare, and one-quarter hectare for the very poor.[13] A youth from Kuphera recounts,

My grandparents used to tell me that land for agriculture was not a problem at all. They had more than enough for cultivation. . . . Large tracts of land remained fallow. The situation changed when their sons and daughters, including my mother, began to get married. They all wanted to have gardens of their own. My grandparents had to redistribute some of their land to them. By the time they died, they did not have enough land to grow crops to last them a year. The land my mother, aunts, and uncles were given cannot support the subsistence of our families either. Our families have grown big and our gardens are simply inadequate.

Even in the three urban settlements, poor people link food shortages to population growth. "In the past some of us had gardens around, so hunger was not a problem as such, but these days we no longer have land to cultivate because of the increase in population," report women in a Chemusa discussion group.

Men and women in all ten communities also associate hunger with declining soil fertility. Typical of many comments throughout the study, a woman in Nampeya observes, "Even the poor used to grow and produce a lot of crops such as maize, sweet potatoes, and cassava, because the soils were very fertile then."

Costly Fertilizers and Devalued Currency

Poor men and women in every study community, urban and rural, mention the difficulties caused by fertilizer prices. A few discussion groups identify the devaluation of the kwacha as the trigger for spikes in the cost of fertilizer and other basic goods. The corresponding benefit of better prices for cash crops such as tobacco emerges only rarely in discussions with poor farmers, who mainly grow maize for household consumption.[14] "The main problems we are facing now are diseases and hunger. Hunger is brought on by the increase in the price of fertilizer. We work as hard as possible, but we don't harvest much due to inadequate fertilizer," explains Mrs. Nasikelo of Chitambi. A group of women in Nampeya says,

In the past we were able to harvest at least four full oxcarts without using fertilizer, and we could sell the excess to buy things like bicycles. But now since the price of fertilizer has gone up and the soils have lost fertility, we harvest just enough for home consumption and not enough to sell.

Beginning in 1999, the government distributed seeds and fertilizer to farmers in an effort to avoid a food crisis, improve soils, and ensure continued support for the country's economic liberalization policies.[15] In at least one village visited, however, the program was less than successful (box 1).

According to women in Mtamba, when the government sent villages free seed and fertilizer "starter packs" for the 1998–99 farming season, some households in the village received several packs while others received only one. Women there say that when a government assistance program is implemented, "Government should administer it because when they leave it to anybody within the village, say for example the chief, he doesn't share the help equally. He first of all gives the help to all his relatives before giving to the rest of the people in the village, which is very unfair."

Moreover, fertilizer is not all that now costs more. According to a woman from Chemusa, "Ten years ago money was not a problem because with little money we could buy so many things, which is not the case nowadays." Participants in a discussion group of men and women in Mbwadzulu say, "Things are expensive now," and stress that they now need to buy maize in addition to other basic goods because "we cannot harvest enough." Box 2 describes a state-run shop that people can turn to when desperate.

The effects of the devaluation of the kwacha are felt very strongly in the three urban settlements as well. A youth from Phwetekere says,

> Not long ago 15 kwacha would suffice to buy relish for the
> whole week, but nowadays the same money buys nothing. . . .
> It is not even enough as pocket money for a single student
> going to school for one day. . . . This is why we are saying our
> currency has lost value.

Precarious Jobs

In villages and settlements, the poorest households are described as landless and having to rely on casual work to survive. Polina Hawa, a poor widow from Mbwadzulu, says, "I earn my living by selling firewood and cooking zitumbuwa [fritters] and selling them. During the rainy season I work hard at casual labor so that I can get something to eat." Many people report that they cannot find informal jobs regularly, however, and that wages for casual labor are very low and sometimes in kind. A youth group in Mtamba explains, "During times of hunger we go around doing casual labor in exchange for maize bran." Other poor people report that they don't have enough strength to undertake this type of work.

The hardship of joblessness emerges strongly in the three urban settlements. Youths in the squatter settlement of Chemusa report, "At the moment the population is high and the number of educated people is also high due to free education, so job opportunities are really scarce."

The privatization of state-run firms is also viewed as contributing to unemployment in Chemusa and Kowerani. "The government has sold some of its companies . . . the new management of the companies has retrenched workers instead of recruiting new employees, as was the case before," says a discussion group participant from Chemusa.

Weather Vagaries

Poor people in every community visited also link their illbeing to unpredictable weather and the changing seasons. Heavy rains in 1998 and 1999 washed away soil, seeds, and crops in many villages, while the previous growing seasons were marked by extended drought. A villager from a discussion group of men and women in Mbwadzulu says, "Rains have been very erratic for the past few years . . . and this has led to poor harvests, especially maize, which is our main staple food. That is why most of us are poor." Chimwemwe Kachala from Phwetekere remarks, "My job is seasonal. I get better money in the dry season when people are building, but in the rainy season no one builds a house and I get nothing." As with farming, the prospects for casual jobs rise and fall with the weather. Wage jobs are most scarce and hunger and illness most often peak during the rainy season.

Seasonal food shortages are a widespread risk. Women in Chitambi note, for instance, that half the population may "miss meals for days, especially in the hungry months of January and February." Study participants also report that lean agricultural times have become more difficult to endure because wild foods are harder to obtain due to deforestation and reduced fish stocks.

Youths from Khwalala village say that wellbeing depends on a household's ability to cope with crisis situations such as "a falling house" and "crop failure due to heavy rains" or other weather problems. Falling houses is a disaster mentioned by poor people in five communities in the study. Made of mud-brick and thatch, most of the houses in these areas cannot withstand the heavy rains and winds that have been typical in the past two years. Chiyambi Mwale, a poor woman from Phwetekere, says, "Our home is in very bad condition. It leaks and looks like it is falling but we cannot afford to maintain it. This has made our life more miserable."

No Credit

Poor women and men describe several activities in their communities in which they are not permitted to participate. While credit opportunities are reported to be growing, in seven of the ten study communities poor people say they are denied access. Beneficiaries are said to be relatives of responsible officers and chiefs, as well as people who are better off because they have collateral and can afford the high interest rates and bribes associated with obtaining loans.

A discussion group of Mbwadzulu youths acknowledges that the change of government has made life better for some households because they are able to run businesses without political interference and can access loans from credit institutions in the area such as the governmental Malawi Rural Finance Company (MRFC).[17] The youths report, however, that individuals getting these loans are those who can raise a deposit fee; most people cannot benefit from the credit services because they lack such funds and "are afraid of its high interest rate." Similarly, a resident of

Phwetekere says that "so many lending institutions have emerged, but their operations are hardly transparent. People do not know how to access them. Those who have tried have been let down by high levels of collateral demanded."

A discussion group of men in Mbwadzulu indicates that credit opportunities such as those offered by MRFC can also sow seeds of disunity in the village:

> We feel things are getting worse because there is segregation of groups other than Yaos. Only Yaos are getting loans and not us Tongas. Among the Yaos, the poor are being segregated. They said that they have to pay a deposit before they give them a loan, but where do they expect them to get the cash?

Women's discussion groups in Mbwadzulu and Nampeya report that the public credit institutions merely register their names, then go on the radio to announce progress without actually providing loans to the women. A woman in Mtamba recalls that some time ago government lending officials came to their community, gave people forms to fill out and collected them, but "we still don't have access to credit facilities."

One of the better-known NGO credit programs in the country is the Foundation for International Community Assistance (FINCA), which makes small business loans exclusively to women. All the women's discussion groups in Phwetekere ranked FINCA as an important institution. FINCA members pay a deposit of K25 per week for five weeks, after which they are eligible for a loan of K2,500 (about US$58 in 1999). Other women in the credit group must ensure that each member pays back her loan. In case of default, property may be confiscated. Payments begin a week after the loan is made at K125 (about US$3) per week.

Some women in Phwetekere speak positively of FINCA: "The welfare of a lot of women in this location has improved because of FINCA's credit. Without it no woman, especially from the poorer groups in the community, would be able to run a small business." But others have mixed feelings: "Much as the loans have helped some of us to become somewhat better off, the terms and conditions force us into psychological slavery." Some object to the deposit, and others believe that payments should not start for at least a month. Women in Chemusa say the loan amounts they qualify for are too low to help them start businesses.

Poor men feel sidestepped by NGO credit programs, which target women. Women's discussion groups disagree that they have any advantages over men in obtaining loans, reporting that the lending officers or wives of politicians and other local leaders have recently been the beneficiaries of credit schemes. In Chitambi a discussion group of men reports that some loan officers demand sexual favors from women in exchange for loans or only give credit to those who have money.

Inadequate Water and Roads

All communities in the study struggle with poor water quality and water shortages as well as lack of good roads. Most communities report that existing wells are either inadequate for their growing populations or sit in disrepair, and nearby streams and lakes are not safe or reliable alternatives, especially during the rainy season when floodwaters carry harmful wastes into the waterways. Although the village of Madana recently received two new wells, participants in a discussion group of men and women say it isn't enough: "We need more boreholes because we rely on unsafe water from streams and unprotected wells. It is a critical problem because most of these streams and wells dry out during the dry season. We have to travel long distances in search of water."

In Khwalala people report that they "have to line up for hours before it is our turn to draw water [from the communal taps]." If the boreholes break down or the lines are too long, residents must get their water from a polluted lake. During the rainy season, people are at greater risk of infectious and parasitic diseases such as diarrhea and schistosomiasis because waste from the highlands flows into the lake. Garbage and refuse also wash in to Mbwadzulu's lake, but the community recently received two boreholes and cholera is said to have declined.

Poor roads are another urgent problem. The roads into the three urban communities are full of large potholes, and both public and private transport operators have suspended service because of the hazard to their vehicles. Women report that this makes their lives "unbearable" because now they "either have to walk [to work] or stay home and earn nothing." Lack of transport also keeps people from accessing medical care and other services.

During the rainy season, roads in seven communities are said to become impassable, and many of these communities say they lack the resources to maintain the roads on their own. In Mbwadzulu a group of men explains, "In the past, we used to be employed by the roads department to work on maintenance and clear the bush along the roads so roads were not a problem, but these days they have stopped employing us, and roads are not being maintained." Similarly, in Kowerani the roads sit in disrepair. Poor people there explain that the government no longer maintains the roads and the community's spirit of self-help has dwindled: "It is very difficult to mobilize for self-initiatives." Villagers in Khwalala and Madana also report that they have tried to maintain the roads on their own but have not been able to do it satisfactorily, as they lack proper resources.

The Reach for Schooling

Study participants express satisfaction with the government's efforts to increase access to education through the introduction of free primary schooling in 1994 and a major school construction initiative. A discussion group of women from Chemusa, for instance, speaks highly of these advances: "In the past schools were very far, about five kilometers away. Our children used to go to HHI, Blantyre Girls, and Dharap because we had no school around. These days our children are walking just two kilometers to Mbayani for school."

Nonetheless, schools remain distant for children in each of the villages in the study and both urban and rural study participants express concern about the low quality of teaching,[18] the lack of learning materials, and the fees that are still required to continue into secondary grades. A group of women in Kuphera explains,

> We hear the government introduced free primary education and provides for all essential requirements, notebooks, pens, and pencils. The pupils have never received these items. We still have to provide them ourselves. We strongly believe it is not the government's fault but is sheer malpractice on the part of the school's management. We have seen several teachers going around selling notebooks and pens. In addition, the teachers are not dedicated to their duty. Often pupils go back home without attending even a single lesson. We hear the teachers are unmotivated because of poor working conditions. Their salaries are particularly low. It is not surprising that they divert free primary education resources to supplement their miserable

*salaries. This has adversely affected the standards of education
at school.*

Poor people also report that school buildings are in serious disrepair. According to a group of men in Mbwadzulu, "In the past we had enough classrooms because we had fewer children going to school, but with the introduction of free primary education, the classrooms have proved to be not enough."

Youths throughout the study communities express despair over the obstacles to obtaining education, especially secondary school fees, and link this directly to their poor employment prospects. "Lack of money to pay school fees for secondary school level leads to illiteracy, which leads to not getting employed. Therefore lack of school fees invites suffering," explains a discussion group of women from Nampeya. Likewise, young men in a group in Phwetekere remark that school is very important because it is the only viable means to gain a livelihood in their community:

> *We have no choice but to rely on school for our futures. We are
> not a farming community. None of our families have land for
> agriculture. If we drop out of school, the only other alternative
> is casual labor. The wages are barely adequate. This means that
> we shall be condemned to poverty indefinitely.*

A women's discussion group in Phwetekere remarks that the future of girls hangs in limbo despite the promise of schooling: "Free primary education in itself is not enough. The constraints for girls to persist in school are quite insurmountable. It will therefore be very difficult for them to break free from poverty."

Endangered Health

Poor people in every community visited say they are very vulnerable to illnesses, and they identify numerous health dangers, including hunger, strenuous labor, extreme weather, leaky shelters, contaminated water, poor sanitation, promiscuity, and unprotected sex. Frequent outbreaks of diseases such as cholera, schistosomiasis, and malaria, together with the killer scourge HIV/AIDS, leave many people orphaned, widowed, and disabled. Hospitals and clinics are very important to poor people under these conditions, but as with schools, the quality of services is reported to be very low. A discussion group of men from Phwetekere says, "Life begins and usually ends in the hospital. In between, we depend on the hospital for good health. There is therefore no more important institution than the hospital. It is more or less a custodian of our lives."

Traditional healers and birth attendants are still active in many communities, but most poor people in the study prefer modern services. "Whenever a person falls ill, the first thing that he or she thinks of is the hospital. We used to also rely on traditional healers, but they have now expired. They are no longer reliable and effective," says a man from Phwetekere. Women in Nampeya rank their traditional healers low and report that they supply "fake medicine" and "cause hatred between people." Women in Kowerani feel that their practices are "unhygienic" and outdated.

Lacking modern services locally, poor people in all three urban settlements and most of the villages lament the time and expense needed to reach distant health facilities. A woman from Mbwadzulu says, "Sometimes a patient dies at the bus stop or on the way to the hospital because it is far from our village." Similarly, a woman from Mtamba remarks, "Expectant mothers deliver under the tree while going to the hospital because it is too far from the village." Even when they are able to reach the hospital, people say they spend hours there trying to get service and then medication and often return home without the necessary drugs because they are not available or cost too much.

In Khwalala participants say that conditions at the hospital—poor sanitation coupled with prohibitively expensive or inadequate drugs, substandard food and bedding, and disrespectful staff—actually worsen the health of people who go there for treatment. This is said to lead to many deaths that could otherwise be avoided.

In addition, the rate of AIDS-related diseases and deaths is very high. In Kuphera participants say, "Both men and women end up contracting sexually transmitted diseases including HIV/AIDS, which incapacitates them." In Madana a participant states, "The people should refrain from promiscuous acts. This has escalated the HIV/AIDS epidemic, which has increased the death rates." Women in Phwetekere observe that those in higher wellbeing categories are more at risk because their extra cash "promotes promiscuity," which can lead to HIV/AIDS and death.

Divorced and Widowed Women

About a third of Malawi's poor people live in households headed by women, an unusually high proportion.[9] Women across many communities depend on their husbands to be the main breadwinner. If divorce or death of the husband should befall the household, women, who have fewer livelihood opportunities, are left with the responsibility of caring for children. Women from Madana indicate that this is why most female-headed households belong to the lower wellbeing classes:

> *Women can be divorced at any time or can get pregnant and be abandoned by men. . . . This normally happens out of men's greed—they always want to have a new taste. . . . The burden of caring for the children rests squarely on women's shoulders. . . . These women become helpless and they lead a miserable life.*

Due to the strong impact of divorce on women, marriage counselors emerge as one of the most important institutions in the study. They are called upon to help with family problems, typically unfaithfulness on the part of husbands and domestic violence. People in Mbwadzulu say, "Without marriage counselors most of the families would have separated; they are uniting families." However, some participants remark that the counselors show male bias or are unresponsive. Men and women in Nampeya say, "Marriage counselors from the male line may favor the husband when actually the husband is the one at fault."

Domestic violence is reported to be widespread in all but one of the communities visited in Malawi. Although women are overwhelmingly the victims, discussion groups of both men and women acknowledge that men are also targets of abuse. Reasons given for domestic violence vary, but many discussion groups mention a decline in traditional values. Men in Chitambi say that "women no longer fully submit to their husbands," and they feel violence is increasing against women who are working and gaining resources of their own. In contrast, women in Chitambi say that it is precisely working women who are most protected from violence because men are more dependent on them.

Widowhood is another severe hardship for women. A woman in Mbwadzulu says, "For some of us, the death of our husbands has left us helpless. [There is] no one to assist . . . and a lot of children to look after." Another participant from the same village explains,

Poverty in this village has affected women more than men be-
cause when a man dies, the woman is left with all the responsi-
bilities of looking after the children. . . . She cannot harvest
enough food because of the poor rains and the little land she
has . . . and she cannot go into the lake on a boat to fish. But if
a woman dies, the man is not affected the same way because he
does not stay with the children. . . . He sends them to grandpar-
ents or other relatives.

Polina Hawa, 37, lives in the fishing village of Mbwadzulu. She never
attended school and married at 18. Her husband died of dysentery in
1996. After her husband's death, his relatives confiscated the household's
property. She says, "They just left me with a blanket and one bedsheet to
cover my children. . . . My children do not have clothes." Two of her children are now married, but she has three others. She tries to support them
by selling firewood and doing casual labor. "But I don't have time to
work in my field and as a result we lack food."

Grandmothers are often left caring for multiple grandchildren
when their own children die and leave orphans. Mrs. Nangilia from
Chemusa says,

I got married at 13 because I wanted to run away from the
troubles I was facing. . . . I had eleven children with this man,
but three passed away. Things changed for the worse when my
husband died and my three children died. The children left an-
other six children whom I was supposed to take care of, so now
I have fourteen children to care for.

Mrs. Nangilia says that she tries to provide for them all by selling
beer, but it is not enough. "I am now a poor woman," she remarks. "I
have no food; I can spend a whole day, even two, sleeping without eating
anything." She had hoped her children would be able to provide for her.

Children Left Behind without Hope

With one of the highest rates of HIV/AIDS in the world, Malawi has a
growing population of orphans. Although reliable data are not available,
it is projected that within the next few years two-thirds of a million
Malawian children may be orphaned.[20] A woman in Mbwadzulu reports,

"Indeed, [orphanhood] is becoming worse due to the killer disease AIDS.
. . . These children lack many things in their lives and we cannot manage
to provide them with everything." According to a participant from
Phwetekere, "Many more children will become delinquents and orphans
because of the impact of the HIV/AIDS epidemic. . . . The children will
invariably be trapped in a vicious circle of poverty."

Mrs. Namasina from Chemusa became an orphan in high school. Previously, she lived happily in the capital city of Lilongwe with her mother,
stepfather, and five siblings. She was in her third year of high school in
1995 when her mother died. She says,

> My siblings and I went to stay with our grandmother in Lilong-
> we. Unfortunately this grandmother who was supporting us
> also passed away and that is when we faced a lot of trouble. . . .
> My aunt also died and left six children, so we were twelve
> orphans, all of us, without anyone to lean on. . . . We were
> suffering. We could spend a whole day without eating anything.
> We lacked soap. . . . We lacked parental care and advice.

Ultimately she married her current husband but feels she married
too young.

Theft and Other Crime

In every community visited, poor men and women report theft, robbery,
burglary, murders, and other acts that pose physical threats to people's
lives. In most communities, participants say crime is increasing, and police services are lax and ineffective.

Several villagers in Kuphera spoke of their lives spiraling downward
after the theft of their cattle. Farmers in Mtamba say, "We can't grow cassava these days to support us when the maize is finished because thieves
will come to steal it." All discussion groups in Kowerani mention a story
of a woman who was caught stealing maize from a garden; they emphasize that women are rarely associated with theft, and view the incident as
a sign of worse things yet to come. In Mtamba and Chitambi, villagers
say that crime is on the rise because police stations are far removed from
their communities.

Crime is reported to be growing more serious in urban areas, as well.
A man from Kowerani explains that he and his wife began with a small

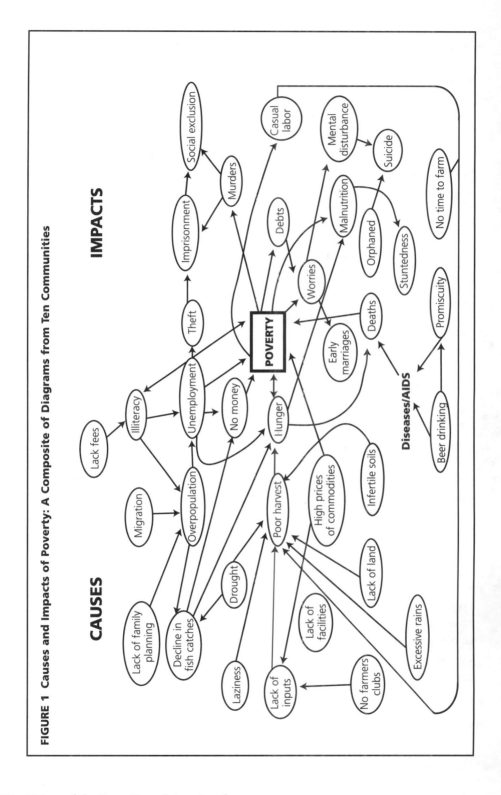

FIGURE 1 Causes and Impacts of Poverty: A Composite of Diagrams from Ten Communities

CAUSES

IMPACTS

business selling charcoal and fresh fish in 1994 and "raised enough money to open two groceries and one bottle store." In 1998 all three businesses were burgled in three separate incidents.

Many study participants are critical of the police and blame them in part for the increase in crime. Most people believe that the police have become more lax about law enforcement and that the country's penal system is weak. According to a participant in Nampeya, "They are of course not entirely to blame. They do not have adequate resources at their disposal, but still the problem is that they are corrupt. They fall prey to bribes; and as a result, they do not prosecute the offenders." Some associate the rise in lawlessness with the reintroduction of multiparty politics in 1994. A few attribute growing crime to the disbanding of the Malawi Young Pioneers and the youth league of the Malawi Congress Party because these groups used to enforce peace and stability, albeit at the expense of people's political freedom.

People in Mtamba and Chitambi say that not only are the police unhelpful, but "Normally, they send us back to catch the murderers and thieves and bring them to the police station. Who dares to try to catch a robber armed with an AK47 rifle?" Yet in some urban and rural areas mob justice has become a common alternative to police procedures. A discussion group in Mtamba explains, "Now the people are just punishing the thieves on their own. They burn them. For example, last week two thieves were beaten to death because the police do not punish them accordingly." Similarly, in Mbwadzulu, a participant reports that "when a thief is caught, he is sometimes beaten up by children or even stripped naked." Thieves may be stoned, beaten, or burned to death. In Phwetekere and Mbwadzulu, participants say they sometimes take the law into their own hands out of frustration at seeing thieves released from police stations a day after being caught. "Just last week a thief was burnt to death," note discussion group participants in Phwetekere. Less extreme measures in Phwetekere include a neighborhood watch started by residents who have banded together to help discourage crime in the community.

Trapped in the Tangle

Figure 1 is a composite of the causes and impacts of poverty identified by discussion groups in the ten study communities. Many of these disadvantages are described as interlinked and are illustrated by study participants as circular, with many impacts becoming causes and many causes becoming impacts, all feeding back into ever deepening cycles of destitution. Hunger, illness, joblessness, lack of money, population growth, and lack of education appear on a number of the discussion groups' diagrams as both causes and impacts of poverty.

As the following three life stories attest, the disadvantages poor people's experience are multidimensional and interrelated.

Orphaned; Married Young; Mother of Five; Robbed; Widowed; Hungry

Nasibeko of Kuphera village says, "My father died a few months before my birth, and upon my birth my mother became blind and died a day later. Hence I was raised by my aunt." Nasibeko's aunt and uncle lived well and provided her with food and clothes, but they did not send her to school. She was married shortly after puberty to a man who became a prosperous farmer. "We were given a large piece of land to cultivate; we usually got bumper yields." They invested in a cow and eventually had a herd of thirty cattle.

> *Our life was fine until one day when our cattle were stolen.*
> *After that, our lives became miserable. . . . Fertilizer became*
> *unaffordable. A year later my husband passed away and left*
> *me the task of caring for five children. . . . Sadly, my son who*
> *was helping me a lot was beaten to death by some thugs. . . .*
> *I sometimes go without food and I lack good clothes.*

Falling House; Abandoned Youth; Hungry, Dirty, and Stressed; Unaffordable School Fees

Yohane Mbalule is an orphan of 16 in the village of Mtamba. His father died in 1996 from "swelling of the legs and coughing." Yohane and three siblings were living with his mother until their house fell down and they were homeless. He says, "My mother decided to go search for a job in order to build another house, and now it's been five months since she left us." His aunt took them in, but he explains, "My aunt has six children and we are four. . . . My uncle is not working, so it is very difficult for him to manage to feed us. It is impossible to buy soap for all of us, so sometimes we go to school without washing our clothes." Yohane is concerned about the lack of money for high school fees. He says, "Due to this fear of school fees I have on my mind, I sometimes fail to concentrate in class. . . . I wish I could continue my schooling through high school or even to the university so that I could take the responsibility of looking after my younger sisters."

Unemployed; Separated from Wife; Homeless; Elderly; Disabled; Begging for Survival

Mavuto Siwinda of Khwalala was born into poverty in 1934. When he was 26 he left for Zambia and found a job as a "houseboy" for a white man. Mavuto married after he believed he was earning enough to support a wife. Soon after the marriage, however, his employer returned to his home country and Mavuto was out of work. Unable to find another job, he returned to his parents' home, but his wife refused to accompany him. "Much as I still loved her," says Mavuto, "I couldn't stay with her because my pride could not allow me to stay in a woman's home."

When he arrived home, he discovered that both his parents had died. With nowhere to go, Mavuto sought refuge with his younger brother, then 63, who is divorced and lives alone. "He has a very small garden," Mavuto says, "where he grows cassava but the stuff lasts us less than a year." The men must often beg from distant relatives, without whose help they would not have food, soap, clothes, or other necessities. Mavuto's health is now poor. His legs are too weak to support him if he stands for more than ten minutes. "I am a weakling," he says. "I am also susceptible to malaria and coughing. I even have a problem of high blood pressure, you see. I am helpless. I don't have my own house. I am weak, I can't work, and I beg from other people in order to earn a living."

A Few Break Free

In a few places, study participants report that things are getting better. In Chitambi, a farming village of 2,300 in the southern region, poor people say that ten years ago 90 percent of their community was in the "suffering" category, while only half is now. They say many people have benefited from credit schemes, farmers clubs that help them obtain fertilizer and seed loans, higher prices for crops, better wages, free primary education, and the transition to a more open political system.

Beyond Chitambi, participants in some discussion groups (particularly in the south, which is the stronghold of the ruling party) report that some households in their communities have improved their wellbeing or that they themselves are actually doing better. Mostly, they associate the gains with the political transition and greater freedom that exists in the country. A group of participants in Phwetekere says, "Nowadays people are free to do any type of business without fearing government interference, unlike in the past when we could be asked a lot of questions about where we got the capital from . . . or who we wanted to compete with." Likewise, a group of men and women in Nampeya indicates that in the past most people were afraid of doing any business and "buried their money in the ground to hide it." Now, they say, people are beginning to start up businesses. Women from this community add, "There has been a change of government such that people are now free to do business, unlike in the past when anyone who was 'doing well' was questioned on how he or she made it to 'doing well' status." Youths in Mbwadzulu echo this idea: "We now have a government that is not oppressive. . . . In the past the government was very oppressive, but these days people are free to go into any business they ever think of."

In other areas of the country, people also sometimes mention new credit programs, public works, and NGO relief and development efforts. Men in Mbwadzulu remark, "Since the new government took over the reins, people have learned to look for loans and have also

TABLE 1 Upward Mobility in Two Urban Settlements

Reason for upward mobility	Chemusa	Phwetekere
There are more casual labor opportunities than before, and wages are better than before	✔	—
People can fetch river sand and sell it to construction companies	✔	—
Some people have access to loans from kinship networks to start businesses	—	✔
Family sizes are smaller than before	✔	✔
Some people are in big business	✔	✔
Retirees and other workers have come to settle in the area	✔	✔
There are more moneylenders	✔	—
More people have secured jobs	✔	—
There is no government oppression, as there was in the past	✔	—
More political leaders have access to loans for members of their parties to start businesses	—	✔

— Not mentioned.

worked hard in their businesses." Remittances from children and relatives are also said to play a role, although such support is reported to be declining and unreliable. Of note, study participants in two urban settlements, Chemusa and Phwetekere, say that some households are doing better because family planning is now more available (table 1). According to a poor woman in Chemusa, "In the past, people were not using family planning methods and this was causing the families to have more members . . . so that it was difficult for most households to budget properly."

Turning to Each Other

Poor people in Malawi have numerous informal and formal institutions that are rooted in or come into contact with their communities. When asked about leading local institutions, people in the ten study communities identified about ninety different ones. While government institutions such as public hospitals, the police, schools, and depots for farm commodities are considered important, they very frequently receive low ratings for effectiveness. Among the institutions that poor people identify, in fact, only two receive mostly favorable reviews: the village headman and the marriage counselor (see "Divorced and Widowed Women," above). Poor people also identify a variety of community-based institutions, many informal, that bring them together and help them cope with disasters.

The village headman is generally ranked high (first to third among the most important institutions) by almost all the discussion groups in most urban and rural communities. People believe headmen are helpful during times of bereavement and illness, and in settling disputes. They also provide their community with a link to the government. In a few cases, however, study participants reveal problems of favoritism and ineffectiveness.

Discussion groups in Phwetekere speak particularly highly of their headman. One man there describes the chief's role this way: "If anything goes wrong, we first think of him as the primary source of assistance. If, for instance, your house has been broken into or you have quarreled with neighbors, you rush to him for assistance. He is simply indispensable." Another woman adds,

> He is quite responsive when help is sought. When, for example, he is informed of illness, he does not hesitate but leaves at once

He assists in finding accommodations. He thus keeps an up-to-date record of individuals renting out houses. . . . He is what we want. He is just, responsive, understanding, and caring.

Such praise is consistent with comments from most other communities. A woman from Mtamba notes, "Whenever we go to the village headman, he provides the help we need. He is always around to settle our disputes and to preside over funeral ceremonies and other important functions in the village." A youth from Mbwadzulu calls him "the protector of our village. . . . He is the one who builds up the village." In two cases, some participants question the impartiality and effectiveness of their local chiefs. In Kowerani a group of women says that the village headman is "corrupt, nepotistic, and ineffective." In Nampeya a group of men reports that the headman does not respond quickly to people's problems; rather, he responds quickly only to receive his salary.

Poor people in many communities organize among themselves to guard against shocks. In Chitambi a group of men and women explains that several households formed a farmers club to work together to prevent hunger in the community. For the past decade this group has been planting sweet potatoes, soya, cassava, and sugarcane alongside their main crop of maize. They also hope to receive credit to purchase more farm inputs.

A women's discussion group in Kuphera explains the function of their Funeral Association:

Our main duty is to offer assistance during funerals. We, for instance, buy food and cloth for wrapping up dead bodies [nsanda], cook, and fetch water and firewood. Although men are not formally recognized members, they still assist us. For example, they are the ones who often go to town to buy pieces of cloth. . . . We extend our services to all regardless of how well off they are, but we mostly assist those who cannot afford funeral services on their own. This association brings unity among ourselves. Every woman is automatically a member.

Study participants from Mbwadzulu indicate that the villagers are united despite the diversity of ethnic groups that have settled there. The Tongas, Tumbukas, Chewas, Yaos, Senas, and Lomwes are reported to be living together and mixing freely. People in Mbwadzulu say, "We work together on community projects like molding bricks for a school project."

Others say, "Whenever there is a funeral, we work together. . . . Women draw water, collect firewood and collect maize flour . . . while men dig the grave and then bury the dead."

Conclusion

Caught in a tenacious web of poverty and buffeted by floods and drought, theft, disease, death, and divorce, poor Malawians must rely primarily on local institutions for help. The state provides minimal services, and families, however broken, are often the only safety net. Women and children bear the heaviest burdens. A group of women in Mtamba says, "We are increasing in number but we have nowhere to get help."

Not surprisingly, most poor people in Malawi are fatalistic and express little hope for the future. A man from Mbwadzulu comments,

> Only God knows the future, but I think the poor will continue getting poorer while the rich will continue getting richer. Because they have money, they will keep doing business. The poor will keep on facing problems. . . . Those that drink tea will continue to drink tea.

When asked about the future, a poor farmer from Kuphera shares his discouragement over high prices for seeds and fertilizers and responds, "We are going to die of hunger."

Yet, poor people in Malawi also speak of opportunities for action. Since 1994 the government has been working through community leaders and organizations to encourage active participation in addressing local problems and combating fatalism. Although less apparent in the very poor communities visited for this study, villages across the country have been engaged in building schools, clinics, roads, and bridges. In areas where action is lacking, there may be value in community exchanges to show those who have given up hope the potential for community-government partnerships to bring change.

Many in the study hope that fertilizer will soon become more affordable, loans easier to get, and safety net programs such as the starter pack initiative better targeted to those most in need. However, the agricultural sector alone will be unable to feed the large and rapidly growing population of Malawi. There is a desperate need for alternative economic opportunities if Malawians are to move out of poverty. Actions that support the creation of microenterprises and small businesses as well as private-sector jobs will be key. Better access to credit and education will also be essential. And finally, greater efforts are urgently needed to combat the spread of HIV/AIDS, provide care for its victims, and support the many orphans the disease is leaving in its wake.

Fatalism for some in the study is tempered by hope in their children's education and employment or in their own prospects of building a business. Mleza Gondwe, a woman of 32 from Khwalala, has suffered through the trials of orphanhood, watching her grandmother die, and seeing her husband lose his job and migrate in search of work. Sometimes her husband sends money, but she says, "It is not enough. I spend it on food because I do not harvest much." Mleza has talked to someone about a loan and hopes to start a small business. She says, "I have not given up to poverty. I will still work hard to see myself better off."

TABLE 2 Study Communities in Malawi

RURAL COMMUNITIES

Chitambi, Mulanje District Pop. 2,300	Like many other villages in the district, this one is surrounded by tea plantations that occupy almost 70 percent of the cultivatable land in the district. The main livelihood sources for men and women include farming (maize, sweet potatoes, sugarcane), small businesses, and agricultural wage labor. The nearest health center is ten kilometers from the village. The community is reached by two feeder roads that become muddy in the rainy season. There is no potable water and no sewerage. According to the village headman, people in the village are mainly Lomwe (80 percent), and most belong to Protestant churches.
Khwalala, Nkhata-Bay District Pop. 2,250	The village lies between the shores of Lake Malawi and the Tunde hills. Most households earn their living by farming and fishing. Until recently, farming was considered women's work; men simply assisted in tilling. The main crop, cassava, was attacked by mealybugs in 1987, which caused food shortages. The community has three roads, a primary school, several churches, and three boreholes. The dominant group is the Tonga (97 percent), while Tumbukas, Nkhondes, and Chewas constitute 1 percent each. Nearly all the people in the village are Christians.
Kuphera, Dowa District Pop. 1,110	The community lies eight kilometers from Malawi's main road that connects the north and south of the country. Almost all men and women in the village are farmers; the main crops are maize and tobacco. Very few households own livestock. There is one old school building that serves as both primary and secondary school. There is no health center and no borehole. Most of the people are Christians, and some belong to an indigenous cult called Nyau. Most people belong to the Chewa ethnic group.

RURAL COMMUNITIES (continued)

Madana,
Ntcheu District
Pop. 1,600

Both men and women in this community depend on agriculture for their livelihoods. The main crops are potatoes, maize, beans, and vegetables. Rearing cattle, goats, and pigs is also common. This community experienced a dramatic population increase due to an influx of refugees from the civil war in Mozambique. There is no health center, no post office, and no borehole, although there is a school. It is predominantly a Christian village with Presbyterian, Roman Catholic, and Baptist churches. The principal ethnic group is the Ngoni, with a matrilineal system of descent.

Mbwadzulu,
Mangochi District
Pop. 3,500

This community lies along the shores of Lake Malawi. Ninety percent of men and women earn their living by fishing, 7 percent by farming, and 3 percent through small businesses. There is a primary school in the village, three boreholes, and a small produce market. Most of the current residents came to the village seeking fishing opportunities. Ethnic groups include the Yao, Lomwe, Tonga, Sena, Chewa, Nyanja, Tumbuka, and Ngoni. Most people are Christian or Muslim.

Mtamba,
Chiradzulu District
Pop. 4,800

For most men and women, farming maize, cassava, tobacco, soya, sweet potatoes, and vegetables is the main source of livelihood. Buildings in the village are constructed from mud-brick and thatch. Access to the community during the rainy season is possible only with all-terrain vehicles. There is no potable water, no health center, and no grocery store, and the school is remote. Most people belong to the Yao group and are Muslim.

Nampeya,
Machiga District
Pop. 3,000

About 70 percent of village households farm rice and maize as their primary source of income, while 30 percent of male-headed households depend on fishing in Lake Chiuta. Most of the land has adequate water supplies, but the water is not safe to drink. There is a market and a primary school, and feeder roads pass through the village. The community has no nearby health center, no telephone, and no post office. The main ethnic groups in the village are the Yao and Lomwe. Half of the community is Muslim, but Roman Catholic, Presbyterian, the Church of Christ, and the Evangelical Church are also present.

URBAN COMMUNITIES

Chemusa, Blantyre city Pop. 15,000	The Blantyre-Lilongwe road runs through this settlement. Most of the houses are small and dilapidated and an average of five houses occupy a standard one-house plot. Most of the men work in the city as security guards and laborers; another 15 percent are involved in petty trade. A majority of the women are housewives. The nearest public health center is in Chilomoni, a squatter area three kilometers away, while a big referral hospital is about five kilometers away. There are some community water taps that charge for potable water. The nearest school is two kilometers away. The main ethnic groups in the area are Yao, Chewa, Tumbuka, Lomwe, and Mang'anja.
Kowerani, Mzuzu city Pop. 2,500	Kowerani is a settlement of Masasa, a suburb two kilometers west of Mzuzu city. It has a rolling landscape with steep slopes and valleys, and many homes are susceptible to collapse during the rainy season. The main livelihood sources for men are casual labor or small businesses such as selling fish or transporting luggage. Most women sell bananas or homemade food products. There is no electricity and no health clinic. Three wells were established in the community, but most people still draw water from streams to avoid paying a water charge. There are several public and NGO schools. Ethnic groups in the area include Tumbuka, Yao, Tonga, and Chewa; ethnic tensions were reported to be on the increase, particularly during the 1999 elections.
Phwetekere, Lilongwe city Pop. 4,000	This squatter settlement is located about four kilometers from the main bus depot in Lilongwe. The majority of men depend on small businesses such as street vending for their livelihood, while others are employed as civil servants or in casual jobs in the city. Most women are reported to be housewives, although some do petty trading in food products. The settlement has a fairly extensive road network, but it is often in bad shape during the rainy season. There is no primary school within the community, but a school is less than one kilometer away. There are several water points, but many are in disrepair. About 70 percent of the residents are Christians.

Notes

1. The Malawi study team was led by the three authors and also included Moreen Bapu, Blessings Chinsinga, Augustine Fatch, Annie Kumpita, Edward Kwisongole, Brenda Mapemba, Dennis Mfune, Esnat Mkandawire, Sylvia Mpando, Ndaga Mulaga, Rodrick Mwamvani, Judith Mwandumba, James Mwera, Lilian Saka, Grace Thakwalakwa, and Susan Tuwe.

2. World Bank, *World Development Indicators 2001* (Report 22099, April 2001), 13.

3. Ibid., 195, 192.

4. The poverty line is determined by a set of daily basic food and non-food requirements of individuals in four geographic areas of Malawi. In April 1998 prices, the rural poverty lines are between Mk 7.76 and Mk 11.16 per person per day, while the urban poverty line is 25.38. It should be noted that 60 percent of daily consumption at the poverty level in rural areas does not involve a cash transaction. National Economic Council, Poverty Monitoring System, "Profile of Poverty in Malawi, 1998: Poverty Analysis of the Malawi Integrated Household Survey, 1997–98" (World Bank report 15437-MAI, November 2000), 9–10.

5. Ibid., 15.

6. *World Development Indicators 2001*, 45.

7. See World Bank, "Memorandum and Recommendation of the President of the International Development Association to the Executive Directors on Assistance to the Republic of Malawi under the Enhanced HIPC Debt Initiative" (Report P7423-MAI, December 5, 2000), 9.

8. IMF and International Development Association, "Malawi: Assessment of Interim Poverty Reduction Strategy Paper," November 22, 2000 (Report 21445-MAI), 1–2.

9. The poverty rate in the southern region is 68.1 percent; central region 62.8 percent; and northern region, 62.5 percent. The rural poverty rate is 66.5 percent and the urban poverty rate is 54.9 percent. See National Economic Council, Poverty Monitoring System, "Profile of Poverty in Malawi," 43–44.

10. Local terms to describe wellbeing include *umoyu umampha* in the Tonga language; *umoyo uwemi* in Tumbuka, spoken in northern Malawi; *umoyo wabwino, kupeza bwino, moyo okoma, moyo osangalara* in Chichewa, spoken widely in central and southern Malawi; and *moyo okatamuka, moyo ovaya, moyo okhupuka* among youths. *Ovaya* comes from the English word "via," and means aloft, on top of, higher, beyond, superior, or exceeding.

11. Malawi National Statistical Office and ORC Macro Inc., "Malawi Demographic and Health Survey," 18.

12. The fee was 4 kwacha per year, about 10 cents at the time of the study. There is now free primary schooling in Malawi, but fees are still required for secondary education.

13. William James Smith, "Spending on Safety Nets for the Poor: How Much, for How Many? The Case of Malawi" (World Bank, Africa Region Working Paper 11, January 2001), 6.

14. For a discussion of why poor farmers have yet to benefit from the recent policy and institutional changes affecting Malawi's agricultural sector, see Mylène Kherallah and Nicholas Minot, "Impact of Agricultural Market Reforms on Smallholder Farmers in Benin and Malawi: Final Report Executive Summary" (University of Hohenheim, Germany, and International Food Policy Research Institute, Washington, D.C., February 2001, draft). With respect to the particular issue of price changes with the devaluation in the mid- to late 1990s, the authors note that maize, the most prevalent crop among smallholders, is not sold for export and its relative market price declined with the devaluation. At the same time, the real price of fertilizer, all of which is imported and used mostly on maize crops, more than doubled between 1994 and 1999.

15. Partially funded by donors, the starter pack distribution program was designed to enable households to produce an additional six-week supply of food. It also aimed at improving nutrition by promoting the consumption of other legumes and nuts and at limiting soil degradation. The *Voices of the Poor* fieldwork took place during the first year of the program; in that year, nearly 3 million farmers received the starter pack, but it has since been scaled back to about 1.5 million farmers. After the first year of the program, the country experienced a bumper maize harvest, which was partially attributed to the use of these starter packs as well as to favorable weather and good maize prices the previous year. See Smith, "Spending on Safety Nets," 21; and Louise Cord, "Cash Transfer Programs in Rural Areas: Lessons from Experience" (World Bank, Poverty Reduction Group, May 21, 2001, draft).

16. For thirty years the government promoted a system of hybrid maize and subsidized fertilizer as a means of promoting food security among subsistence farmers, who were prevented from growing cash crops such as burley tobacco for markets. Before 1987, ADMARC controlled markets for inputs and produce through its large network of depots, which are more concentrated in urban and better-off rural areas. Over the next decade, the farm economy was gradually opened up to the private sector and many subsidies on credit and fertilizers were removed or reduced. Until 1999, however, the government continued to set a price band for which maize could be bought and sold in the country, and ADMARC acted as a buyer of last resort. Of note, smallholders now account for more than half of the total burley tobacco production. See Smith, "Spending on Safety Nets," 5, and Kherallah and Minot, "Impact of Agricultural Market Reforms."

17. MRFC extends loans mainly to tobacco farmer clubs and cash crop growers. It operates like a commercial bank and charges market interest rates, which were above 50 percent in 1995–96.

18. The ratio of pupils to *qualified* teachers is about 120:1; however, teachers without credentials are widely used and reduce the ratio to 60:1. The retention rate is 17 percent in primary schools and the dropout rate is 20 percent. At the secondary level, the enrollment rate is 19 percent and the dropout rate is 17 percent. About 5,000 teachers die of AIDS or are lost to attrition annually, and cannot be replaced fast enough. There is also a shortage of teaching and learning materials. See World Bank, "Memorandum and Recommendation of the President," 6–8.

19. Smith, "Spending on Safety Nets," 6–7.

20. World Bank, "Malawi: A Safety Net Strategy for the Poorest" (December 8, 1999, draft, v).

Nigeria

Illbeing and Insecurity

Foluso Okunmadewa with Olu Aina, Gabriel Bolade Ayoola,
Abubakar Mamman, Noble Nweze, Tanwa Odebiyi,
Dora Shehu, and James Zacha[1]

Chinwe Okoro, 26, is the fourth of five children who were raised by a widowed mother in the small, remote farming village of Okpuje in southeastern Enugu State. Chinwe lost his father in 1982, just as he was entering primary school. With his mother lacking a reliable income and his brothers jobless, Chinwe's schooling was cut short so he could contribute to the household by doing farm jobs and harvesting oil palm.

When Chinwe was 15, a friend of his father's took him to Ibadan in the southwest to work for two years and then sponsored him in an auto-electrical apprenticeship. The apprenticeship required seven long years, and when he completed it, Chinwe scored well on the government trade test. Unfortunately, by that time, his sponsor's business had collapsed and Chinwe lacked the resources and contacts to launch his own shop. Chinwe returned to Okpuje to live with his poor mother. Once again he is helping out with farm work and palm harvesting, but he vows to "return to town and practice my trade if I find money to buy tools and equipment and to rent a shop."

Poverty is spreading in Okpuje, and a host of challenges confront Chinwe and other villagers. Farmland, though once abundant, is becoming scarce as the village's population grows. Land shortages combined with deepening poverty mean farmers can seldom afford to let fields lie fallow, although continuous cropping depletes the soil and reduces yields. Farmers say that illbeing in the community is exacerbated by the seasons. Crops grow only during the rains, which also replenish scarce water supplies. During the lean months, people sell oil palm products and farm animals, and work as farm laborers locally or migrate in search of work. Very poor families in the village borrow from thrift groups and eat their seed yams, which only makes them more vulnerable in future seasons, when there will be fewer yams to plant and eat. Worsening hardship is also leading to theft of farm produce, which participants say was unknown in the community ten years ago.

Distant markets and very poor transportation infrastructure further contribute to farmers' poverty. Young men in a discussion group say they cannot sell their crops "in good time" because bad roads force them to "pay 100 naira instead of 20 naira to get to the nearest market." Villagers report that Okpuje's isolation and bad roads also discourage qualified health personnel and teachers from accepting positions in the community. Those who do take these jobs live in nearby towns and commute to Okpuje "as they please," often irregularly.

Like farmland, water is also scarce and becoming scarcer. A 13-year-old well broke down in 1995 and has not been repaired. In the dry season, women and children travel up to eight kilometers in search of spring water. Some travel to buy water in the nearest town, twenty-two kilometers away. Poor men and women say that, in addition to these problems, they struggle with malnutrition, premature aging, and ill health, and they have few places to turn for help.

With 124 million people in 1999, Nigeria is Africa's most populous country. Its people have endured decades of political turmoil, divided by disputes among political groups as well as ethnic, religious, and regional tensions.[2] Since Nigeria gained independence in 1960, the country has endured a civil war, successive military coups, and conflict-ridden civilian rule. In addition to ethnic and religious rifts, Nigerian political leaders have faced deep regional disputes over the allocation of oil revenues, rising pressure for autonomy in the regions, and the growing power of the military.[3] In February 1999, former military ruler Olusegun Obasanjo won the first presidential election in more than fifteen years, taking power from a military government that had grown increasingly corrupt, repressive, and unpopular. The formal transition to civilian rule occurred in late May 1999 and coincided with the fieldwork for this study.

While the country has vast oil reserves, GDP growth averaged 1.6 percent per year between 1980 and 1990, 2.4 percent between 1990 and

1998, and just 1 percent in 1999. Years of economic mismanagement, macroeconomic instability, and widespread corruption have undermined the country's development prospects and fueled sharp rises in poverty. With donor support, the transition government that preceded the Obasanjo administration took some steps to reduce corruption and improve fiscal controls in the mid-1990s, and it began a program of reforms aimed at a market-based exchange rate regime, privatization of state enterprises, removal of petroleum and fertilizer subsidies, and decentralization of many public services. Many of these reforms, however, were delayed, never undertaken, only partially implemented, or even reversed. The Obasanjo government has also had great difficulty implementing economic reforms, but rising oil prices enabled the economy to approach an estimated 3 percent growth in the year 2000.

Amid political and economic instability, poverty in Nigeria has steadily grown worse since first measured in 1980. In that year, the expenditure poverty rate stood at 27.2 percent, with close to 18 million people classified as poor. In 1985 the rate increased to 46 percent, and then declined slightly in subsequent years. The poverty rate surged again to nearly 65 percent of the population in a 1996 survey, affecting 67 million people. About 30 million of these people are extremely poor and cannot meet their basic food needs. Urban poverty grew at a very fast rate from 17 percent in 1980 to 58 percent in 1996, although it is still less extensive than rural poverty (70 percent in 1996).[4] The northwest region accounts for the largest share (40 percent) of the country's poor people, but the most severe poverty lies across the southern regions of the country.

Eight urban and eight rural communities were selected for this study (see table 3, Study Communities in Nigeria, at the end of this chapter). The communities span sixteen states and were chosen to reflect as much as possible the leading geographic, ethnic, and other distinctive characteristics of each of the country's regions. At least two rural and two urban sites were selected in each geographical area. The communities for the study were selected with the assistance of the National Planning Commission of Abuja and its Macro Department and the Federal Office of Statistics. The Benue State Project office of the UK Department for International Development (DFID) also assisted the team in the North East Region. At the community level, poor people and specific vulnerable groups were identified for participation in the study through social mapping exercises carried out by discussion groups.

Researchers conducted a total of 132 discussion groups: forty-one of men, forty-six of women, and thirty-seven of youths consisted of poor people exclusively; in addition, there were four groups of men and four of women who were not poor and were seen as opinion leaders in their communities. Sixty-four (48 percent) of all the discussion groups were held in urban sites, and sixty-eight (52 percent) in rural sites. Forty-one individual case studies of poor people were conducted in rural communities and forty-three were undertaken in urban communities, for a total of eighty-four. All but twelve of these case studies were with poor men, women, and youths.

A facilitated training/orientation workshop and field trial for the research teams in April 1999 preceded the field research for this study. Fieldwork was conducted between April and May 1999. At the end of fieldwork, a regional workshop and synthesis meeting was held, including representatives from each of the communities visited, NGOs and other facilitating institutions, and government officials. The workshop allowed the stakeholders to engage with the research outputs, enrich them, and identify follow-up action. The workshop also contributed to the preparation of the national synthesis report.

The World Bank and DFID provided overall coordination for the study, and the field research team included members from Obafemi Awolowo University of Ileife, University of Ibadan, University of Agriculture Makurdi, Uthman Dan Fodio University Sokoto, University of Nigeria Nsukka, and University of Maiduguri.

This chapter opens with poor people's descriptions of illbeing and declining local conditions, then moves into discussion groups' ratings of public, private, and civic institutions. Several dimensions of the rising insecurity faced by poor Nigerians are explored, including seasonal stresses, ill health and barriers to health care, environmental degradation, crime, and civil conflict. Difficulties accessing education and jobs are then examined, with a special look at one community where many people see opportunities growing. The chapter ends with a discussion of society's exclusion of poor people, women, and widows.

Downward Slide

Discussion groups in Nigeria say that hardships have pulled everyone down and that even people who are comparatively well off are no longer able to help others as they used to. Across the study communities, poor people define wellbeing as the ability to meet basic household needs, for example, eating three meals a day. Discussion groups generally distinguish four categories of wellbeing groups in their communities: wealthy, average, poor, and very poor.

In urban areas such as Dawaki, *wealthy* people are identified as those who have good houses, are healthy, have a means of transportation, have enough food, dress well, can help relatives in need, and can afford hospital care. Wealthy people also can pay for their children's education, have investments and reasonable savings for emergencies, have a high social profile, and employ other people to work for them. They have peace in their lives. In rural areas, wealthy people are described as having large farms and an easy life, independence, and enough resources to cope with life's ups and downs. A study participant from Aten says, "Just look at their faces; you can see wealth there."

Average wellbeing describes those who have a regular job and can afford to educate their children. In general, a person with average wellbeing lives in a modest home, does not wear expensive clothes, and, in rural areas, has a medium-sized farm. During some periods, however, these groups may struggle to meet basic needs. The extent of material wealth for people in this category varies. In Ughoton an average man might own a car or a motorcycle.

Poor people are most frequently described as lacking the ability to educate their children above primary school, if their children receive education at all. Illbeing is also associated with a lack of adequate food, safe water, and decent clothes, and an inability to afford medical care or obtain justice when wronged. Study participants indicate that the *very poorest* have no money, live in unsatisfactory housing, and must beg for alms. They also are said to "live a wretched life," and they might be "restless," "ill," "lazy," or "alcoholic." Other common definitions include having no means of transportation, being unemployed or employed as a laborer, living in a dirty environment, and being in debt. These very poor groups also are said to have no freedom.

A discussion group of men in Umuoba Road–Aba Waterside, a shantytown area straddling the eastern bank of the Aba river, reflects on changes in wellbeing in their community over the past ten years (table 1). As the table shows, even those considered wealthy are not as well off as they used to be, and the numbers of very poor have grown dramatically.

In all but a very few of the communities visited, there is agreement that poverty has increased greatly over the past ten years. Poor people

**TABLE 1 Decline in Wellbeing, Discussion Group of Men in
Umuoba Road–Aba Waterside**

Ten years ago	Percentage of population	Now	Percentage of population
Wealthy	10	Wealthy	5
Owned cars and houses; ate well; educated children well; helped other people; had investments		Same criteria as in the past but no longer help people because times are difficult	
Struggling	10	Struggling	5
Were comfortable; could meet household needs; some owned cars		Fairly comfortable but cannot maintain cars; eat well but have no savings	
Seasonally poor	15	Seasonally poor	10
Hard work brought success and good pay; could pay rent and eat well		Can barely pay rent and eat all year round; must accept menial jobs	
Poor	30	Poor	20
Could find jobs on daily basis; lived in hovels		Often jobless or do menial jobs; eat poorly; children rarely go to school	
Very poor	35	Very poor	60
Perpetually lazy and poor; homeless		Jobless; survive on alms; children often promiscuous	

identify numerous causes of the increase, but the most commonly cited is the economic downturn, which has led to extensive joblessness. Study participants in Umuoba Road–Aba Waterside stress that the depressed economy has brought inflation, factory closures, and unemployment. Street venders there note that markets are less active because people have lost their purchasing power. Clement Nwokedi, unemployed in Umuoba Road, says he takes casual work whenever he can find it, but jobs are difficult to come by because many people are competing for them. When he does find work, he says, "The pay is low and cannot sustain me under the present rate of inflation."

To cope with unemployment, people in Umuoba Road say they squat illegally on a piece of land or share "hovels" with friends and relatives who can afford rent. Sometimes they send household members back to their villages to live and send word of any opportunities that might develop there. Like their rural counterparts, many urban dwellers are engaged in farming, animal husbandry, and fishing. Some piece together several jobs in hopes that they will add up to a livable income, moonlighting as security guards or "spending the daytime hawking goods" in the business district. A man from Ayekale Odoogun, for instance, supports his wife and three children by driving, farming, and working as a night watchman in addition to his primary job as a grinding machine operator. Abubakar, a civil servant in Dawaki, says he couldn't support his family on his government wages alone, so he took up several odd jobs on the side, including tinkering, farming, and contract work. "I came out of poverty by combination," relates Abubakar.

Poor Governance

Poor governance is a key issue that emerges in poor people's explanations of dire poverty in an oil-rich country. "We are too poor to do anything, and secondly, there is enough money to go round the country and make life worth living, but corrupt practices do not allow us to share in the national wealth," say participants in Umuoba Road–Aba Waterside.

Discussion groups across the sixteen study communities consistently report that, with the exception of a few very local entities, public, private, and civic institutions are corrupt and exclude or abandon poor people. In Ayekale participants suggest that the declining economic fortune of their country is caused by bad governance and mismanagement of public funds. In Dawaki people say that even relatively educated people remain unemployed because of bad government policies and lack of good leadership. Groups in Elieke Rumuokoro express frustration over the government's apathy toward development, the lack of employment, and nonpayment of salaries of public sector workers. When reflecting on the role of state institutions in improving their community, youths in Ughoton remark that their village is more or less cut off from the government.

People are also weary of ineffective public agencies and misappropriation of funds by public officials at the local level, and they give low ratings to their Local Government Agencies (LGAs). LGAs are responsible for managing a range of services to communities, including primary health care, primary education, social development, and other public infrastructure. A discussion group of men and women in Ayekale Odoogun reports,

The Local Government Agency has no positive contribution to the development of this village. As a matter of fact, it is making

living more difficult for us. The water pipes that connected us with the main water supply scheme were destroyed by the local government some five years ago when they were building the road to Ilemona. The LGA has made many promises to put the lines back but we are yet to see it fulfill its promises.

In Umuoba Road–Aba Waterside, participants say the LGA shut down the market, the only means for many poor people to earn a living. They also state that the community's lack of infrastructure is caused by corruption in the public sphere. To make matters worse, the LGA imposes unnecessary taxes and levies, most of which are collected by force. Participants point out that no development projects have been initiated to benefit the people. They link some of the corruption to the fact that LGA employees are at times owed several months' back salary, and are thus more vulnerable to the temptation of illicit income. Nonpayment of salaries also dampens the local economy.

In remote Jimowa participants indicate that the government's presence is felt only during tax collection and at election time. According to a group of women in Jimowa, "The only government we have known over the years is the village head." The weak government presence is compounded by many communities' isolation. People must travel long distances on poor roads to reach telephones and other communications services. Few communities have post offices.

Poorly Functioning Private Sector

Poor men and women also struggle with problem-ridden markets and with corruption in firms and banks, and point out that there is little recourse. Virtually all the communities visited report a lack of regularly held markets and declining demand, and link it to poor government management of the overall economy as well as to lack of support for local markets and traders (box 1).

Markets provide opportunities for self-employment, especially for women who contribute to their families' income through small-scale trade. Women in Jimowa say that when they get up, they milk their cows and prepare dairy produce for sale in the town markets. "I would like the government to intervene in the area of creating a periodic market center for our village. I think if we had markets for our products things would change," says Femi Olorunda of Ayekale Odoogun.

Institutional accountability is another problem. The Ohia Mati bank in Elieke Rumuokoro was capitalized by a group of businessmen and commissioned in 1995.[5] It was open less than one year when, unexpectedly, depositors could no longer draw on their accounts. One Saturday morning, the bank locked its doors for good. Bank officials disappeared, and depositors have been unable to collect their savings. To many, this is yet another case of the rich swindling the poor.

In Ughoton, Shell Petroleum Development Company (SPDC) is ranked the number one institution by a group of elderly men and women, reflecting the importance of the company's activities for the development of the community in the past. Currently, the only oil well in the village has been abandoned because it dried up. The presence of SPDC in the community is conspicuous. While villagers report that they are affected negatively by air and water pollution caused by Shell, the company is widely seen as having helped the physical development of the community. SPDC built a paved road to connect the village with the hinterland, and the company has also provided funding for building secondary schools and for training village youths.

Religious and Community-Based Institutions: Trusted but Noninclusive

Poor people in both urban and rural communities identify a range of local institutions that are active where they live, and with very high frequency rate them more effective and trustworthy than government or private-sector institutions. While these religious and community-based institutions are valued, poor people also say they are frequently excluded from participating in them. Poor women are particularly marginalized from most community activities, but in many villages and settlements they have developed their own organizations.

Table 2 shows the four most important institutions identified by a discussion group of young men and another of young women in Dawaki, an urban settlement in the northeast. The findings are typical of the kinds of institutions and rankings that emerge in discussion groups from other communities visited.[6] In Dawaki researchers note that there were keen debates about institutional evaluation criteria, selection, and rank. The group of young men developed an elaborate list of criteria, including "employment opportunities, income generation, morality and discipline, social security, trust, equality, and access." In explaining the final criteria, the local researchers summarize, "Trust means the extent to which a given organization is reliable or committed to the truth. Equality relates to whether members are treated equally. Access means both physical distance of the institution and ease of benefiting from its services."

Across Nigeria poor people rate community-based institutions as important and effective, and strongly prefer them over governmental and

TABLE 2 Most Important Institutions, Two Discussion Groups in Dawaki

| | Ranking by discussion group | |
Institution	Young men	Young women
Schools	1	2
Places of worship	2	1
Market	3	—
Drivers union	—	3
Tinkers/blacksmiths association	4	—
Tailors	—	4

— Not mentioned.
Note: 1 = Most important.

other formal institutions. These include age grades,[7] village councils, and rotating savings–credit cooperatives, also known as thrift clubs. Age grades in Ikot Idem are valued for rendering social services and upholding the customs and traditions of the community. In Okpuje the community-based Okpuje Development Committee is widely acknowledged for mobilizing resources and implementing development projects in the community. In Umuoba Road–Aba Waterside, thrift clubs receive good ratings from young women because they lend to unemployed members to invest in petty trade or for personal expenses, such as payment of school fees and medical bills. The Olowowo Cooperative Thrift in Ayekale Odoogun provides loans to members by building on savings from weekly meetings.

While savings–credit cooperatives are widely valued, participants say they often exclude the poorest of the poor, who cannot become members without contributing financially on a regular basis. John Nweze, a 65-year-old illiterate farmer from Okpuje, says he has no access to loans and is even too poor to join local rotating savings-credit groups. "Only those who have money can be members of thrift clubs," he explains. Indeed, groups frequently report that poor men and poor women are actively excluded or exclude themselves from livelihood opportunities, social events, and community decision making. In Elieke Rumuokoro, for instance, social exclusion based on caste is reported to be nonexistent and the very poor are not socially excluded in theory. In reality, however, they say their voices are not counted during community decision-making processes. In the southeast, a distinction is made between the "free-born" and "outcasts" in the community, where the caste system excludes all but the free-born from major ceremonies and other community affairs. Intermarriage between free-born and outcasts is forbidden.

In one discussion group in Dawaki, participants assert that such disregard of poor people, who are not recognized at meetings and not served food at gatherings, causes community cohesion to erode. Many poor people share the view that they are invisible to the larger society, and they say that not having money means they will be excluded. Poor people also reveal that because they are not rich and well educated they do not feel encouraged to approach institutions in times of need.

Important gender differences also emerge in the discussions of local institutions. In organizations or events where both men and women are involved, women frequently are described as holding positions of lower status. Women's community responsibilities often tend to be an extension of domestic duties, for instance in contributing to and assisting at weddings, births, and funerals. Decision making at the community level is still very much viewed as a man's responsibility, and women continue to be excluded from civic and religious forums where decisions are made. A poor woman in rural Ikot Idem declares, "If I did not go to school, how can I have mouth in community matters; if I don't have money, who am I to talk?" In Ughoton women claim they have no voice in community matters, despite their perception that they are more industrious in the community than men. In this settlement it is considered a taboo for women to enter the Court Hall because it is regarded a sacred place. Women may sit outside, where they can only listen while important decisions are made. Similarly, only men may worship inside the mosque; in some communities, women stay in their homes and participate in prayer sessions that are broadcast on loudspeakers. Discussion groups in Dawaki say that the mosque provides religious and moral guidance to the community as well as several valued services for its members, such as the collection of weekly contributions to help the needy in emergencies, including fire outbreaks, unexpected travels, or renovations. Access to these resources is limited to men, however.

Women are increasingly creating their own community-based institutions, including rotating savings–credit groups, cooperatives, and women's associations. In Ughoton, for instance, women created a Community Women's Association, responsible for settling disputes among women, making decisions on new developments in the community, and joining hands to help any member facing circumstances such as the birth of a new baby. They also assist men in the community when they have financial problems and provide support for elderly women. Women indicate, however, that despite all of its good works the association remains excluded from community administration.

One of the significant findings across all regions of Nigeria is the absence of competent and responsive NGOs. Indeed, there was no mention of formal NGOs when study participants discussed important institutions in any of the urban or rural communities.

Illbeing

In interviews about their life experiences, Nigerians describe a range of risks, some of which are growing more acute and creating greater insecurity than in the past. In addition to the economic downturn and poor governance, they frequently mention a range of health risks caused by food shortages, lack of basic infrastructure, and insufficient heath care. Participants struggle with land shortages and depleted natural resources, as well as with seasonal hazards such as excessive rains, drought, pest infestation, and fire. Crime and conflict are other widely mentioned sources of insecurity in both urban and rural communities, and groups say the police are ineffective and sometimes so corrupt that they deepen people's insecurity. While becoming educated is often mentioned as a way of escaping poverty and reducing vulnerability to risks such as these, many poor parents struggle with the decision to send children to school and keep them there on account of the high fees, the poor quality of schooling, and lack of opportunities facing those with education and skills.

Bodily Risks

Hunger, illness, and injury are widely reported causes of impoverishment. Many poor Nigerians skip meals and get by with extremely little to eat. The primary strategy for coping with a crisis listed by men and women in Ikot Idem is "eating less." In urban Dawaki youths point out that women experience hunger more than men because women tend to direct scarce food to their children.

In addition to diet, poor people also point to bad water, hard physical work, and very limited access to health care when speaking about health threats. Work accidents as well as malaria, HIV/AIDS, typhoid fever, cholera, fevers, dental problems, poor eyesight, high blood pressure, and complications of pregnancy are hazards mentioned across the study communities. The elderly and children are considered the most vulnerable to illness and injury. Women in Okpuje and Ayekale Odoogun conclude that the ultimate effect of poverty is ill health, leading to death.

Few poor households have the resources to meet increasingly high medical costs; should a breadwinner become ill, the family must bear the loss of income, as well. Most communities lack any health care facility. Among those that do have a clinic or health center, facilities are said to lack staff and equipment and to charge fees that are not affordable to poor people. Men and women in Dawaki mention that there were no hospital fees in the past, and that ten years ago medications were readily available and were inexpensive or free. One woman from this community recently took a relative's child to the hospital but was turned away because she had no money and they would not extend credit. In Okpuje the twenty-bed health center is staffed with a doctor and twenty-six nurses but is unreliable because there are no drugs and the staff work irregularly. Okpuje residents who can afford it use private clinics in neighboring communities. In Elieke Rumuokoro health services are now provided largely by private clinics instead of public ones as in the past.

Eroding Physical Environment and Dilapidated Infrastructure

Land shortages and soil degradation are other major problems in several rural communities visited. According to a man from Elieke Rumuokoro, "All our problems stem from lack of land. If we had enough land we would be able to produce enough to feed our households, build houses, and train our children."

In Bagel groups of women explain that soils are degraded and drought has caused a lack of water and a dearth of fish in the river. Insufficient rainfall and infertile soils, coupled with a lack of fertilizer, have caused poor yields and reduced harvests, leading to food scarcity. In Okpuje, as mentioned above, overpopulation and continuous cropping have depleted soils, resulting in ever poorer yields.

In urban areas, a lack of water and sanitation services creates severe hardships. Broken water pipes and pumps often force communities back to unhygienic or overexploited traditional sources. Ughoton residents must collect rainwater or get water from hand-dug wells and streams. Participants indicate that some years back, the community had a borehole from which water was pumped into a large reservoir for communal use, but the pumping machine often broke, causing water shortages. Now, such a facility no longer exists and people are forced to rely on water from rain or streams, which, they say, has become contaminated by pollution from oil fields and oil exploration activities in the district.

In Elieke Rumuokoro and Umuoba Road–Aba Waterside, appalling sanitation problems are reported. With no sewerage, pipe-borne water, or reliable drainage system, pit toilets as well as open baths expose many residents to serious illnesses such as cholera. The rainy season intensifies people's exposure. In Elieke Rumuokoro, an urban settlement on the coast, seasonal rains and poor sanitation cause dirty wallows to form around the bungalows and tin hovels of the impoverished residents.

Seasonal Stresses

There is a seasonal dimension to illbeing, which is tied to the timing and extent of the rainy season. In Ikot Idem, for instance, poor people regard the months from January to April as the "hungry period." These lean months coincide with the planting season, when farmers, especially poor ones, do not have crops to eat or to sell or money to buy food. According to groups in Elieke Rumuokoro, the period of greatest deprivation extends from January, after all the agricultural produce has been consumed, up until the new harvest in the autumn.

Hunger is not the only hazard of the rainy season. In Bagel people report that rainy months also bring periodic pest infestations, flooding, and cholera outbreaks; meanwhile, periods of drought can be disastrous for crops, farm animals, and household food security. Similar weather extremes threaten villagers in Jimowa, where a drought in 1998 left most households without enough to eat. Men very frequently migrate in search of work during the hungry season, leaving women, children, and the elderly behind in Jimowa to cope with hunger. Villagers describe turning to neighbors and kin for food to survive. The availability of casual work is also seasonal, and many poor people who attempt to work in street vending, construction, farming, or the oil industry find that their jobs disappear with the rains.

The rainy season also exacts a heavy toll on poor communities' precarious roads and housing. People in Bagel and Ikot Idem report having to work communally to clear mud-covered and flooded roads. There are long periods, however, when the roads are impassable and getting children to school, obtaining health care, or visiting the market to buy or sell goods is simply impossible. Dilapidated housing conditions expose poor families to harsh weather and health threats. A poor widow in Ikot Idem wishes someone could "save her from the rains." She says her greatest problem is housing because as a farm laborer she cannot afford to buy a mat every year to repair the rain-damaged roof of her thatched mud-brick house.

Crime and Conflict

Poor people in both rural and urban areas fear crime; armed robbery and food theft are frequently mentioned. In some villages, such as Ikot Idem, crime is considered to be on the rise due to disregard for traditional values, growing impoverishment, and widespread disobedience among local youths. In the southwest, road improvements are said to contribute to the increase in robbery, rape, and street fighting. A shop owner in Umuoba Road–Aba Waterside related his struggles to rebuild his business not once, but twice, after armed robberies. The legal and medical expenses that followed the first robbery wiped out his entire savings; the second robbery involved a gang that received a tip from a former apprentice.

Rivalries among the country's ethnic groups also sometimes lead to violence. In urban areas in particular, ethnic violence and disputes over political boundaries emerge as themes of discussions. Divisions between the Muslim and Christian areas of the country add further tensions. Only in the urban settlement of Elieke Rumuokoro in the southeast are crime and conflict considered moderate.

Corrupt and abusive police are widely mentioned in discussion groups, which report illegal arrests, intimidation, and extortion. Participants in Elieke Rumuokoro declare that police are more interested in extorting money from poor people than in protecting them. In Ikot Idem a group of men asserts that police officers' deplorable attitude and behavior toward the village people have a negative impact on the community, although police are valued for their effectiveness during times of disorder. Similarly, policing is well regarded in Okpuje because it maintains order in the community, but there are complaints about the tendency of the police to take money from people fraudulently. For example, police reportedly make illegal arrests, especially when they have not received their salaries, and demand money before they will free the arrested person. Poor people's inability to pay these bribes often results in detention and missed work. In some cases, the victim is forced to sell a valuable item in order to pay the bribe.

Education's Mixed Promise

"I want my children to have a good education," says a father from Ayekale Odoogun. For many Nigerians, job opportunities seem to be directly proportional to one's level of education, and several participants specifically blame their lack of education as a major factor in their inability to escape poverty. Quite a few poor people with schooling also participated in the study; however, many of their reports about the value of education are less enthusiastic.

Perhaps the most widely shared educational concerns voiced by poor men and women are the unaffordable fees and bribes associated with keeping children in school. In Dawaki, for instance, a group of men reports that whereas twenty years ago the government made efforts to subsidize education, such support has not continued in recent times. Schooling for many children is intermittent and delayed, or abandoned altogether because parents cannot afford the fees. Chidi, a 14-year-old boy in Elieke Rumuokoro, remains in primary school when other children his age are already in secondary school because his parents could not afford the fees for him to take the promotion examination. He hopes "to enter the secondary school in the future, whenever God gives a good job to my father." In the same community, Janet, a 15-year-old girl, had to drop out of school last year because her parents had difficulty paying her school fees and buying the recommended texts. She hawked oranges and performed other jobs to raise money to pay the fees in order to be readmitted this year.

Poor people also frequently comment on the low quality of education. Women in Umuoba Road–Aba Waterside maintain that primary education has deteriorated because of ill-trained, uncommitted teachers, overcrowding, lack of equipment, and dilapidated buildings. According to participants in Elieke Rumuokoro, a public school education does not equip young adults to gain employment or pursue higher education. Other common concerns voiced in many communities are that teachers do not show up at school except to receive their salaries and that most schools are grossly understaffed. Many teachers working in village schools prefer to live in the nearest town, but with poor roads and transport services, teachers' attendance is erratic.

Long distances to school and lack of transportation for students pose added hardships for some communities. In Ayekale Odoogun, Ikot Idem, and Jimowa participants are concerned that there is no primary school located within the village. Schoolchildren have to trek many kilometers daily to and from the nearest school, and most cannot attend in the rainy season or other times the roads become impassable.

For some Nigerians, basic education is perceived as a vital support in poor people's lives. Gladys Usoro, a poor woman turned successful business owner in Umuoba Road–Aba Waterside, credits the little education that she acquired with enabling her to keep proper financial records. She says her education has been a great strength to her and helped her "fight back any form of suppression." Aware of this advantage, she has tried to improve her education by attending adult literacy classes at night.

For quite a few people in the study, however, education has not provided a path to a better life. Hassan, 23, comes from a family of twelve children in the urban settlement of Dawaki. His mother died when he was 11 years old, and his father died when he was 19. When Hassan reached senior secondary school, he worked as a laborer in order to earn money for his school needs. "I struggled to stay alive," he recalls. He was admitted to the state polytechnic institution and earned a certificate in banking and finance; then he went to a university for a diploma in social work. "I have no father, no mother, and all my relatives are poor, and you can't go begging because in our culture it is a shameful thing to beg," he remarks. "I faced many problems. I used to beg motorcycle owners for motorcycles to do *achaba* [motorcycle-taxi service] and pay for accommodations and all that." Following his graduation, Hassan searched in vain for a job that would enable him to care for his younger brothers and stepmother. His continued unemployment has forced him to return to the dangerous *achaba* business despite his level of education.

Signs of Hope

Poor men and women in most of the communities visited in Nigeria have very bleak outlooks on opportunities for the future. People in Jimowa in the northwest and Ikot Idem in the southeast, however, say poverty has declined somewhat and times are easier now than ten years ago. Participants in Jimowa say the local economy is better than a decade ago because people have diversified from raising cattle into farming and trade. They also report receiving much better prices for their cattle, although population growth has reduced land available for grazing.

A discussion group of women in Ikot Idem points to four improvements in their lives: increased possibility for migration to urban centers, more employment opportunities, more factories, and more access to credit. People in this village also say they are better off because of education and skills acquisition, as well as by dint of hard work, honesty, prudence, thrift, and acquiring assets (box 2). Ikot Idem, located in the palm oil belt of southeastern Nigeria, is blessed with abundant wild palm forests and plantation palm. Palm fruit processing is also a key industry. While the men own and manage palm forests, women are chiefly concerned with the processing and marketing of palm products. Women's groups agree that men have more opportunities than women, but that better education, skills acquisition, and women's increased empowerment have brought women more employment opportunities than they had in the past.

> **BOX 2 Breaking Out of Poverty: A Life of Setbacks,
> Determination, and Hard Work**

Udo is a 76-year-old man with two wives and thirteen children in Ikot Idem. Udo's parents died when he was a boy, leaving him property, which he was too young to manage. Udo's uncle took him in and brought him up with his own children. He recalls:

During the period I lived with my uncle, I had no future. When I grew up to fend for myself, I decided to trade soap. My initial capital came from picking and selling palm fruits, and saving the proceeds. My initial capital of 2 manilla [traditional currency] was wisely invested and yielded good dividends. When I had saved 20 manilla, I bought an initial stock of hens for 3 manilla. I continued trading with the remaining 17 manilla. From my savings, I was able to redeem my father's property.[8]

After toiling for many years, I was able to marry. Following marriage, I became poor again. But I continued harvesting palm fruits and tapping palm wine until I saved enough money to stand financially. When I saved 15 shillings, I bought some kernel, which I carried on my head to sell in Azumini. By so doing we successfully combined soap trade with a palm kernel business. I saved up to 20 pounds to buy a new bicycle, which enabled me to ply my trade on a larger scale. My wife and I became adequately clothed. We bought additional farmland and intensified food production. Having acquired enough land, I proceeded to plant palms, which I obtained from the government. These plants I nursed, and with the subsidy received from the government for fertilizer and farm implements, I established my plantation. I have been harvesting palm fruits from my plantation since they reached maturity.

Following my recognition as a hardworking man, the government came to my aid in 1983 with a loan of 3,000 naira. This I fully paid back in installments. The palm estate has enabled me to build a house for myself and to feed my family. I now depend on my plantation as a major means of livelihood.

The Gulf of Gender Inequities

Discussion groups of both sexes in the sixteen communities visited describe partnerships between men and women that are still highly unequal, but they also identify trends that suggest the gap may be narrowing. Both men and women in the study agree that men continue to control household decisions, although men increasingly seek their wives' guidance. Also, domestic violence continues to be a widespread problem, but the levels of physical abuse are perceived to be declining in several communities. However, there are few signs that progress has been made to improve the status of single women and widows, who are repeatedly identified as among the most vulnerable and impoverished. Poverty is much more severe in female-headed households than in male-headed households.[9]

In discussions on changes in gender roles and responsibilities in poor households, most study participants say women in Nigeria are more empowered than in the past, but they still acknowledge sizable inequities. In urban areas in particular, groups mention that women have gained greater liberty to visit friends and relatives, and husbands now sometimes consult them on household decisions. In Dawaki, for instance, discussion groups indicate that men may draw on the ideas and suggestions of their wives before making final decisions on matters such as children's schooling and major purchases. Participants attribute such gains to women's skills, education, hard work, and increased incomes, as well as to external cultural influences. "Before the civil war, it was difficult for women to be heard, but now they even claim ownership of the compound," argues a poor man from Ikot Idem.

In many rural communities, however, there are no reports of even modest shifts in household gender roles or women's participation in decision making. On the contrary, in Bagel and Jimowa, women's work outside the home has been greatly reduced by the adoption of stricter Islamic rules about seclusion. In Bagel women's responsibilities within the household have remained the same over the last ten years, according to both men and women. Both discussion groups explain that women gave advice to their husbands in the past as they do today on issues such as house repairs, choice of schools for children, and sale of livestock, but men always make the final decisions. In two rural sites, Okpuje and Ikot Idem, men and women both farm, but there are crops traditionally cultivated by women and others cultivated by men; this has not changed in the last decade.

Domestic Violence

Reports from many discussion groups suggest that domestic violence against women used to be at very high levels and is now coming down as "ignorance" and "illiteracy" decline. In a few discussion groups, participants even suggest that levels of violence have fallen significantly. Nevertheless, perceptions of the trends in levels of abuse vary considerably across the discussion groups in Nigeria, suggesting that violence likely remains a problem in many women's lives.

In Umuoba Road–Aba Waterside, some study participants indicate that violence against women in households is now low but rises during crises, such as when men are out of work. As male unemployment is widespread in this impoverished community, violence is likely to be higher than a reporting of "low" might suggest. It is significant, however, that in this community and others, such as Dawaki, Ayekale Odoogun, and Elieke Rumuokoro, violence against women in the household is seen to be on the decline. In Jimowa domestic violence is reported to be "unheard of." In this remote village, women live in seclusion, honoring traditional Muslim practices. In Ayekale Odoogun a discussion group of elderly men suggests that men may refrain from abusing their wives because the women are so hungry that they might collapse or even die from a beating. In Bagel the story is also mixed. A discussion group of men concludes that violence has fallen to a level of just two out of ten households in their community, from eight out of ten households a decade ago. The women's group in Bagel, which did not want to discuss the sensitive issue at any length, merely stated that they perceive no changes in the level of violence.

Such conflicting reports may reflect the fact that prevailing social norms seem to sanction various forms of violence against women. In communities such as Ikot Idem, female genital cutting still occurs and is considered a "good practice." Also, the researchers note that physical abuse of women is "not perceived as a serious form of ill-treatment" by many study participants. In some places, a good deal of violence seems to touch the lives of poor women and occasionally poor men. For instance, the researchers reporting on a discussion group in Dawaki note:

> Outside the household men fight women over commercial transactions when men buy on credit and refuse to pay. Violence between women can arise between co-wives over the sharing of things brought by the husband, or such fights may be a carry-over of conflicts between children of different wives. Physical violence between women also results from attitudes of unmarried women toward married women.

The Stigma of Women without Men

Among poor people in Nigeria, single women and widows are particularly vulnerable to exclusion and insecurity. Kezie is a poor woman in Ikot Idem whose husband left her after the death of their only surviving son (out of five pregnancies) led to her emotional breakdown and subsequent ill health. She says,

> In my home village, I have nobody to help feed me except good
> Samaritans who give me money to buy processed cassava. I live
> with a distant relation who only gives me accommodations. I
> would not like to go back to my husband because he does not
> want me at all because I have no child. I am sickly and can do
> no work except to go gathering [palm] kernels in the bush and
> sell to middlemen. Now that I am incapacitated and without a
> helper, I pray sincerely to God to send me a helper who will
> feed and clothe me.

Women's wellbeing often deteriorates quickly after the loss of their husbands, when they suffer threats to both their physical security and property. A widow often loses her husband's property to her in-laws in accordance with traditional family rules.[10] Mary, a 70-year-old widow from Ikot Idem, was stripped of her husband's property upon his death. She earns a living primarily by processing palm fruits, and she also farms part-time. She says,

> The children were still in school when my husband died. There
> was nobody to assist me. Rather, my husband's relations force-
> fully took away my husband's property, which we relied upon
> for survival. I was compelled to take menial jobs in order to
> care for my children. I also pledged some of my husband's re-
> maining property so that my children could go to school. I
> thank God that since my son left school he has been able to re-
> deem some of those properties I pledged.

Conclusion

The voices of the poor in Nigeria reveal the deepening and multidimensional nature of illbeing and insecurity. According to a young man in Dawaki, the impact of poverty is largely cumulative. He states that starvation as a result of poverty leads directly to death, whereas frustration and crime arising from poverty are simply slower routes to death. Some poor Nigerians hold the view that today's urgent problems were not even major issues in the past. They recall times when food was cheaper, wells functioned, school fees and medicines cost less or were free, and educated people found jobs.

Affecting some two-thirds of the country's population, the sharp rises in poverty in the 1980s and 1990s have been fueled by bad governance and political instability. Pervasive official corruption in this oil-rich country, many study participants say, has robbed the country of vast resources that are urgently needed for development. Critical shortages now characterize the daily experiences of many men and women in the sixteen communities visited. Participants everywhere report that they continuously "fight" for meals, water, housing, work, and education for their children, and they give largely negative reviews of public services. In many villages and urban settlements, government presence is described as negligible.

Some in the study do express hope that the economy will turn around, the government will improve, and their community will at last gain more of what it needs. In the majority of communities visited, water, roads, and better schools and health facilities emerge as urgent priorities. In rural areas, many farmers seek assistance to improve soil quality and gain access to land and markets. In both rural and urban communities, study participants seek support for their local businesses as well as job opportunities.

The people of poor villages and slums, however, do not see how they alone might address such needs, especially in the context of rapidly growing populations. A group of young men from Ikot Idem suggests, "We would wish that government or donor agencies intervene directly and establish the facilities because we fear that monies meant for these purposes would go into private pockets without completing the job. We will be willing to contribute labor during construction." These sorts of partnerships will be vital in delivering local services and combating corruption. Adebayo Wahabi, president of the Owolowo Cooperative Thrift in Ayekale Odoogun, expresses his hope that life will improve in the future: "If our local economic conditions improve, we will be able to run society better."

In the absence of government supports and economic opportunities, various local institutions and associations provide limited security and safety nets, and it is these groups that have won the greatest trust and confidence of poor people. Yet, poor men frequently say they find it difficult to influence even these local channels to address leading problems, and women say they have no voice in these institutions whatsoever. In addition to material deprivation, the people in this study speak of lacking dignity, status, security, and hope. The absence of family and social ties also figures prominently in their descriptions of what it means to be poor. Poverty is seen as passed from generation to generation. An older man in one discussion group observes, "We poor men have no friends; our friend is the ground."

TABLE 2 Study Communities in Nigeria

RURAL COMMUNITIES

Bagel, Bauchi State Pop. 5,000	A road from the state capital to the local government head-quarters passes through this farming community, which has one primary school and one dispensary. The people of Bagel belong to the Bankalawa ethnic group; their present village leader was installed in 1998. According to villagers, the rivers around the community used to contain plenty of fish and the land used to be more productive than it is now.
Ikot Idem, Ibom State Pop. 10,600	This farming community, located five kilometers from the main road, is reached by a dirt road. It has two primary schools and a health center, but lacks running water and electricity. While men are predominantly engaged in yam production, women grow cassava, cocoyam, and vegetables. In addition to farming, men work tapping raffia-palm wine and women are traders and process palm fruit. The community is predominantly Christian.
Jimowa, Sokoto State Pop. 400	Men are farmers; about 25 percent also engage in cattle rearing and 20 percent in trade. Women process cow's milk and make mats and calabash decorations. The community is homogenous both ethnically (Fulani) and religiously (Muslim). The village government is headed by the *hakimi*, a leader who is elected by the community. In the last decade there have been a few natural disasters, although participants report that the local economy has improved.
Okpuje, Enugu State Pop. 19,000	This community is located about twenty-five kilometers west of the university town of Nsukka. Men plant crops such as yam, cassava, and cocoyam. Women are responsible for vegetable production, weeding, harvesting, and food processing. Other income-earning activities include trade and handicraft. The small-scale nature of farming is partly a consequence of poor infrastructure and underdeveloped marketing facilities. The community relies on distant streams for water. Health personnel live in the nearest urban center, Nsukka. With an increase in population, land is becoming scarce and most farms are located far from the village.

URBAN COMMUNITIES

Ayekale Odoogun,
Kwara State
Pop. 1,200

Farming is the main source of livelihood for men, although 8 percent work as artisans. Women are mainly engaged in trade, but they also earn their living by processing cassava into *gari*. The community is linked to the national electricity grid and a paved road runs through the site. There is a jointly owned primary school in Alaya village, which is about three kilometers from the Ayekale community. Local people rely mainly on a hand-dug well for water. Yorubas are the dominant ethnic group, and about 85 percent of the population is Muslim.

Dawaki,
Gombe State
Pop. 20,000

The main sources of livelihood for men are farming, metalworking, trade, and grain milling. Women engage in trade, tailoring, and weaving. The community has access to electricity, a health center, a network of roads, and a primary school. It has suffered a number of natural disasters in the last years, including floods and fires. The dominant ethnic group is the Fulani.

Elieke Rumuokoro,
Rivers State
Pop. 5,000

Elieke Rumuokoro is one of five traditional villages in Rumuokoro, which has been absorbed by the rapid urban development around Port Harcourt following the development of the oil industry. A majority of men are low-level wage earners in the public sector and the oil industry; another 20 percent engage in farming and trade. Women also engage in trade, although many are full-time housewives. The community lacks urban planning and is traversed by dirt pathways. It has electricity from the national grid. Although there was running water years ago, water is presently obtained from wells.

Ughoton,
Delta State
Pop. 5,000

The community is eight kilometers from the nearest permanent road. The main sources of livelihood for men are farming, fishing, and petty trade. Women are mostly employed in farming, fishing, petty trade, and palm oil processing. About 80 percent of households have electricity. There is a health center, but it is understaffed and is rarely visited by a doctor. Water supplies come from hand-dug wells, streams, and rainwater. There is a primary and a secondary school, as well as a small Court Hall, where elders preside over community affairs and women are not allowed to enter.

Umuoba Road– **Aba Waterside,** Abia State Pop. 5,000	The neighborhood is peopled by migrant artisans, low-level factory workers, laborers, and the jobless. Women are mostly engaged in petty trade and selling food. Most of the buildings are made of mud brick, and there are no paved roads or streets. Although the community has electricity, water service is extremely erratic and the people rely on privately owned wells. The community has an ill-equipped primary school. Sanitation is extremely poor. Drug use is rampant. Two ethnic groups predominate in the area, the Igbo and the Efik/Ibibio, and a majority of residents are Christians.

Note: The national report is based on analysis of sixteen communities, nine of which are described in the table above.

Notes

1. The study team was led by Olu Aina, Gabriel Bolade Ayoola, Abubakar Mamman, Noble Nweze, Tanwa Odebiyi, Dora Shehu, and James Zacha. Overall coordination was provided by Foluso Okunmadewa, Olukemi Williams, and Dan Owen.

2. There are more than 250 ethnic groups in Nigeria, with as many languages. Under British rule, Nigeria became a federation of three regions that reflected the principal ethnic groups: the Hausa-Fulani in the Northern Region, the Yoruba in the Western Region, and the Ibo in the Eastern Region.

3. Economist Intelligence Unit, "Nigeria: Political Background" (EIU Country Profile 2001/2002, January 2001).

4. Current estimates suggest that the poverty rate in 1999 had changed little since 1996. See Sudharshan Canagarajah, John Ngwafon, and Foluso Okunmadewa, "Nigeria's Poverty: Past, Present, and Future" (World Bank, Nigeria Country Department, December 2000), 2–3, 23; and World Bank, "Memorandum of the President of the International Development Association and the International Finance Corporation to the Executive Directors on a World Bank Group Joint Interim Strategy Update for the Federal Republic of Nigeria" (May 21, 2001), 2.

5. The history of community banks in Nigeria dates to the early 1990s, when governments established such banks in an attempt to encourage banking culture and rural savings.

6. In Dawaki the group of young men listed six other institutions that do not appear in the table: clinics (ranked 5), police (6), industries (7), courts (8), clubs and societies (9), and the grain-sellers association (10). The young women's group only identified and ranked four institutions.

7. Age-grade members are men and women born within the space of one to four years. They construct town halls, repair school buildings and roads, serve as community mediators, and so forth.

8. The West African manilla ceased to be legal currency in the late 1940s; at that time it was worth 3 British pence. Shillings and pounds were used during the colonial period in Nigeria, and the naira is now the national currency.

9. Canagarajah, Ngwafon, and Okunmadewa, "Nigeria's Poverty," 5.

10. National laws do not call for a widow to lose her husband's property to in-laws or other family members, but widows rarely seek legal redress to protect their rights.

Bangladesh

Waves of Disaster

Rashed un Nabi, Dipankar Datta, and Subrata Chakrabarty

Mariam Bewa, a 40-year-old widow and mother of five, lives in Halker-
char village, five kilometers from the headquarters of the Dewangonj
thana (subdistrict) in the northern district of Jamalpur.[2] When the banks
of the river Jamuna eroded in 1998, Mariam's home was swept away by
the river, along with the homes of her 450 neighbors. The community re-
built their village on vacant government land; it has a government-run
primary school, a junior high school, and an informal primary school run
by an NGO. A small market with a handful of permanent stores stands
in the middle of the village. Halkerchar has little transportation infra-
structure, but there is a road that leads to the thana center and another
that connects the village with the flood control embankment, which is
used to access water. Although the land is prone to flooding and erosion,
agriculture remains the main source of livelihood. Poor people supple-
ment their incomes by working in fisheries and by picking up day-labor
jobs, but the availability of these opportunities fluctuates with the
seasons.

Mariam's family used to own a homestead, farmland, and cattle, but
when her husband became ill, they sold their assets to cover the costs of
his treatment. When he died, Mariam was left destitute except for a
house, which washed away in a flood in 1988. Since then, Mariam has
raised her family in a small, thatched house. Mariam is excluded from
most livelihood opportunities because she is a woman. In her younger
years, she supported her family by agricultural work, although it violat-
ed local norms. Recently, Mariam took up work as a domestic for wealthy
households in the community.

Like many parents in Bangladesh, Mariam raised her four sons hoping that in return for the sacrifices she made for them they would support her in her old age. Her three oldest sons, however, abandoned her after they married. Her last hope is with her youngest, unmarried son. At present, Mariam's earning from menial jobs and her son's from wage labor are not enough for their household to get by. In addition, Mariam's only daughter will need to marry, which will require that Mariam pay for dowry and other expenses. Anticipating these outlays, she cuts back on household expenses and saves what she can.

B angladesh has the highest incidence of poverty in South Asia and the world's largest poor population after India and China. Poverty rates worsened in the late 1980s and reached 59 percent in 1991–92, but have since shown small but steady improvements. In 1996, the most recent year for which data are available, 53 percent of the population fell below the upper poverty line, and 36 percent lived in abject poverty without sufficient food.[3] Despite extensive poverty, the country has made important progress on a range of social development indicators, including access to safe water (84 percent) and near gender parity in primary school enrollment. In addition to government poverty initiatives, there is a flourishing NGO community that brings diverse services to poor communities. Both public and civic efforts benefit from large flows of foreign aid into the country.

Bangladesh's economy grew by an average of nearly 5 percent a year in the 1990s, and GDP rose from US$290 per capita in 1990 to US$370 at the end of the decade.[4] However, there are striking urban-rural disparities in rates of economic growth. Agriculture, the core of the rural economy, grew an average of 2 percent a year between 1986 and 1996, while urban growth rates reached 20 percent on average in this period, driven heavily by garment exports.[5] In 1995–96, the rural poverty rate was 61 percent, compared with 45 percent in urban areas. Ninety percent of the country's population with expenditures below the upper poverty line resides in the countryside.[6]

In the early years after Bangladesh gained independence from Pakistan in 1971, the country's development strategies were strongly inward-oriented, seeking to achieve growth through industrialization for import substitution. In the late 1970s, facing a severe financial crisis, the government worked with the World Bank and the International Monetary

Fund to undertake a major program of economic reforms. Throughout the 1980s, economic policies strove to mobilize domestic resources and liberalize the economy in an effort to spur economic growth, create employment, lower inflation, and contain fiscal and current account deficits. Market reforms were deepened in the 1990s by accelerating the growth of export-oriented industries, reducing regulations, reforming tariffs, privatizing state enterprises, and better coordinating industrial and export policies.

The country's political life has been marked by unrest and brief military interventions. A popular movement overthrew the military government in 1991 and the country became a parliamentary democracy. The prime minister at the time of this research was Sheikh Hasina Wajed, elected to a five-year term in 1996. Her government received generally favorable reviews for guiding the country's recovery from a devastating flood in 1998. However, the two leading political parties are enmeshed in deep rivalries, and the Wajed administration has faced ongoing political and economic challenges, including frequent *hartals* (general strikes) called by the opposition party. Corruption and weak rule of law are also pervasive problems, undermining public, private, and civic activities throughout the country.

This chapter is based on small group discussions and brief life histories provided by women and men in eight poor villages and two urban slums in Bangladesh (see table 2, Study Communities in Bangladesh, at the end of this chapter). Communities were selected to ensure socioeconomic and geographic diversity. In rural areas, eight districts were identified that represent six agro-ecological zones, and within each district, one thana was selected based on the rankings provided by the official food allocation and poverty map of the World Food Programme and the government of Bangladesh. The selection of specific villages within thanas was done at the field level with the help of nongovernmental field officers working in the area and after a short visit to the villages. The remaining two thanas were selected in order to capture the distinct dimensions of urban poverty. Communities were chosen where the researchers and their NGO partners had knowledge of local conditions and could undertake follow-up actions.

Within each community, poor people were identified with the assistance of local residents who participated in discussion groups that classified and analyzed different wellbeing categories in their village or slum. Local NGO officers also assisted research teams in identifying and convening discussion groups of poor women and men.[7] A total of sixty-nine discussion groups were held in the communities visited, of which fifty were with poor people. In most locations, discussions were held with at least two groups of poor women, two groups of poor men, and one group of youth. Discussion groups were also held with better-off women for a fuller understanding of trends in gender relations. In addition, a total of forty-six case studies were completed, which in most localities included a poor man and woman, a better-off man and woman, and a poor youth.

The study was carried out by the Bangladesh-based NGO Working Group on the World Bank (NGOWG) as part of its long-term participatory poverty monitoring in the country. Three member NGOs of the NGOWG—Proshika, ActionAid Bangladesh, and Concern Bangladesh—mobilized the resources and research teams for the study. The fieldwork took place in March and April 1999. Research teams spent an average of one week in each location.

Poverty remains widespread in Bangladesh. This chapter opens with an overview of the many severe risks facing poor men and women in the communities visited. It then discusses participant's largely negative ratings of public and private institutions, and their general approval of NGOs that operate in their communities. It concludes with study participants' ideas about what would help them the most.

Poor People's Many Risks

Poor people in Bangladesh are exposed to severe and diverse risks that continually threaten their wellbeing. In rural villages, anxiety and hopelessness about the future form the core of their discussions about their lives. Rural dwellers are threatened by increasing landlessness and population growth, lack of jobs, recurring floods, indebtedness, and dowry. Urban participants also indicate many sources of vulnerability, including the threats of sudden unemployment, homelessness, overwhelming debt, crime and violence, and dowry. In both rural and urban communities, poor people say that their problems are compounded by governmental and social injustices, obstacles to their participation in community decisions, and lack of respect in society. Across the communities visited, participants emphasize that these disadvantages frequently intertwine, making their lives precarious in the extreme.

In Fadli Pur (Gowainghat thana), a poor village in northeastern Bangladesh, people say that their insecurity is rising daily, and they describe having to contend frequently with a multitude of dangers. Villagers report that they are increasingly exposed to misfortune as the local population explodes and job opportunities cannot accommodate the increased number of job seekers. Fadli Pur's worst-off residents are identified as those who are landless and who lack the assurance of food and clothes. Especially at risk, according to elderly women, are women who have nobody to look after them. For poor men in this village, the biggest source of anxiety is the prospect of falling ill and losing the ability to work. By contrast, rich people are said to fear thieves and robbers who can steal their possessions and send them spiraling into poverty. Rich and poor alike in Fadli Pur were hit hard when crops were destroyed five times in the floods of 1998. Fadli Pur discussion groups summarize their greatest risks as:

▸ the earning member of the family falls ill or dies;
▸ there is no work in the area;
▸ crops are damaged by flash floods;
▸ loans are taken and assets are sold to tide over the crisis;
▸ there are marriageable daughters in the family;
▸ family members have to leave the area in search of work;
▸ cattle are stolen;
▸ there is failure to catch fish in the leased *beels* (depressions in the floodplains, where water remains for about eight to nine months); and
▸ there is quarrelling between Hindu and Muslim families.

To Fadli Pur villagers, risk also means that people go to work knowing that they may fall into danger. "I know well that there are snakes in the floodwater even when I go out in search of a job, wading through the floodwater," says Kamini Biswas. Poor fishermen risk their lives to catch fish in the dark of night because they lack permits to fish. When caught by the *mohazans* (big merchants and moneylenders), the night fishermen get a thrashing and lose their nets; sometimes, they are handed over to the police.

According to men and women in Dhaka city's Battala slum, risk means any kind of danger that could make one become worse off during his or her lifetime. In general, discussion groups in the two urban communities visited say that despite some improvements in basic services and job opportunities, they still face numerous risks. For women in Battala, these include "police harassment, no assurance of getting a job or housing, bullies in the road teasing and making trouble, and men throwing acid on women for different reasons." Men and women in Battala and Bastuhara (Chittagong city) say they can be evicted by their landlords or lose their jobs at a moment's notice. The 1998 floods also harmed urban dwellers; in Battala the waters damaged housing and businesses and swept away rickshaws and carts. Later that year, Battala was consumed by a disastrous fire.

The following sections explore in greater depth the leading sources of vulnerability raised by discussion groups in the ten communities. As seen below, a slide into the lowest categories of illbeing is often sudden and can be triggered by any number of events.

Hunger, Weakness, and Poor Health

Many people in rural Bangladesh say they go hungry on a daily basis. Hunger appears to be present in the urban communities as well, though it is less severe. Frequent hunger brings weakness and illness, which can be catastrophic for those who rely on their physical strength to work and who already live perilously close to destitution.

Ziad, a poor man in Purba Rasti village (Madaripur thana), sells fish for a living, but he can afford to purchase it himself only rarely. Ziad's family is chronically short on food. He never has enough to eat in the morning, and his wife sometimes goes without food in the evenings. Jobeda, who lives in the same community, attempts to extend the two and a half kilograms of rice she cooks for her eight-member family every day by adding one kilogram of flour. Often in the evening she and her children go to bed hungry. Similarly, a poor woman in Halkerchar (Dewangonj thana) says, "Sometimes there is no food if there is no work." A woman in Nurali Pur village (Khaliajuri thana), whose house was washed away in the 1998 flood, explained to researchers that she had been without food since that morning and did not know if she would be able to eat later in the day. The baby in her lap was suffering from fever and her husband had gone out in search of work. She says, "If he can bring food for me, I can eat."

Badesh Mia, a 60-year-old man from Nurali Pur, attempts to piece together work to support his family of six. On the day he spoke with researchers, he had earned only 12 taka (24 cents) as a day laborer on a fishing boat. With those earnings he bought one kilogram of wheat, which was the only food for his family that day. If he fails to get any work even for a single day, he has to beg for food.

During the rainy seasons and slack agricultural periods, many participants in Bangladesh say they have little alternative but to go without food. When food is scarce in families, working members and children generally eat first. Elderly women eat only after all the other members of the family have taken their food. In most cases, very little—if any—food is left for them to eat.

Hunger is also mentioned in the urban slums visited. Poor people are described as those who can "hardly eat twice a day" and as "having to go without food sometimes" in Bastuhara and Battala, respectively.

Poor agricultural workers describe a vicious cycle in which inadequate food leads to weakness, reduced energy to work, and illness, which in turn reduces income, and the spiral continues. Men in Ulipur thana say that their level of income and the number of dependents in their households do not allow them to buy enough food. As a result, they rarely regain their energy after the arduous physical labor that their work requires, and this is perceived as laziness by women and by employers. In Nurali Pur a group of elderly men says that they suffer more illness than other people due to hard work and low food intake. When they are ill, they cannot do as much labor-intensive work; consequently, their wages may be reduced or delayed—and so the grip of impoverishment tightens. In Fadli Pur women state that a good quality of life requires "a physically fit husband in the family, and a son for every mother" to earn household income. Similarly, men in Ulipur view wellbeing as having a disease-free, healthy life and the ability to work.

Poor people report that when they need medical attention, they receive deficient treatment at the hands of public doctors and staff at the local health center, so they turn instead to private doctors. According to a group of elderly men from Nurali Pur. "Doctors behave badly with poor people and show reluctance to talk to them." In addition, government hospitals are said to charge high fees, above the stipulated amount. One women's group in Purba Rasti says that going to the hospital costs money but doesn't necessarily result in service. These women report that they pay transport costs and then must spend more money to buy an entry coupon. Hospital attendants do not offer medicines (which are supposed to be distributed free), claiming that the stock is exhausted. The women also state that the doctor ignores them and gives preference to patients wearing good clothes and to those who can afford side payments, referred to as "visit fees."

In Ulipur thana and Halkerchar, people rely on village doctors who provide medicine on credit and respond to everybody's call at any hour of the day. Ulipur discussion groups admit that the village doctor is unable to treat all diseases, but that does not affect their confidence in him because he charges no fee for consultation. Additionally, he sells medicine to them on credit and never pressures them for payments.

Lack of Assets

Ownership of productive assets most often distinguishes those who are rich or in the middle from those who are poor. People who lose their land or other means of earning income are said to descend almost instantly into poverty. In several communities, poor people are further divided into three subcategories that describe their illbeing: the *social poor,* the *helpless poor,* and the *hated* or *bottom poor.*

In Halkerchar and other villages in the study, *rich* people are those who "have their own land and other properties, livestock for cultivation, and money for investments, and can afford sufficient meals, wear good clothes, send their children to school, have jobs and mobility, and are free from disability." In all the communities visited, the rich are described as controlling the area's land and living in houses with permanent structures and bathroom facilities. Those with education may have white-collar jobs in private and government offices both within and outside the village, or they may operate businesses. Rich people in cities are described as being respectable donors to charity, employing servants, and having luxury items, including good furniture and electronic goods such as a TV and a VCR. Everywhere, those with wealth and education are seen to dominate the local power structure.

Assets and a stable livelihood also characterize those in the *middle* category. In rural areas, these are farmers who own or sharecrop a moderate amount of land (between one and two acres), and have their own cattle, animals for plowing fields, and agricultural implements. Fishermen in the middle category in Char Kukri Mukri (Charfession thana) own fishnets and boats. In Hiranadi Kulla (Dhamrai thana), which is close to an industrial zone, some members of middle-strata households earn incomes from factories. In Fadli Pur household members in this category "can live on stored food for six months" and wear good clothes. In the two urban settlements visited, middle-strata households typically have two wage-earners, often a husband and wife both working in garment factories. In Battala some of these families own multiple homes and also earn income from rents.

The *social poor* can turn to the community, including moneylenders, in times of need, unlike the other two categories of poor people who are denied access to credit and loans. According to a discussion group of men in Aminpara (Ulipur thana), the social poor and the rich are joined by their mutual dependence on agricultural labor. These employer-employee connections help the social poor to be considered "trustworthy" and thus they are not completely disregarded by the rich, even though they cannot take leadership positions within the community. The social poor suffer periodic food insecurity and deficits. They commonly combine share-cropping with wage labor or do other jobs to diversify their income sources. They can provide themselves two regular meals during slack seasons, but harvests from their land typically can meet no more than two months' need, at best. In the two slums visited, people in the social poor category often have no assets and no capital, and so are forced to seek credit to cover their daily expenditures. They live in rented tin or bamboo houses, and most work as day laborers or part-time domestics.

The *helpless poor* are largely landless, without homesteads or farm-land. Wage labor and sharecropping are their main means of earning a living. Study participants say the helpless poor are identifiable by their old clothes and pained faces. They can afford neither health care nor education for their children, they do not have the means to entertain guests, and many cannot offer a dowry to marry daughters. In urban contexts, this wellbeing group is referred to as the "hard-core poor." "Most of them are widows, separated, or have husbands with ill health," say women in Battala. The women also say that the hard-core poor often beg, have no reliable income, and live in sublet rooms and tin shacks.

The *bottom* or *hated poor* are terms used to describe households, usually headed by women or elderly men, that have no income-earning members. Disabled people are also among the hated poor. Members of these households often starve. Lacking land and other assets, they do not have access to loans, even from family or friends. In addition, they are not accepted as members of local organizations, and thus cannot benefit from group assistance as a last resort. Women at this level in Aminpara say that they are utterly disregarded and are never invited to any village social event; nonetheless, they go "if there is a feast." In Nurali Par they are not invited to any marriage ceremony in the community because they have no ability to purchase gifts. They explain that this neglect by the people in the village also causes neglect by government functionaries, and as a result poor people do not receive any government assistance. Some discussion groups identify a category even lower than the hated poor, which consists solely of beggars.

Study participants in both urban and rural communities estimate that some three-quarters of the households where they live belong to one of the three categories of poor people. In all but Bastuhara, participants say that the numbers of poor people in the bottom category have grown or stayed the same over the past decade, and in six communities they comprise more than a quarter of the population. Participants report that the helplessness of this group is more permanent than that of the other categories of poor because they receive no support from formal development programs and hardly any help from their neighbors.

Insecure Livelihoods

Poor people in both rural and urban areas view having a job year round as a precondition for wellbeing. Many rural men who participated in the study report that it is common for them to migrate to the cities when farm work is scarce and back to the countryside during peak growing seasons. Those who live permanently in the slums are often relatively recent migrants. A striking feature of the country's workforce is that it includes 6.3 million children under age 14.[8]

Rural Challenges

The supply of labor in the rural economy exceeds demand, which keeps wages low and leaves workers with little bargaining power. Employment opportunities are very few in Nurali Pur, as the whole area remains under water for about seven months and farmers harvest only one crop a year. Most of the families are landless, so they work as sharecroppers or as day laborers in agriculture. Furthermore, rights to fish are leased by the government, effectively locking poor people out of this livelihood. As the labor force increases, men and women in Nurali Pur say wages have decreased. A few years ago, day laborers used to receive food in addition to daily wages. Nowadays, laborers earn wages of only Tk 15 to Tk 20 (30 to 40 cents) per day. Only a few employers offer food with wages during the harvest to attract workers when water starts coming in quickly in the floodplains and crops are endangered.

In contrast, in rural Dhamrai, which lies near the export processing zone at Savar, wages for agricultural day laborers are uncommonly high. Most men prefer working in factories, so there is a shortage of agricultural workers in the area. During the sowing and peak harvesting seasons, wages run from Tk 140 (US$2.30) to Tk 150 (US$3.20) per day, and they do not fall below Tk 100 (US$2.00) even during lean seasons. Although industrial development has expanded employment opportunities, workers say they still must often combine several income-earning activities in order to support their families (box 1).

In order to help with ongoing household needs and with the inevitable periods of crisis, women in nearly every study community say they are assuming more responsibilities for contributing income or food to their households. Women in both villages and cities who work outside the home are typically domestics. Women are constrained by social norms from engaging in agricultural labor in Dewangonj, Ulipur, Khaliajuri, and Madaripur thanas, although there are reports that increasing numbers of women are doing this work. While men frequently migrate (especially in Ulipur and Madaripur) as a livelihood strategy, women cannot migrate unless they are accompanied by their husbands or other family members. Women are not allowed in the markets in Ulipur and Charfession. In Charfession the practice of *purdah* (socio-religious seclusion of women) considerably reduces women's freedom of movement. In Madaripur, again where men migrate for long periods, women move freely in the community, including in the local markets.

BOX 1 Diversifying for Survival

Nurul Islam is a poor man in his late thirties from Ulipur thana. His father had a good amount of land, but lost it bit by bit: portions were sold off to cover the dowry of his seven daughters, some was flooded by the river Brahmaputra, and an uncle took advantage of the father's hard luck and cheated him out of the remaining land. Nurul therefore did not inherit any land, and he now struggles to maintain his household of five, which includes his elderly mother and a divorced sister.

Nurul reports that this year he has been able to sharecrop a quarter of an acre of land and cultivate rice. He also worked as a day laborer during the six-month peak agricultural season. In the off season, Nurul migrates to Dhaka to spend six months of the year pulling a rickshaw or doing any job he can find. Nurul sees little opportunity to increase his household's security. He says he can only hope to earn enough to cover sufficient food for all his household, particularly his infant son and elderly mother.

In most cases, women work for food or in-kind compensation. When women are paid in cash, they typically receive far less than men's wages. "A woman always gets 50 percent less than a man on the excuse that a woman cannot work as hard as a man," reports a woman in Nurali Pur. In Ulipur women receive only Tk 20 or three kilograms of rice, while men receive Tk 30 or more for doing work of a similar type and quantity in the fields. As employers prefer men, women feel they have no scope to bargain.

Urban Opportunity and Insecurity

Poor people in Battala and Bastuhara name unstable livelihoods as one of their most pressing concerns, although they say employment opportunities have increased in recent years. A steady flow of permanent and seasonal migration from the countryside to the cities, however, puts downward pressure on wages and makes job security nonexistent. In Bastuhara a woman says, "Though people work hard they do not get the right wage from the employer."

Most study participants in Bastuhara consider themselves better off than a decade ago. According to a group of women there, when most of them migrated to the slum some ten years ago, they arrived unemployed, unskilled, and illiterate. Since then, they say, the opening of new factories has given them work opportunities and improved their lives somewhat. In addition, NGOs have come to the area and raised awareness of the benefits of saving money and accessing credit. Rokeya, a 25-year-old mother of two from Bastuhara, tells of her success in launching a clothing business with the help of a loan. She not only has been able to pay off the loan, but has also helped her father repay his debts for her marriage.

Urban participants feel very vulnerable despite increased opportunities. People in Battala say that rickshaw pullers lose their rickshaws if they are late with rental payments, and garment workers may lose their jobs for many reasons (box 2). Factory workers may be fired immediately if they miss a day of work, as others can replace them immediately. Workers are also at great risk if they attempt to organize. The owner of one garment factory in Battala cut employee wages to compensate for his losses during a strike.

Child Labor

Participants in more than half the study communities expressed concern about child labor. Although the issue emerges mainly in discussions in the rural communities visited, people in Battala also indicate that

Seventeen-year-old Monira Akhter is the youngest daughter in a poor farming family with six children. When her family could no longer support her, she was sent to live with her married sister's family in the Bastuhara slum. Shafiq, Monira's brother-in-law, earned the family's only income as a rickshaw puller. A year ago, Shafiq abandoned his wife, two children, and Monira without any notice. Monira's sister borrowed money from a neighbor to overcome the immediate crisis of paying rent. Next, the sister took a job as a part-time domestic for Tk 200 (US$4) a month and two meals a day, and Monira found work in a garment factory for Tk 700 (US$14) a month. With these incomes the women were able to pay the rent and provide two meals a day for their four-member family, but nothing more. Shortly before researchers spoke with Monira, she had developed a high fever that kept her from work for ten days. Not only was she fired, but her employer refused to pay her for twenty days she had already worked.

children of the poorest families may have to go out to the streets to work and beg.

In Nurali Pur participants report that about 50 percent of children 8 to 12 years old work for food as day laborers for wealthy families in nearby villages. A child who works for an entire year for a wealthy family may receive an allotment of rice. Other children are involved in fishing and collecting cow dung from fields. In Madaripur children engage in diverse activities, such as chipping bricks or collecting twigs to sell as fuel. Both boys and girls perform domestic and agricultural labor, and their workload is described as heavy and sometimes even as harmful or deadly.

Parents in Ulipur, as noted above, send their children to other households to live and work in exchange for food and sometimes cash payments, which are sent back to the family. They say they are aggrieved by the harsh physical labor demanded of young children, and they worry especially about the fate of the girls. According to a discussion group of women, girls employed as servants in wealthy people's homes are often given workloads that are too heavy to accomplish in the assigned time. Mothers of these girls report that the girls may be beaten by both men and women in the employer's household for failing to finish their work. In addition, girls employed as maids may be sexually assaulted. Once a girl is known to have been violated, it becomes very difficult for the parents to marry her because a very large dowry would be demanded.

Floods and Erosion

Bangladesh consists of a vast delta plain formed by one of the largest river systems in the world, where the Ganges and Brahmaputra rivers and their tributaries drain into the Bay of Bengal. Flooding occurs every year, with catastrophic floods happening once or twice a decade. In autumn 1998 Bangladesh was hit with a devastating flood that submerged two-thirds of the country, left half a million people homeless, and caused more than 1,100 deaths. Businesses, industries, schools, roads and other infrastructure, and crops were destroyed. The floods damaged all of the communities visited; however, some areas were hit much harder than others. In Fadli Pur, where massive deforestation had already increased the number and severity of flash floods in recent years, the 1998 floods sent many better-off households into destitution. Rich families sold off bullocks and land at rock-bottom prices to local moneylenders, and poor people fell deeper into poverty.

Saduadamar Hat, Aminpara, and Hatya are villages in Ulipur thana in northern Bangladesh. Ulipur is one of the poorest areas in the country, and flooding poses an annual threat. Saduadamar Hat and Aminpara are one kilometer from the Teesta river, and Hatya lies on the river Brahmaputra. The Teesta and Brahmaputra rivers play key roles in the wellbeing of people in Ulipur thana. Everyone in Ulipur is endangered by erosion of the riverbanks and the resulting destruction of land and homesteads.

Discussion groups report that there is no middle wellbeing category in this area because of the constant riverbank erosion, which has created extensive land disputes and striking inequalities in landholdings. Study participants there report that the community includes some people who are well connected politically and socially and have very large landholdings, and the larger population that has been left nearly or completely landless by the shifting rivers.

Although Aminpara is not affected directly by riverbank erosion, a majority of the poor households in this village relocated to the area several years ago, after the river Teesta made a major shift. Many families who lost everything in the flood left their children nothing to inherit but poverty. Today, villagers in Hatya live in fear that the Brahmaputra will also overflow its banks and topple their homes. Already the river is eroding its banks, and it is possible that within a few years Hatya residents will also be forced to relocate.

The 1998 flood damaged crops in Saduadamar Hat and Aminpara but spared roads and houses there. In Hatya, however, the flood wiped out roads, houses, and cropland. Table 1 indicates discussion groups' perceptions of the dramatic losses in wellbeing suffered by everyone in Hatya. In the other two villages, the impacts are noticeable but less severe.

While a few households were able to absorb the shock of the flood, men and women in Hatya say that dozens of rich households became "hated poor" overnight as the river submerged their land and homes. Those who were already poor suffered even greater illbeing. The social poor, the only category of poor people with access to credit, attempted to overcome the havoc of the flood by borrowing money to replant rice, but an untimely post-flood rain in November destroyed their crops for a second time and they were unable to pay back their loans.

Crime, Violence, and Police Harassment

Another important risk widely discussed by urban and rural participants is the lack of physical safety where they live. Young women in Bastuhara and Battala, as well as in many villages, say they encounter teasing, harassment, and abuse from "hoodlums" and cannot move freely in their communities. Men in the cities express fear of police abuse and wrongful arrest. In Battala they report that residents are also exposed to hijacking, extortion, and kidnapping in the streets; however, overall insecurity has decreased significantly compared with the past. In contrast, residents in Bastuhara say that insecurity due to crime and corruption is much worse than it used to be.

Police stations receive overwhelmingly negative assessments in all locations where they are mentioned, except for a mixed report in Fadli

TABLE 1 Changes in Wellbeing in Three Ulipur Villages Since the 1998 Flood (percentage of population)

Wellbeing category	Hatya		Saduadamar Hat		Aminpara	
	Before flood	1999	Before flood	1999	Before flood	1999
Rich	24	5	2	3	30	25
Social poor	43	27	—	—	10	15
Helpless poor	10	19	98	87	45	35
Hated poor	21	40	—	10	15	25
Beggars	2	9	—	—	—	—

— Not available.

Pur. Study participants frequently report that the police and judicial systems are sources of fear and insecurity. In Bastuhara and Battala, the police are said to provide little protection against "hooligans and hijackers" and sometimes are said to work in collusion with them. Slum dwellers and villagers alike state that they are frequent victims of false police charges, and that police turn them in as criminals in order to protect the real culprits. Men in Bastuhara call their police officers illegal toll collectors. Study participants also cite numerous cases of false imprisonment of breadwinners in particular, and stress the hardship this brings to poor households when loss of income is combined with legal fees. "The police always catch the innocent people instead of the guilty ones," say Battala residents. "No work is done by police without a bribe. Police do not come when they are informed of incidents occurring in the slum. Sometimes police prevent the poor people from entering into the thana police station." This sentiment is echoed in several rural sites as well. In Nurali Pur participants state that they have little trust in the police: "Without giving money to the police it is not possible to lodge any complaint in the thana police station."

Dowry

Discussion groups of both men and women identify dowry as an urgent problem facing their communities. In the past, only well-off families gave dowry as a gift, but slowly this practice has become a tradition expected of poor people as well. Poor women in Char Kukri Mukri report that the burdens of dowry have grown worse because as girls become more educated, it is impossible to find literate husbands for them without paying high dowries.

The social pressure for dowry is great. In Nurali Pur, Char Kukri Mukri, and Bastuhara, men claim that if they cannot arrange a timely marriage for their daughters, the family runs a very high risk of being stigmatized and their daughters risk being sexually violated. Shitol Biswas, a poor man from Fadli Pur, says he felt compelled to give his oldest daughter in marriage to a 50-year-old man:

> I had no financial capacity. If I had, I would not have given my daughter in marriage with that old man. It was difficult for me to wait to give her to a good marriage as she was young. Bad Muslim boys teased her and I became afraid. Villagers also

blamed me at that time for not giving my daughter in marriage on time.

Shitol gave his second daughter in marriage when she was just 7 years old because he was too old and impoverished to wait any longer, and feared for her safety.

Anxieties over marriage and the demands of dowry are widespread, with many families drastically reducing their consumption in order to save for dowry. In many cases across Bangladesh, saving is impossible because of the diverse risks people face, and families become indebted and must sell their land and other assets to cover dowry expenses. An older man from Nurali Pur says, "Every poor father becomes destitute after giving his daughters in marriage. They sell out all their belongings, even their houses, to give dowry."

Women in Purba Rasti regard dowry as quite a serious problem because of its potential to affect the wellbeing of two families at the same time. When dowry is given, it drains the bride's parents financially, but if her father fails to meet the dowry demand, the bride may be beaten or abandoned (box 3). In some cases, grooms demand dowry over and over, with the meeting of each demand followed by a new demand.

In Ulipur a decrease in physical violence against women is considered to be a result of increased dowry payments, but this does not imply that the ability of parents to provide dowry has increased. On the contrary,

---

BOX 3 Dowry, Violence, and Women's Tenuous Status

Fatema, 20 years old, lives with an infant son at her parents' house in Aminpara. She married before she finished secondary school, in part because she wanted to marry and in part because her parents could not afford the costs of her continued education. Her husband, Moqbul, inherited some cultivable land and a homestead plot. But after her wedding, Fatema's in-laws pursued Moqbul to sell the land and start a business. They also pressured him to insist that Fatema bring a dowry from her father so that he could invest the money in his business. But Moqbul's ambition could not be fulfilled because his wife's father, a poor carpenter, did not have the ability to provide any dowry for her. This harmed Fatema's status in her husband's family. Moqbul was irregularly employed, and soon he spent all the money obtained from the sale of his land. From then on, he began to beat Fatema and threatened to abandon her, which he eventually did. Her in-laws refused outright to keep her in their house, so she had to move with her son to her parents' house.

dowry is considered to be one of the most pressing problems in Ulipur communities, but families yield to the demand in order to save their daughters from violence and repression.

Nurali Pur residents state that only greater public awareness can solve the problem of dowry. The government has already enacted laws to stop the practice, but discussion groups there feel that laws alone will not solve this problem. They suggest that the government broadcast through various media not the punishment for taking dowry, as it currently does, but the effects of the practice on poor families. Participants in Bastuhara state that they would like to see the government strictly enforce the laws to stop dowry. They say that NGOs should take further steps to increase awareness in the society against the practice of dowry.

Sources of Vulnerability and Abuse of Women

The low status of poor Bangladeshi women in their households shows some small but significant improvements. The freedom of women to travel, work, and participate in markets is increasing, as indicated above, but the extent of change varies widely among the study communities. Prevailing social norms continue to leave many poor women exposed to abuse and abandonment by their husbands. Trends in violence against women are very mixed: poor women in some communities report that domestic abuse is lessening, while in other communities women report that it remains a pervasive and even deepening problem due to rising dowry demands and economic stress. In communities where domestic abuse is seen to be declining, women frequently credit the work of NGOs that raise awareness of gender rights and improve women's access to credit and income-earning opportunities.[9]

Despite changes in women's economic roles and sometimes in their social status within the household, relations among men and women in the country remain deeply inequitable. Two obvious signs of this are the widespread reports of domestic violence against women and the additional insecurity women say they face due to polygamy. In Nurali Pur, as elsewhere in the country, women paint a troubled picture. They say the incidence of physical and mental abuse of women in the household has increased two to three times, but the severity of the physical abuse has largely decreased because women have gained awareness, training, and options. Three main circumstances are said to trigger violence against women in this village: (a) parents fail to provide dowry as agreed, (b) wives fail to take care of their husbands when the men return from work, and (c) women do not complete their household duties on time. Women in this village associate the rising rate of violence with growing poverty in the area. They indicate that men are always bad tempered because they cannot eat a full meal after a hard day of work. Women also report that their own income-earning activities are interfering with their ability to finish household duties, for which their husbands sometimes beat them and deny them food. Difficulties managing their increased work burdens are reported by women in many communities.

Discussion groups of women in Basthara conclude that both the rate and severity of domestic abuse are rising. Ten years ago, their husbands typically yelled at them when they were angry, whereas now their husbands beat them. Women in that community report being beaten, raped, and stabbed. These wives say that they may be beaten if they speak up against their husbands' involvement in polygamy, prostitution, gambling, and drunkenness. Like women in other communities in the study, they may also be abused if dowry demands are not met or if household duties are not performed.

The efforts of NGOs and media have increased poor women's awareness of their legal rights in marriage, but people report that the Bangladeshi legal system does not yet enforce these rights with any consistency. In Nurali Pur, for example, discussion groups state that neither the village institutions nor legal institutions such as the court provide any support when women seek redress against polygamy or divorce. In some cases, if a husband does not provide his first wife with food regularly or grant her a divorce after his second marriage, she may try to get her husband to return her dowry money. Some women also file suit against their husbands in thana court, but they do not get any benefit out of it in the long run, participants say.

Women in four communities report declining trends in domestic abuse. In Battala participants say that violence against women, including kidnappings and attacks with acid, has decreased dramatically. They attribute the decline to a number of factors, including women's role as income earners; their participation in *samity* (women's credit groups), training, and literacy classes; their widening social networks;

and their growing confidence and courage to resist abuse. Women from Battala say they join forces and protect one another if any woman in the community is beaten by her husband. Similar declines are reported by women in rural Fadli Pur and Ulipur thana, where NGOs have been active in building awareness of women's rights and increasing women's access to credit. In Ulipur the women named two factors that have contributed to the reduction of violence. One is that bridegrooms now demand and receive from brides' parents a larger amount of dowry than in the past, which may buffer his abuse. The second factor is the increased practice of marriage registration; most marriages used to take place in the presence of community members and by verbal agreement only, which meant that the husband could abandon his wife at any time without legal ramifications.

Polygamy is another source of risk for women. While having many wives increases a man's social and economic status, women say the practice is deeply harmful to wives' security because it can lead to the husband's complete abandonment of them and their children. A man may take income from all of his wives, while his income may or may not be distributed among all the women. Polygamy is reported to have increased slightly in urban areas. One reason is that women who migrate to the cities are often harassed by men, and women may seek the physical protection that marriage brings, even if with a man already married. However, many first wives fear polygamy because husbands sometimes abandon their first wives for women who can earn higher incomes. According to Shabana Begum, a poor woman in Fadli Pur,

> *I do not trust my husband. He may marry again. I have a job only for the next four months. I do not know how my husband will behave when I am no longer able to give money to him. I do not know if he will continue his good behavior with me or not. If I could continue my job for the next three to four years I would be able to make myself solvent. However, this job opportunity has already enhanced my courage to work outside of the village. I will try to do some new job in the future.*

Thus while many women across the country are working harder than ever to earn incomes for their households, their lives remain deeply insecure due to widespread problems of dowry, polygamy, and violence against them.

Institutions in Bangladesh

In the face of such extensive and severe risks, poor people say that institutions that respond promptly in a crisis are more important to them than institutions that provide help with ongoing needs in their communities. Thus, while local public officials and other government institutions are often identified as important, study participants have little trust or confidence in these unresponsive bodies. Poor people depend heavily on local moneylenders because although they are widely scorned, they are responsive and fill needs not met by the many microcredit programs in Bangladesh. NGOs, followed by religious institutions, appear with the highest frequency on study participants' lists of important institutions in their lives.

Failing Grades for Local Government

In both rural and urban locations, local officials receive mixed reviews. Discussion groups view the local chairmen or members of the union *parishad* (UP, local council) and other government functionaries as important, but often corrupt and ineffective. In none of the locations is the UP judged accessible or accountable to poor people. Study participants in Nurali Pur report that thana officials are corrupt, unaccountable to anyone for their "dishonest acts," and show respect only to the rich. They say the UP members and chairmen only visit the village right before elections, and never fulfill their campaign promises once elected. In Fadli Pur poor people report that UP chairmen wrongfully charge fees for nationality certificates and show favoritism in settling community disputes. In Halkerchar, Char Kukri Mukri, Fadli Pur, and Battala, groups report that local authorities helped themselves to food relief and other public assistance intended for poor households. In a few rural areas, however, local chairmen are valued by poor men for their role in settling disputes at the village court (*salish*), distributing relief goods, and issuing citizenship certificates. In Purba Rasti, Hiranadi Kulla, and Battala, local authorities received a relatively positive assessment for helping with relief assistance during the 1998 flood.

Women appear particularly excluded from participation in civic affairs in their communities. Despite legislation that supports women's participation in elections and their right to hold elected UP offices, women in the rural villages visited in Bangladesh report that in practice little has changed, as elected men either suppress women's participation or take over their roles. Women in Char Kukri Mukri and Ulipur thana say that they brave police repression to vote in local elections, but despite their activism, female officials are still excluded from *salish*. In Nurali Pur women have now earned the right to attend *salish* meetings, but they cannot put forward any views. Even in Battala women report that men still play the major role in community decision making, although in some cases they seek women's opinions.

Dependence on Moneylenders

While poor people report various microcredit opportunities in Bangladesh, private moneylenders continue to thrive in both rural and urban communities. Despite their exorbitant interest rates and ruthlessness in recovering loans, moneylenders are valued by poor people because they offer easy access and flexible lending terms. Unlike public, private, and NGO credit schemes focused on supporting income generation or, occasionally, home improvement, moneylenders will make a loan to cover dowry, health emergencies, food, and other pressing needs. Poor people report, however, that their dependence on moneylenders leaves them deeply vulnerable to losing any scarce assets they may have and to rising cycles of indebtedness.

Participants in Ulipur thana say they can borrow money from the moneylender "at any time for any reason." Men say they borrow during the "slack period" to cover travel expenses to town to find work. Even poor children can incur debt from moneylenders (box 4). Moneylenders do not offer credit without collateral or a labor agreement, and as a participant in Nurali Pur explains, "Most of those who take a loan from a moneylender to cope with a sudden shock end up repaying the loan by selling their assets." Men in Nurali Pur report that the moneylender evicts people forcefully from their homes for failing to repay debts on time.

Some in the study describe being hit by a sequence of shocks that send them deep into debt to moneylenders. Abu Ziad, 50, lives in Purba Rasti with his wife and three children. Several years ago, he earned Tk 2,000 (US$40) a month as an installer of tube wells, and his family lived comfortably. But all of a sudden, his employer declared bankruptcy and Ziad lost his job. Shortly thereafter, he began accumulating debt. He had to borrow Tk 12,000 (US$245) to resolve a dispute over his homestead. Then, Ziad developed a hernia while working as a rickshaw puller and borrowed Tk 15,000 (US$305) for treatment. While he was recovering, his wife fell ill, which required another Tk 8,000 (US$160) for medical care. Weakened by his hernia operation, Ziad quit the rickshaw business and borrowed Tk 15,000 (US$305) to start a fishing business. Unfortunately, he had to use much of that loan to rebuild his house and repay his other loans. Then came the flood of 1998. Shortly after that, his eldest daughter married, and he needed to borrow Tk 10,000 (US$200) to pay for the marriage ceremony and dowry. His total debt now amounts to Tk 40,000 (US$815) and he does not know how he will repay it.

Poor people have little trust in, or access to, commercial banks. Participants in two groups in Dewangonj mention that they cannot get a bank loan because they have no land or any other property for collateral. To obtain credit through a commercial bank, participants say they must pay a bribe through a broker. Only a few wealthy families in Nurali Pur are reported to be able to obtain loans from a commercial bank, and they do so with relative ease.

NGOs: Reliable and Trustworthy

Nongovernmental organizations that conducted research in the communities where they had programs found that they were the only institutions to receive consistently high ratings. NGOs inspire favorable reviews because they are responsive in crises, respectful, and include poor people in decision making. NGO programs in the study communities are wide-ranging and include microlending, training, education, employment, reforestation, and disaster relief.[10] Many NGO activities specifically target their programs to poor women who otherwise go unserved. While poor people greatly appreciate NGOs, they also identify corruption in a few of them, and they add that many NGO programs fail to reach, or even actively exclude, the poorest groups.

In all three villages visited in Ulipur, men rated the NGO Proshika as the most important institution because its staff works closely with the villagers and it offers villagers assistance when they deal with the thana administration and court. In Purba Rasti, Proshika is also highly regarded for providing credit, education, and training programs as well as meeting space for men and for women at the NGO-operated school. In addition, poor people acknowledge that NGOs and the *samity* gave them their first opportunity to participate in decision making.

Poor people across Bangladesh also appreciate NGOs in times of crisis. Villagers in Nurali Pur say that Concern responds quickly after natural disasters. In the floods of 1988, 1993, and 1998, Concern provided villagers with food, shelter, clothes, and treatment facilities, along with village reconstruction. In Fadli Pur the organization sought out the poorest women affected by the 1998 floods and offered them jobs as caretakers of roadside trees that had been planted under a reforestation program. Women in Hatya recall that Proshika gave them a new tube well and latrine for the community as well as assistance during the floods. Similarly, discussion groups in Battala say Proshika helped them to recover after their slum was on fire for two days. Some poor women share encouraging experiences with gradually accumulating savings and assets (box 5).

Views about NGOs are not uniformly positive, however. Participants in Nurali Pur say of one group active in the community:

> *The poorest of the poor cannot enroll as members of the group. In a natural disaster, only group members receive relief from them. The relief they get is too inadequate for the members. The NGO staff act badly with the group members if they fail to repay the loan on time.*

In several communities, moreover, poor women indicate that beneficiaries of NGO schemes are typically better-off women who have some assets or a regular source of income that enables them to save money. Those who cannot contribute weekly savings are excluded from many

Anisa married Keramat against the wishes of her family and receives no assistance from them. Early in their married life, Keramat worked in a battery factory, but he lost his job in 1985 and has suffered insolvency ever since. After he lost his job, Anisa worked as a domestic for three years, but she could not maintain her family responsibilities at the same time, and their rent increased. They moved to Battala, and Keramat began to beat Anisa often when he came home drunk. At that time, a fieldworker from Proshika visited the slum and Anisa joined the association on November 1998. She deposited Tk 5 (10 cents) weekly and received development and organizational training from Proshika. She then borrowed Tk 200 (US$4) from a Proshika small-business credit scheme. She earned Tk 300 (US$6) per month by investing the money in an auto-rickshaw garage owned by Keramat's friend. Later, she borrowed an additional Tk 5,000 (US$100) and Tk 8,000 (US$160) from Proshika and continued investing. She paid off the loan and reduced family expenditures. She purchased land and took subsequent loans from Proshika. In addition, she sent her daughter to World Vision, which provides clothes, books, and medical treatment. Anisa now lives well and she has become the owner of land and an auto-rickshaw business.

rotating credit schemes. Aseea Begum, a poor widow in Khaliajuri, says, "Previously, nobody provided me with a loan. If I requested a loan, they gave me one kilogram of rice or Tk 5 to Tk 10 as alms. I did not get any opportunity to make myself a member of an NGO because I had no capacity to deposit savings money."

Other women say that the activities undertaken with the loans, such as raising cattle or poultry, homestead gardening, or petty trade yield only intermittent or small incomes, not enough to pull them out of poverty.

Religious Institutions: Important but Limited

While poor people consider the mosque an important and trustworthy institution in their communities, they often express the wish that local religious bodies would be more forthcoming with financial help during crises. In Fadli Pur people's trust in the mosque stems from their practice of going to an *imam* (prayer leader) to seek a blessing to overcome social problems and natural disasters. In urban Battala discussion groups say outright that the mosque is of no use during crises. Similarly, a discussion group of men in Ulipur thana gives the *madrasa* (traditional Islamic teacher) very little importance because he is not able to provide any financial or social support when a household is in urgent need. An exception was found in Gowainghat, where some poor Hindus live on land owned by the temple and therefore regard it as supportive to their livelihood. Some poor people, including discussion groups of women in Battala and Purba Rasti, express the view that mosques exclude and discriminate against poor people—and especially poor women—in their decision-making processes.

Conclusion

There have been only modest shifts in poverty rates in Bangladesh, and the numbers of poor people are not going to decline dramatically without major economic, institutional, and social changes. Many in Bangladesh say they feel destined to be poor by virtue of being "poor by birth." They remain poor, they say, because of scarce, unreliable, risky, and seasonal jobs at low pay, repeated natural calamities, the trap of indebtedness, demographic pressure, illness, and dowry. Poor women face the additional burdens of earning far lower wages than men while enduring physical and mental abuse in their homes and communities and the threat of polygamy. Participants in all the study communities would like to see caring and trustworthy institutions that work for poor people instead of against them. Poor people do not feel the government is on their side. They appreciate the good works of the NGOs, however modest.

Despite monumental problems, women and men have many creative ideas about what could be done to improve their lives and protect them from shocks. Bastuhara slum dwellers assert that their insecurity could be solved if they could just settle in a permanent place without fear of eviction from government lands. With secure shelter, they hope the government will take further initiative and provide electricity and water; they also want steps taken to protect them from harassment by the police and "outsider hoodlums." Poor women of Ulipur thana believe that their traditional sewing skills can be transformed into incomes with some start-up capital and market assistance from an NGO. Nurali Pur residents state unanimously that they could solve many problems themselves if they had work, and they urge the government, political leaders, and NGOs to step forward and help create these economic opportunities.

It is evident that access to jobs and incomes reduces hunger and vulnerability. Nevertheless, government efforts to create jobs together with NGO income-generation activities are not enough to offset pervasive unemployment, and the question of giving more people access to land and other resources is not on the agenda. Nor is microcredit reaching enough poor people, as communities still depend heavily on exploitative private moneylenders. Meanwhile, the absence of safety nets for flood-affected people who have no assets contributes to their desperate situation.

Many studies have been done of poverty in Bangladesh; the problems they document are well known and have long been part of the country's development debate. The present study lets poor people speak for themselves about their experiences, their views, and their hopes and fears. To address many aspects of poverty and vulnerability, however, poor people's actions by themselves are not enough. Poverty reduction requires system-wide change, which is contingent on political commitment. We end by raising a series of questions:

- ▸ Can the present study make a contribution toward raising political commitment to address the country's urgent development needs?
- ▸ What types of long-term actions are needed to create jobs, enhance poor people's assets, and protect them with effective safety nets?
- ▸ How can microcredit and private money-lending, which coexist widely in rural areas, be redesigned to help poor people build their assets and reduce their exposure to hunger and shocks?

Many sources of poor people's vulnerability and exclusion are deeply rooted in sociocultural practices such as dowry, disregard of poor people in the community, and absence of women from the market. There are no easy and immediate solutions. In addition, there is an urgent need to end discrimination against poor people in government hospitals, by the police, and in the local councils.

- ▸ What types of concerted social actions can help gradually to undermine practices that exclude and degrade poor people?
- ▸ How can public authorities be held more accountable for their disparaging attitudes and behaviors toward the poor? How can the quality of public services be improved?

▸ None of the governmental or NGO programs are reducing the numbers of bottom or hated poor. Across Bangladesh, their numbers are quite large. What can be done to help them?

TABLE 2 Study Communities in Bangladesh

RURAL COMMUNITIES

Saduadamar Hat, Aminpara, Hatya, Ulipur thana Pop. 12,000 (est.)	Ulipur is a poverty-stricken thana in the northern part of Bangladesh. Residents are sharply polarized into poor and rich. The area suffers from riverbank erosion and is extremely dependent on agricultural wage labor, resulting in a high level of migration in lean agricultural seasons. The thana has very good infrastructure facilities and road networks. There is a primary school in Saduadamar Hat as well as a privately run religious school. The three villages do not have easy access to medical facilities.
Diara, Laxmipur, Dion, Nachol thana Pop. 9,000 (est.)	Poor infrastructure isolates this area from the rest of the town. It is dependent on agricultural wage labor, and job shortages are severe. Lands are characterized by low fertility and cultivation is excessively dependent on groundwater irrigation. People in these villages do not have easy access to health or education facilities, nor do they have electricity.
Halkerchar, Dewangonj thana Pop. 2,250	A flood control embankment separates the village from the river Jamuna. Men work primarily as day laborers or in agriculture and fishing. Most of the women are housewives, and many also collect and sell wood and cow dung. The village has one government primary school, one junior high school, and one informal primary school run by an NGO. A very small market is situated in the middle of the village. Most villagers are Muslim.
Char Kukri Mukri, Charfession thana Pop. 7,000	This community, located in a floodplain, is isolated from the mainland and depends on forestry and capture fisheries. The main sources of livelihood for men are agriculture, fishing, and working as day laborers. Women are generally housewives, although they also occasionally fish, collect firewood, rear cows, and sew. The lives and livelihoods of the people of this area are frequently threatened by cyclones, tidal surges, and riverbank erosion. There are five schools, one of them run by the government, and a big market. The area has no electricity. Most villagers are Muslim.

Nurali Pur, Khaliajuri thana Pop. 642	The village is situated on the bank of the Dhanu river; livelihoods depend on agricultural wage labor and capture fisheries. There is no school in the village, no electricity, no primary health clinic, and no telephone. These services are available in the district capital, which is about eleven kilometers away.
Fadli Pur, Gowainghat thana Pop. 259	This area, heavily dependent on agriculture, is also severely affected by flash flooding. Men earn their living as farmers, fishers, and day laborers. Others are involved in petty trade. Most women are housewives, and many also grow vegetables, raise poultry, and weave bamboo baskets. There is one government primary school in the village, but attendance is spotty in the rainy season. There is no post office, electricity, or health center, but they are available twelve kilometers away in the district town.
Purba Rasti, Madaripur thana Pop. 12,000	Located between Madaripur district town and a shifting river, the village is unusually densely populated and there is fierce competition for homestead plots. Men depend heavily on wage labor and work in the informal and urban labor sector. Some women are employed as domestics in the village and town. The village has electricity but only a single hand tube well for water. There is no government-operated primary school, but a national NGO operates informal primary schools in the village alongside a semi-government (registered) school.
Hiranadi Kulla, Dhamrai thana Pop. 2,000	In this village located near an export processing zone,* both men and women depend on factory employment supplemented by agriculture. The village is densely populated and the communications infrastructure is poor. There is a government primary school and an informal school run by an NGO. Apart from the thana health complex, the villagers do not have any access to health care services.

An industrial area where goods for export—mainly garments—are manufactured or processed.

URBAN COMMUNITIES

Battala,
Dhaka city
Pop. 10,000

This densely populated slum has two informal schools, a bazaar, a mosque, and a few stores. Residents work primarily in the informal sector as drivers and day laborers. There are water and electricity connections; however, the water supply is irregular and there is no sewerage.

Bastuhara,
Chittagong city
Pop. 3,000

The slum is situated in the busiest area of Chittagong and most houses are built of bamboo sticks. The main sources of livelihood for men are driving trucks and day laboring. Women work in the garment factories or as domestics. There is an informal primary school and some sanitation services, but not enough. The community is Muslim, and there is a mosque.

Notes

1. The study was coordinated by Md. Shahabuddin, and the fieldwork was led by Rashed un Nabi, Dipankar Datta, Subrata Chakrabarty, Masuma Begum, and Nasima Jahan Chaudhury. The study team also included Mostafa Zainul Abedin, Shukhakriti Adhikari, Dil Afroz, Selina Akhter, Zaed Al-Hasan, Khodeja Begum, Morzina Begum, Hasibur Rahman Bijon, Pradip Kumar Biswas, Lipi Daam, Nikunja Debnath, Bijoy Kumar Dhar, S. M. Tozammel Haque, Emarat Hossain, Tariqul Islam, Iqbal Hossain Jahangir, Roji Khatun, Shohel Newaz, Moshfeka Jahan Parveen, Rajia Pervin, Amjad Hossain Pintu, A. K. M. Azad Rahman, Ashekur Rahman, Mizanur Rahman, Abdus Salam, Shofikus Saleh, Mezbah Uddin Shaheen, Afroza Sultana, and Al-Haz Uddin.

2. Bangladesh is divided administratively into divisions, districts, thanas, unions, and villages. There are 490 thanas in the country.

3. World Bank, "Bangladesh: From Counting the Poor to Making the Poor Count" (Poverty Reduction and Economic Management Network, South Asia Region, April 1998), 6. The upper poverty line is based on expenditures required to consume 2,122 kilocalories a day per person plus a fixed bundle of essential nonfood items. At the lower poverty line, if a person purchases anything besides food it will reduce food expenditures to below the minimum calories indicated above. The cost of the food and nonfood items is calculated for various regions.

4. World Bank, *World Development Indicators 2001* (Report 22099, April 2001), 12.

5. World Bank, "Memorandum of the President of the International Development Association and the International Finance Corporation to the Executive Directors on the Country Assistance Strategy for the People's Republic of Bangladesh" (February 8, 2001), 2.

6. World Bank, "Bangladesh: From Counting the Poor," 6.

7. The government of Bangladesh and the World Food Programme used composite indices of seven sociological and environmental indicators to group subdistricts into four rankings: very high poverty, high poverty, moderate poverty, and low poverty.

8. For example, in the village of Halkerchar, the research team asked the NGO working in this community to organize a meeting with poor women. More than 75 women came to this meeting.

9. World Bank, "Memorandum of the President," 3.

10. As mentioned in the introduction, the sample in Bangladesh includes mainly communities where NGOs are active, and many NGO income-generation and social awareness programs specifically target and benefit poor women. For this reason, the trends in violence in this sample should not be considered representative of wider conditions.

11. It should be noted that the study in Bangladesh was conducted by Proshika, Concern Bangladesh, and ActionAid Bangladesh. They selected communities where they had ongoing programs, both to speed their entry into the communities (given a very tight research deadline) and to facilitate follow-up on the study findings. For information on the overall study process, methodology, and sampling, see chapter 1 of *Crying Out for Change*, vol. 2 of *Voices of the Poor* (New York: Oxford University Press, 2000).

India

Gains and Stagnation in Bihar and Andhra Pradesh

Somesh Kumar[1]

Lokesh Singh, a 40-year-old father of two, is a Bhumij, part of the Singhbhum warrior caste. One of the very poorest people in the remote village of Geruwa, Lokesh has been hit by one tragedy after another. He lost his two brothers in an accident, and his wife died three years ago. Two years ago, he was stricken with tuberculosis. Lokesh no longer owns any land; he lives with his two children in a small, crumbling hut. Neither his son nor his daughter has ever been to school.

Geruwa lies on the fringe of the Dalma wildlife sanctuary in south Bihar. Villages like Geruwa are subject to frequent attacks by elephants as human settlements' encroach on wildlife habitats. Local farmers say that the elephant menace makes it foolhardy to expand or diversify their farming. To make ends meet, many Geruwa villagers travel along a winding twelve-kilometer path to the city of Tatanagar in order to sell goods in the street. Once the rainy season begins and the road is flooded, this source of income is cut off for all but the able-bodied men who can scale the rocky hills.

There is work for Lokesh in a local brick kiln that pays 35 rupees (81 cents) a day, but his health is bad and he hasn't been able to work much lately. He knows very well that without this income he will not be able to feed his children, afford his medication, or survive for very long. To get money for food, the children occasionally go to the forest to cut

147

timber and sell fuelwood at the weekly Jamshedpur market, located eight kilometers away in the town of Maango.

Lokesh's monthly household expenses amount to nearly Rs. 700 (US$16.25 at the time of this study). This includes two kilograms of rice daily, as well as pulses, sugar, salt, and oil. He obtains his ration quota from the PDS (Public Distribution System) shop at Bonta and purchases other household essentials at the Jamshedpur market.

Every time he visits a private doctor, he has to pay a consultation fee of Rs. 40. His medicines amount to at least Rs. 400 per month (more than US$9). He estimates that the foods prescribed for him, including barley and fruits, cost about Rs. 300 (nearly US$7), which is unaffordable. He says he doesn't even think of going for the recommended blood transfusions because every bottle of blood costs Rs. 100 (more than US$2).

The family's hut urgently needs repairs, but Lokesh does not know where to get the resources to accomplish this. He estimates that hay would cost Rs. 950; logs, Rs. 900; rope, Rs. 150; bamboo, Rs. 100 for five pieces; and sticks, Rs. 200. Any additional patchwork using clay would cost him another Rs. 3,000.

Poor men and women from ten communities in the Indian states of Bihar and Andhra Pradesh participated in this study. Like Lokesh, other participants report frequently that illness or the death of a family member sends their entire household into deep debt and turns their life into a daily battle for survival. Even those in the study who have not endured such shocks say that finding a path out of poverty remains extremely difficult because livelihood opportunities continue to be precarious and low paying. At the same time, study participants note that in recent years they have had better access to public services and more engagement with the private sector and NGOs, and that these advances have somewhat eased their hardships. Many people in the study also feel a greater sense of freedom now, and they describe small but important changes in lowering traditional caste barriers and expanding women's opportunities.

India is the largest and one of the most culturally diverse democracies in the world. While India's overall economic growth, poverty reduction, and social gains accelerated after the mid-1970s, weak governance sent the country into a severe fiscal crisis in the late 1980s. The government's response has been to initiate major economic reforms, bringing greater openness and competition to many areas of the economy, and stimulating very high growth rates. The central government is also devolving many responsibilities for public service delivery to the states. GNP growth averaged an unprecedented 7 percent annually from 1993 to 1997, and has averaged 6 percent since.[2] Per capita incomes in India climbed from US$390 to $440 between 1990 and 1999.[3] Recent years have brought economic transition and continued rapid growth, but poverty has abated more slowly than expected.

The government has been strongly committed to reducing poverty and has invested heavily for decades in infrastructure, a large food distribution scheme, and many other anti-poverty programs. As this study attests, some of these initiatives have catalyzed development and reduced extreme hunger and insecurity, yet poverty remains a massive development challenge. According to World Bank figures, India has some 433 million people living on less than US$1 a day, accounting for 36 percent of the world's poor people. India's own official estimates indicate that 36 percent of its population, 350 million people, are poor.[4] Three out of every four poor people live in rural areas.[5]

A key aspect of poverty in India is the great diversity in the levels of deprivation and social development across the states. Table 1 presents data for the two states in this study, highlighting sharp differences in poverty rates and a smaller gap in social development indicators. Andhra Pradesh has one of the country's lowest poverty rates, and Bihar has the highest.

TABLE 1 Economic and Social Indicators, Andhra Pradesh and Bihar

	Population 1998 (millions)	Poverty rate 1993–94	Literacy rate 1997	Infant mortality rate 1997 (per 1,000 live births)
Andhra Pradesh	75.1	21.9	54.0	63.1
Bihar	99.2	55.2	49.0	71.3

Note: Poverty data in this table are based on India's official poverty line.

Source: World Bank, "Memorandum of the President of the International Bank for Reconstruction and Development, the International Development Association and the International Finance Corporation to the Executive Directors on a Country Assistance Strategy of the World Bank Group for India" (June 27, 2001), 2.

Andhra Pradesh is a leading reform state, earning much attention for its Vision 2020 poverty alleviation strategy. About 70 percent of its workforce is in agriculture. Several major industries, including machine tools, pharmaceutical products, shipbuilding, and electronic equipment, operate across the state. Hyderabad, its capital, has been nicknamed "Cyberabad" due to its efforts to promote information technology and the location of major software industries in the city. Despite a well-organized response by the government and NGOs, the growth rate in wages remains low. The third largest state in the country, Andhra Pradesh has high rates of casual agricultural labor and child labor, as well as very high female illiteracy and school dropout rates. On average, 35 percent of the state's children complete elementary education.[6]

Bihar, which lies in the east of the country, is both the poorest and the most rural state in India, with 87 percent of its population classified as rural. It is the only state in which the percentage of people living in poverty increased between 1987 and 1994. As in Andhra Pradesh, the main occupation in Bihar is agriculture, though the southern area has rich mineral resources and bustling heavy industry, including the giant Tata Iron and Steel Company. Despite being the poorest state in the country, investments in education and health are high compared with those of other states. Nonetheless, only half the state's children ages 6 to 10 attend primary school. The state has faced inter-caste conflict for the past fifteen years.[7] Recent political reforms in Bihar have aimed to empower many traditionally oppressed castes. During 2000, the government introduced and Parliament passed legislation creating a new largely tribal-populated state from the Jharkand area of southern Bihar.

This study is based on discussions with poor women and men in six rural, two urban, and two peri-urban communities in Andhra Pradesh and Bihar (see table 2, Study Communities in India, at the end of this chapter). The communities represent varying demographic, environmental, occupational, and social characteristics, and include the most disadvantaged groups in Indian society: women, the landless, and members of scheduled castes and tribes. An overriding criterion was to select places that offered the possibility of program or project follow-up.

The study was undertaken by PRAXIS, a Bihar-based NGO that received support from ActionAid India. Communities were selected in the two states where PRAXIS had ongoing programs or contacts through other NGOs. At the community level, poor households were identified through a social mapping exercise in which residents reflected on the characteristics of wellbeing and illbeing of different households within the community. The researchers conducted fifty-nine discussion groups with women, men, and youths. In addition, forty-six individual case studies were conducted with thirty-one poor people and fifteen people who were once poor but managed to escape poverty. Fieldwork in Bihar and Andhra Pradesh was carried out in February and March 1999.

It is important to understand the complex social institution of caste, which permeates community life. In the caste system, a family's occupation and place in the social hierarchy remain firmly defined generation after generation, and there is little interaction among members of different castes. The reservation, or quota, system in the 1950 constitution gave scheduled castes (the lowest caste, the *dalits* or "untouchables") and scheduled groups proportional representation in the legislature, civil service, and education. The so-called backward castes, numbering more than 3,000, are one rung above the scheduled castes. Accounting for half the country's population, they are a potent political force in the densely populated north. The reservation system was meant to end deeply rooted inequality, but lower-caste people continue to face discrimination from higher castes. Disputes over wages, land ownership, and even the right to draw water from upper-caste wells can sometimes flare into conflict. It is common for upper castes to dominate the center of villages, forcing others to live at a distance. The landless poor often work for abysmally low wages for upper-caste families, who control most of the land and benefit disproportionately from many public services, and who may refuse to relinquish land earmarked for *dalits*. Clearly, caste still influences opportunities. Yet, there are indications that the system is loosening and that opportunities are opening up somewhat for people in the lower castes.

This study reveals poor people's views on the key economic, institutional, and social hurdles they experience in their attempts to move out of poverty. The chapter opens in a poor village of Andhra Pradesh, describing what poor people there consider to be the defining local features of a good life and a bad life. It then examines the leading problems and trends affecting wellbeing in the communities visited. Next, the chapter presents poor people's assessments of the most important public, private, and civic institutions in their daily lives. It closes with a look at changes in gender relations in the study communities.

Experiences of Wellbeing and Illbeing

Pedda Kothapalli is the main village in a panchayat (informal local government unit) of five hamlets in one of the poorest areas of Andhra Pradesh. The mud track from the village to the national highway is in such bad condition that government officials avoid visiting in the rainy season. About half the 153 households in the village are from the dominant Telaga caste of landed farmers, and the rest are mainly from the scheduled, shepherd, and washer castes. Most households earn their living in agriculture, with the Telaga owning 80 percent of the land and many landless poor people working as laborers. Wages are meager, and the younger generation is moving to towns to find work.

Definitions of wellbeing in Pedda Kothapalli center on economic criteria, but also include social and psychological dimensions. The community's *elite* are described as mill owners and moneylenders who own houses, are literate, and are able to eat a variety of foods every day. The merely *rich* or *well-to-do* in the village own shops and eat a variety of foods only once a week. This group also owns property and jewelry, and "their word carries weight." Discussion groups estimate that 15 to 20 percent of the village population is rich or elite.

Those in the *middle class* own three to four acres of land, bullock carts, and good clothing, and they have easy access to credit. Scheduled caste women estimate that 28 percent of the villagers fall into this category.

Poor people are described as those who own less than an acre of land, occasionally have to work as wage laborers, may migrate in search of work, are malnourished, wear old clothing, and are indebted. At 34 percent, according to a discussion group of scheduled caste men, poor people form the largest share of the village population. Below this wellbeing category is a group referred to as the *very poor* or *poorest of the poor*. Participants say that these people go hungry, lack support, and cannot obtain loans. Scheduled caste men simply say that the very poor are "totally dependent on others." Scheduled caste women report that just over 20 percent of Pedda Kothapalli could be categorized as very poor.

Criteria of Wellbeing

Like the groups in Pedda Kothapalli, most people who participated in this study describe wellbeing in multidimensional terms. Possessing assets, land, livelihood, savings, enough food, the resources to afford health care, and housing are elements of wellbeing, as are having the resources to host guests in style, having few worries, having influence in society, and being respected.

People from all occupations—farmers, wage laborers, potters, fishermen, and vendors—see a regular income as important. In urban settlements people are considered happy or rich if they have their own businesses or shops and can employ others. In rural areas the prosperous are considered to be those who cultivate cash crops, own orchards, and lease out land. In many communities those with assured income are called *nischinta*, or worry-free. For fishermen and their wives in Konada, Andhra Pradesh, people are rich if they can afford powerboats and fishing nets. In urban areas, having a business, a vending license, and a legal right to property puts one high on the wellbeing continuum. Vendor women in Patna, Bihar, see people who own their own shops as prosperous. Savings, according to many women's groups, is another indicator of wellbeing. People want to accumulate surplus to cope with emergencies, and having to borrow is a sign of poverty.

Those without property or other assets are forced to depend upon wage labor. This is seen as a leading indicator of illbeing because these jobs are often scarce, irregular, and very low paid. People with few options often must work in dangerous or unhealthy jobs, such as in the bauxite mines in Netarhat, Bihar, or the limestone quarries in Dorapalli, Andhra Pradesh.

Chronic indebtedness is a major determinant of illbeing across study communities, and poor people are identified as perpetual borrowers. Landless men in Jaggaram, Andhra Pradesh, estimate that each household needs about Rs. 2,000 (about US$46) to repay outstanding debts. Dowry obligations are also said to rob savings and send households into debt. Some in the study describe marrying their daughters at a young age because it requires lower dowry. A potter in Konada had to take the socially unacceptable step of marrying off her second daughter before her first because a small dowry was asked.

Many groups define wellbeing as having food year-round or a certain number of daily meals that are complete and varied. In rural areas, droughts, poor harvests, crop and livestock diseases, and lack of work can mean hunger. The members of one landless family in Manjhar, Bihar, say they eat every other day. For another landless family there, lunch consists of "munching some sugarcane."

The elderly, who depend on their children for food, are considered the most vulnerable group. In remote Netarhat, Bihar, where many young people have left the village in search of work, such elderly are called *asahaaya*, those without help. One older woman in Manjhar explains, "I do not have anyone to take care of me and I am alone. . . . I can only eat if I work." In the urban vendor community in Patna, old women are seen as a burden on the family and some are forced to move out to the streets to beg.

Health is another widely used indicator of wellbeing. Fishermen's wives in Konada say that rich people get a doctor "even for small ailments," but very poor people "can't work due to ill health." Participants in Sohrai, Bihar, say poor people "cannot afford treatment for illness." A group of vendor women in Patna reports that poor families incur heavy debt for treatment and endure many deaths.

In Pedda Kothapalli a group of backward-caste women emphasizes good health and small families as signs of wellbeing. They classify the very rich and rich as healthy and able to plan their families, whereas people who fall into the middle, poor, and very poor categories have "ill health" and "more children." Likewise, poor Muslim women in Hyderabad, Andhra Pradesh, describe very poor people as those with "large families and high expenses."

Discussion groups also invariably mention poor quality housing or a lack of shelter altogether as an indicator of illbeing. A woman in Manjhar recounts growing up in a house where her family sought cover in the corners to avoid the water pouring through the roof in the long rainy seasons. In urban areas many people describe unhygienic and unsafe living conditions. Homeless people dream of shelter, urban slum dwellers who live in fear of eviction yearn for legal recognition of their makeshift shacks, and people in thatched huts aspire to own a house made of sturdy materials.

Wellbeing also has intangible dimensions, such as influence over government officials and the ability to command attention in public ceremonies. Both men's and women's groups consider influence, honor, and respect in society to be indicators of wellbeing. Bawri men in Geruwa, Bihar, say people with *shommon* (honor) are well off. Asur women in Netarhat, Bihar, identify "people with voice in the community" as happy. Those whose "word has no importance" are considered by women in Konada to be the poorest of the poor. "If you don't know anyone, you will be thrown in a corner of a hospital," says a Konada fisherwoman. Scheduled castes in particular, who face discrimination from almost all other castes, cite respect as an important criterion of wellbeing.

Figure 1 shows the causes and impacts of poverty developed by a discussion group of poor women in Jaggaram. Many poor people in the area

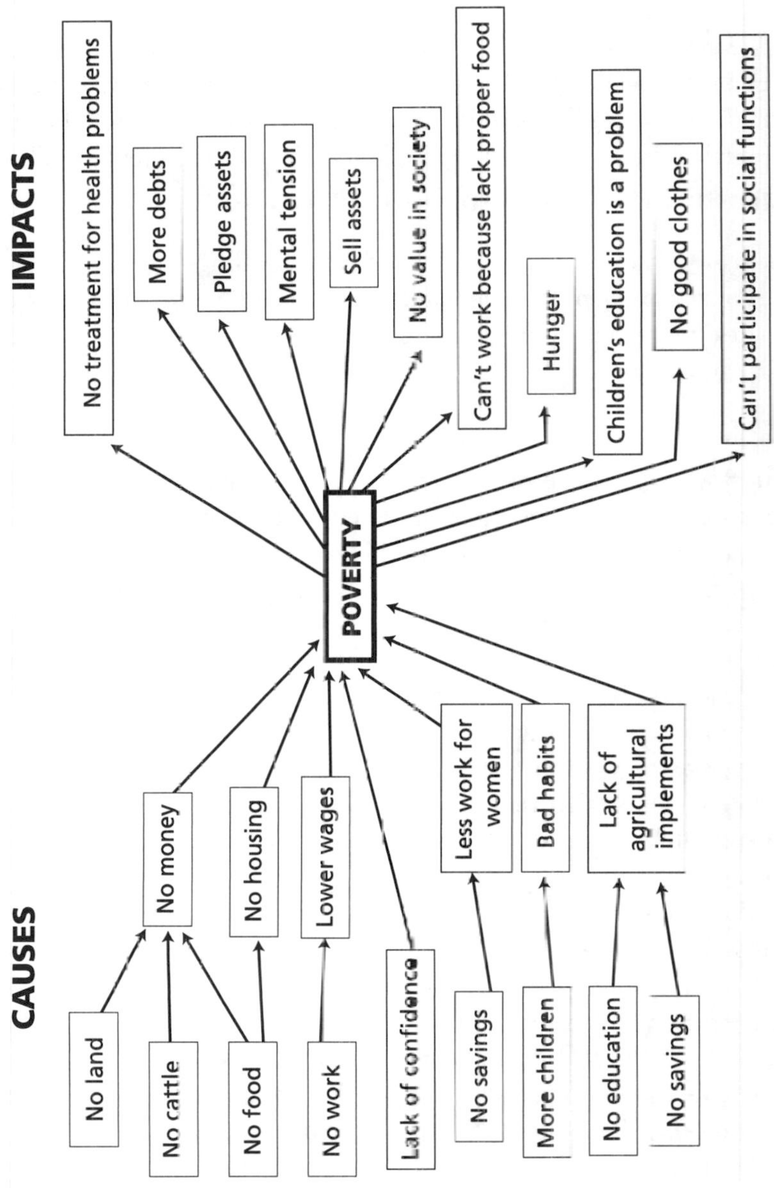

FIGURE 1 Causes and Impacts of Poverty, Discussion Group of Women in Jaggaram, Andhra Pradesh

CAUSES

No land

No cattle

No food

No work

Lack of confidence

No money

No housing

Lower wages

No savings

More children

No education

No savings

Less work for women

Bad habits

Lack of agricultural implements

POVERTY

IMPACTS

No treatment for health problems

More debts

Pledge assets

Mental tension

Sell assets

No value in society

Can't work because lack proper food

Hunger

Children's education is a problem

No good clothes

Can't participate in social functions

earn their living as laborers in cashew orchards, and wages are very low. In lean times, people go to the nearby forests to collect leaves, flowers, tamarind, and other products to sell in the market, but very high rates of deforestation have drastically reduced these livelihood alternatives. For these women, poverty means not only material deprivation, but also "mental tension," "the inability to participate in social functions," and having "no value in the society." Another Jaggaram discussion group says poverty results in sorrow and sickness and may lead to death.

Community Problems and Priorities

Discussion groups were asked to identify leading community problems, and four prominent issues emerged across the communities: lack of water for drinking and irrigation, insecure livelihoods, ill health, and inadequate housing.

Water

Water scarcity is the most frequently identified problem. Where wells are functional, they are often located in areas where higher-caste and more prosperous people live. In villages with several hamlets, wells can be far from the homes of poor people, and lower-caste people may be denied access. Community taps have been installed in Konada, for instance, but the piped supply is erratic and drainage is poor. Only one well has potable water; it serves more than 3,000 people, including those in the three adjacent villages. Only three of Dorapalli's six hand pumps are in good condition, and only two provide potable water. The water problem is particularly severe for the scheduled castes, who are not allowed to draw from the well located in the higher-caste area of Dorapalli.

Poor people in Netarhat and Jaggaram experience acute water shortages in the summer months. Villagers—mainly girls and women—must walk long distances to fetch drinking water. A 14-year-old girl in Netarhat explains that during the rainy season she has to climb over boulders and deal with "wild animals, mainly wolves and hyenas" when she goes for water. In urban areas, poor people, again usually women, must stand in long lines to collect their household water rations.

Some villages have government-installed water pumps and wells, but the equipment is often in disrepair or provides water irregularly. The government installed a tube well in Netarhat after a long delay, but it broke down six months later, and the three government hand pumps are also defunct. The public water supply programs run by panchayats are also described as ineffective in many of the villages in the study. In Hyderabad and Patna, groups call attention to problems with latrines as well as to insufficient potable water.

In rural areas water for irrigation emerges as a concern. Better-off men from Jaggaram who have been able to invest in the lucrative cashew crop identify access to irrigation as their most important priority. In the four rural communities in the study that rely on rainfed agriculture, monsoon rains allow for only one paddy crop a year. In Geruwa and Dorapalli, this meager paddy harvest lasts three months, at most. In times of drought, surviving on yields from the harvest is especially difficult.

Livelihood

With very high frequency, discussion groups identify lack of work opportunities and low wages as among their most pressing problems. People directly relate their precarious livelihoods to exploitation, indebtedness, and lack of skills. With the decreasing availability of land, fish, and forest resources, traditional sources of food and income are disappearing. Land ownership is pivotal in rural areas. People frequently remark that the size of landholdings is reduced as land parcels are divided among children and sold to cover debts. Sharecropping is common. In many areas, outsiders are buying land, and absentee landlords leave productive farmland fallow.

Landlessness and depleted natural resources cause many people to migrate to towns and cities in search of daily wage labor. Women in Sohrai say that migration was unheard of twenty-five years ago but is very common now and widely considered to be hard on family members left behind. Moreover, employment for migrants is rarely assured and income hardly ever steady. In Hyderabad employers handpick laborers they need for the day from early-morning queues, passing by the visibly weak. In Geruwa and Dorapalli, long journeys into town in search of work can often mean long journeys home empty-handed. Jobs in Dorapalli are scarce and low paid, and travel into the nearby town of Dhone is difficult along the winding five-kilometer road, which is not passable in the rainy season. The lack of jobs locally is reported to be a particular problem for women, who find it difficult to travel in search of work while managing household responsibilities.

For poor vendors, hawking on the streets is full of hazards. The police and "local goons" are the greatest obstacle to making ends meet for vendors in Patna. Male vendors say that police harassment, extortion, and blackmail outweigh all other problems. Rag pickers report being locked up and tortured. Vegetable vendors say there are strong connections among police, contractors, and local criminals. Stability is important for urban vendors, who hope for licensing to avoid harassment. Seasonal rains and flooding also devastate business in the streets.

Child labor is mentioned in discussions and interviews with very poor men and women in both Andhra Pradesh and Bihar. Some of the households with working children are struggling with a breadwinner's prolonged illness or death. Landless women in Dorapalli list child labor as a pressing problem for their community. In Jaggaram a group of woman notes that child labor is an impact of poverty. Researchers met with street children in Hyderabad who say they survive largely by scavenging for metals, plastic, glass, and other recyclables. They live in sheds near a busy commercial area and market. Most are illiterate.

In some areas poor people say they have increasing access to employment opportunities. In Geruwa men report earning much more at a coal tar factory outside town than they made in agricultural wage labor. Outside business owners have established prawn farms on the fringes of Konada. Many people from the fishing community work there and sell prawn seed they collect from the sea to these companies. Other sources of private employment reported by rural groups are paper mills, dairies, brick kilns, bauxite mines, and a granite pulverizing factory.

In Patna and Hyderabad, poor people describe a range of wage labor opportunities as well as hawking, vending, and other petty entrepreneurial activities. Over time, some of these people have been able to accumulate assets and develop their own small businesses. Discussion groups in Patna report that wage labor opportunities are growing, with work in construction very popular. Youths work as "go-betweens" in government offices and firms. Many poor people in Patna work as venders and hawkers, operating from kiosks and mobile carts stocked with myriad items—vegetables, tea, eggs, flowers, newspapers and magazines, utensils, groceries, and stationery. Others are home-based workers who offer laundry, bookbinding, glass framing, and repair services, and run small shops. Discussion groups in Hyderabad also describe diverse income-generating opportunities, including tailor work, cycle shops, vegetable and cloth vending, and mechanical repairs.

Health

For poor people, illness and injuries that keep them from work mean a loss of income, as well as depleted savings or increased debt to cover the high costs of medical treatment. From Dorapalli comes this account:

> *Lakshmi's troubles started when her husband contracted a skin disease and her family separated from her in-laws. She had to borrow Rs. 8,000 to pay for her husband's treatment for his disease as well as for a leg he broke accidentally. She borrowed the money from moneylenders at an interest rate of 2 percent a month. She had to sell the family's land to clear the mounting debt, which still stands at Rs. 4,000.*

Six of the communities visited list ill health as a main cause of poverty. Many people consider households with disabled and elderly people to be the poorest of the poor because these members cannot engage in physical labor, and they often require unaffordable medical treatment. Like Lakshmi, many people are forced to go to moneylenders for high-interest loans, as well as sell jewelry, land, and other assets to pay for doctors and medicines. They may never clear their debt, which passes to the next generation.

The high cost of treatment is closely linked to the lack of government health facilities. For four of the six rural villages visited, the nearest public health center is eight kilometers away and impossible to reach during the rainy season. When a family member falls ill in these communities, there are few choices, and poor people often must resort to expensive—but more easily accessible—private doctors.

Housing

Both rural and urban groups identify dilapidated housing as a widespread problem. Most poor people in rural areas live in thatched huts that are vulnerable during monsoons. Typically the huts must be repaired every two years, a major expense for poor households. People who must rent are considered especially poor, and several groups list home ownership as a priority. In Patna and Hyderabad, several discussion groups identify "no permanent home" as their single most important problem. Increased migration has created a housing crisis and extensive homelessness in the two urban communities visited for the study. Many people have built huts illegally and fear being forcibly moved. Other urban groups draw attention to rising rents.

Mixed Trends

Across the study, people distinguish between poor and very poor people. Most discussion groups report that very poor people are better off than they were a decade ago and that their numbers are declining. For poor people who are not at the very bottom, the findings are mixed: those in urban areas seem to be better off than they were a decade prior to the study, but in rural areas there is no consensus across discussion groups, and most groups view the numbers of poor people as having changed little or even increased in that decade.

Participants widely acknowledge that improvements in the overall living standards of their communities have made a noticeable impact on the lives of very poor people. These people are said to have relatively better access to resources and services from the government and from NGOs than they did ten years ago, when "getting cooked lentils, rice, curry, and vegetables was a dream," as a woman from Manjhar puts it. Roads have been laid in several communities, connecting villages to the outside world. State-run PDS shops in Patna, Geruwa, and Konada have helped people obtain essential grains and fuel. Further, there is more demand for and access to education. Several discussion groups in Netarhat, Sohrai, Pedda Kothapalli, and Jaggaram identify a reduction in the numbers of very poor people in their communities. Food subsidies and government entitlements have benefited many groups in these communities, especially those from scheduled castes and tribes. In addition, study participants speak of favorable changes in the social status and freedom of the very poor to undertake occupations that are not traditional for their caste.

For poor people who are not utterly destitute, however, findings are mixed, especially from rural communities. In Geruwa the numbers of poor people are reported to have increased slightly, due in part to the limited availability of land. A discussion group of poor men in rural Manjhar says that the percentage of poor people in their community has increased from 25 percent ten years ago to 45 percent today. The men say that a lack of resources keeps them poor. Most discussion groups in rural Netarhat, Sohrai, Pedda Kothapalli, and Jaggaram also indicate that they lack the means to move up into the middle wellbeing categories. In Jaggaram, for instance, discussion groups state that there has been a clear increase in the number of better-off groups due to the booming cashew economy, but poor people who rely on wage labor or who have very little productive land have not benefited from the cashew trade. Women agricultural workers there earn only Rs. 25 a day, and their male counterparts earn Rs. 30.

Similar wages are reported in Netarhat, although people laboring in the dangerous bauxite mines can earn Rs. 40 a day.

People in the two urban communities, Hyderabad and Patna, as well as in peri-urban Konada, report that the numbers of poor people have declined somewhat over the past decade. Participants in Hyderabad, for instance, say poor people now have daily wage labor opportunities, own bicycles, live in tin-roof houses, and own black-and-white televisions. Men report earnings of Rs. 50–100 a day (US$1.16–$2 32) loading trucks, or Rs. 130–150 (US$3.00–$3.48) as masons. Unskilled laborers earn Rs. 60–70 (women) or Rs. 70–80 (men). Unskilled workers in Patna reportedly earn Rs. 50–70 a day, and skilled workers can command Rs. 100–120. People also report that it is now easier to get loans from rich people. These advances notwithstanding, poor and very poor people are finding it difficult to move out of poverty.

Contribution of Institutions to Wellbeing

Several types of institutions affect the wellbeing of poor men and women in the communities visited: local and national government agencies and programs, NGO income-generating and social initiatives, and community self-help groups. The communities depend on government agencies for many support services and consider them important in reducing poverty. Nevertheless, many public programs and services receive poor ratings because they are inefficient and untrustworthy. The institutions that generally score the highest in overall importance among both rural and urban groups are community-based initiatives, some of which are supported by NGOs. Given that this study covers areas of Bihar and Andhra Pradesh where NGOs are active, these findings are not necessarily representative of poor communities elsewhere in these states or in the rest of the country.

Leading Institutions in Netarhat

The State Bank of India has a branch in Netarhat, but only twenty people use its services. According to the discussion groups, no villager is known to have received a loan there, although people know about this service. Netarhat falls under Palamu District but is much closer to the district headquarters of Gumla, whose services the villagers are not eligible to use. Study participants believe the block office is corrupt, and the block development officer is hard for villagers to find if they want to air a grievance. In any case, the cost of a trip to the block headquarters is Rs. 100, including food and travel—far too expensive for a poor man or woman. Although the local panchayat was dissolved long ago, the caste panchayat is widely trusted. The former village head, or *mukhia*, is still called on to resolve most village-level conflicts. The Netarhat villagers in the study say they prefer to keep their distance from the police, perceiving them to be corrupt.

Unlike the other communities in this study, no NGOs are working with local groups here. Discussion groups report that a branch of a religious organization came to the village five years ago to campaign against the conversion of tribal people to Christianity, but it is no longer active. The local traditional healer, or *bhagat*, enjoys the confidence of the villagers because he is always accessible in medical emergencies and sometimes helps people with money in times of crisis. The traditional birth attendants are extremely popular with the women in the village, who prefer their services to those of the health centers. The village farm provides employment and even extends veterinary care. Many villagers buy household consumables on credit from local shops, which also sell their farm produce.

The discussion groups use a range of criteria to evaluate the institution: efficiency and trustworthiness, day-to-day importance, role of women in decision making, and extent of community control. Figure 2 shows the institutions most valued by a men's group from an area of the village known as Jamtoli. They rank the caste panchayat, or *chata*, as the most efficient and trusted institution. It has a five-member elected committee, and the men say that any village dispute can be referred to the *chata* to be resolved. It is also the institution over which the men feel people have the most control. The men's group ranks the official panchayat much lower because there has not been an election for many years and the body is presently inactive. The two local shops emerge as the institutions of greatest "day-to-day" importance. In addition to selling goods, the shops provide loans to villagers up to Rs. 500. The men note, however, that high interest rates are charged.

State Institutions

State institutions have built roads, installed drinking water systems, set up schools and primary health care centers, and delivered subsidized food rations to some of the most remote communities in this study. Poor

FIGURE 2 Evaluation of Local Institutions, Discussion Group of Men in Jamtoli, Netarhat Panchayat

INSTITUTIONS	Description	EFFICIENCY	TRUST	DAY-TO-DAY IMPORTANCE	WOMEN'S PARTICIPATION	PEOPLE'S CONTROL
1. SARNA	The religious tree for worship. The community has strong faith and belief.	5	4	10	1	2
2. CHATA	The caste panchayat, a committee of five elected members, is trusted by the community. Any village dispute can be referred to chata and settled.	1	1	6	–	1
3. SHOP	There are two shops in the village for household commodities. These shops also provide loans to villagers for up to Rs. 500.	3	2	1	2	3
4. POST OFFICE	Villagers recognize the post office as a public service used by some individuals. Not all rely on the post office.	7	8	4	6	4
5. POLICE STATION	The police station is not close to village community. Police are not viewed as helpful and supportive.	12	11	1	–	–
6. SCHOOL	A co-ed primary school with 45 children from Jamtoli. The teacher appears very irregularly, so children have problems continuing their studies. Villagers don't know who to approach for improvements.	9	6	2	4	7
7. BANK	State Bank of India at Netarhat. There are only 15–20 people in the village who use bank services.	10	7	3	7	8
8. PANCHAYAT	There has been no panchayat election for a long time, and there is no active panchayat system at present.	6	10	9	–	9
9. BLOCK	The long distance from the village and the indifference of the officials make the block office inaccessible to the villagers. They may spend the whole day travelling — which may cost Rs. 100 — hoping to meet with the BDO, which rarely happens.	8	9	5	5	10
10. VANVASI KENDRA	A wing of the RSS (Rishtriya Swayam Sevak Sangh, National Self-help Group) formed five years ago to curtail the rapid conversion of tribal people to Christianity. It also provided children's education, medical support, and free medicines, but it hasn't been active for two years.	11	12	12	–	–
11. BHAGAT	A local traditional healer using herbal methods. Villagers have more faith in him than in the health center located outside the village because he is always available during times of need.	4	3	7	3	5
12. MUKHIA	The village chief. The same man has been the chief for several years; however, there are no panchayat elections through which to elect another one. He plays an important role consulting and advising on various village matters.	2	5	3	–	6

people appreciate such services and consider them vitally important for improving their quality of life, but they very often rate public services poorly for being inefficient and untrustworthy.

Some study communities are still missing basic services; in communities where they are available, people repeatedly report problems with quality. Participants consider these gaps—such as the lack of bridges and all-weather roads in Geruwa, or drinking water and latrines in Netarhat—a major factor in their impoverishment. Some government officials are seen as corrupt, withholding information and directing benefits only to better-off groups in their communities and to those with influence. When discussing whether they can exert any influence over government institutions, poor people in the study very often feel they have no effective channels to press for more or better government services. These findings are consistent with a larger qualitative study of thirty communities in the states of Bihar and Uttar Pradesh, which concludes that "many of the anti-poverty programs as well as basic services like health and education are serving the wealthy and powerful far better than the poor. Most of the programs are under-resourced, poorly supervised, and poorly targeted."[8]

Panchayats were created after independence to devolve responsibilities from the central to the local government level. While this is beginning to take place, panchayat management is still considered ineffective. Like the men's group in Netarhat, a small number of discussion groups elsewhere in the study give panchayats low to fair grades for their overall importance in the community. Most discussion groups, however, do not even mention these bodies on their lists of institutions that are important in their daily lives.

For many people, the main interaction with the panchayats comes through attendance at political meetings. A ward member in Konada says these meetings do not include discussion or sharing information: "We will be offered tea or coconut water and sent back." When he tried raising the demands of his constituents for water taps and roads, he was told by the panchayat president, "You are drunk and disrupting the peace." According to this man, the panchayat president is biased in favor of his own caste, and about 80 percent of the benefits go to the rich. He is not enthusiastic about contesting the next elections. Women in the same village see no benefit from the panchayat and dismiss it as of no consequence. "The village headman has usurped the benefit of government programs for his own benefit," says one.

India has a range of anti-poverty programs, which include, for example, childcare and early childhood education, health services, free public schools, and a large subsidized food distribution program that operates through local ration shops. *Anganwadi*, a midday meal program for preschool children that is provided at nutrition centers, receives mixed reviews by poor people in the study, and women tend to rank it higher than do men.[9] In Dorapalli the local *anganwadi* generally scored low for usefulness and impact by most discussion groups, with the exception of a group of scheduled tribe landless women, who ranked it third in overall importance. Another Dorapalli group of scheduled caste landless women ranked *anganwadi* eighth in overall importance, and stated that they would prefer to have a separate *anganwadi*, as the current teacher belongs to the Brahmin caste, treats scheduled caste children badly, and does not give them food. Jaggaram is the only community where most discussion groups consider *anganwadi* important. In Sohrai, Patna, and Hyderabad, *anganwadi* is not mentioned at all. These findings are somewhat more favorable than those reported in the thirty-community study of Bihar and Uttar Pradesh, where the *anganwadi* program was functioning in only one of the study communities.[10]

Many urban men's groups rank hospitals among the most important institutions, perhaps because hospitals are the only resort for the seriously ill. Discussion groups in Patna, for instance, report that people avoid government health clinics even for "petty illnesses" because the

---

BOX 1 Private Heath Care an Expensive Risk

Discussions in the study communities reveal that health care expenses are a major cause of impoverishment and a significant barrier to accumulating savings. Although public health services charge lower fees, many participants consider them a last resort because they are located too far from their communities or offer low-quality services. In Patna participants report that the government hospitals are in such a bad state that only the very poorest people use them, and then only when "on the edge of life and death." Yet private care sends many households into deep debt. Vasuman Pandey, whose prosperity was once the envy of people in Manjhar, lost his wife to an illness and then suffered declining health himself. Now poor, he considers his illness to be the sole reason for his downfall because he depleted his savings and sold his property to cover the fees of the local private doctor. Andhra Pradesh and Bihar have the highest rates in India of private spending on health.[11]

facilities are poorly supplied and medicines marked for free distribution are sold. Salaries are not adequate to keep health staff in their posts, and absenteeism is reported to be common. A vendor woman in Patna describes the bind in which many poor people find themselves: "There is no proper health facility for the poor. Government hospitals do not have regular doctors or medicines. Private clinics charge a lot for fees and medicines" (see box 1). In Netarhat villagers rely on traditional medicines to treat most ailments. For treatment of major diseases, and for deliveries, they use the services at the Netarhat hospital. People say the local primary health center has become commercialized, and villagers are charged exorbitant amounts of money even for ordinary immunizations such as the tetanus vaccine.

All urban groups and most rural groups assign high importance to the schools in their areas. Many hope that educated children will have better access to wage employment. They value the government primary schools and are willing to incur the cost—about Rs. 318 (US$7) a year per student—to send their children there.[12] Extensive teacher absenteeism compromises the quality of state-run schools in most of the locations visited. A mother in Jaggaram says the schoolmaster is rarely in the classroom and hardly bothers about the children's education. In Dorapalli the schools are closed much of the time by strikes.

In nearly all the communities visited, the state-run PDS shops are valued, particularly by women's discussion groups, but are considered to be poorly operated. According to the thirty-community study in Uttar Pradesh and Bihar, which asked participants to comment specifically on the PDS, the ration shops

> were nearly always found in the wealthy communities in shops owned by high-caste shopkeepers. The poor were discouraged by irregular hours of operation, lack of information about when the ration would be available, insults from shopkeepers, and transportation costs. Despite this, the [food distribution program] appeared to have lowered the price and increased the flow of food grains to the poor in the study areas.[13]

Andhra Pradesh devotes more to the PDS than any other state in India. Families below the poverty line receive white ration cards entitling them to twenty kilograms of rice a month at a subsidized issue price of

Rs. 5.50. Those above the poverty line receive pink cards to buy rice at an unsubsidized issue price.[14]

Across the study, discussion groups scorn and fear the police for their inefficiency, corruption, and negative impact on society. In urban Bihar the problem is particularly acute because the livelihood of unlicensed street vendors is constantly threatened by police raids and a demands for bribes. Vendors in Patna report that daily police bribes have risen 25-fold in the past decade. A teashop owner described being forced to pay extortion to the constables of the railway police, who also drank tea at his shop without paying. When the police illegally detained him and seized his shop and utensils, his wife had to borrow money with interest from a neighbor to pay the Rs. 920 ransom. Many poor people take it for granted that the police are not on their side. Rarely would they go to the police to report any crimes.

Government support provides mainly short-term relief, which is valued. With much less frequency, poor people describe public services as tools that help them reach the wellbeing and security to which they aspire. Poor people in the communities visited would like to see services that are more accessible in terms of cost, reach, and availability: police who protect them, doctors who care enough about their health not to exploit their desperation, schools with teachers, and reliable roads and transportation. In the absence of effective government services, poor people say they often turn to other providers.

Local Institutions

The communities in this study are divided by the traditional caste system and other deeply rooted social barriers and inequities, and these rifts are mirrored in the limited development of local institutions that represent poor people. In many cases there are caste-based organizations, and in some localities these are reported to be functioning effectively. Caste panchayats are rated favorably in a few communities. In Andhra Pradesh self-help groups are beginning to emerge primarily through the activities of NGOs.

Participants in some areas report that caste panchayats are serving well as a traditional system of justice. These bodies are an important adjudicating and licensing agency in the self-government of Indian castes, sitting as courts of law for breaches of caste customs and sometimes handling criminal and civil cases. Traditional potters in Konada, for instance, mention their caste-based organization as a source of pride and assistance.

Nearly half the discussion groups in both urban and rural areas put moneylenders in the top cluster of valued institutions. People in Patna and Hyderabad value the informal moneylenders, for their availability in times of need, despite their high interest rates. A woman in Hyderabad says her family has taken loans from the local pawnbroker at an interest rate of 4 percent a month (with gold pledged as security) and 5 percent a month (with silver pledged as security). A poor woman in Kothapalli reports that she took a loan of Rs. 5,000 from a private moneylender for the marriage of her eldest daughter.

Researchers selected communities where NGOs are active, and in the nine communities where NGOs are present, discussion groups generally regard their work very favorably; women's groups frequently rank NGOs among the five most important institutions. NGOs are most often valued for helping people accumulate savings and gain access to the tools and skills needed to earn a living (see box 2). NGOs also provide many other services to poor communities, including health care, and they raise awareness about leading social concerns.

In Geruwa the Tata Steel Rural Development Society, which distributes malaria medicine and provides health checkups, is described by scheduled caste women as the most reliable institution in times of trouble. An impoverished Sadai woman in Sohrai expresses strong

---

Box 2 Climbing Up in Jaggaram

Raju, a young man in Jaggaram, was orphaned at age 16. His parents had a half-acre of cashew trees, which he extended by encroaching on forestland. In addition to taking care of his own land, Raju worked toward a better life by laboring as a contractor for two years. He motivated his brothers, who collected timber for a living, to save and pool their money; with these funds they bought five acres of land, four of them under cashew cultivation. ACTIVE, a local NGO, supplied free saplings to plant on the remaining acre. A year later Raju bought three more acres of land and established another cashew farm with saplings and funds provided by the Integrated Tribal Development Authority. Raju is now able to lend money to others. He built a house and acquired a television, a bicycle, and the only double cot (rope bed) in the village. His position as the secretary of the local savings group has strengthened his status in the community.

appreciation for SSVK, an NGO that has helped women become more aware of the risks of child marriage and child labor In Patna the local NGO Nidaan is praised for understanding the needs of street vendors and helping them in times of crisis. In Pedda Kothapalli poor villagers have participated in entrepreneur development activities with the support ARTIC, a local NGO.

There has been a rapidly growing movement of self-help groups (SHGs) in Andhra Pradesh, and there are now more than 100,000 SHGs in the state registered with government.[15] SHG members pool their savings and lend the funds to members on a rotating or as-needed basis. These groups are the only option for many landless people as well as those who may lack adequate land or legally recognized titles that can serve as collateral for formal credit. SHG group members include better-off people, as well.[16] In some cases, the SHGs are reported to be catalyzing the start-up of new community initiatives to address local needs. The self-help groups can potentially provide people with important links to government and private sector institutions, bringing further resources into communities.

SHGs are rated among the top one or two most important institutions by various discussion groups in four communities visited in Andhra Pradesh. By contrast, only one discussion group in one community in Bihar, Sohrai, mentions SHGs. An uneducated Sadai woman of Sohrai describes her early life as tending goats all day in the forests and often going to bed hungry until SSVK came to the village to promote a women's collective. She is now a member of the group, attending meetings and contributing Rs. 5 a month.

Study participants frequently trace the origins of their SHGs to the local organizing and training activities of NGOs. In Jaggaram women say that ACTIVE has worked through SHGs to support many poor people. A poor woman in Pedda Kothapalli joined the self-help group initiated by ARTIC five years ago. She has saved Rs. 2,000, borrowed Rs. 1,000 for a family planning operation, and already repaid Rs. 500 of the loan. A Muslim woman in Hyderabad is a member of a SHG promoted by a local NGO. She saves Rs. 20 a month and repaid a loan of Rs. 2,000 to begin a firewood business. An SHG member in Dorapalli says she regularly saves Rs. 30 a month with the goal of starting a small shop, from which she hopes to earn enough to build a house and cover the dowry for her 14-year-old daughter.

Many women note that participation in SHGs has had a positive impact not only on their level of savings, but also on their self-confidence and social status. A Musahar woman from Sohrai in Bihar says,

> *Women hardly had any say in the outside world. Now, things are different because of the passage of time and the strengthening of the women's collective. The women's role is very important now. In fact, it is the women who mount demonstrations and visit offices, especially the ones people don't like to go to, such as the police station and block office.*

Gender Relations

Across the study communities, women's participation in community activities and access to community institutions is limited. Women from scheduled castes and tribes have greater mobility outside the household out of dire necessity to earn income, but stringent patriarchal norms in higher castes restrict women's mobility. Until they are elderly, women can participate in community ceremonies, such as weddings and festivals, only in the company of other women. In Patna urban slum girls are rarely sent to school.

Nevertheless, study participants report changes in women's roles and responsibilities in recent years. Men and women in fisher and potter castes from Sohrai, for instance, report that women have had to assume a larger role in managing their homes because many men are migrating to the cities for work. Women work as merchants and agricultural laborers and are involved in SHGs. Geeta and Seema, two women in Sohrai, say that twenty-five years ago

> *there was no education. Women could only count. Now a few in the village can sign their names. . . . In the past the responsibilities of the women were cooking, as well as planting seeds and other such agricultural work. Earthwork [construction work] was avoided and shopping was taboo. Now the women tend cattle, collect grass, go out to shop for the home, and accord priority to earning money.*

More Varied Livelihoods

Group discussions reveal that women across castes and economic groups are compelled to work outside the home to contribute to family income. Women's income is particularly important among the more disadvantaged castes and tribes, and their economic responsibilities are more pronounced. Two men's groups in Hyderabad say that women's need to work signifies a decline in wellbeing, a matter of necessity in hard times. Similarly, groups in Dorapalli say that the lower the social or economic status of a group, the more significant the women's role in earning money.

Even the tradition-bound Kumhar women in Geruwa have begun venturing out to earn incomes. "Who would feed my children and invalid husband if I did not go to the market to earn?" asks one woman. In Manjhar the women do more agricultural work than the men. Women work in the mines of Netarhat and sell fuelwood in Geruwa. They are vendors in Patna and home-based workers in Hyderabad, making incense sticks and wire baskets. In many other rural and urban communities they are wage laborers and agricultural workers.

Women's groups report that the pressure to contribute to household income does not exempt women from their household responsibilities—cleaning the floor, walls, and yards in the early morning, fetching water twice daily, gathering fuelwood, preparing meals, washing children and cattle, and carrying food to men in the fields. Women throughout the study describe days that begin very early in the morning and end very late at night. In Jaggaram women estimate that they work eighteen-hour days. In Netarhat the working day of tribal women ends long after the men and children have finished their dinners and gone to sleep.

Women in all communities say they still do most of the chores at home. In Dorapalli, Netarhat, and Jaggaram, however, groups note an increase over the past decade in the contribution of men when they are asked to cook, clean, and look after the children.

Changes in Household Decision Making

Many participants say that earning income gives women higher status and makes their husbands consider their opinions more often in family decisions. Increased male migration is, in many cases, forcing women to become the de facto heads of households. Women's groups in eight of the ten communities report that they are beginning to be asked for input about the marriage and education of their children, not only about the family budget. Greater exposure to the outside world and NGO interventions have led younger women to question their role, and many men resent this. "Earlier the women used to help move the farmyard manure from the pits to the field and help the men lay it out. Now they ask for pay or tell us to find a wage laborer to do it," states an older man in Dorapalli. The extent of the shift in decision-making roles is relative. Groups in Netarhat and Geruwa report smaller changes, and say, "Women are rarely consulted in matters of consequence." Even if women are consulted, men still have the final say in major household decisions.

Beyond the household, few changes in women's roles are identified. In Geruwa women plant saplings, weed, or pick pears at the local pear farm, and as many women as men work in the mines, for the same compensation. Yet women are barred from the affairs of the traditional panchayat unless the cases involve women.

Domestic Violence

Women's increasing economic role is not always seen as bringing them greater security. The most traditional families, along with displaced or unemployed men, express the most doubts on this score. The Mallah men's group in Sohrai reports that as more men migrate, women have a greater role in society than they did in the days of *purdah* (seclusion) a decade ago, but the group also says that there is more wife beating by alcoholic husbands. In all communities the most commonly reported reason for violence against women is alcohol abuse.

In Konada and Jaggaram, men's and women's groups report a decrease in domestic abuse since women began participating in self-help groups. In Patna it is said that women are more aware of their rights and do not hesitate to resist male violence. Nevertheless, domestic abuse against women, ranging from belittling and mocking to physical assault, persists. A Hyderabad woman says that violence occurs when "the husband is not ready to accept the increasing awareness, exposure, and participation of the wife in spheres outside the household and as a result beats the wife to demonstrate his supremacy." In Sohrai a men's group reports that "on return after a hard day of work, if immediate attention is not paid to the men, it invites their wrath. "

Still a Long Way to Go

While participants report that women's access to health and education services has improved, especially in urban areas, their access to education in rural areas is still abysmally low. One of only three girls in Netarhat who attend school says, "If my father did not have a job in the school, I would never have had the chance to study." A participant in a Sohrai women's group confidently says that there is less domestic violence now because women have learned to show resistance from working with the local NGO, but the group admits that girls in most households are not sent to school. The low female literacy rate (16.6 percent in Andhra Pradesh in 1991)[17] will make it difficult for rural women to meet the skill requirements of future jobs in a nonfarm economy. And despite progress, the Mallah women's group in Sohrai describes women as still having only 25 percent of the duties in a social context compared with men's 75 percent. Women in Geruwa find it absurd to question their traditional roles.

The changes women want to see are reflected in their hopes for their children. Geeta of Sohrai says she wishes to have her children educated and employed. They would then become good citizens and lead happy lives. She hopes to have a beautiful and educated daughter-in-law. She would like her son to buy land, build a house, and have whatever she missed in her life.

Conclusion

Many men and women in this study acknowledge improvements in wellbeing over the past decade: more money, more children in school, more job opportunities, more services, more savings, and a larger scope for women's participation. While these changes are indeed helping people cope and survive better—especially the very poorest in their communities—participants report that few rural people are managing to break free and leave poverty behind. The numbers of poor people remain very large, and in some villages are continuing to grow rather than diminish.

Sharp inequalities in social relations, reified in India by the caste system, influence access to economic opportunities and public services and to the social life of the community. Poor people see better livelihoods opening up around them but say they don't have the means to access them. They remain stuck, eking out a living on small and unproductive farm plots or in precarious daily wage jobs that pay very poorly. Lack of employment in farming and fishing forces many people to migrate, and wage insecurity drives people into debt. Men and women in the study clearly show that they know how to cope with destitution, but their challenges are growing. In villages, population pressure has brought environmental problems and caused landholdings to be subdivided into smaller and smaller plots. In cities, homelessness is a rising problem. Drinking water has become scarcer. Schools and health centers are short-staffed and poorly equipped. Police harassment is reportedly on the rise. Problems of dowry remain vexing. In discussions about their lives, people in the study repeatedly emphasize that the causes and impacts of poverty are multidimensional and interconnected.

When reflecting on the various government institutions that interact with their communities, study participants consider them important but often ineffective. Many discussion groups express appreciation for public entitlement programs, but in their evaluations find the assistance more helpful in easing their struggles than in enabling them to climb out of poverty. Poor people report that many public services and programs have problems of governance and weak accountability.

Participants rarely describe any role for poor people in influencing public agencies, although they can cite specific measures that they feel would greatly improve their lives. Women in Sohrai and Geruwa, for instance, blame the liquor trade for the ruin of so many households and for the rise in domestic violence; they would like to see it more regulated. Men's groups in the Hyderabad slums say they have waited a long time for the local administration to honor requests to regularize their illegal constructions. India's slow pace of change in the face of its large antipoverty programs illustrates that the government working alone cannot bring faster poverty reduction. Support for decentralized decision making at the panchayat level and the inclusion of women in leadership roles are important first steps. However, unless poor men and women can strengthen their capacity to participate actively in this framework, the panchayats will not be representative. If capacity is built, poor people can acquire more influential roles in setting government priorities, defending their rights, and obtaining better public services.

In both urban and rural areas poor people are engaged in a variety of entrepreneurial activities. This work often yields low and precarious returns, and in urban areas vendors report that they face repeated harassment by the police. Given the large numbers of people engaged in petty trade, home-based work, and other informal activities, policies related to private sector development should focus on actions that enable poor people's entrepreneurial initiatives to become more productive. It is important to link rural non-farm producers with urban distributors and markets.

For most people in the discussions for this study, wellbeing means work that is stable and safe, food for the family regardless of the year's scant rainfall or the morning's poor catch at sea, and a surplus to rely on in the future. In the struggle for a better life, poor people say that government schemes help somewhat, but it is the local civic groups that are their greatest supports. In these bodies, poor people find "value for a poor man's word" and, according to an expression from Jaggaram, receive help in fulfilling their "aspiration for a life that has not been experienced so far."

TABLE 2 Study Communities in India

Dorapalli Pop. 1,962	This rural village, located near a town with government services, has high rates of poverty and infant mortality. It is largely agricultural, though many scheduled castes and tribes rely on wage labor. Most landholdings are less than an acre per capita, and most land belongs to nonresidents. Two-thirds of the population consists of backward castes who live in thatched huts. There are no medical facilities or ration shops, and only two of six wells have potable water. There are self-help groups, and one NGO.
Hyderabad Pop. 3.6 million	Researchers visited four areas in Hyderabad: Hamaal Basti (pop. 3,500), Bondalagadda (pop. not available), Satyanarayananagar (pop. 2,500), and Monda Market (pop. not available). The literacy rate in these communities is 25–50 percent for men and is often much lower for women. Hamaal Basti suffered from flooding in 1997 and 1998. The population is largely Muslim. Men are back load workers, truck drivers, tailors, shopkeepers, and mechanics; home-based women workers make incense, cut betel, and sort rubbish. The community's electricity access is mainly illegal. An NGO opened a school and a clinic. Bondalagadda comprises migrants from many different areas; they face the threat of eviction. Many children work and have little education. Satyanarayananagar is a relatively new community that comprises six castes, only a few of which are practicing traditional occupations. The mason caste is economically prominent. In the busy commercial area of Monda Market, researchers met with a group of male rag pickers 10 to 24 years old, who scavenge materials, sort them, and sell them to scrap dealers. An NGO brought an orphanage and school to the area. The market experiences frequent police harassment.
Jaggaram 100 households	This rural community has electricity, roads, regular bus service, a drinking water tank, and primary schools. It has a cash-crop economy based on cashew orchards, and there is also trade in fuelwood, timber, and non-timber forest products. The area suffers forest depletion.

Konada Pop. 3,400	This peri-urban village is home to seventeen castes. Male and female literacy is very low, and infant mortality is high. The village has a market, a panchayat office, a homeopathic dispensary, *angarwadi* and numerous shops, including a ration shop. There are primary, private, and secondary schools, as well as savings and credit programs established by an NGO. Prawn seed cultivation farms have been established outside the village. Water supply is poor and hygiene is bad. Many men migrate and leave women in charge of households. There is alcoholism and domestic violence.
Pedda Kothapalli Pop. 153 households	This rural area suffers acute poverty and lacks government services. Village affairs are controlled by a landed elite, though intermediate caste groups are gaining power. The local economy is largely dependent on agriculture, and 80 percent of the land is controlled by upper castes. There are land disputes and many landless laborers. The area faced a severe drought in 1993–94. The community has poor housing, and there is electricity only in upper-caste settlements. Low wages cause youths to migrate.

BIHAR

Geruwa Pop. 500	The residents of this peri-urban village are mainly scheduled tribes, scheduled castes, and potter castes. Confusion over jurisdiction means that villagers pay city taxes but have no access to government institutions. The economy is forest- and agriculture-based. Most land belongs to nonresidents, and scheduled castes and tribes are mainly contractual wage laborers. Some youths work in paper mills. The reservoirs flood in the rainy season, and elephants from a wildlife sanctuary sometimes cause destruction. The community has a small shop, and one public and one private primary school. There are no medical facilities.
Manjhar Pop. 550	Livelihoods in this rural village include fishing, sharecropping, and wage labor. Flooding is a problem. The village's administrative headquarters is six kilometers away, but there is a primary school to class five, panchayat, and *anganwadi*. Some villagers are well educated, but better-off people tend to leave.

Netarhat Pop. 924	This remote, scenic, resource-rich panchayat is in a tourist area, close to a main road. Residents are mainly aboriginal Asur and Nagasia, who work at unskilled and dangerous labor in mostly illegal bauxite mines. Daily agricultural wage labor is also available. The district headquarters is 150 kilometers away. There is a caste but not a government panchayat, a pear farm, and two primary schools.
Patna Pop. 2 million	Many poor people in Patna, the state capital, work as vendors, hawkers, and construction workers. Scheduled and backward castes work as wage laborers, and there are also many child laborers. The city has extensive social infrastructure, but much of it is inaccessible to poor people. There are government primary schools and thriving private doctors. Roads are frequently ruined by rain, and many people live in unhygienic conditions. Consultations here were conducted with eight groups of poor people, including male and female vendors from Kamla Nehru, R-block, and Gaya Gumti areas; construction laborers from Shri Krishna Puri; and children from the Kurji Balupar locality of West Patna.
Sohrai Pop. 927	This rural village has mainly fisher, farmer, and potter castes. Work opportunities include wage labor, sharecropping, and dairy production. There are many absentee landlords. There is access to transport, a market, primary health care centers, a primary school to class five, nearby secondary schools, a road on the river embankment, and good potable water. Land disputes and out-migration are common.

Notes

1. The study team was led by Somesh Kumar and also included V. C. S. Bahadur, Anindo Banerjee, Ronnie Barnard, Mr. Bharterdu, B. Rama Devi, Shirsendu Ghosh, S. S. Jaideep, H. K. Jha, N. J. Joseph, Madhumati Katkar, Jyotsna Kumari, Neelam Kumari, P. S. Lalita Kumari, Kumari Mridula, G. Muralichar, K. S. N. Murthy, Mr. Nagendra, Murali Krishna Naidu, Amitabh Pandey, Harshavardan Patnaik, K. J. Prabhavati, Anamika Priyadarshini, B. Saroja Rajashekhar, D. Rajeshwar, Netala Rajeshwari, R. Venkata Ramana, V. V. Ramana, V. Paul Raja Rao, E. S. Rathnamma, M. Rajashekhar Reddy, N. Laxmi Narsimha Reddy, Surendra Sain, Neelam Sharma, Shailesh Kumar Singh, Shipra Singh, Surisetty Sreenivas, and C. Upendranadh.

2. World Bank, "Memorandum of the President of the International Bank for Reconstruction and Development, the International Development Association and the International Finance Corporation to the Executive Directors on a Country Assistance Strategy of the World Bank Group for India" (June 27, 2001), 4.

3. World Bank, *World Development Indicators 2001* (Report 22099, April 2001).

4. World Bank, "Memorandum of the President," 1.

5. World Bank, *India: Policies to Reduce Poverty and Accelerate Sustainable Development* (Poverty Reduction and Economic Management Unit, South Asia Region, Report 19471-IN, January 31, 2000), 4.

6. World Bank, "Andhra Pradesh: Draft Report of the Rural Poverty Reduction Task Force" (South Asia Region, May 17, 2000).

7. According to the National Commission for Scheduled Castes and Scheduled Tribes, caste clashes are frequent in Uttar Pradesh, Bihar, and Tamil Nadu.

8. Valerie Kozel and Barbara Parker, "Poverty in Rural India: The Contribution of Qualitative Research in Poverty Analysis" (World Bank, Poverty Reduction and Economic Management Unit, South Asia Region, 2000).

9. Nutrition is a problem area in India, especially for weaning children. Despite a comprehensive public food distribution program, 53 percent of all children under age 4 and 75 percent of children under 4 in the poorest consumption quintile are malnourished. World Bank, *India*, 15. As part of the Integrated Child Development Services program implemented since 1975, village nutrition centers provide supplementary feeding and sometimes early childhood education. See Anthony R. Measham and Meera Chatterjee, "Wasting Away: The Crisis of Malnutrition in India" (World Bank, May 1999).

10. Initial survey results showed that less than 3 percent of eligible children in the study area are benefiting from the program. See Kozel and Parker, "Poverty in Rural India," 37.

11. Government of India, *Morbidity and Treatment of Ailments* (National Sample Survey Organization, Department of Statistics, Ministry for Planning, New Delhi, 1998). Cited in World Bank, *India*, 20.

12. World Bank, *India*, 15.

13. Kozel and Parker, "Poverty in Rural India," 33.

14. World Bank, "Andhra Pradesh," 23.

15. Ibid., 25.

16. A government survey found that scheduled castes, who make up 16 percent of the Andhra Pradesh population, comprise 22 percent of the members in six of seven districts. Weaknesses of the groups found in the survey include poor bookkeeping and record keeping by largely illiterate members, a low participation of widows and destitute women, and training confined only to the leaders. World Bank, "Andhra Pradesh," 25.

17. Ibid., 20.

Indonesia

Coping with Vulnerability and Crisis

Nilanjana Mukherjee[1]

Wulan and her husband, Joko, come from poor families that have always eked out their living in the informal sector. They reside in the densely crowded squatter settlement of Tanjungrejo in East Java, where most people work as scavengers, day laborers, rickshaw drivers, and petty traders. Wulan is the ninth of thirteen children, only four of whom have lived to adulthood. Although Wulan's mother sold snacks for a living, her children were never allowed to taste any. Wulan sold rice illegally as a young girl, and she often had to run for cover with a heavy rice basket on her head during police raids on unlicensed traders. She never attended school. Wulan married Joko when she was 21; she has two children who are now 8 and 12 years old.

Joko works as a becak *(three-wheeler) driver. He rents his vehicle from the owner at a daily rate of 40,000 rupiah (about US$5 at the time of the study). Before the economic crisis, he could earn a profit of Rp. 8,000 to Rp. 10,000 a day (US$1 to $1.25). Now, though, he has very few customers. He sometimes comes home in the evenings without any earnings at all and even asks Wulan for money to pay the daily* becak *rent. If he defaults on the rent, the owner may not let him operate the vehicle again. Joko once tried to break out of this cycle by going to Malaysia as a migrant laborer, borrowing Rp. 1.5 million (US$191) from a money-lender for the trip. However, because he did not go through legal channels he could not get a regular job. During the year he spent abroad, he only once sent home money, which Wulan used to pay off most of her debts.*

Their landlord, in addition to charging rent, requires that all house-holds sell any scavenged material to him at whatever price he determines. Households that work for him are allowed to use the local well that he built rather than a public well half a kilometer away. Wulan used to collect scrap materials to help earn income for the family, but with no one at home to care for her children, they became sick and malnourished. She stopped working in order to care for and spend time with them, but now she has no money for daily necessities, nor can she afford to send her children to school. Whenever she is completely out of money, Wulan pawns her clothes at a government-run pawnshop for Rp. 5,000 (75 cents) apiece. She has no other assets and very few clothes left. She dreads the day when she will be forced to borrow from the local moneylender, who charges 20 percent interest per month. She knows that once she resorts to this she will inevitably sink deeper and deeper into debt.

Throughout the Indonesian communities visited for this study, poor people report that they live on the brink of disaster, and they describe many factors that contribute to their extreme vulnerability. The economic crisis of 1997 and 1998 sent millions of Indonesians into abject poverty, with the most developed and populated island of Java suffering the most. In all areas of the country, however, poor people identify inadequate assets, unreliable livelihoods, indebtedness, and environmental and seasonal stresses as sources of insecurity. Poor infrastructure and governance compound their vulnerability. Women's lives are doubly insecure due to poverty and entrenched gender inequities at both the community and household levels. This chapter focuses on these sources of vulnerability as described by poor men and women, and explores the ways in which these disadvantages combine to keep people like Wulan and Joko all but destitute.

The *Voices of the Poor* research was conducted during May and June 1999, a tumultuous period for Indonesia. Devaluation of the rupiah precipitated a disastrous economic crisis in August 1997, which in turn sparked public unrest and opposition to the Soeharto regime. In June 1999, amid recession and political protests, Indonesia held its first free and open election since the 1950s. The People's Consultative Assembly elected a moderate religious leader, Abdurrahman Wahid, the new president. The recession lasted two years, with per capita GNP falling by half to US$580 in 1998. The economy began to recover faster than expected, however. After plummeting by 13.2 percent in the fiscal year ending in

March 1999, the GDP rebounded to 0.8 and 4.8 percent growth in the following two fiscal years.[2]

In the twenty-year period before 1996, Indonesia had made striking gains in reducing overall levels of extreme expenditure poverty. The proportion of the population in extreme poverty fell from over 60 percent to less than 12 percent during the two decades.[3] Then, with the onset of the economic crisis in August 1997, poverty as measured by expenditures more than doubled, peaking at 27 percent of Indonesia's 207 million people in late 1998/early 1999. Among those who are poor, 60 percent work in the agriculture sector, 75 percent live in rural areas, and 87 percent live in households headed by someone with a primary education or less. The crisis revealed that a large number of people live close to the edge, cycling in and out of extreme poverty. A recent study finds that over a three-year span, from 30 to 60 percent of all Indonesians face a greater than fifty-fifty chance of periodically experiencing extreme poverty.[4]

This research is based on discussions with more than 900 poor men, women, and youths from six rural, four urban, and two peri-urban communities in Indonesia (see table 2, Study Communities in Indonesia, at the end of this chapter). Eight of the twelve communities are on the island of Java, which, with nearly 60 percent of the country's population, has both the highest concentration and the largest numbers of people living in poverty. Four other communities were chosen from the eastern provinces of Nusa Tenggara Barat and Nusa Tenggara Timur, which are less populated islands but have more severe poverty than Java as well as very different climatic and livelihood patterns.

Upon entering the study communities, research teams approached the village chief with an official introduction letter from the central government. At the village chief's office, they examined a community map to identify neighborhoods where the poorest households are located. To identify participants for the discussion groups and case studies, researchers walked through poor neighborhoods and met with community members in their homes, fields, water points, and shops. They also met with neighborhood chiefs and local religious leaders. Appointments were then made with community members for group meetings of ten to fifteen people. Before leaving each community, the team reported outcomes of the discussions to larger groups of community residents.

A total of fifty-seven discussion groups were held. In addition, between eight and thirteen individual and institutional case studies were collected in each community, for a total of eighty-four. Among these, fifty-five were individual case studies of poor people, better-off people,

people who used to be poor and are now better-off, and people who used to be better-off and are now poor.

The Indonesia research team was coordinated by the local World Bank office and comprised members from the World Bank, the Indonesia National Development Planning Agency (BAPPENAS) of the Government of Indonesia, the Population Research Center, Gajah Mada University in Yogyakarta, the Social Research Center at the University of Indonesia in Jakarta, the Center for Urban & Regional Development Studies, the Institute of Technology in Bandung, and the Institute of Social & Economic Research, Education & Information in Lombok. The research teams, which each included two men and two women, spent five to seven working days with each community.

"When the present is at stake, the future can be sacrificed," is a predominant theme running through the discussion groups, which were held while the economy was still struggling to recover from the East Asian economic crisis. The chapter opens with a look at both old and newer sources of vulnerability that poor people say force them to focus on daily survival. Next are poor people's assessments of public, private, and local institutions. The chapter concludes by examining both improvements and enduring inequities in gender relations at the household level.

Exposed on Many Fronts

Poor people throughout the communities visited in Indonesia say that their greatest sources of vulnerability are unstable and inadequate livelihoods; lack of assets, including savings; indebtedness; and seasonal and environmental threats. Since the economic crisis, people in many communities visited describe dramatic declines in security as jobs have become scarce and the price of basic daily necessities has risen. Study participants frequently say that a day's income, if they receive any at all, is usually just enough to meet that day's needs. Insecurity is widely defined as having to borrow money and fall deeper into debt on days when there is no income. People report that even those with seemingly steady employment in factories or the construction industry can lose their jobs at any time. The rainy season also deepens the vulnerability of poor households as jobs in agriculture and many trades disappear during this time, and high winds and floods destroy crops and property. In addition, poor people worry immensely about illness striking their families and about lacking the "the strength to make a living."

The leading sources of vulnerability vary by region. The economic crisis of 1997 and 1998 is the overriding source of insecurity described by men and women in West Java. They identify large numbers of "new poor" in their communities and say that wellbeing has declined significantly compared with ten years ago. People in East and Central Java identify pressing needs that relate both to the effects of the financial crisis and to longer-term development problems. They report marginal improvements in wellbeing over the last decade due to new infrastructure such as roads, bridges, electricity, and water supply. In the communities visited in Nusa Tenggara Barat and Nusa Tenggara Timur, the effects of the financial crisis are more limited. People there list precarious livelihoods, lack of assets, seasonality, and environmental risks as more important concerns.

Market Shocks

None of the Java communities visited for this study was spared the effects of the severe recession of 1997 and 1998. There were massive layoffs from urban industries that closed or went bankrupt during the economic crisis. In addition, many rural areas in Java that have close ties with urban centers felt the effects of the crisis through labor force reductions, as well as through sharp increases in the prices of basic goods and of inputs needed for farming and other occupations. Other effects included a severe credit crunch and a flood of people returning to their villages, competing for scarce local jobs in an effort to survive.

In West Java many construction projects came to a halt, and thousands of jobs disappeared in Galih Pakuwon, Harapan Jaya, and Padamukti. Most factories with large labor forces, including those in textile, rubber, and oil, scaled down or closed operations, affecting populations in both urban Harapan Jaya and rural Padamukti. Auto industry employees from rural Galih Pakuwon lost their jobs. In urban Pegambiran, where unemployment was high even before the crisis, many people lost jobs in the animal feed and food industries. Many in Galih Pakuwon earn their living working at home making leather bags, purses, and shoes, and the skyrocketing price of raw materials and difficulties accessing credit after the economic crisis led to bankruptcy and unemployment for many of the artisans.

Layoffs abruptly pushed thousands of urban and rural low-income workers out of the formal sector into the informal sector, where poor people were already making only a barely adequate living. Informal workers such as laundry women, motorcycle taxi drivers, food vendors, and housewives with rooms to rent found that their customers suddenly declined in number. Describing their livelihoods in the informal sector, poor men and women say that competition for jobs and clients is fierce.

The crisis also sent shock waves through the agricultural sector. Farmers in Galih Pakuwon report that their rice harvests could not be sold for good prices or properly stored; consequently, they could not purchase sugar, coffee, or other daily necessities. Farm laborers there report that employers used to provide one meal a day, but now workers receive only wages. In Banaran, a village in East Java, Bambang, a 23-year-old father, says that he lost his job of two and a half years in a chemical fiber enterprise tending plants that provided raw material. Discouraged about finding other work locally, Bambang has applied and paid a deposit to participate in a migrant worker program that would place him at an oil palm plantation in Malaysia. While new workers are not yet needed in Malaysia, he has been waiting for six months and hopes that he will get word soon. Bambang says his greatest hope in life is for his children to have a better education than he received because he doubts he will be able to leave them with any possessions.

Many people, unable to make a living in urban areas during the economic crisis, returned to their villages, adding to the pressures on resources and scarce wage labor opportunities in the countryside. This trend is devastating for poor villagers such as Neneng and Cecep, landless farmers in Padamukti. The couple is raising two sons, both of whom recently dropped out of primary school because the family can no longer afford the cost of schooling. Neneng has never known life without poverty, but until the 1997 economic crisis hit Asia, she says she had not known constant worry about where to get her family's next meal. She used to serve three meals a day, usually rice with vegetables and sometimes fish. The family can now eat only once a day, a meal of rice with salt when they can afford rice. Usually they eat cassava or corn porridge, which are cheaper. Neneng often has to borrow from her neighbors or the village grocer for the day's meal. Their savings are gone.

Before the crisis both Neneng and Cecep could find daily work, and they could even save a little. At that time, they could cope with the rainy season or unexpected floods because Cecep was able to find construction jobs in a nearby town. Since the economic crisis, construction projects have come to a standstill. Both Cecep and Neneng now work as farm laborers from dawn until midday. Cecep is typically paid Rp. 6,000 a day (70 cents). Neneng gets 25 percent less, in keeping with local wage differentials between men and women. However, increased competition for farm jobs from people who fled back to Padamukti means that work is not available every day even in the peak agricultural season. What's more, wages have not kept pace with the sharp increases in food prices. Adding to farm workers' insecurity, rice fields have remained flooded for months by excessive rains. Neneng tries to keep her family fed by doing laundry for better-off families in the village, earning Rp. 2,000–4,000 a day (25–50 cents).

Like Neneng, many people in Indonesia cope with poverty by diversifying their sources of income. Yet, many say they earn barely enough to live from day to day. Youths in a discussion group in urban Tanjungrejo (East Java) explain that they are always looking for work, for whatever is available. Yanto, a man from the dense settlement of Pegambiran (West Java), explains that his job as a scavenger is uncertain, so when he has no work, he looks for additional income by pedaling a *becak*, which he rents for Rp. 1,500 per day. When he is not scavenging or on a *becak*, he can sometimes look after a vendor's stall to earn extra money.

The economic crisis has greatly affected poor people's purchasing power. Pak Sujud, from Pegambiran, says he had trouble coping even before the crisis, when he could afford to buy two kilograms of rice at Rp. 1,000 a kilogram and a few side dishes on his daily earnings of Rp. 3,000. Now, a single kilo of rice costs Rp. 2,500, and he can no longer afford to buy enough rice, let alone pay for other daily needs. "I don't even think about saving; my earnings are not even enough to eat sufficiently," says another man in Pegambiran.

The communities visited in Nusa Tenggara Barat and Nusa Tenggara Timur are more physically remote and have few ties with commercial centers. Study participants there describe relatively minor effects of the economic crisis, although some report paying higher prices for basic goods as well as receiving higher prices for local goods such as fish, candlenut, cocoa, and other crops. Instead, poor people from these outer islands mainly point to seasonal hardships, weather-related disasters, and their remoteness as sources of insecurity in their lives. They also say they are vulnerable because they lack the tools or working capital to run their own businesses, as well as the skills needed to pursue more promising livelihoods. Most have very few assets and rely heavily on low-paying day jobs. In Waikanabu and Kawangu (both in Nusa Tenggara Timur), poor people perceive limited opportunities for improving their lives or those of their children. Outlooks are somewhat better in Renggarasi (Nusa Tenggara Timur) due to infrastructure improvements, as well as in Ampenan Utara (Nusa Tenggara Barat), where there is now greater access to credit.

Lack of Assets and Access to Common Property Resources

Kampung Pondok Perasi is part of the poor peri-urban coastal settlement of Ampenan Utara on the island of Nusa Tenggara Barat. Most poor men in the community work as wage laborers on fishing boats, and many poor women process and preserve fish or engage in petty trade. For the study, small discussion groups of older men and younger women worked to identify and rank the most important problems in their community (table 1). Explaining why they can't break out of poverty, both men and women stress that they cannot afford to purchase their own boats and fishing nets. Seasonal, environmental, and other stresses noted in table 1 also heighten vulnerability in Ampenan Utara.

For the discussion group of older men, a pressing problem is that "the small income does not compensate the fuel and production costs" of fishing. Lacking their own boat, engine, and fishing nets, poor fishermen must rent their equipment and typically must give half of their catch to the boat owner. According to the discussion group,

> Poor fishermen have no option but to use the wealthy fishermen's fishing equipment on a fifty-fifty basis. This is a very unfair arrangement because up to nine fishermen have to share one boat. The catch after a four-day trip might be worth Rp. 1 million. After deducting operating costs and fuel [from the poor fishermen's 50 percent], each man would get only Rp. 20,000 [approximately US$3]. And this is only during eight months of the year. In the three to four months of the rainy season there is no alternative income available because we have no skills or experience except in fishing. To make things worse, rich entrepreneurs are now catching all the fish near the coast with trawlers and large tuna fishing nets. They leave nothing for the poor fishermen.

The use of gill nets by wealthy fishermen with powerboats in Ampenan Utara is dangerously diminishing local fish stocks. For poor

TABLE 1 Leading Community Problems, Two Discussion Groups in Kampung Pondok Perasi Settlement, Amperan Utara

Problem	Ranking by discussion group	
	Older men	*Younger women*
Income does not cover expenses for fuel, equipment rental, etc.	1	—
No fishing equipment (boat, engine, tackle)	2	1
Nothing to do and no income during three to four months of rainy season	—	2
No capital to start business other than fishing	3	3
Not trusted by the rich to borrow money	4	
Too many children	—	4
No other experience and skills to earn income except fishing	5	—
Children drop out of school to work	—	5
Fish are scarce due to the use of gill nets in waters near the coast	6	—
When husbands return from sea empty-handed, arguments ensue	—	6

— Not mentioned.
Note: 1 = Most important problem.

fishermen who only use traditional nets or simple fishing tackle, the catches are becoming ever smaller in terms of the size of the fish and the volume of the total catch. Small fishermen have pressured the local government for regulations prohibiting the use of gill nets, but they have received no response. Study participants say wealthy fishermen often contribute money and resources to official functions and community activities and have special connections with relevant government officials. Although not reported by study participants, it is known that fishermen who are desperate for a catch are resorting to cyanide and potash bombing of coral reefs.

Poor people in other rural communities in the study describe being disadvantaged by increasing pressures on farmland and other common property resources such as forests. In Renggarasi "sterile land" is mentioned as a cause of poverty, along with outright lack of land. Study participants in Waikanabu say that opportunities for clearing fertile new lands have diminished considerably as forests have receded, and plant diseases and declining soil fertility have greatly reduced yields on available lands. Youths and older men in groups in Waikanabu say that farmers are overworking the land "without being able to replenish it or let it recover by moving to other lands, so they do not have good produce."

Poor people say they have few options for protecting their assets. Most hold their life's savings in the form of livestock, but there is no animal insurance. Thefts by gangs from outside the village are common. Protective services against livestock disease are located far from villages, necessitating unaffordable expenses to procure these services. A man from Kawangu notes, "When our cows are sick and it is suggested that we give them injections, we do not always follow the suggestion. When there is a traditional option, we would use it rather than going to buy the medicine. We have to use the money for other needs."

Remoteness, Isolation, and Lack of Bargaining Power

Some of the more remote villages visited in Nusa Tenggara Timur are particularly disadvantaged because they lack transportation infrastructure. Inadequate roads and transport limit villagers' access to markets and information and leave them vulnerable to abuses by middlemen. According to a group of women from Waikanabu,

> The traveling merchant is our only source of loans to buy thread for weaving ikat [traditional textile]. He also comes to the village to buy our ikat. He gives us very low prices, but we are forced to sell to him alone because he provides the cash and thread and because it is difficult for us to go to the market to sell our own fabric. The road is so bad that no public transportation reaches our village.

Discussion groups of men and women, young and old in Waikanabu list "difficulty in transportation" as the most important issue affecting their community's standard of living. A group of older men explains that without good roads, "it is difficult to transport farm and plantation products, such as coffee, betel nuts, bananas, and vegetables to market."

The situation is similar in Kawangu. Participants there say,

> When people from the village can reach the market, they find the prices are surprisingly high. But when that trader comes to the village to buy our harvest of candlenuts and cocoa, his

*prices keep changing. Sometimes high, sometimes low. We do
not understand it.*

Seasonal and Environmental Stresses and Shocks

Indonesia is richly endowed with fertile agricultural land, abundant rainfall, forests, marine resources, and mineral and fuel deposits.
However, every poor community visited in Indonesia is vulnerable to
both seasonal and environmental stresses, notably flooding, erosion, and
depleted soils in rural areas, and problems with water, sanitation, and
flooding in urban areas. Poor villagers emphasize that the more well-to-
do groups have been able to shield themselves from increasing pressures
on natural resources, while poor people have become more exposed and
insecure in the face of environmental and seasonal changes.

Each year the rainy season brings greatly reduced work opportunities,
along with hunger and illness. Hambali, an 18-year-old fisherman in Ampenan Utara, says his income falls drastically during the rainy months; he
copes by collecting brushwood, which can be sold as packaging for preserved fish or as fuel, and by working in fish processing. In Renggarasi all
discussion groups report that natural disasters such as high winds and long
periods of drought and flooding are urgent problems because they increase
illness and hunger, destroy crops and animals, and keep children from
being able to travel to school. In four rural communities, poor people describe increased hardships due to more severe and unpredictable storms in
recent years. In Padamukti the most recent floods are reported to have lasted six months, forcing people to use small boats for travel and to cope
with extended outbreaks of diarrhea as well as skin and eye diseases
Three discussion groups in Padamukti ranked the yearly flooding and its
health consequences as the most pressing problem facing the community.

Environmental and seasonal hardships also touch the urban poor
Many urban and peri-urban communites sit in low-lying areas with little
drainage and inadequate or nonexistent sanitation. Poor women lose days
of wages when they must miss work in order to protect their homes and
belongings from polluted floodwaters. Pegambiran is situated on a
coastal strip where high tides and storms regularly flood homes with sea-
water. A nearby river is choked with silt and garbage from the city up-
stream. Drainage is also a problem in Semanggi and Tanjungrejo, where
rainwater stagnates for days in stinking puddles and presents a health
threat. All urban communities in the study report a shortage of latrines

and deteriorating sanitation conditions. Some wells are so badly polluted that people are forced to spend their limited resources to purchase drinking water from vendors.

Poor people in both urban and rural communities report that many resources are being bought up, polluted, or overexploited by those who are better off. Study participants in Genengsari, Harapan Jaya, Galih Pakuwon, and Padamukti talk about receiving inadequate payment for land they sold for housing projects. Farmers from Galih Pakuwon, for example, indicate that people in their village were forced to sell productive agricultural land for a governmental housing construction program, receiving compensation far below the land's market value.

Participants also describe unequal labor arrangements and poor governance in Indonesia, which further their vulnerability to seasonal and environmental risks. Padamukti sharecroppers, for instance, report that they have been greatly disadvantaged by crop damage and reduced yields resulting from severe rains, torrential winds, and flooding in recent years. Inequitable sharecropping arrangements have meant that wealthier landowners in the community have been able to protect their incomes from these hazards by shifting all the risk to the sharecroppers. As one farmer explains,

> Sixteen of us sharecrop a 200-hectare rice field owned by a rich landowner. Before the annual floods started in 1996, there were two to three harvests each year and the yield was 2,000 metric tons of unhusked paddy. The landowner's share was set at that time at 800 tons per year. Now half the rice field is flooded for six months a year and yield has come down to 1,000 metric tons. Out of that, 800 tons must still be given to the landowner. Two hundred tons are shared among sharecroppers. All the production costs such as fertilizers, pesticides, labor, and so forth, are the sharecroppers' responsibility [which they pay out of their 20 percent share], whereas the landowner is getting 80 percent of the net produce. With recent increases in prices for agricultural inputs, we have hardly anything left in our share.

Through these highly inequitable arrangements, poor people bear the brunt of environmental and seasonal risks in their communities. As seen in the next section, institutions that are in a position to help reduce people's vulnerability to such abuses and stresses are by and large not effective in their jobs.

Reducing Insecurity: Role of Formal and Informal Institutions

Working in small groups, poor people evaluated and ranked institutions according to four criteria: the institution's *importance* to people; its *effectiveness* in providing support, solving problems, or helping; people's *trust* in the institution; and the extent to which people have *control* (or influence) over the institution. Although a large number of institutions touch the lives of poor Indonesians, not many score well across all four dimensions. Religious prayer and learning groups, neighborhood associations, and formal and informal savings and credit organizations are among the few that do.

In reflecting on the qualities that she values in institutions, a woman from a discussion group in Kawangu remarks,

> What is most important about an institution's activities and assistance is its usefulness to the people. Assistance does not have to be in the form of cash or goods. Even when an institution provides a large sum of money, it cannot be considered effective when it does not address the problems the community is facing.

A woman in Waikanabu agrees: "Only after an activity and its results are proven first of all in the community's life can it be trusted and evaluated as good." Similarly, poor people say they must trust an institution in order to feel comfortable using it. In Waikanabu, for example, groups of both older and younger men say that when an institution is honest, its programs are known to the community and are managed and carried out with the community's involvement. "If you are not honest," they explain, "you are not trusted any longer to do anything or implement any activity and will no longer be granted power." Poor Indonesians from different communities made clear that an institution's effectiveness in helping alleviate their problems largely depends on its willingness to consult with them and adjust forms of assistance accordingly. As shown below, only a few institutions have these qualities.

Little Trust in Public Institutions

Poor people consider government institutions and their staffs to be important in their lives. Yet they frequently stress that most government programs aimed at reducing poverty fail to do so because poor people lack any capacity to influence them or to hold officials accountable when problems arise. There are some government-sponsored programs, however, that are reaching poor people.

During the three decades of the Soeharto regime, government-sponsored community organizations were established and nurtured by the state. These structures were mandated in every community and represent different social groups, such as the village council (LKMD), village elders (LMD), women (PKK), youth (Karang Taruna), and so on. The purpose and rules of these organizations are the same across Indonesia. With the exception of the PKK in Java, these organizations are not considered effective, important, or trusted by people in the study.

Study participants, with the exception of urban women's discussion groups, generally identify the neighborhood association (RW/RT) as the most important, effective, and trusted community organization.[5] The RW/RT is not a government body, but tends to function as a support to local administrators and as a first point of contact between the government and community members. The RT chief is a respected and usually better-off local resident, not appointed by the government (as distinct from the village chiefs, who were appointed until 1998). In the past, however, one needed to be publicly loyal to the ruling political party to be elected to lead even a neighborhood association.

Among other responsibilities, the neighborhood association and village officials issue identity cards and certificates needed for obtaining jobs or fee waivers at government-run institutions such as clinics and schools. Frequently, they also provide information about job openings in the area. In Harapan Jaya men report that they first turn to their neighborhood association chief when faced with difficulties: "He is responsible for getting aid . . . for our neighborhood. He has lived in the area all his life and is a known and trusted person who puts common funds to productive use for the benefit of all residents."

Poor people generally view village councils (LKMDs) negatively. The government at the village level is made up of the elite, who tend to make decisions on behalf of, rather than in consultation with, the poorer majority. Although poor people are often asked to attend village meetings, their participation has little effect on the decisions made. Recent efforts to decentralize government responsibilities are leading to changes in local governance structures; however, the hierarchical legacy and lack of accountability of government institutions persist. A poor man from Renggarasi explains,

*When the LKMD calls a meeting, all the decisions about a
project or program have already been made that it should be
this way and that way. Even an old, helpless, and blind man
like Umbu Tamu will be invited to this meeting along with the
rest of the village men. Poor men would all remain silent and
only listen. This is despite the fact that we all live with and
relate well to each other in the village.*

The feelings expressed by poor men in Waikanabu are common
throughout Indonesia: "Although many institutions can be influenced by
the community, not all levels of the community can influence them. Only
people with high social status, the village officials or the rich, are able to
have influence." Poor women have virtually no influence or voice even in
community institutions (box 1). In Kawangu local institutions are

---

BOX 1 No Voice for Women

While women are at the forefront in carrying out development programs, often
providing the bulk of the voluntary labor, they have little or no say about the content and types of programs that are implemented. Few programs ever ask for the
opinions of poor people, and if they do, they ask only men.

In more than half the villages visited, men feel they can at least talk to their village government officials, the LKMD, religious leaders, and neighborhood chiefs.
If women try to express their opinions, however, they are ignored. A poor man
from Renggarasi says, "When women are invited to the meeting, they are only
given the task of preparing and serving refreshments." A group of women in
Waikanabu explains, "The husband's responsibility for *edat* [traditional rituals
and ceremonies] is always in the front, while the wife's responsibilities are only in
the kitchen." Women and men seem to concur that "community decisions are the
rights and responsibilities of menfolk. Women's role is only to accept and implement them." Only in Harapan Jaya, a suburb of Jakarta, do women say that they
attend community meetings and speak up when necessary. However, even they report that the local government officials "turn a deaf ear to what women have to
say." In Nusa Tenggara Timur a poor woman speaking up at public meetings is
considered irreverent and draws male chastisement.

Women's influence is limited to women's institutions within their own communities, such as the PKK. Among women's discussion groups in Java, the PKK is
highly ranked and its services are valued. It organizes monthly health clinics where
women have easy access to family planning and health services (including services
for children) and government credit initiatives, and it organizes local rotating credit and relief initiatives. Even in PKK processes, however, women who have a voice
are either from economically well-off families or are the wives of important people such as the village chief, the religious leader, or the traditional *adat* leader. The
poorest women have little voice.

considered completely unresponsive and out of reach of the poor. When discussing both local officials and traditional clan leaders, a Kawangu villager says, "These two institutions exist, but in reality they are not there for us. These institutions pay no attention to the various problems the community faces."

Poor people also say they are often afraid to speak up against their community leaders, fearing that the limited resources they do gain could be lost if they are considered disruptive. "The village administration is the authority that rules the community. We dare not disobey them. . . . We have to go to them whenever we need any official papers, and then we do whatever the village administration tells us to do," says a poor person in Ampenan Utara.

Government-Provided Safety Nets

It is estimated that slightly more than a quarter of the people in Indonesia's poorest expenditure quintile receive some form of social assistance under the government's safety net program.[6] In 1998 the government launched several centrally designed and operated Social Safety Net (JPS) programs aimed at crisis response.[7] Poor people in most communities visited express appreciation for whatever aid they receive, and some components of the safety net program fare well in discussions. However, JPS initiatives such as the educational subsidy and a special loan program for poor communities, discussed below, are not well regarded by participants in most of the communities visited.

Frequent charges include poor targeting, favoritism, and lack of transparency in the delivery of these programs. According to a man in Galih Pakuwon, "In the end we always see and feel that the activities were not transparently implemented." He gave examples of subsidized rice and scholarships that did not reach the targeted beneficiaries, and asphalt for road repairs that was not provided as promised.

Scholarships to keep children of the poorest households in schools are one component of the JPS program. During 1998–99, 3.3 million Indonesian children received these scholarships. However, poor men and women knew about these scholarships in only three of the twelve communities visited, and poor children actually received them in only a few households in Pegambiran, West Java. Meanwhile, the children of neighborhood chiefs and the village head invariably received scholarships, although they were not poor. Poor parents were told by community leaders or school officials that the recipients of scholarships had been decided "from above" (at the district level or higher), or that poor children were not smart enough to qualify.

Another targeted poverty-reduction program of the central government is Inpres Desa Tertinggal (IDT), which provides a revolving loan fund for income-generating activities in poor villages. In several communities visited by researchers, the poorest households say they have been denied loans. Local officials told researchers that they were "afraid that the poor would not be able to repay loans." The loans instead were given to people they considered capable of repaying them, that is, to those with established business or trade activities, who were definitely not poor, and were often the friends and relatives of the officials themselves.

IDT first reached the peri-urban settlement of Kawangu in 1996. The sub-district administration reports that over a two-year period Rp. 40 million has been disbursed to benefit 175 Kawangu families organized in seven different income-generating activity groups. In the community of Kampung Hunduburung in Kawangu, however, only eight of the forty-eight families classified as poor received IDT assistance. For these reasons, study participants gave very low ratings to their IDT facilitator, although he is paid to work in the community and ensure that the funds are directed to the most needy groups and to promising activities. Poor people say the facilitator approved loans without consulting community members. According to Bapak Hawula Windi, a local resident, "The aid did not even touch the hands of the poor, let alone help the poor."

In addition to faulty targeting, some of the facilitators' income-generating requirements have been disastrous for participants. One woman in Kawangu explains that her group had decided to use the money to assist its weaving activities, either for marketing the finished product or for buying raw materials such as thread. The facilitator rejected this idea because, in his opinion, weaving and selling cloth would make the recycling period of the funds too long, so fewer people would benefit. He advised the group to use the money to raise poultry, instead. However, poultry raising failed because immunization services were not readily available and many birds died from disease. The net result was a waste of everyone's time and no benefits for poor families, despite the expenditure of IDT funds.

Waikanabu is the only community where poor families report that they received and derived sustained benefits from IDT as well as from Sapi Banpres, which provides aid for livestock breeding. They also report good experiences with the Food/Cash for Work program in 1998, which provided emergency relief work during the drought, along with agricultural tools. Study participants say that the village chief has been instrumental in ensuring equity in the distribution of government aid in the community.

Protecting the Body: Health Care

Government spending on primary health care facilities is equitably distributed across the consumption quintiles in Indonesia.[8] Despite the presence of these facilities in or near many communities visited for this study, however, poor people rate primary health care services low, and many say they do not use them. In the eastern island communities of Waikanabu, Kawangu, and Renggarasi, study participants indicate that they see no point in investing effort, time, and transport costs to get to health centers because they do not receive medicine there. In Kawangu participants report that the nurse always says medicines are out of stock. Even if they are available, the prescribed medicines cost many times more than an herbal mixture supplied by a local traditional healer.

Similarly, the village birthing clinics built for the government midwife with community contributions at Waikanabu and Genengsari remain unoccupied. The midwife visits the villages only once a month, and women obviously cannot time their deliveries to her monthly visits. Instead, they entrust their deliveries to an untrained traditional midwife (*dukun*). They also consult the *dukun* for children's illnesses. According to a woman from Kawangu, "We are doubtful of the *dukun's* capability in treating our ailments. The medicine she provides for different symptoms is just all the same. Yet, since there is no choice and the *dukun* is more accessible, we just resort to the *dukun*."

Public health expenditures for hospital care in Indonesia heavily favor well-off income groups, with the top expenditure quintile receiving 40 percent of government spending while less than 10 percent goes to the bottom expenditure quintile. In nearly every community visited for the study, poor men and women say they can receive more reliable treatment and access to medicines from hospitals, but they often avoid hospital treatment because it deepens debt. Some people in the study report that hospital expenses have left them destitute. In Padamukti a poor woman says her mother was treated for breast cancer at the hospital in Majalaya (about four kilometers from their village) and died three months later. To pay for her mother's treatment, medications, and other debts, the family was forced to sell its rice field and house. A discussion group participant in Semanggi says, "For more serious illness, people should go to the hospital, yet the high cost required has made poor people see the hospital only as their last resort, after the illness gets really bad."

Struggling to Get Credit: Formal and Informal Sources

In addition to the poorly targeted government credit programs discussed above, study participants in Indonesia mention a variety of formal and informal credit channels and say they depend primarily on informal credit mechanisms, both for helping them cope with daily needs and in times of emergency.

NGO and private credit programs receive favorable reviews, but they are available in only two of the communities visited. The NGO Yayasan Wahana Tani Mandiri/FADO assists poor people in Renggarasi with credit to support crop diversification, and it also provides training, seedlings, and guidance for small businesses. Poor people feel that their wellbeing has improved significantly through this assistance. Likewise, mobile private banks in Nusa Tenggara Barat are showing that microcredit services can help poor people change their lives (box 2). Small, local cooperative or private bank vehicles come to the communities every day to offer small weekly or monthly loans and to receive daily repayments. Communities visited in Nusa Tenggara Timur report that local churches also offer credit and savings services for small businesses.

BOX 2 Wiranadi Mobile Bank: Tailoring Services to Poor Clients' Needs

Wiranadi Bank is one of several mobile financial institutions operating in the Narmada subdistrict of Lombok island, serving residents of Pondok Perasi in Ampenan Utara daily from morning until afternoon. According to one customer, "The borrowing system is very easy; the borrower only needs to sign an agreement with the bank staff." Agreements may be "signed" by stamping the borrower's thumbprints on a loan record card.

Loans are available to anyone, rich or poor, without discrimination. Honesty and regular repayment are the only requirements. Loan sizes range from Rp. 15,000 to Rp. 200,000 (US$2–$25 at the time of the study), with 5 percent interest per month. Repayments are made daily, as most fishermen prefer it that way. Subsequent loans are available based on the regularity of repayments. One customer says, "If I borrow Rp. 25,000 then I should repay Rp. 1,000 daily for thirty days. The bank deducts Rp. 2,500 per loan as an administrative fee." Mutual trust and the desire to maintain a continuing credit relationship keep repayments regular.

To meet day-to-day needs, poor families seek credit from pawnshops in urban areas and from the village store in rural areas. Village stores are valued for offering goods, even when cash for purchases is not immediately available. In Genengsari the local shops and stalls are ranked as the most important credit institutions by three out of four discussion groups. Steep rises in food prices since late 1997 have made these resources all the more important for poor households. Shopkeepers and their poor clients operate with high mutual trust, as all credit transactions are informal.

For poor people in urban areas, moneylenders and pawnshops are often described as necessary evils, the only sources of loans when one needs money urgently. Exorbitant interest rates of up to 30 percent per month, however, cause borrowers to sink into debt with little chance of escaping. The pawnshop is preferred over moneylenders because, though the pawnshop pays less than market value of the pawned item and charges 10 percent interest per month, there is the possibility of buying back pawned items. In Kawangu women rank the pawnshop as the most important institution because there are not many rich people or other institutions to lend money in the community. Women in a discussion group in Tanjungrejo explain, "The moneylender and the pawnshop are like husband and wife. One month we borrow from the moneylender and pay the pawnshop. Next month we borrow from the pawnshop and pay the moneylender."

Traders may be a source of credit, but on very disadvantageous terms. The fish trader (*pelele*) in Ampenan Utara lends money to rent motorboats and buy fuel. In return, the fishermen must sell their catch exclusively to the *pelele* at lower than market price. The traveling textile merchant (*populele*) provides the same kind of binding credit to women weavers in Waikanabu and Kawangu.

Poor people also rely on wealthy neighbors for credit, sometimes on good terms, but often at a high risk. A woman from Ampenan Utara reports, "Neighbors who are willing to help are especially favorable since the loans are speedy, almost routine, without interest, and can reach Rp. 1 million. Moreover, a compromise is normal when the repayment is not available, and at times we are invited into a joint business."

Building Informal Survival Networks

With few supports provided by the government, the private sector, or civic groups, poor people across the study communities say they feel closest to and rely most heavily on mutual support and self-help groups that they form themselves. A 1996 survey of development activities in Indonesian villages found that local initiatives without any external partners accounted for 38 percent of all development activities. More specifically, the study found that local groups themselves carried out 53 percent of all credit projects, 47 percent of all infrastructure projects, and 36 percent of all projects involving public facilities.[3]

The most popular local institutions identified by study participants are weekly prayer and learning groups, which exist in most communities across Indonesia. For instance, in six of the eight communities visited on Java, *pengajian*, or Islamic prayer and learning groups, score very high among institutions valued by poor people. Members of these groups are of the same gender and share a common ethnic origin, neighborhood cluster, or occupational category. Activities include reading and discussion of religious texts and communal prayers, combined with savings and credit activities. Members relate their misfortunes, find caring listeners, and may even receive small amounts of material assistance. These groups are especially highly valued in urban areas, by both women and men.

Poor people also generally trust the more formal religious institutions that exist within their communities. The predominantly Catholic people in the eastern islands of Nusa Tenggara Timur, for example, explain that churches are "always ready with support during crises such as typhoons and earthquakes. Also, they teach the truth and the community follows them." In Ampenan Utara most community decisions are said to be made at the mosque after the Friday midday prayer.

Arisans, or rotating savings and credit groups, are regarded highly in nine of the twelve communities visited in Indonesia. Members of an *arisan* group meet regularly and contribute small sums to a common savings pool. Periodically one member, chosen by lottery, draws the total pool. This continues until every member has won once, at which time a new rotation begins. This is the most accessible source of interest-free credit available to poor people, and it is a vital means of saving for those who find it difficult to set aside money without regularly pulling some out to cover daily needs. *Arisans* are popular among women, especially those involved in petty trade, who use it for their capital needs. Women in Galih Pakuwon view *arisans* as important "at this time when prices of basic goods are very high." In Semanggi a poor woman says that the local *arisan* made it possible for her to build a home by providing a loan of Rp. 1 million in 1996. So far, she has been able to pay back Rp. 600,000 in weekly installments of Rp. 10,000. A poor man in Tanjungrejo says he belongs to an *arisan* that will pay him Rp. 210,000 when he wins the lottery.

Jimpitan is a community mechanism in rural Indonesia that provides credit and protection to the most vulnerable members of society. Rice and cash *jimpitan* are the two most common types. Rice *jimpitan* requires every participating household to contribute one cup of rice every month to a common fund from which loans are made to poor families. The amount of rice loaned is repaid when the borrower is able. Rice given to elderly, disabled people requires no repayment. Cash *jimpitan* requires participating families to contribute Rp. 200 per week. The pool is loaned to those who need additional capital for business. Repayments include a small administrative fee and may be made in installments after the business yields some profit. *Jimpitan* systems are established in every neighborhood of Galih Pakuwon and are administered by a cluster of neighborhoods.

Gender Relations Increase Women's Vulnerability

Gender relations in Indonesia are far from equitable. Poor women are disadvantaged by both gender and economic status throughout their lives. The story of gender relations in the family, however, is complicated; there are variations across regions of the country, with general improvements in some areas affecting women's status and persisting patterns of inequity in others. Women in all communities, and particularly in Nusa Tenggara Barat, stress the economic and social vulnerabilities of female-headed households, and single out divorce and the destitution it brings as an urgent risk facing women.

Poor women in Indonesia have typically been supplementary earners. Today, they are likely to be primary earners in many areas where large numbers of men have lost jobs at factories and construction sites. This has not necessarily changed traditional gender roles, however. Women report that, for the most part, they have added the increased earning responsibilities to their existing household labors. Men's and women's discussion groups in every community visited confirm that women still shoulder a heavier and more diverse physical workload than men, yet men are still the principal decision makers both within and outside the household. As a woman in Nusa Tenggara Timur says, "Women have more responsibilities because they have dual functions, managing the household and also generating income. Besides, women must obey their husbands as well."

Women's groups report that men over 40 still do not share household work or child care if a woman must work outside the home. As a woman in Ampenan Utara states, "It is our destiny as well as ancient tradition that women should do more for the household." Older men from Renggarasi confirm that "a man who takes care of his young children or prepares food is branded as incapable of training his wife properly, or as dominated by her. Such a man is looked down upon by the community." Younger men, however, appear more accommodating. According to a young man in a discussion group from Renggarasi, "Ten years ago it would be impossible to see a man preparing food or pounding rice grain, yet it should be possible now."

Improvements over Time

Groups everywhere agree that women today are better off than they were ten years ago, although the extent of change and the reasons for it vary widely. There seems to exist a graduated scale of changes in gender relations across Indonesia, with the most inequitable situation reported in the eastern provinces of Nusa Tenggara Timur and Nusa Tenggara Barat. Moving westward, the situation is better in East and Central Java, and at the high end of the scale, the West Java communities, both rural and urban, are the most equitable.

According to the men's discussion groups in Renggarasi, Nusa Tenggara Timur, "Woman is a low or a second-class creature," whom a husband buys by paying a bride price in cash or cattle to her parents. A man in Kawangu explains the commodity value of girls and women: "We keep girls from school to protect them from being kidnapped by outsiders, as that will mean the family will lose the bride price the girl would have brought them." Here the gains made by women have been relatively small, but still important. Women in Kawangu consider their lives better today than in the past because they face fewer forms of physical violence from their husbands. Also, a woman is now allowed to hold money of her own and buy something by herself. Furthermore, though ten years ago there was a common saying, "The river must flow backwards before you can go to school," now some girls are permitted to attend school.

In East and Central Java, women speak of additional gains in status and influence. In addition to having better access to education, women are now consulted before their husbands decide about "taking big loans, choosing mates for children, sending children to school, and making contributions for community functions." Men still often make unilateral decisions about buying and selling animals, land, and agricultural produce, however.

In West Java women today are more vocal in decisions at home and even speak up in community meetings. They have gained more power in the domestic sphere because they earn more cash income and manage landed assets more often now than they did ten years ago. In the villages of West Java, women have had to assume traditionally male tasks in crop fields and in forests for much of the year because men have migrated to the cities to work.

Power for women, however, is generally understood by both women and men across Indonesia as "shared authority with men" for solving household problems and making family decisions. As women in East and Central Java explain, "Women now fight back against injustice by husbands and warn men if they are wrong. Husbands are also more understanding now if the food is too simple and sometimes they even help with housework if the wife has to go out to earn."

The Devastation of Divorce

The ease with which husbands can divorce their wives in some parts of the country is emphasized by women across the study communities as a major cause of women's and children's poverty and illbeing. Divorce can cause a woman and her daughters to lose ownership of assets that were acquired during marriage with the woman's contributions. The man usually keeps the tools of production, the home, fruit trees, and furniture. The woman might get consumable assets such as stored grains, her own jewelry, and kitchen utensils. Whether the husband will pay any child support is left to his discretion, according to the women of Ampenan Utara. In other places, community leaders reportedly force husbands to make some child support payments. Female-headed households with small children are said to be the worst off because they cannot send a family member to the cities to search for work when no work is available in the village. After all assets have been pawned off and no further loans are available from any source, desperate single mothers send their children to different village homes at meal times in the hope that someone will feed them.

Siti was born in Straten, Central Java, 45 years ago. She is a widow with six children, three of whom are already married. The other three live with her and are still in school. Siti's family used to be the richest in Semanggi village. Although she was well off, Siti was never happy because her husband was an alcoholic and often engaged in illicit affairs. He was, however, very generous in providing money for community functions and the development of their neighborhood, which won him high social status.

Siti's husband sold their land and household furnishings without telling her and gave the money to his mistress in another village. After losing all the property, Siti finally asked for a divorce because she did not want to share her husband with a second wife. By this time he already had four children with his mistress. From the divorce settlement, Siti received Rp. 4 million (US$509), calculated as Rp.1 million (US$127) for her and Rp. 500,000 (US$63) for each of her children. Her husband sold all her jewelry and burned her good clothes.

Across Indonesia, men say that due to religious teachings over the last ten years, adultery has decreased. However, women in several communities report that men are still having affairs outside marriage, in some places more so now than ten years ago. While men attribute the decrease in adultery to improved education levels and religious teachings, women explain that the underlying reasons are economic. In Genengsari women explain, "The economic crisis has made men more mindful of saving money. Therefore, they are now more loyal to the first wife. Earlier, if they had extra money they would immediately look for a new wife." A decline in livestock ownership has reportedly resulted in fewer affairs in Kawangu. Ten years ago men owned more cattle per family and could more easily afford to pay the penalties imposed by community leaders for adultery, which were paid in cattle. Women explain that the likelihood of adultery can be reduced to a simple equation: If men have surplus resources, they will womanize.

Widows are also extremely vulnerable in Indonesian society. Old, widowed women in Galih Pakuwon village say they have become used to living with constant hunger. They are dependent on their children, who are themselves facing increased hardships due to loss of jobs and lowered earnings. In these conditions, the widows are ashamed to ask for a little more to eat.

Domestic Abuse Declining but Still Prevalent

Discussion groups in eight of the twelve communities visited indicate that levels of domestic abuse against women are declining; however, men and women differ over the extent and forms of household violence in Indonesia today. While most men say that violence against women has decreased significantly over the past ten years, women report a more mixed picture.

In most communities, discussions about violence encompass injustices of all kinds against women. Women list more types of injustice than men do, including beating, verbal abuse, cheating and lying, and polygamy; women may be thrown out of the house, abandoned, or divorced, and left to bring up children alone. In addition, women in specific communities mention the following practices: wives being sold as prostitutes (Tanjungrejo, East Java); wives being prohibited from going out of the house without the husband's permission (Ampenan Utara, Nusa Tenggara Barat; Renggarasi, Nusa Tenggara Timur); and wives being shackled with ropes (Waikanabu, Nusa Tenggara Timur).

In contrast, men mention verbal abuse, infidelity, and "beating when a woman acts beyond reason" as the only violence against women that occurs. While men argue that violence has decreased, they express the need to control the lives of their wives and daughters. Men of Kawangu, Nusa Tenggara Timur, explain that even now "men forbid their wives to go out of the house because it would only make them neglect their household work." They also express the opinion that "men beat their wives because they love them."

In Renggarasi, where large declines in violence against women are acknowledged by both men's and women's discussion groups, women say that things are better than in the past largely because they are no longer starved or tied up by their angry husbands:

In the past, when a woman made a mistake, or even made no mistake but the husband was upset, she would be the target of her husband's anger. Women could be beaten, abusively shouted at, tied up with a rope, or given no food. When a woman ran to escape, seeking refuge at her parents' house, her parents would

simply tell her to go home, since such a situation was a com-
mon thing in every household. The woman's parents would be
embarrassed because their daughter had already been belis, or
bought, by her husband.

In addition, while adultery attracts severe social sanctions for women, the consequences of adultery are less severe than in the past (box 3).

In Tanjungrejo (East Java), where both men's and women's discussion groups also indicate declines in violence, men credit the influence of Islamic teachings, which discourage physical abuse. The men admit, however, that women continue to be abused verbally, slapped and beaten, and abandoned for other women.

Conclusion

Across all the communities visited, poor people say the primary hallmark of wellbeing is owning or having access to tools that enable them to earn their livelihoods and reduce their vulnerability to destitution. In the rural plains, these tools include land, livestock, and the means to irrigate; in coastal areas, they are a powerboat and fishing net; in the hilly and forested regions, they are fruit trees and gardens of coffee, cocoa, and rubber. In urban areas, the key is employment that pays regularly, or capital for trade. People with wellbeing in Indonesia also have peace of mind, harmonious family relationships, and the respect of their neighbors. They can bring up their children to be religious and dutiful. An old man in Padamukti village even states that "wellbeing enhances one's faith in God, and develops one's patience and the ability to save resources."

By contrast, poverty and illbeing in Indonesia mean lack of assets, powerlessness in the face of exploitation or abuse, deepening indebtedness, seasonal risks, dependence on dwindling and degraded natural resources, poor infrastructure, and lack of harmony in the family. The economic crisis has made the lives of many people even more insecure. Together, these disadvantages leave poor people at constant risk of destitution.

The men and women who participated in the study shared a host of recommendations for reducing poverty in their villages and cities. Study participants in Renggarasi suggest that greater access to formal savings, credit, and venture capital services directly targeted to poor families would enable them to acquire the assets they need for stable employment and to break the cycle of increasing debt. In Ampenan Utara people say that poverty has eased in their fishing village due to improved fishing equipment, better access to small business loans, the availability of long-term government and NGO credit for outboard engines, and higher fish prices due to the crisis. Urban groups cite access to credit and also say that their conditions could improve if there were more opportunities in the informal sector and in formal jobs requiring low education and skills, as well as formal and informal job training programs. A participant in a discussion group in Renggarasi village states, "As you can see, the most important thing to us is to work."

Study participants report extensive governance problems and provide concrete suggestions for their authorities. They say they have little information about government programs, including safety net initiatives, and they report pervasive favoritism and corruption in the delivery of services. In their view, government programs are largely ineffective because poor people lack channels for influencing them and ensuring accountability. They suggest, for instance, that food-for-work programs be made available yearly between planting and harvest periods, and that information and targeting be improved for cheap rice and free health care programs. In their daily lives and during emergencies, poor men and women say that they rely most heavily on their own local networks of family, kin, neighbors, religious groups, savings and credit groups, and informal community organizations. These are valuable foundations upon which a more decentralized government can form partnerships to address community needs.

Raising the status of women in the family and in the broader community is another important task that lies ahead. It will require adjusting entrenched norms of behavior and traditional beliefs about gender roles in society. To reduce the most extreme sources of vulnerability, a helpful beginning would be legal and social actions to protect women's economic and social standing in cases of divorce or adultery. Also crucial are expanded—and enforced—penalties for men who abuse their wives and children, physically or otherwise. Further initiatives are needed that focus on enhancing women's participation in community decision making.

TABLE 2 Study Communities in Indonesia

WEST JAVA

Galih Pakuwon Pop. 4,579	Forty percent of the villagers are farmers, and the rest are wage laborers in agriculture or livestock rearing. There are eighteen private telephone connections in the village, including one at the village head office, but there is no public phone. Ninety percent of the households have electricity. There is no health clinic, only an integrated health post that serves children under 5. The area suffers from landslides in the rainy season.
Harapan Jaya Pop. 49,776	In this densely populated urban settlement on the outskirts of Jakarta, a majority of residents are migrants from rural areas. Nearly half the men and women work in the informal sector; others work as laborers and civil servants. The settlers have access to most services, including electricity, telephones, schools, and a health center.
Padamukti Pop. 6,123	The population of this predominantly Muslim village is evenly divided among agricultural workers, laborers in garment factories, and private trade/business people. Half the women are housewives, and the rest work as agricultural or factory laborers. The village has many amenities, including telephones and a health center. The village floods every rainy season and floodwaters remain on crop fields for months.
Pegambiran Pop. 14,891	This densely populated urban settlement is in a coastal zone, near a river estuary. More than 60 percent of men work as industrial laborers, some engage in petty trade, and a small number are farmers. The area is prone to frequent flooding. Population growth is 6–8 percent per year. Ethnic groups include Javanese, Chinese-Indonesians, and people of Arab descent. There are private and public telephones, a post office, a health clinic, and several health posts.

CENTRAL JAVA

Genengsari Pop. 3,400	The village is near teak forests, seven kilometers from the nearest road. Half the houses have electricity. The population is 100 percent Javanese Muslims, 85 percent of whom are farmers. There are three telephone connections in the village—at the village head office and in the homes of the primary school teachers who are not natives of the village. There is no health clinic, but there is a village midwife. Floods, earthquakes, drought, and fire have damaged the area in the last decade.
Semanggi Pop. 30,285	In this densely populated urban settlement on the banks of the Bengawan Solo river, the population is engaged in factory labor, informal sector services, construction, and petty trade. The area floods every rainy season. There is an NGO working in the community. All houses have electricity, some have telephones, and there is a health clinic.

EAST JAVA

Banaran Pop. 1,863	All the residents of this village are Javanese Muslims, and 95 percent of them are farmers. Twenty-five percent of houses have electricity. Many families have sent members abroad to work. There is a maternity center and a midwife, as well as a primary school. The village is three kilometers from the nearest permanent road.
Tanjungrejo Pop. 24,091	This is a densely populated urban community where people work mostly as scavengers and laborers; there are also some civil servants. Ninety percent of the houses have electricity, and there is a health clinic and school. The nearest telephone is ten minutes' walking distance. The community is mostly Muslim, with a few Christian households.

NUSA TENGGARA BARAT

Ampenan Utara
Pop. 16,763

In this coastal peri-urban settlement, the main occupations are fishing, carpentry, masonry, trade, and civil service, as well as private sector employment. To supplement family income, many women are involved in petty trade, mostly selling fish or selling vegetables from a stall. The majority of the population belongs to the Sasak ethnic group, who are Muslim. Other ethnic groups include the Buginese, Balinese, Timorese, and Chinese. All households have electricity, and there are three practicing doctors as well as a health clinic.

NUSA TENGGARA TIMUR

Kawangu
Pop. 2,764

Although this is a peri-urban settlement, most people engage in agriculture. Every rainy season, especially during February and March, the area is flooded, damaging plantations and crops. Crops are also prone to pest attacks. Most people are native to the region and belong to one of fifteen traditional clans. Most are Christian, and missionaries have been active in the region for many years. There is a health clinic, but no post office or telephone. Seventy percent of households have electricity.

Renggarasi
Pop. 2,000

This is an entirely rural community in which 90 percent of the families are farmers. Three main clans are the Moa Kolo, Laki One, and Wedonoi; all of the population is Catholic. Natural disasters such as floods and earthquakes are frequently endured. There is a primary school and a health clinic but no electricity and no post office, and the nearest telephone is forty-four kilometers away. NGOs are actively working in the community.

Waikanabu
Pop. 888

This remote village is reached by walking for four hours from the nearest bus route. Ninety-eight percent of households are engaged in farming, on both dry land and rice paddies. Other jobs include animal husbandry and handicraft. Women make *tenun ikat* (a handloom textile from tie-dyed thread) and plait mats, although their main occupation is farming. There is no electricity in the village, but there are three integrated health posts, and a school, as well as five churches and a local market.

Notes

1. The Indonesia study team was led by Nilanjana Mukherjee and also included Alma Arief, Ratna I. Josodipoero, Sita Laksmini, I. Nyoman Oka, Amin Robiarto, Setiadi, Joko Siswanto, Ronny So, Devi R. Soemardi, Suhardi, Nyoman Susanti, Herry Widjanarko, and Susi Eja Yuarsi.

2. World Bank and International Finance Corporation, "Memorandum of the President of the International Bank for Reconstruction and Development, the International Development Association, and the International Finance Corporation to the Executive Directors on a Country Assistance Strategy of the World Bank Group for Indonesia" (February 8, 2001), 5; and World Bank, "East Asia Update: Regional Overview, Special Focus: Financial and Corporate Restructuring, Poverty Reduction and International Development Goals, Environment" (East Asia and Pacific Region, March 2001), 15.

3. These poverty figures are based on the international poverty line of $1 a day per person at 1985 prices. World Bank, "East Asia: The Road to Recovery" (Report 18475, September 1998), 3.

4. World Bank, "Poverty Reduction in Indonesia: Constructing a New Strategy" (East Asia and Pacific Region, Environment and Social Development Sector Unit, October 2000, draft), 5.

5. Rukun Tetangga (RT) is the smallest neighborhood unit, consisting of 30–40 households; Rukun Warga (RW) is a larger unit grouping several RTs.

6. Unless otherwise noted, all references in this book to the poorest or richest 20 percent of the population refer to statistics that rank people by how much they consume rather than by how much they earn.

7. The initial performance reports being disappointing, revisions were made to introduce greater transparency and better poverty targeting in the Safety Net programs in 2000. They are, however, difficult to justify as "emergency" programs three years after the economic crisis. Poverty reduction strategies now need to shift their attention to programs and policies involving far larger resources and impacts on the population: for example, the safety net budget is far less than the Rp. 28 trillion allotted to a fuel subsidy program that heavily benefits wealthier groups in the country. See World Bank, "Poverty Reduction in Indonesia," 48.

8. World Bank, "Poverty Reduction in Indonesia," 47.

9. World Bank Local Level Institutions (LLI) study, cited in World Bank, "Poverty Reduction in Indonesia," 20.

Bosnia and Herzegovina

War-Torn Lives

Dino Djipa, Mirsada Muzur, and Paula Franklin Lytle[1]

Senad is 49 years old and a metalworker by trade. He lives with his wife and two young children in Zenica's inner city in an area known as "the Chinese Wall," a complex of ten high-rise apartment buildings joined in a wall-like structure. Senad was given the apartment by the steel factory where he worked for twenty-nine years before the war. In those days he paid his bills regularly, and in the summer he took a short vacation with his family at the union vacation center. During the war, Senad was on work assignment instead of in combat. "I worked in special production for three and a half years and did not receive any pay. I got a few parcels—flour and canned food," he says. The war years were hardest for him because he could not explain to his children why there was nothing to eat.

Senad is now on a waiting list for employment. No one else in his family works. His children are in primary school, and he is not able to afford all of their necessities, particularly clothes "It is very hard now. There is no money. I cannot steal—I just can't, and I won't because of my children—I would not want them to start stealing. It is most important to keep one's dignity," he says.

When he can find work, Senad chops wood, unloads trucks of flour, or does other manual labor. When he gets paid, he pays for electricity and spends the rest on food. He has large utility debts. "I have never been in debt, and now I am in a situation where I may have to go to court because of my debts."

When it is absolutely essential, Senad buys clothes for his children, and he stresses that he does not spend anything on himself or his wife.

Purchasing furniture does not even cross their minds. The only electronics left in the apartment are an old TV and an old radio; the family's other possessions were sold during the war to buy food. "This TV is about to give up, but I don't think that I'll be able to afford to fix it, let alone buy another one."

Although Senad believes that the war is the major cause of his decline into poverty, he is nonetheless very disappointed with the steel factory and the state for their lack of concern for workers. "I do not hope for anything better, as things can only get worse. The war has brought about this situation, and I really do not know how it will all turn out."

Like Senad, many people in Bosnia and Herzegovina see the war as the cause of their distress. During the war from 1992 to 1995, more than half of the country's 4.5 million people were displaced: most were displaced internally, but approximately 800,000 fled the country. In addition, an estimated 200,000 people were killed. Widespread atrocities were committed during the war, and far more civilians than soldiers died. While physical infrastructure has been reconstructed, people's lives remain shattered by the loss of livelihoods and continuing social dislocation. Most of the country's workers lost their jobs, many lost savings when bank assets were frozen, more than half of the housing was damaged, and children lost years of schooling.

Of the total population, close to one-half are Bosniac,[2] approximately one-third are Serbs (Orthodox), and about one-sixth are Croats (Roman Catholic). Under the 1995 Dayton Accords, Bosnia and Herzegovina was divided into two entities: the Federation of Bosnia and Herzegovina, composed primarily of Bosniacs and Croats, and the Republika Srpska, mainly Serb. At the national level, tripartite governance arrangements are in effect but hold limited powers. The most important policy decisions have been devolved to the two entities, where ethnically based political parties have won most postwar elections and there is little consensus, including over policies needed to support the transition to a market economy. Despite the difficult political situation, peace has been consolidated, economic growth has been restored, and the reconstruction program has been largely successful.[3] Much of the economic activity has been driven by the very large and heavily donor-financed reconstruction program.

Bosnia and Herzegovina is now one of the poorest countries in the Europe and Central Asia region. Per capita income fell from US$2,429 in

1990 to US$456 in 1995, recovering only to US$1,080 in 1999. Reliable poverty data are not available, but the best estimates suggest that 27 percent of Bosnians fell below a relative poverty line in 1997, while 11 percent were extremely poor and could not meet their immediate food needs.[4] Before the war, income distribution was relatively even and there was little abject poverty.

Researchers spoke with poor people in five communities in the Federation and three in the Republika Srpska (see table 2, Study Communities in Bosnia and Herzegovina, at the end of this chapter). In choosing communities for the study, researchers aimed to achieve geographic distribution, rural and urban diversity, and inclusion of different groups of displaced people. Researchers thus included a typical medium-size town where a specific industry, now closed or working at reduced capacity, had dominated the area and its employment options, as well as an area with refugee camps. Finally, researchers included areas in which World Bank programs operated, based on recommendations from the World Bank's Resident Mission. Study participants belong to various ethnic groups and also include displaced people, refugees, and returnees. At the time of the research 860,000 people were still internally displaced.

The fieldwork for the Bosnia and Herzegovina study, conducted during March and April 1999, was carried out under particularly difficult circumstances. NATO bombing in neighboring Yugoslavia restricted travel to some areas. For instance, a village selected on the border between Russia and the Federation had to be substituted with another, and not all members of the team were allowed to enter the Serbian entity of Bosnia and Herzegovina. Mountainous and icy roads added to the difficulties.

Participants for discussion groups were identified through a variety of methods, including using existing formal and informal networks established by the research team in local areas. A total of seventy-two discussion groups were organized, including forty-nine with poor men, poor women, and poor youths. The remaining twenty-three discussion groups focused on special population groups such as the elderly, refugees, and groups that combined different generations and genders. In addition, a total of sixty-two individual case studies were completed, including four with people who used to be poor but are now better-off.

Prism Research, a private company providing services in marketing, media, and social research, carried out the study in partnership with an American social scientist with previous research experience in the country.

This chapter looks at the war's long-lasting effects on the people of Bosnia and Herzegovina, including the destruction of the middle class, widespread illbeing, loss of industry and infrastructure, a large displaced population, tensions in gender relations at the household level, and the very limited capacity of various institutions to meet the needs of so many people plunged into poverty.

Loss upon Loss

The war in Bosnia and Herzegovina ravaged the lives of most of its people. While a few prospered, the majority fell from the middle class into poverty as jobs, homes, and possessions were lost. Men came home wounded, and others did not return. Numerous civilians were killed or wounded. A war widow in the Serbian village of Tisca says, "In 1993 I lost my husband. He was killed in battle defending what was his. He left two children [ages 3 and 5] who were unaware of what was happening at the time." She had worked in a factory in Sekovici but lost her job when the war began. The widow says,

> *In order to feed two children, I sold all the valuable things I had in the house. Now I work in a store and do all I can to en-sure that my children have decent food to eat and clothes that are warm and clean. We are at the bottom of society. What is my future and that of my children? What prospects do we have? Sometimes I ask myself why I live at all.*

Life, property, livelihood, health, and spirit are the many casualties of war. Years after the Bosnian war ended and the death count was officially estimated, people's lives are still devastated by the many other losses they endure. "Those who have lost their property have fallen to the very bottom," says a discussion group participant in Sarajevo. Another poor person in Sarajevo says, "Even if I were to work for over a hundred years to establish a household, I would never have what I had before the war destroyed everything." A discussion group participant in Capljina says, "The main thing is that, before, those who wanted to work could find work. Now they cannot." In Sarajevo a participant told researchers, "The biggest problem is always money. A bad financial situation causes loss of sleep, and if you are sleeping poorly, in a certain sense you are ill."

Physical and Emotional Suffering

The aftermath of war affects both physical and emotional health. A middle-aged poor man in Tombak says, "The rise in the number of people with heart complaints, high blood pressure, and depression has become normal for us. There is not a person in Tombak who does not suffer from at least one of these illnesses. All of this has been brought on by poverty and war." A young participant in Vares says, "It is horrifying how many sick people there are. My mother is very young, but she is ill and is now on a disability pension. There are many people who are only 40 years old but suffer from serious illnesses."

Study participants very frequently report extreme stress. "We all suffer from two illnesses: high blood pressure and nerves," says an old woman in Glogova. An old man there says, "I can barely breathe; nerves are suffocating me. The doctor told me that my life hangs from a thread and that I am not allowed to get stressed—but how?" An older woman in Tombak explains,

> I have burned out because of fears and worries for my family
> in the war. I had to send a husband and two sons to the front
> lines and wait for them to return—or not. I did not think about
> eating, sleeping, dressing, or anything. I would lie down and
> awake in tears. . . . You can never recover from spiritual
> impoverishment.

A displaced woman in Vares agrees: "Our souls, our psyches, are dead."

Destruction of the Middle Class

War, displacement, and unemployment have virtually destroyed the middle class. One woman from Tombak had a job for twelve years at the Payment Transfer Bureau, and her husband was a construction worker. "We did not see a single day of suffering. We knew how to enjoy the coast, vacations, and restaurants," she says. But, "Today we are extremely poor. We don't have enough to take the kids to ride the play cars in the park."

A poor man in Sarajevo says,

> I am now among the humble, but before I lived like a normal
> man. I had a car, a VW Golf. I visited many countries; travel

*was my pleasure. I would take both summer and winter vaca-
tions; we would go to the coast, to Turkey. Now I can't do anything. We barely make ends meet.*

According to a participant from Mostar West,

*The middle class were ordinary people who lived off their
salaries. . . . We could afford a car, an apartment, or a house.
We had credit. Unions provided opportunities for summer and
winter vacations. Our children had free education. There were
even scholarships provided by the state. Work was rewarded
and stimulating.*

Another adds, "The middle class constituted 79 percent of the population. They were people without debts; their refrigerators were full, and
they could travel." Now the overwhelming majority are poor, and a few
are rich. Very few discussion groups indicate that there is any middle class
in their communities today (table 1).

Participants around the country echo the Mostar West groups' con-
clusions regarding the very large inequalities. In Glogova: "Now the two
most notable categories of the population are the rich and the poor; the
differences are enormous." In Vares: "There are people who live super-
well, maybe 1 to 10 percent—the owners of cafés, for example—but the
vast majority are barely surviving, are barely making ends meet, and only
10 percent live normally." In Sarajevo: "There are very few who can ensure themselves a normal life with honest work, but there are many impoverished people living in fear of losing their crust of bread."

The War Is to Blame

"The war is the basic reason for the worsening of our situation," says
Nata, a Serb by nationality who is married to a Roma (gypsy) in Sarajevo. "My husband and sons were wounded but did not seek disability payments. You need a lot of papers and you have to pay. . . . Things are a
thousand times harder now than they were during the war. You can't earn
anything; there is no money, and no more humanitarian aid. Nothing."

Similarly, a discussion group participant in Zenica remarks,

*How can I not blame the war for all of this poverty? I had a
decent job, I was nearing retirement, my children had almost*

*completed their education—I was to have enjoyed the rest of
my life, and now look at what I'm doing. My children have
qualifications but they work in cafés as wait staff. My pension
is meager and I have to work to make some extra money. . . .
All my savings were melted by the war. I could have been happy
now, living a normal life.*

TABLE 1 Levels of Wellbeing, Four Discussion Groups in Mostar West

Discussion group	*Criteria*	*Percentage of households*
Middle-aged and younger women	**Very rich** Politicians; owners and directors of large firms criminals; returnees from abroad (Western countries).	10–20%
	Poor Everyone who survives on a salary, pension, or social assistance.	80–90%
Older women, pensioners, widows of former military officers	**Rich** Have material stability and comfort; employed. Own a house or apartment. Healthy, and have healthy families.	10–20%
	Poor Unemployed; pensioners: refugees/displaced people. No health insurance.	80–90%
Young, mixed gender	**Upper class** Have two or three expensive cars, a house and an apartment. Privileged children. Completely secure existence.	20%
	Lower class Have income of KM 300–400, insecure housing, no social or health insurance. Cannot afford vacations.	80%
Ethnically mixed younger couples	**Rich** Those with good, secure employment; profiteers. Have health insurance, house, apartment, family property.	5%
	Poor Those with irregular and insecure income, and the unemployed. Poor housing, no health insurance. Fear of not being able to pay bills.	95%

Unemployment and the Collapse of Industry

Before the war, the entire economy of Bosnia and Herzegovina underwent wrenching changes as Yugoslavia moved away from socialism and began to fracture from political, ethnic, and economic stress. Inflation reached 2,000 percent in 1989, eroding the purchasing power of wages. Efforts to privatize state enterprises began in 1990 and were still incomplete when the war broke out. Most industry shut down during the war; production dropped to between 5 and 10 percent of the prewar level.

Although difficult economic changes preceded the war, study participants widely consider the war to be the immediate cause of the economic turmoil they now face. According to a discussion group participant in Sarajevo, "Before the war, it was not like this; anyone who wanted could find work. But now everyone is scrambling to keep their job." Registered unemployment reached 37 percent in the Federation and 36 percent in Republika Srpska in 1998.[5]

A mine and a 100-year-old steel factory tower over the road leading into Vares. "Vares used to be an industrial town, and now there is no industry," says a discussion group participant there. Before 1991 the steel factory and mine employed 3,000 residents. One recalls, "When the steelworks were operating, the workers would head home at 3 P.M. It was an impressive sight, a river of people; literally thousands would walk up the main street."

The economy of Vares crashed before the war, and the steelworks closed in 1991. "When the steelworks stopped working," a resident says, "the economic status of the entire city changed because 70 percent of the population depended on the steel plant. That had a big impact, and now, after the war, the effects of this are magnified." A timber processing plant employed 320 before the war, but while 180 people are still on the books, only about fifty work in that plant now. The mine currently employs only seventy people.

In other communities, the destruction and chaos of the war left many industrial plants shelled and equipment looted. As a participant from Capljina describes,

> In the war everything that was of any worth was stolen. In the
> factory where I worked almost everything was new. The war
> had not even started and the Serbs took everything. Then our
> own criminals took what was left. It was this way everywhere.

Now people do not have work, and the few who do work do not have salaries. Everything will fall apart. Nobody will invest here when they see what it is like.

Agricultural resources throughout the country also suffered during the war. In rural areas, farming now sustains many who used to work in industry. For example, about half the residents of Zeljeznik (mostly men) worked in the factories of Sekovici, but now subsistence agriculture sustains over 90 percent of the community.

The Displaced: Seeking House and Home

More than half the population of Bosnia and Herzegovina was displaced during the war. Many people were still in refugee camps at the time of the study, unable to find work and waiting to return to something resembling a normal existence. For some people in the three camps visited by researchers, it seemed that day would never come. Since the study, displaced people and refugees have returned at a higher rate.

Organizing in Glogova

The small village of Glogova lies outside the town of Bratunac and has a collective center (camp) for displaced Serbs in the Republika Srpska. Glogova is the only study community where the majority of inhabitants are displaced people. Glogova's prefabricated buildings house 100 families who left central Bosnia as a group. When they left their homes in 1993, they traveled first to Banja Luka. A resident of Glogova recalls, "When we came to Banja Luka by bus they told us we would be temporarily housed in a collective center and that they would soon find us decent accommodation. That has taken a little longer than they expected. Here I still am today."

Residents set up a system of self-administration with a president, vice president, and in-camp social service; the camp is neat and orderly. Despite their efforts and the promises of many potential donors, only in 1998 did residents receive water and electricity. "When we got electricity and water there was nobody in the world happier—nor at the same time as bitter—as we were," says another discussion group participant. "For five years, nobody thought to help us. Our children threw stones at the light bulbs because they didn't know what an electric light was."

Another displaced woman, Milena, says her children completed secondary school while at the camp, and they are now unemployed. "I dreamed of sending them to the university so they could be somebody, but I am afraid that secondary school is as far as they can go," she says. She is a chemical technician by training and her husband is an economist. Now, her husband and other men from the camp cross the border to Serbia to work as farmhands or construction laborers, earning 10 convertible marks (about US$5.50 at the time of the study) for twelve hours of work. Milena recalls, "I left behind twenty-two silk blouses and a heap of lovely clothes and shoes. Now I wear someone else's torn tracksuit."

Branko, 53, says, "Before the war, I lived like a lord. I worked in the military industry in Bugojno and had a really good salary. My wife never worked . . . I worked and earned enough for the whole family." Now his wife and daughters collect snails or mushrooms to sell in Bratunac.

Squalor in Tombak

The deteriorating old buildings of Tombak contrast sharply with the buildings of Glogova. Tombak is one of the oldest neighborhoods in the city of Bijeljina. Gypsies lived there before the war; now it is filled with 250 to 300 displaced Serbs. Paint is peeling, roofs are caving in, and windows are broken and patched with boards. Rubbish litters the narrow streets, as it did before the war. Running water and electricity are available, but there is no sewerage.

Before the war, most people in Bijeljina were Bosniac, but now the vast majority are Serbs. Ibro, 64, is an exception. Ibro is Bosniac, born and raised in Bijeljina. In 1993 the Serbs forced him and his wife, Fatima, out of their house in the center of the city. "When they forced us out we had nowhere to go. Some friends told us that here in Tombak there were empty houses. Even if my wife and I were disgusted by this settlement, we were happy because at least we had somewhere to sleep . . . We live on my pension and on what the children send."

Ibro's former house is only about 500 meters from where he and his wife live now, but he avoids passing by. He says,

> When I look at everything, it pains me. All of the life and love
> I invested while I was building it. I see that the people living

there are not taking care of it. Well, they figure it is not theirs. Will I ever enter my own house again or not? I don't know. The way this state is, it seems to me that it will never be.

Displaced People in Capljina

Stipe is a displaced Croat man living in a camp outside Capljina in the Federation. He holds no hope of returning to his home in Jablanica. "I will try to exchange my house in Jablanica with someone from Capljina or the surrounding area who is now living in Jablanica," he says. He and his relatives were forced out of Jablanica during the Muslim-Croat conflict of 1993–94. Formerly Capljina was composed of 52 percent Croats, 40 percent Muslims, and 8 percent Serbs, but now it is almost entirely Croat. He and his wife live with about twenty-five other families in a camp of prefabricated houses outside Capljina. They live on humanitarian aid and occasional part-time work in the greenhouses or construction sites nearby.

Zlata is a retired Croat woman who was forced out of the industrial town of Vares, waited out the war in a refugee camp in a high school gym, and has since returned. During the war, first the Croat army and then the army of Bosnia and Herzegovina occupied Vares, and the town therefore received successive waves of refugees. Many Croats like Zlata tried to return to their homes in 1995 or 1996 but found them inhabited by displaced Bosniacs. Zlata has been trying since April 1996 to get her apartment back. Her family was one of the old families of Vares, but Zlata's siblings and their children did not return to the town. She explains, "I am a displaced person in my own city. I don't have anyone left here. I never married, so I am completely alone. Anyway, I don't care about me; what upsets me is the way young people have to live. I was born here and I will die here. I am just counting the days."

Struggling to Cope

The battle for survival has transformed the people of Bosnia and Herzegovina. Strained social ties, including in gender relations, have reduced trust among people. Men and women relate to each other on new terms, as the war and harsh economic circumstances have drastically altered gender roles. For various reasons, women in Bosnia have been thrust into assuming both breadwinner and caretaker responsibilities for their households, and they are doing this with far fewer public supports than they enjoyed under communism. Men, meanwhile, are struggling with unemployment and alcohol abuse, and domestic violence against women is reported to be a problem in every community visited. The hardships of life in Bosnia and Herzegovina have also dashed the dreams and aspirations of young people, and most see little hope but to migrate.

New Roles for Women and Men

A middle-aged man in Sarajevo points out, "In the war, a soldier's wife had to care for the family and collect wood. She had to be both male and female. . . . Women in the war really were heroes." Likewise, a man in Zenica comments, "Women suffered in this war; you go to the frontline and she is left to care and worry about the kids."

In the postwar period, many women continue to shoulder a heavy work burden both in and outside the home. Despite their new responsibilities, however, poor women do not perceive that they are gaining greater authority over household decisions or increased protection from domestic violence. Men express similar views about persisting gender inequalities.

Before the war, both Kosana and her husband worked in the metal factory in Sekovici, and they also tended their land and animals in the village of Zeljeznik. Kosana's husband became an invalid in the war, and now Kosana must support her husband and two children. She says,

> I started to work twice as much on the land so that I could manage to produce some to sell—I sell milk, cheese, cream, but it is all very little. The money leaves the house far more easily than it makes its way in. The children always need textbooks or sneakers. . . . I buy my husband medication every seven days as with every change in the weather he is struck down with pain. I am lucky he has not started to drink the way others do.

In Sekovici, people report that heavier workloads are not the only reason life is much harder for women. Many public services that women relied upon before the war are no longer available or have become unaffordable; these include health care, social benefits, child benefits, maternity leave, and advisory and support services. A particularly high number of war widows live in Tisca, and many are bitter that they receive scant help from the state. "Our husbands gave their lives for this state," remarks one woman. "They gave what is most valuable, but all of the victims were soon forgotten. Now our alternative is to become whores and prostitutes—that is the only way that we could earn enough for a normal existence."

Men also are struggling to cope with difficult memories and dramatic changes in their lives. "I lived through some terrible things in the war, which I prefer not to talk about because I do not like to burden others," says a 30-year-old man from Zenica who was wounded. In addition to being traumatized by their war experiences, many men express anger and depression over the lack of jobs for them. A displaced man in Tombak relates, "Before the war I couldn't imagine not getting up at six, shaving, dressing, and going to work. For eight years now my ties have hung on the door, for eight years I have not gone to work. This is killing me; I feel useless to myself and my family." A woman from Zenica says, "Now that the men are not going to work, they just sit at home. . . . It is harder for him not working. Women always find themselves something to do in the house." A woman in Capljina agrees, "The thing I would like most is for my husband to find a permanent job, any kind of work. The worst is not doing anything."

Violence in the Home

To escape depression, many men seem to be turning to alcohol. A woman in Sarajevo says, "The little bit of income that is earned, if you don't hide it, he drinks it away. But what can you do? Life goes on. You sit in the corner and cry." Poor men and women also report with great frequency that drunkenness often leads to domestic violence against women. "Under the influence of alcohol a man puts his wife in second place. He spends the money and sometime he beats his wife or abuses the children. This creates enormous insecurity and fear in a woman," says a participant in Tombak.

The level of domestic violence is higher than or the same as before the war, according to many discussion groups. In explaining the abuse, people often refer to economic and alcohol problems as well as to long-standing social norms that condone violence against women. In the Serbian village of Sekovici, for instance, discussion group participants report little change over the last ten years in women's decision-making roles in the household or in the incidence of domestic violence against them. Reflecting on trends in levels of violence, a young woman from Sekovici observes, "I cannot say whether men beat their wives more in the war than now, but I personally know individuals who beat their wives when they come home drunk, and sometimes they beat the children. That is something that has always existed and always will." Similarly, a woman in Mostar West associates domestic violence with traditional norms, many of which are particularly prevalent in village life:

> There is violence, even in marriages. Still, it depends on individual people; people are different. There are the urban folk, and there are the newcomers [dosle—a derogatory term] from the villages who consider wives to be a necessary evil, existing just to cook, clean, and bear children.

According to many, deepening poverty also fuels violence. One person in Sarajevo explains, "Children are hungry, so they start to cry. They ask for food from their mother and their mother doesn't have it. Then the father is irritated because the children are crying, and he takes it out on his wife."

Young People Lose Hope

Nenad, 23, lives in a refugee camp in Glogova. He works with his father as a day laborer. Nenad has a few friends in the camp, but he laments their lack of social opportunities: "Nobody wants to hang out with us because we don't wear good sneakers or name-brand tracksuits, have a lot of money, drive a good car. . . . I cannot even have a girlfriend because I cannot afford to take her out to a café for a drink, let alone out for pizza." A young person in Vares says, "We have no entertainment because we have no money. It is very sad that our parents don't have any money to give us, it makes them sad and they say they would gladly give us money if they had any. I am afraid to have any hope."

Adults across Bosnia and Herzegovina express sympathy for the plight of the young people. In Vares a participant says, "Young people are only here because they have nowhere else to go. . . . Young people cannot survive here, not psychologically or materially. This society kills you."

Many feel pressure to migrate. "My personal opinion is that if I do not enroll in the university course I want, I will leave here and go to Sweden. . . . Here, even with qualifications you cannot do anything. Look at the example of this young man who is a mechanical engineer; he works as a waiter in a café," remarks a young Vares man. Similarly, Goran, a 19-year-old man also from Vares, works five hours a day, seven days a week in a video store, but he works "on the black," that is, he is not legally registered as employed. On Saturdays he works as a bouncer at a local club. He alone supports his mother and younger sister and brother. In the future he hopes "to escape from here and go abroad," as do the majority of his peers.

Nowhere to Turn

Poor men and women in Bosnia and Herzegovina are angry. Rada, a retired chef living among displaced people in Tombak, says,

> I live in this misery and poverty, and I really do not care for living anymore. Sometimes when I awake in the morning I wish I would never wake up. Look at what the evil ones have done to us. We are a good people, we never hated each other, but the politicians got between us. May they rot in hell!

Before the war Nina lived comfortably in a small apartment on her pension. Now her pension is only KM 29 (about US$16) per month, and even with the help she gets from her sister and brother-in-law in Serbia, she cannot make ends meet. Nina condemns the politicians for the war. She also calls them criminals and blames them for the corruption that now reigns. Others direct their anger not only toward politicians, but also toward war profiteers and returnees from abroad.

The Failure of State Institutions

A woman from Sarajevo says, "In essence, we don't have help from anybody. We help ourselves. If we don't have anything to wear, we find something through family or the neighbors. I don't trust any state institutions." Across discussion groups, poor people agree that they cannot count on the state. While a handful of relief organizations are cited positively, most study participants emphasize that they rely almost solely on family, especially family members abroad who send money.

A participant in Glogova says, "The war is to blame for what we are now, and after that, this incompetent government." There is universal agreement among the discussion groups that state institutions are ineffective, and there is intense frustration with politicians, especially those who are also involved in businesses and take advantage of people's desperate situations. "There is no state, there are only individuals who are using the chance to get rich in the name of the state," maintains a young man from Capljina.

Similarly, a discussion group participant in Sarajevo says, "The role of the state is almost nonexistent. Before it was much better and more secure. Now it asks everything of you, but gives you nothing. Things have returned to peacetime, but still they give you nothing." In Zenica a participant says, "Institutions, ha! What institutions? When there is no state, there is nothing else. . . . This state is in the embryonic stage. The institutions cannot deal with the complexity and volume of requests."

Poor people are particularly discouraged by the lack of support from the municipality. According to a participant from Zenica, "It is hard to get to the right person in the municipality, and when you do he says, 'I'm sorry I am not able to help you.'" Another participant in Zenica concurs, saying, "The people from the municipality are constantly coming and writing things on papers. But nothing ever comes of it." According to a single mother living with her parents in Zenica, "The only people that you can rely on are your family. The documents and paperwork you need [for social assistance] are more expensive than the value of the help it would get you."

Discussion groups in Zenica mention repeatedly that in order to get assistance from the government, one needs good connections and money to pay bribes: "Everything here is done through contacts," says one person. Another adds, "Only if you have someone of your own . . . a cousin, uncle, close friend—and money plays a big part."

In addition, many services that were provided under the socialist regime are no longer free of charge, and this puts an extra burden on poor people. Unaffordable fees and expectations of bribes deter many poor people even from seeking services. A participant in Vares says, "Before, everyone could get health care, but now everyone just prays to God that they don't get sick because everywhere they just ask for money." According to a discussion group participant in Sekovici,

If you need the doctor, you have to pay. If you need the police and want them to react, you have to give the policeman something. If you need the courts, you have to pay for even the smallest service. Social services and health care are truly at rock

bottom. You have to pay for everything—water, electricity. Everything has changed for the worse. A person has nowhere to turn, and if he does he has to be ready to pay.

In Zenica participants worry about the quality of health care and say that "now you can't go to the doctor because you need money. Where to get the money?"

Business Owners, War Profiteers, and Returnees

Participants also had few good words for the role of the private sector in their lives, and they relate many stories of exploitation, corruption, nepotism, and abuse. As seen below, interviews with several entrepreneurs and employers who have managed to do well in the current economy largely confirm these problems. Participants also comment openly about the intense resentment toward war profiteers and returnees who escaped the war and are now running successful businesses (box 1).

Study participants often refer to wealthy people and business owners as "war profiteers." Quite often returnees who have come back with money to open businesses are also lumped into this category. A poor man from Sarajevo defines war profiteers as those "who used the carelessness of the state to become wealthy at the state's expense in various ways." A war widow from Tisca argues bitterly that "the wealthy are those who never went to war, those who did not lose anything, but rather just grabbed as much as they could during the war from those who had paid with sweat and blood for everything they had."

BOX 1 Resentment of War Profiteers

"Those who were not in the trenches got rich in black-market trade or in politics over the backs of the ordinary people."

—A discussion group participant, Tombak

"We were fighting the Bosniacs while [war profiteers] were buying chocolates and biscuits from them. I would kill the lot of them."

—A Serbian man, Bijeljina

"Before the war it was absurd that a politician or functionary owned a gas station, restaurant, casino, building material yard, or such. Now this is completely normal!"

—A discussion group participant, Glogova

With the collapse of state industries, private businesses now offer many of the current jobs to be had, but poor people say that they prefer state jobs to jobs in the private sector. A participant from Zenica remarks, "Private business people exploit workers for small salaries." A young woman in Capljina says, "Now all the private business owners employ only their own relatives. There are no state jobs any more."

The demise of large enterprises in Bosnia has also weakened the role of trade unions, and there is now no means to negotiate for better wages and benefits. Discussion groups from Zenica explain that trade unions used to play an important role before the war, but that has changed, and only two discussion groups even mention unions on their lists of relevant institutions. "In my firm there is no trade union presence at all. Trade unions exist, but they do very little and are essentially ineffective," reports a poor person in Zenica. In Sarajevo a participant says, "Before the war, people cared. There were the trade unions and the firms, and now there is no one to help."

Slavojka, a cake shop owner from Zeljeznik, says that others call her a war profiteer, but she disagrees, though she acknowledges that her business in Sekovici did very well during the war and now she considers herself to be fairly wealthy. "That was the first cake shop ever in Sekovici! I had the good sense and fortune to start with that enterprise." Initially a friend worked for free to help Slavojka make the cakes, but later Slavojka paid her. "Her pay was not large, but enough to shut her mouth about how I was getting rich off her back."

The role of special connections in obtaining jobs and keeping businesses running emerges frequently in interviews with those who have become better off since the end of the war. Ljubo is from Sekovici. Before the war he ran a small café-bar in Sekovici, and he lived simply. "I made just enough for food, to pay bills, and to take my wife out every once in a while," he says. But he prospered during the war years and renovated his bar several times. He explains, "With the start of the war and the arrival of the army in Sekovici, the consumption and sale of alcohol was banned. But since I am a local and a personal friend of the commanders of the army and police, I sold alcohol in my bar the entire time." Ljubo then built a big house with a large garage and a garden. "Before the war I was an average citizen, like most people here, but now I am rich—I have everything. Even though my bar does not work with the same intensity as during the war, I really can't complain."

Edin is a 31-year-old man who left Zenica for Germany in 1992. "At the end of 1992, I went to Germany so that I would not be mobilized.

There I worked in cafés, discos, and restaurants." He met his wife—who is also from Zenica—in a German restaurant. Her father had started a private business back home, and after they married, they returned to Zenica and went into business with her father. "We started with one café and a video store, and after that we opened a boutique." He credits his success to luck and hard work, but he regrets that his prewar friends do not look at him the way they used to.

Although some money is brought back into the economy as refugees return from abroad, it is not enough to salvage strained relations between returnees and those who stayed at home during the war. A poor man in Mostar West says,

> I have awards and medals for my participation in the war, but the problem is that I cannot eat them. When I was good enough to shoot at someone, they would pat me on the back. But now there is no place for me. People come back from Germany, they buy themselves a job, and I am supposed to wait.

An old woman from Sarajevo says, "Things are much better for them as they have been given houses because they are returnees. They have brought back all sorts of things, cars, money, other goods, and then they tease us." And in Zenica a poor man tells researchers, "I stand there for hours waiting for the returnee from Germany to pay me 20 convertible marks to work all day. . . . We fought for this country, and there we wait like animals hoping to earn something to feed our families."

Humanitarian Aid Falters

While most express disillusionment with nongovernmental aid agencies, some participants report that humanitarian aid did come through for them, particularly during the war. Now, however, much of that assistance has dried up, although for many it is still very much needed.

An old woman in Glogova says, "The Red Cross is the only organization we got something from concretely, unlike the other organizations, and that is why we trust them." A participant in Sekovici concurs, "Only the Red Cross gave us flour, sugar, and oil. That is the only institution that has helped us in these years of misery." Although it sometimes receives mixed reviews, participants generally speak highly of Caritas, a Catholic relief organization.

One refugee camp in Glogova appealed to many aid agencies with little success. A resident of the camp says, "A thousand times I met with various foreign organizations and government organizations. They promised all sorts of things. And what have we received until now? One big fat nothing." However, another participant in Glogova notes, "The French helped us bring water into the camp . . . They paid us three convertible marks a day to dig ditches. Everyone worked then, even the children. The state did not bat an eye."

In Sarajevo a participant says, "International organizations operate through the municipalities, but the people [who work for] the municipality keep everything for themselves. An Italian organization donated bathroom fixtures, but no one who needed them got them, only some crumbs." Another person there says, "The municipality received 40,000 convertible marks to fix people's homes, and they took it all for themselves. . . . What they were supposed to hand out to people, they took for themselves and sold later."

Relying on Relatives Near and Far

With nowhere else to turn, study participants all over Bosnia and Herzegovina say they must count heavily on family and sometimes friends to survive. Eight discussion groups in Zenica identified and ranked local institutions that are important in their daily lives; all the groups but one ranked family at the top. "Parents will always help their children, children will always help their parents," says a study participant from Sarajevo. The remaining discussion group, which consisted of unemployed steelworkers, ranked family second to friends.

Although they trust friends, poor people say it is often difficult to ask their friends for help because they, too, are struggling. "The relations between people have changed," says a discussion group participant in Zenica. "When you go to visit someone you have to think hard what to say, or you don't know whether they have anything to eat that day. Depression catches hold of you, you wonder how you will manage tomorrow."

More striking, perhaps, is the fact that most participants whom researchers spoke with receive some help from relatives abroad. A participant from Sarajevo says simply, "If my relatives abroad did not help, we could not get by." Similarly, a displaced Serbian man says, "If it weren't for some relatives in Australia who send me 200 to 300 convertible marks every three months, I would have died of hunger by now." Another poor person in Sarajevo comments, "I have a sister abroad and she buys clothes for my children and sometimes she sends money. People who have no one abroad have to make do with what they get."

Conclusion

The intense emotional, physical, and economic disturbance of the war and postwar period has taken an immense toll on the outlook of those in Bosnia and Herzegovina. In Vares researchers heard the same sentiment from both an old woman and a young girl: "Hope dies last, but for me, even hope has died."

Rebuilding hope across the communities visited in Bosnia and Herzegovina requires that urgent governance issues be addressed to ensure that services reach poor people and that there is a stable environment for private investment. Hope is particularly tied to recovering jobs and housing, two losses that have impoverished huge portions of the population. In Glogova researchers heard, "If we had a real roof over our heads and a job, then maybe we could live normal lives, even if we had to work from morning until tomorrow." In Zenica a participant believes, "If people could work, everything would be different and things would go back to the way they were." Similarly, in Sarajevo a participant says, "I still believe something will change in the future, when the factories start, when one can get a job, when money is invested in industry."

Poor men and women everywhere in the study feel the government could do more to help them heal from the war and recover some of their losses. A participant from Zenica says, "The government could do something, but they do nothing. Take the steelworks as an example. If they were to fix it, 20,000 people would return to work, but instead of that they build religious objects." In Vares another person says, "Those in the municipality care only about their salaries and themselves, and not at all about others."

Zlatko is a gaunt and restless young man. He and his wife and baby live with his mother in Zenica. "I would place myself on the lowest rung of the ladder; there is no way there can be any lower," he says. He has been unable to find a permanent job but works as a day laborer when he can. "I still have hope in life," he insists. "My goal is a modest job and to be surrounded by people dear to me. When there is work, I work, and when there is not, we struggle to survive. During the war I turned to others for help, but now I rely only on myself." Of the future he says, "It has to get better, surely."

TABLE 2 Study Communities in Bosnia and Herzegovina

FEDERATION OF BOSNIA AND HERZEGOVINA (BOSNIAC AND CROAT)

Capljina Pop. 8,500	This agricultural town near Mostar is known for fruit and tobacco production. The town did not suffer much damage during the war and is currently very clean and well kept. Before the war, the population was a mix of Croats (52 percent), Bosniacs (40 percent), and Serbs (8 percent). Now the inhabitants are Croat, and 40 percent are displaced people from other areas. Discussion groups were held both in the town and in a refugee camp of displaced people from central Bosnia a few kilometers outside of town. The camp consists of small prefabricated buildings surrounded by rubbish.
Mostar West Pop. 10,000	The entire city of Mostar had a prewar population of 76,000. Today Mostar East is dominated by Bosniacs, and Mostar West by Croats. Many parts of the city were destroyed in the war, and the effects of heavy shelling are still visible. The city remains deeply divided along ethnic lines. Discussion groups were conducted in four communities around the Croat-dominated Mostar West, including a special group of ethnically mixed couples.
Sarajevo Pop. 400,000	The capital and most populous city in Bosnia and Herzegovina, Sarajevo was the scene of heavy shelling and severe destruction during the war, including the destruction of heavy industry. Discussion groups were held in four communities in the city: Gorica, a Roma (gypsy) settlement of both returnees and people who remained during the war; Marin Dvor, home to ten households that have no sewerage or indoor plumbing; Soukbunar, one of the most populous neighborhoods and one highly exposed to fighting; and Vogosca, where Bosniacs were expelled and have since returned.
Vares Pop. 8,800	This industrial town suffered an economic crash after the steel industry and mines closed in 1991. There are now two industries providing some employment: a timber processing plant and a spare-parts factory. Despite the predominantly working-class and heavily industrial character of the city, it has the highest proportion of university graduates per capita in Bosnia. It was alternately dominated by Croats and then Bosniacs during the Bosniac-Croat conflict in 1993–94. Researchers spoke with a special discussion group of Croat returnees.

Zenica Pop. 96,000	Before the war, Zenica was the fourth largest city and among the most industrialized in Bosnia and Herzegovina. The steel-works and associated industries employed 38,000 people. During the war, Zenica was not as heavily bombed as other cities, so an estimated 50,000 refugees fled to its comparative safety. Research was conducted in four communities around the city, with one of the discussion groups consisting of laid-off steelworkers.

EPUBLIKA SRPSKA (SERB)

Bratunac and Glogova Pop. 100 households	Bratunac is a municipality located near the Montenegro border; Glogova is three kilometers outside the town. There is a camp for Serb refugees and displaced persons in Glogova. The camp consists of approximately 100 small prefabricated buildings, with one family per house. Until November 1998, the camp was without water and electricity. Most of the families are from central Bosnia and left there in 1993. Among them are several highly educated people, including men who were employed in the military industry.
isca and Zeljeznik, Sekovici Pop. 230 households	These two rural Serbian villages are in eastern Republika Srpska, in the municipality of Sekovici. Few people left during the war, and there are no refugees or displaced people; however, much of the male population was actively fighting. Both villages are entirely made up of Serbian Orthodox residents. Tisca, which is nine kilometers away from Sekovici, has no health center or police station, although there is a primary school, a Serbian Orthodox church, and a gas pump used only for military vehicles. Zeljeznik is only two kilometers away from Sekovici; it has no school and no health center. A special discussion group of war widows was held in Zeljeznik.

REPUBLIKA SRPSKA (SERB) (continued)

Tombak,
Bijeljina
Pop. 250–300

Bijeljina municipality consists of an urban area surrounded by villages. Before the war, primarily Bosniacs lived within the city, while the surrounding area was mixed Serb and Bosniac. Now the area is mainly Serb. Within the city, one of the best known and oldest settlements is Tombak, located beside two better-off areas. Before the war, it was a Roma settlement, but almost all the current population are displaced people from the Federation. The special group here consisted of unemployed male war invalids.

Notes

1. The study team was led by Dino Djipa, Mirsada Muzur, and Paula Franklin Lytle, and also included Dado Babic, Vesna Bodirogic, Sanja Djermanovic, Faud Hegic, Milos Karisik, Maida Koso, Elma Pasic, Marko Romic, and Mladen Vidovick.

2. *Bosnian* includes all the ethnic groups living in the country, whereas *Bosniac* is the preferred term for Muslims of Bosnian citizenship.

3. Phones, roads, and water service in urban areas had regained more than 90 percent of their prewar capacity by 1998, and power service was at 73 percent. Primary enrollment in schools was higher than before the war. See World Bank, "Bosnia and Herzegovina, 1996–1998, Lessons and Accomplishments: Review of the Priority Reconstruction Program and Looking Ahead Towards Sustainable Economic Development" (Report 19632, prepared for the May 1999 Donors Conference co-hosted by the European Commission and the World Bank), 2.

4. World Bank, "Memorandum of the President of the International Development Association to the Executive Directors on a Country Assistance Strategy of the World Bank Group for Bosnia and Herzegovina" (Southeast Europe Country Unit, Europe and Central Asia Region, June 14, 2000 , 3–4.

5. Ibid., 4.

Bulgaria

Reeling from Change

Petya Kabakchieva, Iliia Illiev, and Yulian Konstantinov[1]

Milena is 35 years old, divorced, and the mother of one child. She lives with her parents in Jugen, one of the six municipalities of the southern city of Plovdiv. Milena graduated from a technical secondary school in 1982 and immediately found a job at a chemical plant. After a few months she was shifted to an administrative position. She married soon after and had a son. She and her husband used their own savings and money from their parents to buy an apartment.

In 1991 the director of the chemical company reduced administrative staff to lower production costs. Milena was offered a chance to return to the production unit, but she declined. "We had to deal with all sorts of chemical poisons. I saw how the men working there were passing away one after the other," she says. She also observed that the economy was changing and that "nobody could survive on the salary," so she looked for new opportunities.

Milena retrained as a waitress and was immediately employed in a prestigious restaurant where the staff earned large tips. "People had more money then," she says. Three and a half years later she was fired and replaced by a 17-year-old girl at a lower salary. "This was a child right from school, still living with her parents. She would accept any pay. For her it was like pocket money—she had a room and food at her parents' apartment."

During the next three years, Milena found temporary jobs as a waitress and shop assistant, working overtime for even lower wages than she received at the chemical plant. For the past year and a half she has not held any job, and feels disadvantaged in the job market because she is no longer in her twenties. "Each time, the owner looks at me and says, 'OK.

239

we'll see, I'll call you next week.' Then he looks at my passport, sees my birth date, takes another look at me and says, 'Sorry, it's not your fault. The fault is on the second page of your passport.'"

Milena was divorced a year and a half ago after her husband began complaining that she would not accept low-paying employment. "He kept protesting all day long, 'Look, so-and-so has found a job as a cleaning woman. She is cleaning lavatories. Why don't you accept the same?'" He also accused her of being less diligent at housekeeping than she should have been, and Milena admits he was somewhat justified. Milena often spent long hours smoking, chatting, and drinking coffee with her friends, most of whom were also unemployed:

> *The more things you have to do, the more things you do. And when you are unemployed you can't do anything. When I stay half an hour at home, I start to say to myself, "Milena, why are you staying at home like this, as if everything is all right with you? Stand up, do something." So I go to see my friends. Other days I can't do anything—I start one thing, then I leave it half done and start another one, so I end up doing nothing.*

After the divorce, her husband married a colleague. Milena and her son moved to her parents' house and rent out the apartment. In addition to this income, Milena receives social assistance benefits. Her parents have a small garden in their yard, which produces enough vegetables for the household. Milena continues to look for a new job as a waitress or shop assistant. She says, "I'm not that old. Tell me, do I look thirty-five?"

Almost a decade after democracy and privatization were supposed to deliver undreamed-of advances, life in today's Bulgaria is marked by massive unemployment and disillusionment. Disappointment and low expectations pervade conversations with many men and women in the nine poor communities visited for this study.

Bulgaria entered a turbulent period of political and economic change when communist rule ended in 1989. The country's leadership changed hands six times before 1997. That year a political crisis, marked by month-long street demonstrations, was sparked by public dissatisfaction with poor governance and 200 percent inflation. The electorate forced the Bulgarian Socialist Party government to resign. A center-right government took over and stepped up free-market reforms and opened up Bulgarian industries to foreign investment. Despite macroeconomic stabilization and growth, lack of tangible improvement in living standards for many in the country paved the way for another change in government in June 2001.

On the economic front, Bulgaria's failure to move ahead with reforms after an initial surge in 1991 left the country behind other transitioning nations in Central and Eastern Europe. The previous system had been dismantled, but the transition to a market economy proceeded haltingly in the face of political discord, high taxes and inflation, restricted access to credit, and legal insecurity. Gross domestic product dropped at an average annual rate of 2.7 percent between 1990 and 1997, and then grew at an average annual rate of 4.5 percent between 1998 and 2000.[2] Per capita GDP for the country's roughly 8 million people plummeted from US$2,260 to $1,380 over the course of the decade.

Spurred by the requirements for membership in the European Union, radical reforms were introduced in 1997. The government achieved financial stabilization through the introduction of a currency board arrangement. Other policies included accelerated privatization, liquidation of unprofitable state-owned enterprises, price liberalization, and increased labor market flexibility. In parallel, major social reforms were initiated, including introduction of a multi-pillar pension system, new health care and health insurance programs, and an overhaul of safety net and child welfare assistance. Poverty and unemployment remain pressing issues, however. In 1995, 18.2 percent of Bulgaria's population lived below the international poverty line of $4.30 a day [3]

To find out how poor people are coping, researchers visited three villages, three small towns, and three cities in Bulgaria (see table 1, Study Communities in Bulgaria, at the end of this chapter). The selection of particular communities was based on recent poverty surveys and on criteria for geographic and ethnic diversity. Poor participants were identified with the help of ministry officials, local welfare offices (which supplied lists of welfare recipients), the mayor of Kalofer, and the Center for Independent Life, an NGO that works with disabled people. Once present in a community, researchers also worked with residents to identify poor people. Study participants included retired people; young people; single mothers; members of large families; members of the Roma (Gypsy) and Bulgarian Turkish ethnic minorities, as well as Bulgarian Muslims; children in state institutions; people with disabilities; and the unemployed. Additional discussions were held with rich people and with working people of average means to explore how perceptions of poverty vary among social groups. The study team also met with three special groups: Roma heroin users in Varna, nurses in Sofia, and homeless people in Sofia.

The study team spent a minimum of six days in March and April 1999 in each of the communities, often returning to the communities after completing the main fieldwork to cross-check the findings with study participants. A total of 121 discussion groups were conducted. Mini–case studies of people's lives were gathered from fifty-four individuals, including twenty-four men, twenty-two women, and eight youths.

Poor people's reports about their current lives and past experiences were often very intense and emotional. Their views are shaped not only by rocketing increases in unemployment in their communities, but also by the loss of many state services and benefits that brought security to their lives, as well as by the humiliation and loss of status that accompanies a fall into poverty. They describe a new world full of fears and strife, and often contrast this with easier times that they remember and long for.

This chapter opens with a look at the large slide in living standards that most Bulgarians experienced in the 1990s. The study then examines the effects of the economic transition on disadvantaged children and ethnic minorities. Next, the chapter highlights the growth of subsistence agriculture, the informal economy, and other coping mechanisms of poor Bulgarians. It then reviews people's heavy reliance on friends, relatives, colleagues, and neighbors, and their generally unfavorable assessments of elected officials and public services. The final section looks at the rising hardships faced by poor women in their homes, workplaces, and communities.

The Struggling Majority

Asked to describe a good life, most study participants mention economic, physical, and psychological security. "If you have money, that doesn't necessarily mean that you'll be happy. But if you don't have it, that certainly means that you won't be happy," says a woman in Etropole. Other material dimensions of wellbeing include adequate food, clothing (especially shoes), and living conditions. Many of the groups stress that wellbeing and wealth are not synonymous, and no one in the study expressed a desire to be wealthy. "You might be poor and still live well because wellbeing depends on other things," say men and women in

Sofia. "The rich live in constant fear because that's how the times are—everybody's trying to poke out everybody else's eyes," says a student from an institution in Dimitrovgrad for mentally retarded and orphaned children. Security also comes from good health, the ability to pursue intellectual interests, satisfying relationships with family and friends, professional fulfillment, the respect of the community, and social cohesion—described by a Roma youth as "common understanding." Above all, as a man in Razgrad puts it, wellbeing is "to know what will happen with me tomorrow."

Few people can live such a life now. In a society in which most people formerly considered themselves equal, many groups now identify five or six wellbeing categories in their communities: *very rich, rich, normal, struggling, extremely poor,* and *those who have fallen out.* Discussion groups from the various study communities generally classify the very rich and rich as comprising 1 to 5 percent of their communities, and another 5 to 10 percent of the population is typically classified as "living normally," or as middle-class. There is no consensus among the discussion groups, however, on the distribution of the remaining wellbeing categories. Those who are struggling or "doing poorly" are said to be the largest group, reaching 80 percent in some cases. Those who are "extremely poor," "desperate," "destitute," or "living in misery," make up 5 to 30 percent. At the lowest end of the scale, the fallen out comprise 1 to 5 percent.

A few *very rich* own private firms and enterprises and have wealth, power, and freedom. Poor people in the study express deep suspicions of this group, often scorning them as people who have been unscrupulous in their climb to the top. The participants question the speed with which many became wealthy, and some suggest that the very rich may have been involved in laundering dirty money. Some also feel that this group's tremendous wealth goes against the strong egalitarian attitudes formed in the communist period. The *rich* are described more favorably as well-connected businessmen or government employees who have stable positions, relatively high salaries, and, according to a participant in Plovdiv, the security to "think of their spiritual interests."

Next comes a somewhat larger group who are considered to have a *normal* standard of living. They have well-paid, regular jobs, savings, and their own apartments, houses, or land. They can plan for the future and are fortunate enough, according to a group in Plovdiv, to "meet with friends and relatives, have a cup of coffee with women colleagues, or offer a glass of beer at the end of the day," or to be able to "afford the cost of a railway ticket to visit their relatives." This is the life to which most of the people in the study aspire, the life many say they left behind a decade ago.[4]

Most of the participants say that now they belong to the next, and largest, group—those who are *struggling* to make ends meet. Many can no longer afford social activities, savings, or new purchases, and they have to make considerable personal sacrifices. They are often described as "normal people" who are no longer able to live a "normal" life. In many cases, poverty in Bulgaria is discussed in the context of the strains that it places on family life, particularly on parents of very young and school-age children (box 1). A youth in a Sofia discussion group explains, "The problem of young families is very acute. . . . If you marry, you can't raise a child decently in small housing, living together with your parents." Similarly, young Roma men from Sofia report that they are "living in horrible conditions," with "no chance to get a better apartment" and that their children are "permanently ill." Poor men and women also describe increased conflict in family relations. "When parents can barely make ends meet and this leads to arguments, violence, and problems at home, this leaves a deep mark on the children, who turn to crime," states a pensioner from Sofia.

The *extremely poor* include large families with a single income, pensioners in poor health, unemployed people, and orphans. Many of these participants relate how they struggle to retain their dignity and sense of

---

BOX 1 Let the Children Be All Right

A Roma father wishes above all, "Let the children be all right." While children are partly valued for the help they provide to aging parents, nowadays many Bulgarian children expect to be supported by their parents well into their adulthood. Meeting the demands of children consumes a great deal of energy in economic hard times and a growing consumer culture. "A teenager is more expensive than a Mercedes now," says a resident of Plovdiv. Many parents from this city and elsewhere worry more about maintaining their children's status among their peers than about giving them better education or meeting household needs. Men report giving up smoking to pay for their children's social activities, and women say they are eating less to be able to buy them presentable clothes. A father in Plovdiv confides, "I feel ashamed if I cannot give my son [about 50 cents] each morning. He does not say anything when I don't. He comes home early and watches TV, but I know that his peers are together somewhere and I feel really bad. This is the thing that I fear most, even more than illness or death."

security even in desperate circumstances. An unemployed Plovdiv man relates an occasion when he was too ashamed to help himself to a "clean piece of bread" left on a garbage can: "I looked around and thought somebody will see me, and I left the bread just like that. I passed by a couple of hours later and the bun was not there anymore." A woman from Plovdiv says she is lonely and wasting away in her apartment, afraid to leave for fear her place will be robbed while she is out.

At the lowest end, according to participants in Plovdiv, are *those who have fallen out*, people reduced to scavenging or begging for food. Such people are considered the worst off because they have lost the respect of the community and face social exclusion

Unkept Promises

People in the study invariably relate rising inequalities to the end of the Zhivkov regime in 1989. The pre-1989 era is associated with job security and the ability to plan for the future despite commodity shortages and restricted movement. Most people had adequate living standards and security, say participants in Plovdiv, although there were a few rich and poor people then. "My bag was bursting every evening when I came home, bursting with food," says a woman in Plovdiv. Most Bulgarians had salaries, however modest, and managed after long years of saving to buy large appliances and apartments for children ready to leave home, and they enjoyed safety on the streets. "We were like everybody else," says a man in Etropole. "We had everything we needed, we had security, we were calm. At that time you had to be very lazy or a drunkard to remain poor. And there was solidarity. If you were in trouble there was always someone to help you."

In contrast, the past decade has brought unpredictable upswings and downswings. Participants associate large social changes with the coming of "democracy"—a word used pejoratively, especially by rural people, to refer to the collapse of law and order and a dramatic fall in living standards. All discussion groups portray the large population in the middle wellbeing category as having a much more difficult time since the fall of communism. People once had "paid leave, free medical services, including rehabilitation facilities, and when they recovered, they would find their jobs waiting for them, and their colleagues would even have prepared a welcome party," says a man in Plovdiv. But 'now a sudden illness will bring ruin to the family, and in the end you will be fired by your employer."

Groups interpret the reasons for Bulgaria's present economic hardship differently. Women in Sofia speak of the socialist legacy of government mismanagement, the absence of civil society, and the withering of personal initiative. A group of pensioners from Dimitrovgrad associates economic hardship with the new social order that is being established: "See where this wild capitalism has brought us? Freedom, democracy—actually that's lawlessness, crime, a chance for people who'll stop at nothing to get the better of us." Participants from the group single out "those who hold power" and say that they are national traitors. Similarly, a group of women from Dimitrovgrad focuses on former communist functionaries, describing them as having overseas ties "in the money flow" and engaging in illegal businesses. A woman in Razgrad cites privatization: "We were all equals before. Then privatization came and everybody began to steal." A woman in Plovdiv singles out the corruption that accompanied privatization: "Why should they close the enterprises just so they can buy them more cheaply during privatization?" Whatever reasons people find for the difficulties of the past decade, all agree that the most serious effect of the economic turmoil is mass unemployment, a new phenomenon that has created widespread insecurity.

Unemployment: The Double Loss

Discussion groups across communities identify the loss of state employment as the most significant factor that has changed their lives for the worse. In Razgrad, for example, 80 percent of the working population in the Roma quarter was unemployed after several state enterprises closed. In Dimitrovgrad the jobless rate is highest among middle-aged people, and more than half of the unemployed are said to be women. In industrial areas such as Kalofer, many people are formally employed but go unpaid because their enterprises are idle. Some have been laid off as long as nine months. Workers in the study say they never know when they will get paid or how much, or when they will be laid off permanently.

High unemployment is considered by study participants to be the root of poor health, social isolation, crime, and lack of faith in the future. A homeless youth in Sofia says, "If you have work, you'll have everything else." As jobs were lost, so were the fringe benefits that went with them— free medical services, state-sponsored holidays, subsidized food and clothing, and child care. Such benefits, attached to lifelong guaranteed employment, meant considerable peace of mind. "Money is not just paper, it is also a form of security. In the past, with your salary you also got security—security that you would have free health care and access to a trade union sanitarium, that nobody would steal your money, and that the bank would not go bankrupt," says a man in Plovdiv.

Although wage labor and temporary jobs are available (more in urban areas than in villages), they are described by participants as typically low paid and unreliable, and often involving demeaning or even illegal work. They are frequently accessible only to those with connections. Most participants do not consider such labor to be a legitimate alternative since it does not provide steady income and social insurance. Men and women in Dimitrovgrad say there are always jobs available at coffee and pizza shops and on building projects, but employers usually look for young men and women. Many employers take advantage of people desperate for work by refusing to give contracts or written agreements so that they will not have to honor salary promises or cover benefits. Participants from Plovdiv explain that some workers prefer oral contracts, though, because they can continue to collect unemployment benefits and be paid wages up front without having taxes or social insurance deducted.

Alienation and Humiliation

Along with the loss of security that comes with reliable work, people say they have lost their identity and moorings. Many poor Bulgarians are experiencing a lack of purpose and demoralization as a result of massive unemployment. No one seems to have a clear idea of the ultimate objective of the changes or of what to expect—and restitution is not complete,[5] laws promoting business are restrictive, and many enterprises are not yet privatized. People talk of "going back in time" and "going wild." For many groups the most worrying impact of the changes is not so much material as interpersonal. Discussion groups in Etropole and Plovdiv say people have become more "estranged," which is associated with "becoming like savages," or losing civilization. Alienation, humiliation, and degradation are described in personal, social, and even national terms.

Participants stress that unemployment has exacted a high emotional price. Students in Dimitrovgrad describe people without reliable livelihoods as "lifeless faces without self-esteem." "Older people are more resigned to it," they say, "but younger people are more rebellious." It is a great loss of face for older men to have to ask younger relatives or employers for work. "There is a nephew of mine who has a small firm. He always has to give orders. . . . How could he give those sorts of orders to me?" asks a man in Plovdiv. Family relationships crumble over quarrels about money and land restituted from state agricultural farms. People have lost the esteem of friends that gave life much of its savor, drifting away from them because traditional social gatherings require gifts and reciprocal invitations. For the young, the lack of a social life is most poignant. "I am young, this is my time to live, but how?" exclaims a girl in Etropole. Colleagues and neighbors avoid each other, unwilling to be involved in other people's troubles. "Even if you have something good to say, you are afraid that the other will start to envy you," says a woman in Etropole.

A middle-aged woman from Plovdiv relates her deep anxiety as she struggles to make ends meet:

> Every day I wonder what will happen the next day, and even the pettiest obstacle could bring a disaster. Say my salary is one week late. Ten years ago I would laugh at it, I would not even notice—who cared? We used to have our money in the drawer, and it was never finished at the end of the month. Now they will cut your electricity or your telephone if you are late with the bills. And I start worrying one week earlier whether I will have money in time. I start planning whom I shall ask for a short loan. And I've started to have headaches. I have to take pills for my heart.

"We Are Like Refuse": Child Outcasts

The research team held discussions with three separate groups of youths who are living under the most difficult of circumstances: institutionalized children, homeless children, and drug addicts. All report extreme isolation from the larger society and most do not see how their future might improve.

In many countries in the region, orphaned, mentally and physically disabled, and other "socially disadvantaged" children were secluded in special state institutions during communism. With some 35,000 children in institutions at the close of 1999, Bulgaria has among the highest national share in Europe of institutionalized children.[6] While new laws and assistance programs are now being put into place to protect these children and a rising number of street children, the legacy of decades of abandonment and exclusion persists.[7]

In a state institution in Dimitrovgrad for children with mental retardation, few of the sixty-eight child residents are actually retarded. A third are orphans, sent to the institution for its full board and vocational training. Most of the students in the radio and television engineering course are intelligent but physically disabled and are taking the course as an alternative to conscription. Many of the other children have been abandoned and have nowhere else to go. The children say that in the institution they have decent meals, clothing, and student grants, but that once they leave, they are stigmatized because of where they came from and their lives get much worse. The girls say they have few prospects besides prostitution, and the boys end up in severely underpaid jobs. In the past ten years only one student is said to have married after leaving the institution. Orphans in an institution in Kalofer report, "We're at the bottom; we have nothing." Still, they say they try to be optimistic that their education will help them in the job market, and they hope to find work at McDonald's.

The Sofia railway station is home to a second generation of children being raised by homeless girls. The Bulgarian, Turkish, and Roma youths interviewed have lived at the station for a decade. They attribute the beginning of their nightmarish existence to their parents' divorce or abuse, often in the wake of unemployment. "It's my parents' fault—they're poor, too, and they abandoned me," says one youth. "We used to lead a normal life. We could afford food thanks to our parents. Things got bad when they fell out and got divorced." The young participants report that they are regularly preyed on by mafia henchmen who beat them and force them into prostitution. Skinheads are said to be their worst menace. These young people readily call themselves social outcasts. "We are like refuse, like animals," says a homeless girl.

With no families and able to count only on one another, homeless youths show a striking resignation and hopelessness. "In time," a boy says, "you'll get used to anything." Police in Sofia are reported to round them up, return those they can to their families or to the institutions from which they have run away, and release the rest to the street. The young people at the railway station say they are ambivalent about the police, who neither abuse nor help them except when skinheads attack. They appreciate the food religious charities sometimes bring them but expect little help from the local welfare office. The government runs a shelter in Sofia for people over 18, and a Bulgarian NGO runs another for homeless children up to 16. A foundation plans another shelter to provide food, medical consultations, and vocational training to people 16–25, but the youths are cynical about this happening soon.

Study participants estimate that 750 heroin users live in the Maksouda quarter of Varna, two-thirds of them between the ages of 15 and 25. "What boys they used to be! When I look at them here around the market, they are melting like ice cream," says a relative of an addict. The users describe a progression from smoking the drug to "chasing the dragon" (inhaling the fumes through a paper tube) to injecting. Degradation and social exclusion are among the highest-ranked problems for heroin users. "Heroin is my boyfriend," says one girl. To get money to buy drugs, most depend on their parents, or turn to theft and prostitution. Women users are said to suffer the most extreme forms of abuse—beating, rape, and even murder.

Heroin users in Maksouda associate the rise in drug use with greater ease of travel across borders and the lure of fast money that the trade offers, but they also mention that the harsh economy is a factor. Wedged between Europe and Asia, Bulgaria has become a major drug trafficking hub. Users say heroin came into their country when the "road to Poland" opened in 1989 and cross-border trading was assisted by wholesale corruption of police, border control agents, and customs officials. A heroin user describes how Roma drug dealers took advantage of the new economic opportunities:

> People from our mahala [Roma quarter] made some money, especially when they started going abroad. They came back here and had to invest the money in something; some started trading in the market, others went into gold, but these are all difficult. Some had heard you could make a lot from heroin dealing and decided that if they started that they could make very easy money.

Study participants say dealers make a lot of money, usually in Poland or the Czech or Slovak republics, and then lose it all.

Users report that addiction problems began to emerge in full force in Sofia after the initial wave of unemployment in 1991–92, and affected the Roma most severely. To get off drugs, some addicts turn to a clinic in Sofia for help. Others simply leave or are sent away from Sofia by their parents to remote villages or out of the country altogether. Heroin is reported to be much more costly in Poland. A father in Maksouda says about his addicted son, "I want to take him away from all of this. . . .

Here the good life is only for bandits, for the rest it is impossible." Both the users and their parents also see a remedy in tougher laws and enforcement. "It is necessary for the police to have a very strong grip . . . but how, when this is the sweetest business?" asks a 19-year-old addict.

Continuing Struggles for Minorities

Bulgaria has two large ethnic minorities, the Turks and the Roma, as well as a small group of Bulgarian-speaking Muslims, often referred to as Pomaks. According to 2001 census data, ethnic Bulgarians number 6.85 million and make up just over 85 percent of the population. Ethnic Turks (745,000) account for 9.3 percent, and Roma (370,000), 4.6 percent.[8] Minority groups face far higher poverty rates than ethnic Bulgarians. The Roma are the most disadvantaged, with unemployment reaching 80 percent among men and 100 percent among women in some places. While many legal rights (for example, to publish Roma newspapers, to form associations, and to speak Romany) were restored to the Roma in 1990, their living conditions continue to be extremely difficult and participants in this study report rising discrimination on many fronts. Pomaks also have greater freedoms under the new constitution; however, they too encounter prejudice both from ethnic Bulgarians and from other minority groups. The attitudes of ethnic Bulgarians toward Turks are more tolerant, although some Turks report discrimination when seeking work.[9]

Ethnic Turks and Pomaks live mainly in rural areas where jobs have been lost to deindustrialization and the dissolution of state farms.[10] These groups have a higher rate of unemployment than do ethnic Bulgarians. Turkish communities in Bulgaria maintain their Turkish and Muslim identity and their language. While most land has been restituted, many ethnic Turks and Pomaks did not have legal claims to land in the first place, nor can they buy it given the lack of any real land market or funds for such a purchase. Many men now migrate seasonally to larger towns, often in search of construction jobs. A young Turkish woman from Kalaidzhi reports looking for work in the nearby town of Elena: "When clerks heard my Turkish name, the look in their eyes would change and they would say that there was no work there."

Pomaks, although they speak Bulgarian, also often experience pressure to live separately in their own communities. One Pomak man shared that his family "threatened me this way and that way" for dating an ethnic Bulgarian and warned him against any future with her:

> *"Wherever you go, ethnic Bulgarians will realize you are a Pomak and laugh behind your back," my parents would say, "and you will have to leave your girlfriend in the end. . . . All your kin will be against you." Mind you, my girlfriend was going through the same thing with her own parents who were horrified she might marry a Muslim. So the greatest event in this period of my life has been the breakup with my girlfriend.*

Although many Roma live together in segregated villages and urban neighborhoods, they are a heterogeneous group. Some are Muslim, others Orthodox, and still others Protestant. They speak different languages, including Romany dialects, Turkish, and Bulgarian. Roma households on Krajezerna Street in the Maksouda quarter of Varna, for instance, are mainly Turkish Roma, who speak primarily Turkish; but there are also Bulgarian Roma, who speak Bulgarian and Romany and are Christians, as well as Vlach Roma, who speak Romanian and a Romany dialect and are also Christians. Some Roma, such as the cattle traders near Kalaidzhi and Sredno Selo, live in villages and towns. Some preserve their traditional crafts and culture. Others have modern jobs and are well integrated into Bulgarian mainstream society, such as the Roma visited in the town of Kalofer.

There are striking contrasts between the official image of Bulgarian cities and towns and actual life in the destitute Roma quarters visited for this study in Sofia (Filipovtsi and the former Vietnamese hostels), Dimitrovgrad, Varna, and Razgrad. According to public records, for instance, Dimitrovgrad has a more or less excellent infrastructure, but this does not apply to the poor sections and, in particular, the Roma neighborhoods. The latter have neither roads nor telephones, the plumbing is disastrous, many houses have no electricity, and a bus arrives every three hours. The situation is the same in Sofia, where the Roma quarters lack adequate sewerage, drinking water is dirty and stinks, and there is no garbage collection or other public services. The physical isolation of Roma areas reinforces the stigma and exclusion. "We're worse than a nobody," states a Roma man from Dimitrovgrad.

Social exclusion is compounded by what the Roma keenly perceive as growing racial discrimination since the end of the socialist state.

Participants in Varna report, "The Gypsies are worse off now than during communism. During communism there were no drug addicts or drug dealers, there never was stealing on the present scale. Everyone had a salary because everyone had a job."

Roma frequently mention encountering discrimination when seeking services, and being targets of emotional and physical abuse. "They don't pay any attention to us at the hospital. Once they see we're Gypsies they throw us out like dogs," says a Roma man from Dimitrovgrad. In Sofia, Roma participants report that they are victims of skinhead attacks and police abuse: "The police are racists. When skinheads attack Gypsies and police turn up, they start beating the Gypsies, too, and let skinheads walk away scot-free. The skinheads are pampered rich kids. That's why the police don't protect us." While schools can sometimes be powerful supports for helping minorities participate in the wider society, Roma children often attend segregated schools; they have a high illiteracy rate (16 percent) and a low rate of primary school completion. Roma participants in Dimitrovgrad say their children are forced to go without education because they have to earn money or are too ashamed to be seen in their ragged clothes at school. Just over 7 percent of Roma youth attend secondary school, and they are virtually nonexistent in higher education.[11]

Discrimination is felt most keenly in employment. Roma were the first to lose their jobs when downsizing began in 1990–92, partly because they were less educated than the Bulgarians. "Before, we were obliged to go to work," says a Roma in Dimitrovgrad. "Now we simply can't get a job even if we beg for it." Another man in the same group remarks, "When you send your [job] application in writing, they'll invite you for an interview if you have a Bulgarian name, but once they see you're dark they kick you out." A Roma man in Varna similarly states, "Whenever [Bulgarian employers] see you are a Gypsy, they don't give you work, although there is work." "They consider us subhuman and thieves," says another. Some Roma in the study work as unskilled laborers in minimum wage occupations. A man in Krasna Poliana, Sofia, explains, "If somebody's needed to carry or dig something, it's us Gypsies—we're now hired to do such dirty jobs only."

As a result of difficult livelihood prospects in the formal economy, Roma say they have turned to informal activities: working abroad illegally; selling on consignment; cross-border trafficking in drugs, small arms, stolen cars, antiques, gold and jewelry, and endangered species; and prostitution. "Why didn't we steal before?" asks a Roma participant in

Dimitrovgrad. "It was a disgrace to be summoned to the police station but now it's become a habit. We're summoned every other day. Of course I don't like being summoned in front of the kids. But how could I live through the night when there's no bread?" "Many people steal—you can't starve to death. When the wolf's hungry, he goes to the pen," says a Roma in Dimitrovgrad.

Some Roma in the study do not deny that they steal, but they contend that theft is a solution to discrimination in employment and lack of work. This, in turn, upsets many Bulgarians, who regard "Gypsy" as synonymous with "troublemaker," "criminal," and "thief," someone who is jobless and does not work but opts for the easy way out. Such attitudes fuel a vicious cycle of increasing discrimination, further isolation, a high school dropout rate, and mounting tensions.

Navigating the Changes

Poor people in the communities visited have been extremely resourceful in finding ways to survive the turbulent and unpredictable past decade. Most turn first to family networks for money, food, clothing, and housing. They economize on household expenses, going without new clothes or buying them secondhand, making their own bread and yogurt, cooking late at night when electricity is cheaper, or leaving their utility bills unpaid. For many, especially the young, the only way to cope with poverty is to find work abroad or marry a foreigner. Many people count on welfare, but not on welfare only, or they would starve, as they state frankly. Private business is not an option for most poor people, who lack start-up capital and collateral for loans. The most effective strategies people have found to cope with the loss of state-guaranteed jobs are the subsistence economy in rural areas and small towns, and the informal economy, with varying degrees of legality, in both rural and urban areas.

The Return to Subsistence Agriculture

Groups in all the villages and towns covered in this study report that they cope with unemployment, low wages, and insufficient welfare benefits by raising food for their own consumption. In the mid-1990s, at the peak of the economic crisis, home gardening accounted for more than a quarter of household income, but it fell to about 18 percent in

1999.[12] Households with unemployed workers and with people who are not in the workforce are most likely to rely on farming to help make ends meet.

The subsistence economy takes different forms. Poor people without land or animals gather wild food. Those with gardens or land plots usually grow some vegetables and keep some animals for family consumption. Many people live from what is called the "jar" economy, growing food in the summer and preserving some to carry them through the winter. This food source is extremely important for pensioners and welfare recipients whose benefits barely cover the cost of their utilities.

The dismantling of state farms forced many rural workers to look for alternative ways to survive. Restitution of land that was formerly incorporated into state farms began in 1990. The 1991 privatization law provided for voluntary formation of cooperatives by private landowners, and the new cooperative institution was quickly and successfully adapted to subsistence agriculture. Private plots are vital to the domestic food supply. In Razgrad members of the village cooperative have retained some private land independent of the cooperative to raise animals and cultivate crops for their own use. An important advantage of the cooperative is access to farm machinery that is too expensive for individual farmers to rent or buy.

Even townspeople and city dwellers also resort to subsistence agriculture to supplement their welfare benefits or reduced salaries. They collect edible plants, and those with access to some land cultivate small gardens. It is also common to depend on food grown by relatives in towns and villages. In Kalofer nearly all participants tend gardens, cultivate fields, or breed livestock for their own use. "If you don't grow something, you're dead," says a pensioner. All families in Plovdiv, women's discussion groups say, produce canned food, even the relatively well off. In urban Dimitrovgrad, collecting firewood and edible plants is the only option for many destitute people. Most families in Etropole have some members engaged in subsistence agriculture. Agriculture "can help eke out a living" says Katerina, a teacher in Etropole who raises pigs, but it is not the way to prosperity.

The "Real" Economy

While subsistence agriculture is an important survival strategy, the informal sector is the main source of livelihood for many poor men and women in the study. It often takes multiple jobs for people to earn as much as they did in the public sector, and even this does not make up for the lost social benefits. "I work twice as hard since being laid off," says a woman in Etropole. People are constantly on the lookout for jobs through networks of friends, relatives, and neighbors. A teacher in Etropole who estimates her normal workday lasts eighteen hours says, "Today you need to work at several places if you want to feel like a normal person. I work at the coffee shop, but I wake early in the morning to feed the animals, then I have classes at the school." Her only "formal" work is teaching at the school. Another woman in Plovdiv says even two salaries are not enough to pay for anything more than food and utilities—she needs a third one to be able to buy things for her child.

Men and women say they work in cottage industries and on construction sites, repair cars, forage for scrap that can be resold, work on farms in the summer, or find summer jobs in Greece or Turkey. Middle-class professionals supplement their regular jobs by moonlighting as night watchmen, shop attendants, or waitresses—occupations considered degrading, especially because they eat up time for interaction with family or friends. Nurses work as cleaners for three times their government salaries. All pensioners who are able to work do so. In Plovdiv they have even replaced the Roma in the business of selling recyclables.

With opportunities for employment limited, study participants in five communities (Dimitrovgrad, Sofia, Plovdiv, Sredno Selo, and Varna) report a rise in semi-legal and even criminal activities. Many express the view that there is no way to earn adequate income by honest means, and that those who have prospered in the new economy have done so through shady dealing. Older women in Dimitrovgrad explain, "Those who've made it are those who had access to party funds and went into business with public and party money. They used to be *komsomol* [party functionaries] and trade union leaders."

Many ethnic Bulgarians and Roma have capitalized on the opportunities for trading within and across borders and on other more or less illicit activities made possible by the liberalization of travel after 1989. A discussion group of older women from Dimitrovgrad explains: "The border is quite close, and smuggling routes run through this part of the country. . . . The money is then distributed via companies that report a false turnover, and the bulk goes to party safes regardless of political allegiance." In the Roma quarter of Maksouda in Varna, a young man describes his father's cross-border trade: "We buy jeans from Poland for two to three German marks apiece and sell them here for [the equivalent of twenty to twenty-five marks], and thus with a single pair you make a day's wage." A group of youths in Sofia states that such shady dealing is the norm: "Speculation—you buy something cheap and sell it at a high price—that's what 90 percent do, at other people's expense." At the Sunday market in Dimitrovgrad, the largest in the country, the line between legal and illegal activity is blurred and public officials are said to demand large bribes for well-placed stalls. Much of the merchandise there is sold at low prices because it comes from unlicensed firms and cross-border smuggling.

Discussion groups also report that there are many risks involved in these deals. A Roma man from Varna recounts,

> *In the* mahala *[Roma quarter] on Saturday . . . they came with the BMWs and Mercedes—seven or eight people, the big ones with the thick necks. They were Bulgarians, and their cars didn't have license plates. They caught one who was a dealer, to beat him—he owed them money—and they beat him with tools. It was very frightening.*

Similarly, participants in Dimitrovgrad state that there is "big money" in drug trafficking, prostitution, and gambling, and that "now and then there's some shooting and killing, you know, they threaten each other, car bombs blow up and God knows what, but they somehow manage to get even. That's their way of doing business."

The enormous spread of the informal sector is a result of the collapse of the state economy and underdeveloped conditions for private business. Many participants do not disapprove of private business and would like to go into it if they could. For example, women pensioners in Kalofer make Brussels lace that would fetch a high price if there were a market in town. They say they would like to set up an association of lace makers and try to sell elsewhere but don't know how to go about this, although they have calculated the cost of yarn and labor and potential profits. With an unpredictable market, however, and no start-up money or security for borrowing, the pensioners concluded that such a risky venture was not practical. Other participants share similar problems in launching business ventures. The problem, say many, is not that they don't understand how competitive markets are supposed to work, but that there are no reliable financial or market mediators or purchasers with any cash on hand.

The Helpful Institutions: "Your Own People"

Study participants identified the most important institutions in their communities and then rated them against several criteria, including whether they were effective and trusted. From their point of view, institutions such as the municipality, the mayor, and the office that distributes social assistance were considered important, but they often rated low on criteria of effectiveness and trust. Schools and health care centers generally scored higher. The institutions considered most effective, trusted, and supportive in the present situation proved to be informal social networks of friends, relatives, colleagues, and neighbors. It is through these *vrazki* (connections) that people say they cope with problems such as finding a job or obtaining services. Reports of exploiting *vrazki* are more common in discussion groups in large communities, while participants in rural villages and small towns are more likely to refer to patron-client relationships.

"If you are alone, you are dead," says a group of Roma in Sofia. With rising unemployment, the family is essential for psychological survival as well as material support. A middle-aged woman from Etropole says, "I like money and nice things, but it's not money that makes me happy. It's people that make me happy—my children, my husband, my sister, my father, and my sister-in-law. To be well . . . is to feel secure, loved, and happy." "If it weren't for Mother to help me support my daughter at the university, I don't see how I could possibly manage," says a woman whose situation has worsened in the past ten years. "People support each other in the family only—that's how we survive," explains a young woman in Etropole. Friends and associates are expected to provide small loans, credit, information about jobs, and access to the institutions where they work. Neighbors are expected to help poor people gain access to public offices. Some groups say these networks of kin, friends, and neighbors can no longer be counted on because everyone is equally poor, but they are clearly valued by most of the participants.

Accounts of using *vrazki* to look for jobs, consumer goods, and services are common in all the urban group discussions. Making use of connections requires knowing the right people in the right places, but *vrazki* are called on in the short term, when need arises, and are not taken for granted. "To be upwardly mobile in Bulgaria you've always had to fight tooth and nail, to be well connected," says an older woman in Sofia. While connections were once needed to help people buy apartments and cars, they are now widely mentioned by study participants as important for survival. A middle-aged man in Plovdiv who was unemployed after a collective farm dissolved says he has only one real *vrazka*—a syndicate leader who owns an apartment in the same building. "I keep him for an extreme case, only if the worst happens."

Rural participants report that they would be lost without long-term arrangements of mutual obligation with influential patrons. "Both before and now you have to be on good terms with those in power, otherwise you are lost," says a subsistence farmer in Kalaidzhi. If the owner of a hay mower has the goodwill to mow your hay for you when it is ripe, they say, you have a store for the whole year. To ensure this, the client tries to gain the patron's favor. "Not only do we pay through the nose . . . but we have to go and ask day after day, take a bottle of brandy to him, humor him." Such patronage relationships are also important to cultivate with people who sell firewood or plow fields. People say they also employ these informal networks when seeking work, protection, and credit.

State Institutions

Vrazki and patronage have become so deeply rooted in Bulgarian institutions that study participants often report that the only way to deal with public agencies is through social ties. Many see public officials as patrons who need to be cultivated with favors or bribes to deliver benefits and services. "If they like you, they will help you," says a villager in Kalaidzhi of the forestry department. A man in Etropole says, "If you have connections in the police, you will always go free." For trader-tourists without travel documents, having one's "own people" to bribe in the customs office is reported to be crucial. A young man in Varna explains, "If one has money one can cross any border without a visa." Another man in Varna says, "Luckily, people from the tax office of the municipality . . . don't come here so often . . . but nevertheless I have a patron there to whom I give from time to time."

Most participants rank the state as the most important, though disappointing, institution overall. "The state is obliged to take care of us, to ensure stability and jobs," says a young man in Dimitrovgrad. Expectations of the state remain high even though trust and confidence in it are greatly diminished. State institutions are judged harshly by poor men and women in the study for not following through on their responsibilities. Comments about the public institutions most often mentioned by participants—the municipality, the social welfare office, and the police—reflect people's high expectations and their disillusionment. "They don't keep their promises," says a Roma man about the mayor's office and the welfare office in Dimitrovgrad.

The municipality, which collects taxes and redistributes the social benefits allocated by the government from this revenue, is the most visible public institution for most groups. The institution receives mixed reviews for its performance. Participants in Etropole rank the municipality highest in importance and evaluate it positively. "They receive some money from the state, so they have to distribute it honestly," says one of the participants. Most other groups do not distinguish between the municipality as an institution and the mayor or municipality staff as individuals. Mayors are seen as the people who make all the decisions. In Kalofer and Dimitrovgrad participants criticize their mayors as weak. "He's too nice and can't cope," says an older woman in Kalofer. Other groups cite unfairness or corruption. Groups in Razgrad accuse the mayor of arbitrarily enrolling the Roma in temporary employment programs, although the mayor says they are the neediest and in any case few young ethnic Bulgarians are left in the town. The borough mayor is important to Roma groups in Sofia because he makes major housing decisions, but they evaluate him negatively because he stays behind barred doors and sees only other officials and visitors with appointments.

Social Assistance

The National Social Assistance Service is an executive agency within the Ministry of Labor and Social Policy, but many people confuse its local offices (referred to as SAO) with the municipality offices where it has local branches. Local SAO branches distribute assistance for heat, along with welfare, maternity, and child benefits, to families with incomes below the national poverty line, as well as occasional cash or food. To apply for SAO benefits, applicants must declare their sources of income and present their previous or current work papers. Unemployment and pension benefits are distributed through separate channels.

Groups who depend on welfare either take the SAO for granted, see it as a necessary evil, or resent what they consider unfair allocation of benefits. No participants in Kalofer, for instance, volunteered the SAO as an important institution, even though one in ten residents receive welfare benefits. Some find applying for benefits humiliating. In Kalaidzhi a young woman says, "I cannot demean myself and go beg any more from them." Some Roma rank this office as ineffective because to receive benefits they must prove they have not engaged in cross-border trading. "They want us to show work books [which document previous employment] and we do not have such, and that is why we cannot qualify," says a woman in Varna. A Roma man in Dimitrovgrad asserts that "the welfare office is keeping an eye on us around the clock—am I home, do I have furniture, why do I have a ring? Of course I'll never ever sell my wedding ring!" Many accuse the SAO of favoritism. "It is the mayor who decides. When he does not like somebody there is no assistance for them," says a poor woman from Razgrad. A Roma in Etropole states, "They give only to the haves while we, the have-nots, do not receive anything."

A high share of Bulgaria's population consists of pensioners, and discussion groups from several communities identify the elderly who rely on their pensions as among the poorest. It is widely reported that welfare benefits have not kept pace with inflation and are too small to support those who receive them: "My pension is enough for bread and milk—the cheap sort," says a pensioner in Kalofer. In Dimitrovgrad pensioners report that not only are their pensions "miserable," but they no longer have free transport.

Elderly who live alone without money to buy firewood or pay heating bills are more afraid of not having fuel for the winter than of going hungry. Olga, a 72-year-old widow in Razgrad, says she bought a very modest amount of coal because she was not sure if she would receive her social assistance benefits for heating fuel. To conserve warmth, Olga reports: "I put on five covers and I stayed in bed as long as possible. When the goat would start bleating, I go to give her some fodder, then go to the bathroom and come back in the bed. And thus all the day, all alone. I do not know how I did not go crazy."

Many pensioners share their pensions and produce from home gardening with their children. A 70-year-old man from Dimitrovgrad explains, "When I retired, both my kids were still students, and my pension was enough to support them. Thank goodness I paid for their education. All I can do for them today is supply some food. When I slaughtered the pig there was sausage and some meat for everyone."

Raised under a different ideology, many pensioners resent the fact that well-educated people who worked a lifetime for the state are now destitute, and they find the promises of free markets especially galling. The collapse in health infrastructure is keenly felt by the elderly, for whom the high prices of medicines and bribes mean having to forgo much needed health care. One woman in Sofia, a pensioner, states that there has been "a true genocide of pensioners." Another serious problem is the rise in assault and theft of food and property from the elderly. Others report that their pensions are not being paid in full and suggest that corrupt politicians are depleting pension funds.

Health Care

Many participants besides pensioners also express strong concerns about health services not operating as well now as they did ten years ago and about drug prices soaring to the point that most people cannot afford them. A poor woman in Plovdiv explains, "Even if the doctors deliver a diagnosis and a prescription, the drugs are so expensive. That's why I asked the doctor to explain the diagnosis to me and then started to ask what kind of herbs are recommended by popular medicine for that illness."

Physical access to health care can also be a problem. Young mothers report that the health care center for the villages of Sredno Selo and Kalaidzhi has closed, and they need to travel to Zlataritsa for checkups and advice. Since the capabilities of the unit in Zlataritsa are also very limited, patients are usually sent to Elena, especially for obstetric care. All this adds up to some 45 kilometers and, given the limited bus service, poses serious problems. Unable to afford the time and expense, several women remarked that they had given birth at home with the help of "old women." One woman said she had given birth in a car on the road to Zlataritsa.

Corruption in the provision of health care is also reported. "Each time I go to the polyclinic I put on my oldest trousers. If I look better, they will ask me for bribes," remarks a Plovdiv man. A woman from the same city reports,

> You wait for two hours and when you finally enter, the doctor says to you, "Sorry, lady, but there are several dozen people waiting for me. I see that your case is not very urgent. You can take these and these medicines. But if you want me to deliver a proper diagnosis you can visit me in the afternoon at this address," and he gives his business card with the address of the private office.

Roma participants report discrimination at hospitals. According to a Roma in Sofia, "Now the hospital won't admit Gypsies even in a critical condition unless you pay a bribe."

Police

Theft and crime are major problems for many participants, and they frequently rank the police as an important institution although ineffective in providing protection. Some poor people in the study think well of individual police, but problems of police harassment and corruption are reported with high frequency. A villager in Kalaidzhi says of the police, "Only people who cannot give them anything are put in prison." Roma in Razgrad quote the adage, "There is no mercy for you if you have stolen a chicken. There is no prison for you if you have stolen a million." Yet another Roma in Dimitrovgrad values the police for being humane, saying, "The only respect the Gypsies get is at the police station because officers know people have no other chance and steal only as a last resort." Groups in Etropole say the police take bribes and let criminals go, but explain, "What will a policeman do who barely makes ends meet? Obviously, he will close his eyes and not risk getting killed." Men and women in Plovdiv say,

> *The policemen on the streets are young boys, still scared (the old ones stay behind the desks) and they do not know how to react. They are risking their lives every day, and every week there are articles in the newspapers that another policeman was wounded or killed. Now all the mobsters have guns.*

"We Are Afraid of Those on the Top"

Almost all discussion groups in this study say they have no control over government decision making. Women in Dimitrovgrad say, "Of course nothing depends on us—the statutory framework [laws] must change." A man in Etropole paints a picture of powerlessness in the face of officialdom:

> *We the Bulgarians are serfs. . . . We all know that if you are down. . . . We are afraid of those on the top. The people cannot gather together to put them in their place. There are some young ones who wanted to make a debate with the mayor on the local TV; they announced that everybody could ask him questions and what happened? He asked them not to interrupt him when he was speaking, they cut the telephone lines, he delivered a speech, and he went home.*

Paradoxically, the discussion groups that express a sense of being able to exert some influence over state institutions are among the least empowered: the Roma and people with disabilities. With the fall of communism, Roma were allowed to form citizens' associations and publish newspapers addressing Roma issues. They now have deputies in every party in Parliament and support from international civil rights activists and humanitarian organizations. Roma votes are courted at election time with food and promises of jobs, a practice they universally resent as humiliating. "They hand out a free bowl of soup and throw us wafers as if we were animals—all for the sake of winning our votes," says a group of men in Dimitrovgrad. Some Roma believe they can have an institutional impact through their vote: "It's up to us to decide who will be mayor. That's one hundred thousand votes." Disabled people talk hopefully of the nongovernmental organizations that have begun to lobby for their rights.

NGOs Stepping In

While all groups agree that the effectiveness of state institutions needs to be strengthened and overall governance needs to be improved, several new civil society institutions are becoming more active in Bulgaria.

The activities of NGOs—mainly distribution of humanitarian aid— are known to most people in the urban areas visited in this study, although they are virtually unknown in the rural areas. The Red Cross is one of the most visible. Participants in Plovdiv say this agency's policy of distributing assistance through hospitals and polyclinics is inefficient. "Who has the right to get this aid?" they ask. "Well, those who happen to be in the hospital that day." They are also critical of NGOs that choose local representatives ("the *vrazki* channel") to distribute aid, because this is seen to favor the representatives' relatives and neighbors. Other NGOs ask municipalities or SAOs for lists of possible beneficiaries, which the Plovdiv groups say is subject to favoritism. In reply, SAO officers in Plovdiv say, "The aid is not enough. . . . There are 23,000 pensioners [in the municipality], so you tell me how to make a list that will satisfy everybody."

Most Roma are familiar with NGOs that work for Roma rights, although many are skeptical about their motives and accuse them of patronage. Men and women in Varna dismiss Roma NGOs, saying, "They play their own game. Waiting for something from them is the same as waiting for a letter from a dead person." Another Roma man in Varna mentions that "Everything's been shared out at the top—all organizations are committed on the basis of either political or family allegiances."

Nevertheless, during group discussions Roma participants in both Sofia and Dimitrovgrad discussed the possibility of establishing their own NGOs to distribute aid.

Disabled people in Sofia see NGOs as a chance to uphold their rights and fight for real social integration. They say that unless they do something about their rights, no one else will. In Sofia there are just two special minibuses for people in wheelchairs in a city with a population of more than one million; no such luxuries exist in the countryside. If it weren't for family members, disabled people say, they could not go out at all, and even then such helpers must be quite strong as there are no ramps for wheelchairs. Disabled participants also report other hardships: employment discrimination, problems accessing polling stations, and requirements that they continuously renew their certifications for benefits.

Many people with disabilities in Sofia are members of an NGO that is helping them to organize and advocate legislative reforms. Most members of this NGO have university degrees, and half were disabled in car accidents. They are working to end discrimination in hiring practices and what they perceive to be official disincentives to working. They have won some policy victories, although much remains to be done. Bulgaria has passed a Disabled Persons Act (though disabled people say no one complies with it), and NGOs have succeeded in putting their concerns on the public agenda. A young disabled woman in Sofia explains their campaign: "We don't want to get social assistance, to be socially disadvantaged—just see how discriminatory those terms sound. We don't want preferential treatment; we want equal opportunities." A disabled young man says NGOs "can help cultivate the self-awareness that you can be independent and you can fight."

The Legacy of Patriarchy

Social and economic conditions have deteriorated for women in Bulgaria since 1989, and many of the hardships of the economic crisis have fallen heavily on their shoulders. They earn less than before, must cut back on household expenses, and have to find additional employment, sometimes in demeaning or dangerous occupations. In addition, women suffer growing abuse by idle or desperate husbands. They have seen little change in traditionally unequal relations between men and women, and they have experienced an erosion of many rights and services designed to protect and support them.

Communist regimes greatly emphasized the emancipation of women and provided both legal protections and supportive services. Groups in Sofia agree that there is generally no gender discrimination in choice of career, and participants in Dimitrovgrad report that many women are employed in local government and business, although none of them are "power holders." In Kalofer all the officials at the town hall and welfare office are women. The more senior positions, however, are still held by men. Women are regarded as good civil and domestic servants, but not as people who should hold real authority. Thus, most decisions outside as well as inside the household, as a youth in a Sofia discussion group observes, are made by men. Household chores and specific types of farm work are still considered women's work, and husbands contribute little. Asked "Who tends to be the master—the husband or the wife?" a Roma woman in one of the discussion groups in Dimitrovgrad answers, "The husband. That's how it's supposed to be, isn't it?"

Women say they are expected to manage household expenses with insufficient budgets, to "do miracles with nothing," as a participant in Plovdiv remarks. In traditional rural households in Kalaidzhi, gender roles have become more clearly divided with unemployment. Women who lost their jobs when state enterprises collapsed are now expected to stay at home; since most have received secondary education, this confinement is considered particularly onerous.

The rate of women's unemployment is high in many urban areas—100 percent among some Roma groups—and women are working harder in the informal and subsistence economies than they did when employment was guaranteed by the state. Women under age 20 have the best chance of finding work, mostly in the service industry as waitresses, barmaids, shop attendants, and secretaries, or in the sex industry. Several women report that expectations of sexual favors are common in the workplace and fuel discrimination against all but very young women. "They want just young girls and they keep them working until midnight. The neighbors see the girls in their bosses' cars—at least they save money on transport," relates a participant in Plovdiv. A woman from Plovdiv states,

> *Only the young girls 20 to 22 years old can find a job. If they are 25 years old or more, nobody wants them. I am 35 years old, and when I applied for a job as a waitress, they told me "Go away, you old* babo *[grandmother], there are 18-year-old girls who are waiting for that job." I am a very good waitress,*

but the boss wanted somebody who would also do another kind
of job just for him.

Middle-aged women say they can find work only as cleaners or in door-to-door sales. Professional women have had to accept low-paying jobs and work that would have been unthinkable a generation ago, such as waiting tables or cleaning toilets, while some formerly prestigious positions have lost their status. "Now a young girl, even if she does well in her studies, cannot keep her head above water," says a Sofia nurse.

Some women find the most lucrative employment in the burgeoning sex trade. Very young women are increasingly recruited by employment contractors as sex workers in the domestic and overseas markets. In Varna and Dimitrovgrad prostitution is described as a coping strategy for Bulgarian women and a normal livelihood for Roma women, with pimps a frequent subject of complaint. A Roma man in Dimitrovgrad says that women support the family through prostitution: "She'll dress up, do her face, and pick up some rich guy. We'll beat them up afterwards—we'll lose face if we don't—but we know there's no other way."

Deteriorating health and child-care services add to the insecurity. Women continue to receive child benefits, but these currently amount to less than \$5 per child per month. Divorce has surged in the past decade, and child support is a serious problem. A participant in Dimitrovgrad says,

> *The rule that might is right still applies—it's all up to the man.*
> *When they get divorced, what's the wife supposed to do with*
> *the two kids and half of the property? And token child support.*
> *There's no law to oblige men to pay the support money, and it's*
> *practically impossible to sue them for more money. It's up to*
> *you to track him down—meanwhile, he's changed his residence*
> *five times.*

Many participants commented on the emotional difficulties that men face with rising unemployment. Some state that men are less resilient and resourceful than women when faced with economic changes. In Kalofer participants report that four men in their thirties had committed suicide in the four months since January 1999. "They can't take the tension, having no job, supporting three kids, so they take a rope and that's it." Men are less likely to take on demeaning and very poorly paid work.

Participants in almost all communities report a rise in violence against women both outside and within the household. While much of the violence is attributed to economic insecurity and less strict social control by neighbors and police, some participants emphasize that domestic violence is a long-standing problem. "Brutes have always beaten and will go on beating their wives," says a discussion group of men in Sofia. More men are beating their wives, say Roma women in Razgrad, because "when a woman is employed and the man is not, he is jealous." In families where both partners have jobs, say women in Plovdiv, "no more than 20 percent of husbands beat their wives."

Wife battering seems particularly widespread in urban areas. In Varna, Dimitrovgrad, and Sofia many participants talk about domestic violence in their apartment complexes. Men in Sofia say that one man used to lock his wife up in the bathroom and beat her savagely while she wailed. An older woman in Dimitrovgrad says, "As you can see, women are harassed in all sorts of ways; wife battering is quite common, too. . . . There's no one to advise them, no one to turn to if they're abused. The police won't even show up if you report a husband's beating his wife."

A lawyer practicing in the Varna Roma quarter says that police and prosecutors are reluctant to interfere in family affairs, and many women refuse to sue the men who terrorize them:

> There is no law that defends the wife, child, or husband in cases of domestic violence. The prosecutor's office says, "This is not a problem of ours," and the police find an excuse in saying that they cannot interfere in family affairs. Being afraid, the women refuse to sue the men who terrorize them. For Roma women, it is absolutely out of the question.

Conclusion

"To be well, this means to be calm about your children . . . to have a house and livestock and not to wake up at night when the dog barks, to know that you can sell your produce, to sit and talk calmly with friends and neighbors. That's what a man wants," remarks a man in Razgrad. For poor men and women in Bulgaria, wellbeing is also associated with knowing what tomorrow will bring. Almost all groups describe their present situation as a reversal, as going backwards. People who once had responsible technical jobs find themselves "plowing with donkeys and cows" or foraging for scrap. Survival for most depends on their success in the informal economy, sometimes bordering on illegal activities and crime.

Unemployment and loss of security are the main problems cited by all groups. Many participants express interest in expanding their farm production or informal business activities but are deterred by the risks. There is a general need for greater understanding of how markets work and for the shift in mindset that underpins entrepreneurship. To move forward, the state must provide a far more supportive environment for the private sector: the economy must remain stable and growing, laws must be clear and enforced, and taxes must be affordable. Poor entrepreneurs and agricultural producers identify the major bottlenecks to be the unpredictability of markets and lack of information and financial services, and in rural areas, the inaccessibility of markets.

Participants also link the present widespread insecurity with the decline in public services and infrastructure and the state's withdrawal from its basic responsibilities. Systemwide improvements in governance are desperately needed to ensure that what basic services and social assistance exist reach those for whom they are intended. Pension reform and recent initiatives for institutionalized children are important steps. More effective measures are also needed to reverse the extensive exclusion of Roma from work opportunities and state services, problems that they say have intensified with the transition. Turkish and Pomak groups also identify discrimination in job markets as an important obstacle. Poor children and children of ethnic minorities need better educational opportunities.

Men and women in the study communities realize that state-owned enterprises are a thing of the past and that the level of state benefits they once enjoyed is irrecoverable. Reflecting on past habits of depending on the state, a group of men and women in Sofia says this dependency reduced people's initiative and responsibility needed to succeed in the new economy. Some participants acknowledge that there are more opportunities for social mobility now than under communism, but they also perceive that much of this upward economic mobility is still due to connections, "bootlicking," and shady deals. People in the study are fluent in the new jargon of competition, profit rate, value added tax, market, purchasing power, and so on. Nor are they averse to the idea of establishing interest groups to press for reforms. It is, they say, the lack of opportunities for democratic participation in decision making and the incomplete transition to a market economy that are proving so frustrating and harmful. To recover a "normal" life, Bulgarians need effective and honest institutions. For the time being, however, a Sofia participant states, "Your career depends on your resources—money and connections—not on your skills and qualities."

TABLE 1 Study Communities in Bulgaria

VILLAGES

Kalaidzhi,
Lovech district
Pop. 260

This highland village is a Bulgarian Muslim (Pomak) enclave in the country's second-poorest district. The road connecting it to other villages is in poor condition. The village has 80 percent unemployment since the liquidation of collective farms and the closure of other industries, and most people now live by subsistence farming. Villagers sell milk to a local private dairy, collect timber, and gather wild forest products.

Razgrad,
Lom municipality
Pop. 1,150

Razgrad is a northeast lowland village in one of Bulgaria's poorest regions. The population consists of 800 ethnic Bulgarians (mostly pensioners since the exodus of younger people to towns in the 1960s and 1970s), and 308 Roma. It has two primary schools, and high schools are located in nearby towns. Over 30 percent of Roma children under 15 do not attend school regularly. An NGO program based in a neighboring village provides Roma children with free food. A doctor and nurse come daily from Lom, and there is also a medical auxiliary who lives in the village. There are telephone lines in most houses and bus service to Lom. Only twenty-four people in the village are officially employed; most villagers survive in the subsistence economy.

Sredno Selo,
Lovech district
Pop. 130

This isolated highland village is in the northern foothills of the Balkans. Inhabitants are almost exclusively Bulgarian Turks, with three Pomak households and no Roma. There is abundant grazing land, and people cultivate potatoes and hay for livestock. The village has a reputation for backwardness. Most people survive by cattle breeding augmented by farming small plots, gathering wild forest products, and finding odd jobs in timber extraction. Transportation infrastructure has declined drastically.

SMALL AND LARGE TOWNS

Dimitrovgrad,
Haskovo
Pop. 53,229 (1998)

This town in southeastern Bulgaria has a large Roma quarter. The main livelihoods are in mining, construction, and chemical industries, which are now downsizing. Mining operations have polluted agricultural land. There are many state-owned companies and five municipal commercial corporations. The town also has several hospitals and dental clinics, primary and secondary schools, theaters, museums, a library, an art gallery, many community cultural clubs, and several Sofia-based NGOs. It is home to the largest Sunday market in the south.

Etropole,
Sofia
Pop. 15,408 (1997)

Located in mountainous central Bulgaria, this highland mining town is 17 percent Roma. Unemployment is high. Four enterprises have closed, and there are rumors that the town's main source of employment, the Elatzite copper mine, may also close. The town has a primary school and two high schools. Thirty-five percent of the children under 15, mostly from the Roma community, do not attend school. There are many pensioners.

Kalofer,
Plovdiv
Pop. 4,200

Ethnic Bulgarians are the main population group in this highland town, but there is social cohesion between Bulgarians and Roma. Industries laid off heavily in 1996–97. Many people are temporarily unemployed and receive only part or none of their pay. There is a secondary vocational school, a boarding school for orphans and disadvantaged children, and an idle tailoring factory.

CITIES

Jugen municipality,
Plovdiv
Pop. 78,000

One of six municipalities in Plovdiv (pop. 350,000), Jugen has railways and bus stations, public and private telephone posts, twelve kindergartens, ten schools, a nearby university, and several industries. There are 23,000 pensioners and 20,000 welfare recipients living below the poverty line. An estimated 8–20 percent of children ages 15–18 do not attend school. There is a Roma quarter, although it is not Plovdiv's largest.

CITIES (continued)

Krasna Poliana borough, Sofia Pop. 62,000

Krasna Poliana is the poorest of the twenty-four boroughs in the capital city and has the largest Roma community. There are high expectations of state social welfare; most welfare recipients live in the Roma quarter in decrepit hostels built for Vietnamese workers in the 1980s. Disabled people are also extremely disadvantaged.

Maksouda Roma quarter, Varna (30,000 plus households)

One of the largest urban concentrations of Roma in the world is found in this poorest district of Varna. The shipyards, a textile factory, and the Black Sea tourism industry, all prominent in the socialist period, have declined. The informal economy and daily wage labor dominate livelihood opportunities, with some men working in ship repair and construction. Unemployment is 80 percent for men and 100 percent for women. The tiny houses have electricity but no sanitation. There is no school or health center in the area. There are a number of heroin users. Researchers visited Krajezerna Street in the Quarter of Maksouda, which runs along the shore of Varna Lake and includes thirty households. The street is inhabited primarily by Turkish Roma (Turkish speaking and usually Muslim), but there are also Bulgarian Roma (who speak Bulgarian and Romany and are Christian) and Vlach Roma (who speak Romanian and a Romany dialect and are also Christian).

SPECIAL GROUPS

Nurses, Sofia

The group consisted of four nurses working at a polyclinic, two school nurses, and one school dental nurse. Bulgarian schools used to have doctors, nurses, and dentists, but this system has been dismantled.

Homeless youth, Sofia central railway station

This group included seven young people ages 18 to 24 (Bulgarian, Turkish, Roma) living at the railway station. Most of them have lived there for ten years.

Heroin users, Maksouda Roma quarter, Varna

About 750 people in Maksouda are heroin users, two-thirds of them between 15 and 25 years old. Travel to Central and Eastern Europe is common; parents often send children to rural villages for detoxification.

Notes

1. The study team was led by Petya Kabakchieva, Illia Illiev, and Yulian Konstantinov, and included Kristina Andonova, Gyulbie Dalova, Vera Davidova, Dimitar Dimitrov, Milena Harizanova, Toni Mileva, Raitcho Pojarliev, Ivan Popov, Dessislav Sabev, Venelin Stoichev, Vesselin Tepavicharov, and Milena Yakimova.

2. National Statistical Institute and World Bank estimates.

3. At the international poverty line of $2.15 a day, 3.1 percent of the population fell below poverty. World Bank, "Making Transition Work for Everyone: Poverty and Inequality in Europe and Central Asia" (Report 20920, August 2000), 5.

4. Poor people's views of those with a "normal" life stirred lively debates among reviewers of this chapter. One group of reviewers felt that the participants had forgotten what their lives were really like under communism. The other group felt that poor people were remembering that they used to be able to meet their basic needs and that the state provided a safety net. Participants recall those times with great longing despite the disadvantages that accompanied them, such as long waits for goods and services and a repression of some rights.

5. Land restitution was completed after the fieldwork for the study.

6. World Bank, "Project Appraisal Document on a Proposed Loan in the Amount of Euro 8.8 million (US$ 8 million equivalent) to the Republic of Bulgaria for a Child Welfare Reform Project" (Report 21012-BUL, Human Development Unit, Europe and Central Asia Region, February 9, 2001), 3.

7. Ibid. A new Child Protection Act has passed the Bulgarian Parliament, and there is a newly functioning Agency for Child Protection. The government is also reforming its child welfare program and has launched activities to deinstitutionalize some children and improve conditions for those remaining in institutions. External aid agencies, including the World Bank, are supporting many of these initiatives.

8. The data are based on self-identification of ethnicity, and there is likely some under-reporting of the Roma population and over-reporting of both ethnic Bulgarians and Turks.

9. G. Fotev, ed., *Neighborhood of Religious Communities in Bulgaria* (in Bulgarian) (Sophia: Bulgarian Academy of Science, 2000).

10. For example, the 1992 census found that two-thirds of ethnic Turks lived in villages.

11. "Project Appraisal Document on a Proposed Loan in the Amount of Euro 8.8 million (US$ 8 million equivalent) to the Republic of Bulgaria for a Child Welfare Reform Project," 107.

12. *Household Budgets in the Republic of Bulgaria 2000* (Sofia: National Statistical Institute, 2001).

Kyrgyz Republic

Crumbling Support, Deepening Poverty

Janna Rysakova, Gulnara Bakieva, Mariam Edilova,
Nurdin Satarov, and Kathleen Kuehnast[1]

Temirbek is a 38-year-old father of four living in Tash-Bulak, a hilly farming village in the region of Jalal Abad known for its long and severe winters. Tash-Bulak is a Muslim community and a relatively new home to its 600 residents. Like every community, it has its own set of problems. But Tash-Bulak stands out for its steep topography, which creates a constant threat of landslides and mudslides. People migrated here after a mudslide devastated their former hillside village, Kainar, in 1987.

When Temirbek lived in Kainar, he lived well. He worked as a tractor operator on a collective farm and owned cattle, sheep, and a house. He says the period of resettlement after the landslide was difficult, but manageable. The government gave out free land in the relocation area, regularly brought in fresh drinking water, and provided other support for the new villagers. "Our lives were fine until 1994," says Temirbek. That's the year the villagers endured a second mudslide.

The 1994 disaster dealt a devastating blow to the villagers because the government assistance that aided recovery from the first mudslide was no longer available. Official plans for irrigation and a vineyard for Tash-Bulak also evaporated. The villagers now are left to themselves, coping with dirty water, infertile soils, and isolation. Land taxes pose an additional new burden. After twelve years, the community's only formal institution is still a single elementary school with just four grades. The nearest school where children can continue their education is ten kilometers away, so children who lack transportation drop out of school after fourth grade. Temirbek says many children simply grow up illiterate.

With the fall of communism and transition to a market economy in 1991, many livelihood opportunities and public services simply disappeared in Tash-Bulak. The end of the collective farm has been painful for Temirbek:

> When collective farms were disbanded, we thought everything would be fine. We could be masters of our own land and would enjoy good profits and become rich. It turned out to be the other way round. It turned out that we were used to having problems solved for us. When we faced problems, we realized that we were not prepared for the new way of life. Formerly, jobs, salaries, and prices were stable. Everything was available in the stores. When the so-called "market" economy came down, it ruined everything old. This has resulted in poverty.

Temirbek now struggles to support his wife and four children. He has tried to cultivate his two hectares of land, but the land is not fertile, and without irrigation his harvests are meager. He explains,

> When you sow you hope to harvest at least the minimum, but unfortunately my efforts were in vain. I have to feed my children and so I sold some cattle to buy wheat and clothes. Three years ago, one sack of flour was worth one sheep. There are six of us in the family. One sack of flour will last us for twenty days. So, we had to sell one sheep every month to buy flour, and in the end we had no sheep left. One can patch torn clothes, but how can one patch an empty stomach?

Temirbek also worries about illness and medical expenses:

> During the Soviet period, we liked to get sick because we were paid for each sick day, and we would have some rest. At that time, medical services were free of charge. Everything was free of charge. Now, I fear to think about getting sick. Once you step into the clinics or the hospital, you start spending money. One cannot afford to get sick now. Many sick people do not go to the hospital because medical services are expensive. They have to treat themselves without professional help.

*In addition to worrying about lack of work, poor crops, hungry chil-
dren, high taxes, and medical care, Temirbek confides that he is deeply
concerned about rising conflicts and the emotional toll of people getting
"poorer and poorer every year." He says, "People's psychology has
changed because of poverty. They used to be kinder and smile more.
Now many people do not smile, they look sad. . . They quarrel over
petty things."*

Like Temirbek, other poor men and women in the Kyrgyz Republic
also describe a harsh life in which poverty has become widespread
since 1991. They speak of persistent hunger and declining health. In their
daily struggles to survive, study participants say they must depend exclusively on family and kin because permanent jobs have disappeared, as
has once-reliable government support. With many children of poor
families unable to continue their schooling, the prospect of mounting
illiteracy is an enormous blow to this country that once boasted 97 percent literacy. Men and women in the study report that they were ill
equipped for the extreme economic changes and downturns that have
occurred since the end of communism, and they see few prospects for
reversing widespread destitution.

The Kyrgyz Republic was one of the poorest republics in the Soviet
Union. Since independence in 1991, the country has become known for
having the region's most open political system and for taking market-
oriented policies the furthest in Central Asia. The consolidation of political and economic reforms, however, has not always been smooth. At
various points in the 1990s, opposition parties have been banned,
parliamentary powers curbed, and voting irregularities and high-level
corruption alleged. Although inflation was successfully reined in from
extremely high levels (falling from 700 percent in 1993 to 10 percent in
1998) and tax systems were reformed, the economy has steadily contracted, with the exception of a two-year upswing in 1996 and 1997.
The decade closed with a recession caused by the Russian financial
crisis of 1998. It is estimated that real GDP at the end of 2000 was only
65 percent of the 1990 level.

In 1999 close to two-thirds of the country's roughly 5 million
people lived in poverty, and the average per capita income was US$300.
Almost a quarter of the population is so destitute that they cannot meet
their basic food needs.[2] Eighty percent of poor people, including a large

share of the country's most severely deprived households, live in the country-side. Recent surveys indicate, however, that the Russian financial crisis hit cities and towns the hardest, causing sharp rises in urban poverty.

Three of the poorest regions in the country were selected for this study: Talas, Jalal Abad, and Naryn (see table 2, Study Communities in the Kyrgyz Republic, at the end of this chapter). In addition, research was carried out in Bishkek, the country's capital. Within these areas, eight rural and two urban communities were selected based on locations of markets and roads, population size (to include large, medium, and small villages), levels of poverty, presence of NGOs that could support the study team, and geographic diversity.[3] Most of the communities are small villages of farmers (private and collective), animal herders-breeders, dairy farmers, pensioners, and a few traders.

Within each community, participants for group discussions and individual case studies were selected in consultation with leaders of the local self-governance committees, chairpersons of block management committees, leaders of local non-governmental organizations, community leaders, and community members themselves. Researchers conducted field interviews and discussion groups with 1,100 people, or approximately 100 people in each community. A total of ninety discussion groups were conducted: fifty with only poor people and another forty with both poor and non-poor and special (elderly or refugee) groups. In addition, researchers completed sixty case studies of individuals who are or were poor.

The experiences of local and international organizations, statistical data, and research also informed the study. Sources of information about the communities and institutions included state administrations, schools, village committees, village heads, the Constructor Community NGO, the Center for Support of Non-Governmental Organizations of Naryn Region, and the Ministry of Labor and Social Protection of the Kyrgyz Republic. Fifteen researchers from Counterpart-Kyrgyzstan, a national NGO, were trained in participatory poverty assessment methodology. The study was conducted from February through May 1999.

This chapter opens with a look at the collapse of a mining town after independence and the perceptions of those who experienced firsthand the resulting poverty. It goes on to examine poor people's struggles against deteriorating livelihoods, failing infrastructure, and rising social problems across the study communities. The chapter then reviews the hardships created by collapsing public institutions. In the absence of government support, study participants indicate that the local institutions of family, relatives, friends, neighbors, and the mosque are vital but are also under increasing stress due to rising poverty. The concluding section examines difficulties in gender relations due to unemployment among men and the increasing importance of women as household breadwinners.

Kok Yangak, a Town in Crisis

Kok Yangak sits in a mountain valley 1,500 meters above sea level. A nearby coal mine once employed 80 percent of the town's labor force. With the breakup of the Soviet Union, the mine lost its large Soviet client, and the town lost generous Soviet subsidies. With the collapse of the business, salaries were constantly three to six months late, and in some cases were never paid. Many other institutions that operated in the area during Soviet times, such as clothing factories, recreational facilities, and a clinic, have either shut down or are functioning poorly as privatized facilities.

Unemployment and lengthy wage arrears are the most urgent problems identified by discussion group participants in Kok Yangak. They testify that they—and indeed most of Kok Yangak's estimated 15,000 inhabitants—are sliding deeper and deeper into poverty. "I've been working in this mine for twenty-seven years, and I had some property but sold it all when they stopped paying us. All we have in our house now are two beds with mattresses; my wife and son are hungry all the time," reports a 47-year-old miner.

For this study, nine discussion groups from Kok Yangak were asked to analyze changes in the community's wellbeing over the past ten years. Each group developed its own categories and criteria of wellbeing. While perceptions differ among the groups regarding the precise criteria for and percentage of those who are better off or poor, all of the groups conclude that there have been dramatic increases in the numbers of poor people in the last decade, and that the middle class has all but disappeared.

Table 1 shows an analysis of wellbeing trends by a discussion group of women ages 30 to 55 in Kok Yangak. The group defines wellbeing as a function of wealth, and indicates that most people in Soviet times were considered "middle class" or "wealthy." Currently, however, a majority of people (79 percent) fall into the categories of "poor" and "beggars," compared with 14 percent ten years ago.

TABLE 1 Changes in Wellbeing since the Soviet Period, Women's Discussion Group in Kok Yangak

	Percentage of population	
	10 years ago	1999
Very wealthy	1	3
Wealthy	25	8
Middle class	60	8
Poor	10	76
Beggars	4	3

People in the community who fall into the lower groups are said to lack money, a steady job, land, and farm animals, along with tea and other basic items. Those considered among the very poor may lack a house or a family and may need to beg and scavenge for food in garbage cans. One discussion group describes beggars as "on the verge of death." It is frequently said that poor people suffer the effects of alcoholism, laziness, crime, drugs, hunger, and vulnerability. The small share of people who are now considered middle class or better possess a job, a house, a family, livestock, land, happy children, peace, good health, friends, and "enough of everything." Study participants say that they experience illbeing now, and that their wellbeing would improve with "timely payment of wages and pensions, reopening of factories, restoration of roads and transportation services, free health care services, and some cash in hand."

Many people in the study associate wellbeing with the Soviet period and illbeing with post-Soviet times (box 1). Several discussion group participants suggest that those who now are rich likely became that way through illicit means and special connections. Older people are especially prone to speak of the newly wealthy with great suspicion. "We hear all the time that bank owners steal millions of *som* [local currency] and nobody cares," remarks one elderly woman.

Communities in Struggle

Throughout the country, discussion groups rate unemployment as the most pressing problem facing their communities. Mirlan, a young man from Kok Yangak, reports, "Everybody is busy trying to earn some

"Wellbeing is what we had in the past; we had enough money then, prices were low, health care was free, and doctors were very polite. Education for children was free, too. People respected each other. There were a lot of children and youths. Everybody had a job, wages were paid on time, nobody's rights were abused, and nobody wanted to leave the town."

—An elderly man from Kok Yangak

"Life was just under communism, but we did not realize that. People had good food; every day we had four to five invitations from friends and relatives. We frequently visited friends and invited them. Now it has become difficult because of financial problems. In the past we did not worry about the future, nor did we have problems with unemployment."

—An elderly male pensioner

"During the Soviet period, there were fewer crimes. Everything was cheap. People lived in the same predicaments, like everybody else. There was no division into the rich and the poor."

—Ulan, a young man in Tash-Bulak

"Every family had a radio, every other family had a telephone, wages were high. Now people are poor again."

—Anara, an old woman living in Urmaral

"In Soviet times there were no beggars, no poor people, ever. Everybody lived well."

—Ethnic Kurd in Beisheke

"Those who don't feel sorry about the collapse of the Soviet Union have no heart, but those who think that it may be restored have no brain."

—An elderly person from At Bashi

"In the Soviet Union there was enough wheat, and people—just common people—were taken care of much better than they are now."

—Gulnar, an elderly woman living in Ak Kiya

money, but the chances to make some money are very poor. All these problems are getting more serious every year. The only goal that people have nowadays is getting something to eat, that's all." Many poor people are turning to informal jobs and growing their own food; however, these efforts are greatly impeded by a lack of markets, credit, and agricultural inputs as well as by crumbling infrastructure. People in both urban and rural communities indicate that rising crime and alcoholism are consequences of the deteriorating economy.

Precarious Livelihoods

Since the privatization of collective farms and state industries, poor people have endured great insecurity and a nearly total lack of permanent jobs. Nurzat, a young woman living in Bishkek, says, "Jobs must be the first priority. It will give people the possibility to have decent living standards and will gradually alleviate the poverty."

A 1998 survey found that 40 percent of the working-age population in the country is engaged in informal labor activities.[4] Both skilled and unskilled workers appear to be resorting to informal livelihoods. According to a discussion group of teachers in the village of Uchkun, "There aren't enough jobs, so many trained teachers sell items at the market or just stay at home, and the old teachers who long ago reached pension age keep working." Earnings from informal activities appear to be extremely low. The same survey revealed that informal work, despite its prevalence, accounts for less than 15 percent of all household income.

Agricultural Hardships

Given the precarious state of self-employment and wage labor, people throughout the country are turning to agriculture to survive. Almost half the total work force is currently employed in agriculture, up from 33 percent in 1990. In addition, about two-thirds of the population is now engaged in some form of farming or livestock production; however, more than half of farm output is for home consumption or is exchanged informally.[5] When discussing obstacles to more profitable agricultural livelihoods, people in the study draw attention to problems accessing inputs, markets, and credit.

"There are no fertilizers, and the soil is getting more and more barren. There are no chemicals against weeds, so we have lots of weeds and lose many of our crops this way," reports an elderly participant from the village of Uchkun. Although once available, agricultural equipment and the network of irrigation channels are in disrepair in some of the villages. Veterinary medicine is also said to be more difficult to obtain.

In the Naryn region, the poorest area of the country, people assert that the transition to a market economy has been exceptionally difficult. Many struggle to earn a living in a marketplace that lacks a critical mass of buyers, sellers, cash, and in some cases, an actual physical space where all can convene. In the village of At Bashi, people without cash must resort to exchanging valuable livestock for staples such as flour and wheat. A discussion group in Achy explains that they must sell their labor-intensive agricultural products to retail traders who offer very low prices because farmers lack the time, money, and connections to seek out better markets. Similarly, men from the village of Uchkun say, "Prices of grain and livestock are very low in autumn. We have to sell cheap, because we need cash to buy school supplies and clothes for children. The traders know it and set low prices or exchange goods and products, such as tea, oil, and vodka, for grain." Sluggish markets take an especially hard toll on the poor.

Lack of Credit

In several communities, access to credit is a pressing priority, as there are many barriers that keep poor people from obtaining financing. In rural areas, people are frustrated by a lack of information about available loans, by obstacles to obtaining the documents necessary to get a loan, and by transportation difficulties that prevent them from conveniently accessing these services. The following comments from a discussion group in Uchkun are typical:

> Many people want to obtain loans, but they're afraid that their crops will be too poor and that they won't be able to repay the loans on time. Besides, to obtain a loan, one needs to provide a whole lot of documents, and to get all these documents one has to go to the town or to the neighboring village where the village council is. Sometimes the right official isn't there, and people go back without the documents they need, and have to pay 15 som for transportation. For many of us, it's not affordable.

Sonun, a mother of three living in Bishkek, says, "Common people can hardly obtain a loan. They cannot receive a cent unless they bribe someone. Everybody is eager to work the land, but in vain, because of lack of money. If people had money, things would be better."

Absence of Basic Infrastructure

Many poor communities lack basic infrastructure. In particular, inadequate transportation and lack of water stand out in many discussion groups as two problems that greatly impact daily life.

Poor people frequently report that crumbling roads, unreliable transport, and broken or nonexistent communication technologies limit their economic opportunities and access to vital services, such as health care. An elderly man from Kok Yangak says that because government agencies are no longer located in town, to reach authorities one must go to the district center, which is fifty kilometers from Kok Yangak and virtually inaccessible due to inadequate transportation. Similarly, the village of Urmaral has no local shops, and with bus service to nearby towns canceled, residents are left walking the five kilometers to Bakai Ata, the district center, to buy food. Urmaral villagers also say they are concerned because their telephone service has fallen into disrepair and placing a phone call now also requires a trip to Bakai Ata. A villager in Achy says, "There's no transportation to the town of Jalal Abad where I get goods to resell here. Gasoline is very expensive, so transportation is expensive, too. Public phones don't function, so it's impossible to call an ambulance."

In 1999 slightly more than half the rural population had access to running water, compared with 85 percent of the urban population.[6] Among the communities visited for this study, all but one lacked access to safe drinking water. Some of the villages and urban neighborhoods never had water service, but for others this problem is more recent and is linked to water channels built during Soviet times that have since broken.

In Beisheke villagers must get drinking water from a spring outside the town because there is no pipeline; they consider the poor quality of this water to be one of their major problems. Obtaining water from local rivers and springs can be risky, especially in the winter months. In some of the newer urban communities of Bishkek, people must also travel to retrieve water. Residents of Kok Yangak are concerned about the safety of their drinking water. They say that intestinal diseases are becoming more frequent, especially in summertime and among children. In Tash-Bulak a discussion group of women and men reports, "Our problem is water, both for drinking and for irrigation. There is no water for people, no water for animals. We were lucky to have a rainy month. We use snow water and rainwater, and the animals drink out of puddles." Chinara, a 50-year-old woman living in Tash-Bulak, where poor people must buy their water, says, "In my opinion, people need water as badly as they need air. There is no life without water. Water means health." Asel, an elderly woman also from Tash-Bulak, agrees: "I often dream of clean spring water in my sleep. Clean water is life, it is happiness, it is health."

Mounting Social Problems

With increasing economic stress, alcoholism and crime are commonly perceived to be growing in poor communities. A woman in Ak Kiya says, "There are a lot of people in this village who drink vodka in the morning and then go do something bad, commit crime." Reports of increased theft of crops and animals are also common. Sulputay, a widow from Kenesh, says, "The council of elders is based in the neighboring village. I think it is useful to have it, because theft, especially cattle-stealing, has increased. My son's peers are idle, they drink alcohol, gamble, watch videos." Elderly people in Bashi claim, "Young guys steal . . . chickens, or bedclothes that are drying in the sun, then sell them or exchange them for vodka and cigarettes." People in Uchkun report, "Because of unemployment, young people start drinking, commit crimes, rape, [and] steal cattle." Women and men in Urmaral state that "thieves put their health and even lives at risk and steal because it's the only way for them to survive . . . they don't have food and clothes."

In sharing their lives, study participants often identify multiple disadvantages that, together, are especially difficult to overcome. A middle-aged man from Kok Yangak, for instance, draws linkages between poverty and unemployment, alcoholism, crime, hunger, and illness:

> Wellbeing means work and the ability to work. Work improves you and makes you feel happy. Other things that contribute to wellbeing are peace and good health. In this town there are no jobs and there are a lot of unemployed people. Illbeing is alcoholism and laziness. We can't feel protected even in daytime. Crime and drugs are growing problems, people are killed. When people are hungry, they are likely to steal from others, rob others, even kill. My relatives often get ill; I haven't enough money to support my family and children. I feel sorry for myself and my children.

When asked about the consequences of poverty, the same man says, "Poverty results in suicide, hunger, death, lack of money, lack of hope. Things are getting worse every day. People are afraid of starvation, lack of heating, ethnic unrest. People bite one another like dogs."

Limited Institutional Support

"Half my life has passed in misery. I may finish this life in misery too," says Nazgul, a 30-year-old woman from Tash-Bulak. Many poor people express concerns that government institutions are failing to perform basic functions at a time when they need such services more than ever. Nor does the private sector seem to play a meaningful role in helping poor people. Daniyar, of Kenesh, says, "In the past, during the Soviet period, government took care of the nation. Now, under the market economy, each person must take care of and provide for themselves." An old man in Beisheke says, "We're in transition now, but we weren't prepared for it, weren't used to working independently. We expected every problem to be resolved by the government, so we need to change our mentality now."

Poor men and women describe extensive problems with public agencies and programs. The prevalence of government corruption leaves them little hope that pressing for improvements would do much good, and they seem largely resigned to relying on informal coping mechanisms, which are also strained. Participants in Kenesh say that they have no hope of outside help, even from the village government, and nowadays relatives may be unable to help. "Relatives and friends have their own problems," says Sulputay, a poor widow.

State Institutions: Fractured and Lacking Accountability

State institutions are generally viewed as dysfunctional and lacking in accountability. Most discussion groups raise the problem of government corruption, which is viewed as widespread. A refugee now living in Tash-Bulak asks,

> Why ask the village self-governance authority, regional administration, or state administration for help when they live at our expense, collecting taxes? When we apply to them they tell us there is no money, yet at the same time they build themselves houses, buy imported cars, and the like. Therefore I do not trust them.

Ulan, a disabled man also from Tash-Bulak, says, "Now everybody steals everything. In the past government officials who stole or embezzled public property were prosecuted and imprisoned. Now they only indict petty criminals, but those who steal millions escape with impunity."

Most discussion groups express a profound distrust of politicians and officials, and indicate that obtaining services often requires family ties, personal connections, or bribes. Elderly people in At Bashi report, "If you have no relatives among high government officials, people treat you as second-rate. If you have any problem with your business, or get in trouble with the police, you will lose your case and won't have any problems resolved. Those who have money and power always win."

In rural areas, villagers still look to the heads of their local self-governance bodies to resolve a wide range of economic and social problems in their communities. Their patience, however, is growing thin. Participants in Uchkun say, "We all apply to the head of the self-governance body for seeds, equipment, and fuel, but he has never given us anything, and he wants money. If we had money we would buy everything ourselves, and there would be no use for him."

Not only politicians, but police, post office employees, and tax collectors are viewed as corrupt and uncaring. In urban settings, study participants held particularly long discussions about unsatisfactory police performance and judicial corruption. Younger men and women raised concerns that the police lack resources and staff to enforce laws effectively and that they may even break the law themselves. Young men in particular feel that personal safety is a growing community problem and that police offer little protection. Some say that the police do more harm than good. A group of participants in Urmaral exclaims, "Instead of protecting public order, the police just provoke further disorder because they take no measures against those who violate the law." An unemployed 27-year-old man asserts, "Now even murderers can avoid punishment. Their relatives give huge bribes to law enforcement officials, judges, and even relatives of the victim. What can a district police officer do in such a situation? Nothing, not even on a village level."

Post office staff and other local officials responsible for distributing pensions and other social assistance benefits are described as corrupt and disdainful of poor people. One elderly participant in Ak Kiya indicates that "Pensions and social benefits are paid late and in-kind. We receive oil and flour instead [of cash], and they are overpriced, 210 *som* per sack of flour that can be bought at the market for 160 to 180 *som*." A participant from Uchkun reports,

We go to the post office to receive pensions and other social benefits, but instead we get vegetable oil. Now we have so much oil in our houses, there is no extra room to store it. Also at the post office they make us buy two-month-old newspapers. Even if we don't buy them, they will still deduct the price from our pensions. One newspaper costs 5 som. If someone protests, they will not get a tractor or a combine harvester in the spring.

In the absence of pensions and a strong economic environment, households headed by people 60 years old and above have the highest poverty rate in the country. During fieldwork in Kok Yangak, researchers for this study observed a long line of elderly people outside the post office at 4:30 in the afternoon. The researchers noted that the pensioners looked tired and sad, had weather-beaten hands, and were dressed in worn-out clothes. One of the pensioners explained that they had been waiting since five A.M., while post office employees refused even to confirm that pensions would be paid that day. One of the pensioners began to cry and said that his wife would not let him in the house if he returned without money, and the others mocked him, saying, "Don't cry. You aren't a woman, are you?" Another in line indicated that the post office staff might throw some money at them "as if we were dogs," but that there wouldn't be enough for everybody.

The topic of taxes and tax collectors also raises the ire of many discussion groups. Not only are tax rates deemed too high and an unreasonable burden on people struggling just to survive, but many rural participants report that tax officials refuse to acknowledge changes in land use and adjust rates accordingly. Explaining that his land no longer has irrigation or even drinking water, a young man from the village of Tash-Bulak says, "We still have to pay taxes as if this land were irrigated. The rate of tax for irrigated land is three times as high as for non-irrigated."

Study participants also draw attention to difficulties obtaining health care due to the introduction of fees in recent years. Erjan, a 67-year-old retired factory worker from At Bashi, tells researchers that he has just been denied a much-needed eye surgery because he lacks the money. Similarly, Nazgul, a 30-year-old mother living in Tash-Bulak, says she cannot afford treatment for her kidney disease, and now her health is in rapid decline. She remarks, "Wellbeing is health above all. I lost my health without realizing how it happened and lost everything with it. I want to be able to work in the field like others, but I have no strength."

Education is another pressing problem. The long distances to schools and the costs of books, school supplies, and clothes present formidable obstacles to poor children's education. A 1997 survey found that education expenditures represented 14.1 percent of poor people's total consumption.[7] For poor children in rural communities, schools can be inaccessible. Erkinbek, a man from Achy, says, "We have only a primary school. After the fourth grade, our children have to go to other schools. The schools are far away and there is no bus service, so the kids have to walk. It's very difficult for them, especially in the winter." Saltanat, an elderly school teacher in Achy, concurs:

In the school where I continue to work, the situation is getting worse. When I see children who are poorly dressed and suffer from cold in the winter, it makes me feel really sorry for them. The children come from different sites located five to six kilometers from the school, and it takes them half an hour to an hour and fifty minutes to get to the school. In winter, in cold weather, some children did not attend school for weeks and even months. I found out that they just didn't have warm clothes or footwear.

It is also hard to retain instructors. Women from Achy note,

Teachers from our school are in a desperate situation. They don't receive their wages for months. The school is far from the center of the village, and there are no cultural institutions and no shops near it. To buy things, people have to go to the town of Jalal Abad. Turnover in the school is very high because of all these difficulties.

Communities in several areas forge and retain bonds over children's education. In Achy the director of a local school in urgent need of repair describes the practice of *ashar,* the pooling of funds and labor:

Our school is one of the first schools in Achy. It needs complete remodeling, but neither the local authorities nor the central government have money for it. We tried to get some money for remodeling, but it was hopeless. The money that parents of the schoolchildren collect is just enough for minor repairs. But we are trying to do something about it. We began construction of a new building by the ashar *method.*

Young men in Urmaral say, "We can't live without the school. We have to think about our children, and we're grateful to the teachers for their patience and hard work."

Social Networks: Invaluable but Stretched

People in the Kyrgyz Republic place heavy emphasis on helping one another and overwhelmingly view their network of families, relatives, friends, and neighbors as the most important and valuable institution in their lives (box 2). Participants in all communities report that they rely heavily on these ties and the continuous exchange of food, money, labor, information, and support that they facilitate. The mosque is also a key institution in many communities.

Across communities poor people come together to address local needs. Urmaral, situated in the northern region of the Kyrgyz Republic, is a small community of 640 people. The residents of Urmaral value working together to address common problems, and all but two families in the village belong to a collective farm. At one point, the villagers joined forces to build a mosque. A group of elderly participants proudly reports, "We built the mosque ourselves, without any support. We get together at the mosque to pray, promote Islam, and, together with the council of elders, resolve disputes that arise in families or in the community as a whole." Kuban, an elderly man from the same village, says, "The mosque is our court, school, and lawyer, while the village council is of no support, and policemen just provoke disorder."

Poor people speak highly of their local mosques, for both the spiritual and material aid they provide. In rural villages such as Uchkun and At

---

BOX 2 Kyrgyz Proverbs on the Ties that Bind

There is a long tradition of valuing kin and neighbors in the Kyrgyz Republic. In discussions, participants relate many local proverbs that illustrate their importance:

"Relatives are the most precious people in the world."

"Buy a neighbor, then buy a house. A good neighbor will always come to help."

"Don't look for a good house, look for a good neighbor."

"It is better to have a hundred friends than a hundred rubles."

"It is better to have a good neighbor than a bad relative."

Bashi, there are young, active mullahs who perform ritual services. They also educate children and young men in the basics of Islam and sometimes give advice on local problems and personal health issues. Similarly, a woman from the urban community of Kok Yangak says, "One institution that I trust is the mosque. Respect to the mosque is respect to the tradition, you know, when you feel your identity, have that sense of belonging to the Muslim world. . . . Women don't enter the mosque, and yet the mosque is a sacred place for me."

Unfortunately, the dismantling of the state and a breakdown of the economy may prove overwhelming to these local bonds and institutions, which are showing signs of stress in the face of prolonged hardship. Social relations are fraying as many people are unable to reciprocate gifts, money, food, or even tea and sugar. A middle-aged woman from Uchkun village believes that "people no longer trust each other. Even relatives don't trust each other any more because when you lend money, you may never get it back, and a distant relative may even bring a thief into your house."

An elderly woman in Ak Kiya observes, "There is no unity now in the village. We don't visit each other. We used to help one another by raising money together, and now we don't because people don't have enough for themselves." An ethnic Uzbek living in At Bashi says, "People think only about themselves and their families nowadays; the rich and the poor alike, they no longer think of others. In the past, people participated in celebrations, helped those who had problems, while now everybody just thinks about ways to survive."

Many parents and children make great efforts to support one another as help is increasingly rare outside the family. A participant in Ak Kiya says, "My only support is my children. I rely on myself and my family, nobody else." However, widespread unemployment of young adults has strained even these family bonds because many children cannot support their aging parents, but instead are supported by them. An old man in At Bashi asks, "Is it acceptable that the elderly have to support young adults? My sons occasionally do some work, but it's quite rare."

Conflicting Gender Roles

Women in the Kyrgyz Republic have long worked outside the home. They make up half the work force formally employed in agriculture, and they also contribute most of the labor needed to maintain household plots. With high male unemployment, many poor women in the Kyrgyz Republic have also taken up petty trading and other informal jobs to help bring food to the table. This shift in breadwinner roles is proving to be a difficult adjustment, particularly in rural areas, where cultural traditions remain entrenched and gender inequalities are often severe. In the six communities where the sensitive issue of domestic abuse was discussed openly, most acknowledge that it occurs, and discussion groups from two communities report worsening trends.

Unsettled Times for Households

A 50-year-old woman from the remote farming village of Tash-Bulak expresses confusion and dismay over changes in women's roles and responsibilities:

> *A woman must obey her husband, as the man is head of the household, father of the children. Older people say, don't look upon your husband, don't threaten your husband, or else you will go to hell. Wherever men get together, women must go round. Girls were taught from their childhood to be obedient, never walk without head covering, wear long dresses. Now girls have opened up; they wear trousers. Women seek work in the cities. I can hardly understand what is going on. I always obeyed my husband, even though he was good for nothing.*

Discussions about gender responsibilities and decision making at the household level generated heated debates. A few participants assert that Kyrgyz women have always worked diligently both inside and outside of the home, and that there is a strong tradition of nomadic women's active participation in important household decisions. More generally, however, men and women believe that women's status has risen in recent years. Views on whether this social change is positive or negative vary widely among young and old, urban and rural, men and women.

Many participants indicate that a reversal in men's and women's roles as breadwinner and caretaker seems to be taking place in some households in their communities, and they express great discomfort and sometimes even anger and despair over this trend. A discussion group of women from Kok Yangak says, "We work in clinics, schools, and other institutions. Our salaries are low, but we are still afraid to lose our jobs.

Employment is important for us because it elevates our status in the family, but it hurts our husbands."

An elderly man from Kenesh, however, expresses outright alarm:

Before, it was clear that the woman is to keep the house and take care of the family while the man earns the daily bread. Now, the woman buys and sells stuff irrespective of the weather and earns the income for the family, while the man is sitting at home taking care of the children, performing the traditional women's work. This is not right; this is not good.

Many, nevertheless, seem resigned to women's increasing confidence, decisiveness, and power. "Today wives rule over their husbands. Even the president's wife rules over her husband. What can we do? We just have to put up with it," observes a young man from Bishkek. Some men seem to welcome the support that women contribute. A man from Kok Yangak says,

Women now play a much more important role in family budgeting than they used to. It's because now women, rather than men, earn the money. Women are better at dealing with tax inspectors. For example, when they don't have an official permit to trade, or don't have the money to pay taxes, they just cry and talk to the inspector, and the inspector is most likely to say that it's okay.

Reports of Domestic Abuse

Despite some gains, men and women in the study paint a troubled picture of trends in domestic violence. Although the evidence is uneven because women hesitate to discuss this sensitive issue, domestic abuse of women appears to be widespread. Some women and men argue that men in their society have always beaten women. A 44-year-old woman from Urmaral, for instance, told the researchers that men in her village beat their wives periodically for disobedience or out of jealousy. Others in the study indicate that rising poverty and changing gender roles are also major causes of domestic abuse.

In some communities, such as the small and isolated mountain village of Ak Kiya, domestic violence is too sensitive an issue to discuss openly with outsiders. When one of the younger women in a discussion group began to name victims of domestic abuse in the village, other women cut short the discussion. In their report on the community researchers explain,

> *Sharing problems of this kind with outsiders is viewed as a disgrace, so the women who were beaten by their husbands felt rather awkward when it was discussed in public. In addition, people believe that only those women who can resolve family problems without conflicts can be called* tyn ayal, *good wives capable of taking good care of the household, so it is quite unpleasant for the women to admit that conflicts do occur in their families.*

Similarly, a woman in Uchkun says, "Very few women go to the health care center if they are physically beaten by their husbands. If there is an apparent trace of beating on a woman's face, she would rather invent some story than admit that she was abused." Silence and secrecy allow abuse to persist, and cultural imperatives forbid women to draw attention to a troubled relationship or to leave. Women report that they are taught from a very young age that a failed marriage is tantamount to a failed life and that women without men are worth nothing. Relatives also may feel they ought to conceal an abuser in order to protect the family's reputation so that the abuser's job prospects are not reduced.

In some contexts the topic is so sensitive that research teams chose not to raise it directly. Instead of analyzing the issue of domestic violence against women, discussion groups reflected on "abuse of rights in the household," with the definition of "rights" left open to interpretation by the groups. A middle-aged woman from Ak Kiya contributed to the topic of "abuse of rights" by mentioning domestic abuse in passing. "My old man could hit me when we were younger," she says, "but now we're no longer kids; we respect one another and don't quarrel." Six of the eight discussion groups in Ak Kiya found that, in general, abuse of women's rights in the household has increased in the last ten years.[8]

In the larger communities, frank discussions about violence against women were possible, and in these communities both men and women indicate that the extent of domestic abuse is the same or worse since the transition from communism. One refugee living in Tash-Bulak explains, "Many women are involved in trading and making money, and they rule in their families. There is abuse against women, it happens in those families, especially where the husband drinks a lot."

Study participants associate the rise in abuse with deepening poverty and increased reliance on women's earnings: men may resort to alcohol abuse and violence out of anger and humiliation at being unable to support their families. An elderly woman from Uchkun village believes that "unemployed men are frustrated because they can no longer play the part of family providers and protectors. They live on the money made by their wives and feel humiliated because of that." Some women feel that they contribute to family conflict. A participant in a discussion group of women from Beisheke explains, "We women start quarrels when there isn't enough food or clothing, and our husbands are very well aware of these problems themselves; they don't need our lecturing. So when they ask us to stop and we don't, they may hit us a couple of times."

Study participants indicate that divorce is now more common than in the past, despite the fact that divorced women are vulnerable to impoverishment and social ostracism. Formal laws ensure that women retain some property rights when households break down; however, women very rarely assert these rights. Making such legal claims is considered shameful because it violates local customs that give full property rights to men and their families. The costs of legal representation, travel, and court fees further limit poor women's access to the court system.[9] Nurgul, 21, says she divorced her husband because he drank to excess and beat her. Her relatives helped her find a room in a dormitory, but she says women there are humiliated, insulted, and sexually harassed by local men who know that the women have no husbands to protect them.

Women and Men in Society

Gender relations at the community level also reflect discouraging trends. A young woman in Kenesh, where discussion groups report that violence against women is increasing, says there are fewer state programs and protective services for women than existed under communism. She remarks, "The state now does not think about women. The woman has to resolve her problems herself and that is very difficult to do now." Similarly, an older man in a discussion group from the same village says, "Women have to deal with raising children. Before, various institutions like the Pioneer Organization, school, and the government assisted her in that, but now she has to rely only on herself."

With the rise in poverty since the Soviet period, many people indicate that women's participation in village or neighborhood organizations has declined. According to a middle-aged man from Uchkun, "Men actively participate in the social life of the community, while women do not attend meetings." Several participants suggest that there was greater gender equality in Soviet times than there is now. An elderly woman from Kenesh reports, "Before, the *kolkhoz* [collective farm] meetings without us would not be valid. We had the right to express our views and participate in making decisions concerning village life. And now no one even listens to us." A middle-aged woman in Bishkek says, "Men and women could be elected to state agencies and organizations on equal grounds. Now, women are practically never elected to represent people in the parliament; the number of women elected is rather insignificant." A woman in Uchkun remarks, "We were really equal with men during the Soviet period, and we should not lose this status now. Kyrgyz women have always been energetic." An old man in Uchkun concurs, "I think there are a lot of clever women in the community, and their words should be taken into account. Sometimes a woman is more intelligent than a man."

Conclusion

In the Kyrgyz Republic, poor people's wellbeing seems to be spiraling downward, and many face increasingly desperate situations. In their daily struggles they see the state as more of an obstacle than an ally, and they are forced to rely heavily on family, relatives, and friends. These social networks, however, also have limited resources and are showing signs of strain. Even the forces of nature seem to be working against many people, as landslides, polluted waters, and meager harvests send already-poor communities deeper into destitution.

People generally believe that during the Soviet period the state governed much more effectively, and many participants argue that the government should recover many of its previous responsibilities and help restore economic life and address urgent community needs. After discussing current problems in his neighborhood, a poor man in Bishkek asserts, "These things do not depend on me. It is the state that must resolve these problems."

The magnitude of poverty in the Kyrgyz Republic requires a variety of approaches to restore economic growth, enhance poor people's security, and create more accountable and effective public services.

Farming and raising livestock are of particular importance to the country's poor population, and programs are needed to make credit, farm inputs, and extension services more accessible to small producers, including women. To improve markets, better roads and transport as well as access to information are needed, especially in remote areas. These investments will also boost self-employment and wage labor opportunities in poor communities. In addition, participants stress that they must have access to clean water to curtail disease and illbeing.

The high levels of human capital in the country are increasingly jeopardized by the protracted economic crisis. In the short run, stronger social assistance programs are needed to keep people out of abject poverty. However, people report many problems with corruption, as well as delayed and in-kind payments of the little social assistance that is available. Decentralized safety net programs that build on community leadership and local organizations can provide a mechanism for more transparent and accountable delivery.

Parents are greatly concerned that their children are not staying in school beyond the early years because schools are remote and parents are unable to meet the expenses of school supplies and clothing. While education is a critical means for people to move out of poverty, there is little social assistance or educational investment available to help poor girls and boys stay in school. The current outlook remains bleak.

Poor men and women who participated in the study often feel overwhelmed by the many hardships in their lives. They try to manage their problems on a day-to-day basis while waiting and hoping for outside assistance. Expressing a sense of helplessness and despair, a middle-aged man in Kok Yangak says, "We were unprepared for such drastic changes in our lives. We have no knowledge that could help us adjust to the new situation. There is nobody to give us advice about it. . . . People are dying every day." A mother in At Bashi sums up the current crisis this way:

> If it goes on like this, I just don't know what to do. My children
> have no decent clothes now, and as they grow, the problem will
> double. . . . We can't even dream about university education for
> them because it's so expensive. The children of the rich are
> going to be rich, too, and have good education, and the children
> of the poor will stay poor.

TABLE 2 Study Communities in the Kyrgyz Republic

URBAN COMMUNITIES

Bishkek, capital city Pop. 670,000	Many new districts have been created for migrants from the countryside. Infrastructure lies in disrepair, roads have deteriorated, and there is no public transportation. Unemployment, low wages, and precarious informal work opportunities are leading concerns. Many recent migrants are not officially registered as permanent residents and are therefore unable to participate in public life.
Kok Yangak, Jalal Abad Pop. 15,000	Situated in a mountain valley at an altitude of 1,500 meters, this town has severe weather and little arable land. Once a prosperous town supplied with goods directly from Moscow, it is now in serious decline. The mine and two key factories closed in 1991, and there is 85 percent unemployment. Infrastructure is collapsing.

RURAL COMMUNITIES

Achy, Jalal Abad Pop. 7,500	Landslides and mudslides forced people to relocate in 1994. The resettlement and privatization of a collective farm led to increased poverty.
Tash-Bulak, Jalal Abad Pop. 600	There is a lack of arable land and clean drinking water. Unemployment is at 95 percent. Taxes are high. Communicable diseases are on the rise, and health is declining. Many of the villagers are refugees from Tajikistan.
At Bashi, Naryn Pop. 12,300	This agricultural village is located in the mountains and faces extreme temperatures in summer and winter. There is a main road through the village, but the streets are dirty and poorly maintained. Villagers are primarily Kyrgyz with a small (3 percent) ethnic Uzbek minority.
Ak Kiya, Naryn Pop. 600	A collective farm was dismantled a few years ago, leaving people worse off than before. Irrigation water used to be provided with the help of a pump, but the pump is broken. People are farmers, but have poor harvests. A mountainous pass separates Ak Kiya from the rest of the country.

Uchkun, Naryn Pop. 2,500	In this remote farming community, most people look somber and tired. There are several joint farms. Most houses were built in the 1960s and now look worn down. Many people are living in *dachas* (cottages with small gardens) in winter in order to save money on heating. Temperatures in summer and winter are extreme.
Beisheke, Talas Pop. 7,000	In this farming community and administrative center, residents are poor farmers who used to work at a collective farm. The village lacks water, and the power supply is unreliable. There is a small Kurd minority.
Kenesh, Talas Pop. 560	The village has little infrastructure; a water reservoir was planned but never built. An elementary school is the only formal institution. Farmers keep cattle and grow grain, potatoes, and corn.
Urmaral, Talas Pop. 635	This farming community is near the Kazakhstan border. All but two families take part in a collective farm. Independent farmers are unpopular. There is some trade with Kazakhstan, but problems with customs officers are common. Infrastructure is underdeveloped.

Notes

1. The study team was led by Janna Rysakova and also included Bakhtiyar Abdykadyrov, Janyl Abdyralieva, Gulnara Bakieva, Mariam Edilova, Takhir Hamdamov, Sagyn Kaimova, Esenkan Osmonaliev, Nurmamat Saparbaev, Nurdin Satarov, Turdububu Shamuratova, Lira Tantabaeva, and Kunduz Ukubaeva.

2. World Bank, "Kyrgyz Republic: Poverty in the 1990s in the Kyrgyz Republic" (Report 21721-KG, Human Development Department, Country Department VIII, Europe and Central Asia Region, January 2001), ii. The value of the poverty line is 8,340 *som* per year (US$170), and the extreme poverty line is 3,849 *som* (US$79). Population and per capita income data are from World Bank, *World Development Indicators 2001* (Report 22099, April 2001).

3. The sample design was especially informed by World Bank, "Kyrgyz Republic: Update on Poverty in the Kyrgyz Republic" (Report 19425-KG, Human Development Department, Country Department VIII, Europe and Central Asia Region, June 1999).

4. World Bank, "Kyrgyz Republic: Poverty in the 1990s," 30.

5. World Bank, "Kyrgyz Republic: Agriculture and Agribusiness: Growth Opportunities and Obstacles" (Poverty Reduction and Economic Management Unit, Europe and Central Asia Region, June 30, 2000, draft), vii.

6. Sanitation facilities are even more limited, with 94 percent of the rural population and nearly half the urban population using latrines. See World Bank, "Kyrgyz Republic: Update on Poverty," iii.

7. World Bank, "Kyrgyz Republic: Update on Poverty," 13.

8. Participants in the two remaining groups estimate the situation to be unchanged over the same period.

9. See R. Giovarelli, C. Aidarbekova, J. Duncan, K. Rasmussen, and A. Tabyshalieva, "Women's Rights to Land in the Kyrgyz Republic" (World Bank, June 30, 2000).

The Russian Federation

Struggling against the Tide

Alexey Levinson, Olga Stouchevskaya, Oxana Bocharova, and Anton Lerner[1]

Svetlana, a 43-year-old mother of three, lives in Ozerny, a farming village founded in the late 1930s in the Ivanovo region. "I used to work at our school as an instruments and equipment keeper," she recalls. "When they started to delay our salary and then stopped paying it, I left." She took a job at the local bakery, but "you had to knead two to three times more than the norm, and they paid you only 270 rubles (about USD$11), half of what they pay you in Ivanovo," she says. The harsh working conditions and low pay caused her to leave the bakery job. Now Svetlana works as a dishwasher in a retirement home cafeteria. In addition to her work at the cafeteria, Svetlana raises pigs, which provides extra income that helps the family survive. Svetlana's earnings are important because while her husband has a job at a boiler house that supplies the village with heat, his employers do not pay him on time. Svetlana says,

> *Our life is hard and we watch every penny. I'm lucky my husband doesn't drink. I don't know how we're going to carry on. The only way is to keep farm animals and grow vegetables. We rely on ourselves—no use hoping someone will come and give us something. We are not well off, but we manage. Our only concern is for the kids to make it in life.*

Poor children bear the stigma of poverty. Because Svetlana's younger son, who is 15, is embarrassed to wear handmade clothes,

Svetlana recently led him to believe that she bought his new jacket at the market, although she had sewn it herself. Having to wear handmade clothing is not the worst effect of poverty on children. Many children from Ozerny's poor families go to school hungry. "What can they understand, what can they learn, if the only thought in their minds is 'How can I get something to eat?'" asks an Ozerny study participant. Svetlana's oldest son has just returned from the army but has yet to find a job. She is afraid her son might take to drinking if he does not soon find something to do.

Last year, many Ozerny residents became officially unemployed when the peat factory finally closed after several years of paying wages very late or not at all. The collective farm remains, but the few people who still work there have not been paid in over a year. Economic problems have made material deprivation a key element of people's daily lives. "It's not life; it's just barely making ends meet," explains one participant when asked to define what it's like to be poor. "We sometimes don't eat bread for five days, and we are so sick of potatoes that we don't know how to ram them down our throats," says another Ozerny resident.

Most housing in Ozerny is dilapidated, mainly due to lack of regular maintenance. A poor man says, "Our apartments badly need renovation. The plumbing is leaking. If the wiring gets short-circuited, there is a danger of fire. There are houses where wiring hasn't been changed in fifty years."

Some key institutions in the village, such as the hospital and the daycare center, have closed. The peat factory used to provide such services at no charge, but a few years ago the responsibility was transferred to the municipal administration and, lacking secure funding, these services soon disappeared. A discussion group describes the terrible blow of losing the local hospital:

> The old hospital was small, but it was there. You could put your mother there. Then they started building a new one, wanted to have a bigger hospital, but didn't have enough resources, and closed it altogether. Now we have to go to Novotalitsy, fifty kilometers away. They seldom agree to admit us to the Ivanovo hospital [twenty kilometers away]; they say we are from a different district.

For 70-year-old Valentina, who lives alone, medical care is out of reach for several reasons:

Now I have gotten old, my eyes are poor. I have glaucoma and a bad heart, but no money to buy medicines. The hospital is in town; it's a long way, and we don't have an eye doctor here. At the hospital they tell me I need surgery, but my pension will not be enough for that. You have to bring everything with you: clothing, food, and even drugs.

Poor men and women from Ozerny say they now feel insecure about the future and find it impossible to plan ahead. "Now we care only about this day. I live today and don't know if tomorrow will come or not," says a young villager. Like many others in Ozerny, old and young alike, a 19-year-old correspondence school student named Sergey sees no future for himself in the village:

This summer, after I pass my exams, I'll go somewhere to look for a job, maybe somewhere at a construction site. . . . In the village it's boring, nothing to do, only a disco on Saturday and drinking. I'm anxious to leave. You can't expect anything good here. The village is dying. But I don't know where to find a job. And I don't want to leave my mother; it'll be difficult for her to be alone.

Poor women and men elsewhere in Russia share many of the same concerns as Ozerny villagers. Like Svetlana, many women report that they support their families, often through a strenuous patchwork of jobs. Many people who have regular employment indicate that they are often paid in kind or that their wages are delayed or eroded by inflation. Many parents now find themselves struggling to provide their children with food, clothes, and education. The elderly report that they are hungry, cold in the winter, and cannot afford medical care. In all ten communities visited for this study, people say that public services are disintegrating.

After seven decades, the Soviet Union broke apart in 1991. The new Russian Federation's transition to a more open political system and economy has been extraordinarily difficult for most Russians. The initial post-Soviet years were plagued with frequent government shake-ups under President Boris Yeltsin, as well as three- and four-digit inflation. In the ten-year period up to 1999, the country's GDP contracted by an average annual rate of 6.1 percent.[2] In 1999 the GDP grew by 3.2

percent and per capita income was US$2,250.[3] Estimates of the proportion of Russia's 147 million people living in poverty ranged from 19 to 49 percent in 1998, depending on the methodology and data used.[4]

Russian governments have generally pursued market-friendly macroeconomic policies and resisted internal protectionist pressures. In the course of a rapid privatization program, however, scandals surrounded many of the transactions transferring ownership, and great numbers of enterprises collapsed after being privatized. Also, many of the remaining state-run enterprises have failed to find markets for their products. With the rule of law generally weak, government corruption and organized crime have escalated, and the environment for private business remains very difficult. In 1998, the year preceding the fieldwork for this study, a financial crisis rocked the economy after a period of relative stability following the 1996 reelection of President Yeltsin. Men and women repeatedly refer to August 17, 1998, the day they say a sharp currency devaluation triggered the "uncontrollable surge of prices" that has left them very insecure. The economic crisis also sparked a shake-up of cabinet leaders. Lack of popular support and political uncertainty continued to surround the Yeltsin administration until the president resigned on December 31, 1999.

The study was conducted in seven urban and three rural areas in seven geographic regions across Russia. Areas were chosen to represent a cross-section of poverty levels and to insure geographic and urban and rural diversity. Study communities included industrial cities, a small mono-industrial town, a street marketplace in Moscow, remote cities in the extreme northeast, and small and large agricultural villages (see table 3, Study communities in Russia, at the end of this chapter).

A total of seventy-five discussion groups were held. These included twenty-one with poor men, twenty-two with poor women, six with poor youths, and twenty-six groups composed of youths, women entrepreneurs, women in remote areas, staff of a youth camp, elderly, and others. A total of seventy-five individual case studies were completed, including thirty-eight with poor women, men, and youths. Another thirty-seven institutional case studies were completed with location-specific individuals and institutions, such as shopkeepers, local authorities, the crafts industry, medical institutions, the church, and the media.

The Russian Center for Public Opinion and Market Research coordinated the fieldwork, which took place from March to May 1999.

Lack of money and loss of livelihoods, decaying infrastructure, unaccountable governance, and weak public institutions are creating intense hardships for poor women and men. The chapter begins with a closer look at the people made recently poor as well as the "new Russians," those who are thriving in the post-Soviet era. It then turns to poor people's struggles with unemployment and wage arrears, crime, alcoholism, and health risks. Next, the chapter explores the failure of Russia's institutions to address the needs of poor people, and it concludes with a brief look at how the rising economic and social strains are affecting gender relations at the household level.

The New Poor and the New Elite

Almost all of the poor men and women participating in Russia's *Voices of the Poor* study say they were not poor in childhood. Instead, they link the beginning of their decline with the beginning of *perestroika*, the process of economic and governmental reform launched in the 1980s. Across communities, most discussion groups report that the "average" wellbeing group, which they equate with the middle class, has become impoverished, while a smaller, wealthy group with close ties to the former Communist elite has become enriched. Residents of Dzerzhinsk assert that before the transition "we, the majority, lived well. Now we live in misery."

The Unraveling of a "Normal Life"

It is striking that participants from many communities refer to wellbeing as the capacity to have a "normal" life. Men and women in a discussion group in Ozerny explain that a 'normal life" for them is characterized by what they had under communism, and includes a "car, housing, and work . . . enough money, and being able to buy food, clothes, and shoes for one's child and for oneself." Participants in Teikovo similarly define a normal life as "having a regular job with a good, regular salary, and the possibility to buy food, new clothes, and medicine." In Belasovka participants say that "a good life is when you drink coffee every morning," "butter your bread," and buy sugar "to make life sweet."

Poor people in Russia frequently express the notion that they were looked after under communism and feel that now they are paying the price for the "Western" ideal of democracy without having the privileges that a more open society and economy are supposed to bring. They stress that the rapid transition to a market economy allowed no time for preparation. "We were taught differently, and we do not know what to do in this new market economy. We are not prepared for this new life," state participants in Magadan. In addition, the whole state system is seen to have collapsed due to institutional weaknesses. In Dzerzhinsk, for instance, some of the causes of poverty listed by discussion groups include bad government, political instability, bad laws, no social protection, inactive trade unions, unfulfilled promises of deputies, "Gorbachev, who ruined the economy," and privatization. In Belasovka participants say, "The constitution doesn't guarantee us anything. You can lose your job and no one will help. We are helpless. . . . We were just as helpless before, but at least we had jobs." Residents of El'mash explain, "Your main objective is to survive, and you couldn't care less about the rest."

Two discussion groups, one of older men and another of younger men, described and categorized levels of wellbeing in their poor neighborhood of Ivanovo, a city well known for its textile industry (table 1). Study participants compared the present with ten years ago, and analyzed changes in the size and characteristics of various wellbeing groups. The discussion groups' analysis reveals generational differences in perceptions of wellbeing trends over the past decade, with older men identifying larger declines for people who are in the middle and poor categories, and younger men perceiving a shift toward a larger population at the top and very bottom of society. The younger men, for example, say a new group of people has emerged in recent years in Ivanovo, whom they label "the successful," and they put entrepreneurs and those with "a good job" in this upper category. Older men in Ivanovo estimate that 73 percent of the population is poor, a much larger proportion than the 40 percent estimated by the younger men. Both groups say homeless people, a recent phenomenon, lack incomes and are actively excluded by the larger society (box 1). The younger group, however, puts the homeless at 10 percent of the population compared with the 2 percent estimated by the older men.

The Ivanovo discussion groups, and indeed those in the other nine communities visited as well, identify very steep declines for the large middle group since the end of communism. The older men, remembering a time when they were taken care of by the state, say the middle category enjoyed many public services "free of charge." Today, a greatly shrunken middle group is mainly characterized by being able to count on "stable wages," according to both the older and younger men. Other Ivanovo discussion groups portray the middle wellbeing category variously as having "scarce food"; living "from one payday to another"; and having

TABLE 1 Levels of Wellbeing, Two Discussion Groups in Ivanovo

Men ages 36–60

Before Communism ended	Percentage of population	Now	Percentage of population
The Rich *Obkom* officials (regional Communist Party bodies, former authorities).	5	Directors of enterprises, administrators, organized crime, bankers. Have luxury cars, expensive furniture.	5
The Middle Intellectuals, workers. Many things came from the state free of charge.	80	Active people who have connections, mid-level officials, entrepreneurs, employees who get more or less regular wages.	20
The Poor Collective farm pensioners.	15	Doctors, teachers, pensioners, invalids, workers who do not receive their wages, the unemployed. Live on reserves put aside for lean times.	73
The Homeless –	–	Alcoholics, vagabonds, those who sold their apartments to crooks. They no longer want anything from life.	2

Men ages 25–35

Before Communism ended	Percentage of population	Now	Percentage of population
The Rich Former Communist Party officials who became capitalists.	7	Rich entrepreneurs, directors of enterprises, administrators. Have cottage or several apartments, luxury cars, vacations abroad, wives not working.	5
The Successful –	–	Small entrepreneurs and people who have stable and well-paid jobs such as dentists. Have an apartment and a car.	10
The Middle Rich were few, "folks were all equal."	90	Workers, clerks, those who get stable wages and can make both ends meet; they live from one payday to another.	35
The Poor Beggars and drunkards.	3	Teachers, doctors, pensioners. Don't have enough money to live; they buy the cheapest products.	40
The Homeless –	–	The unemployed if they have no earnings on the side. Have no money, eat mostly bread, live on the pensions of their aged relatives.	10

– Not applicable.

Poor people's perceptions of the most destitute in their community are very unfavorable. "They beg, eat cats and dogs, and steal," claims a resident of Ozerny when talking about those who are the worst off. People in other communities observe that the poorest families often have many children and lack the resources to take care of them. They also note that the "drunkards and homeless" and "beggars" largely do not interact with other members of society. "Who will deal with those who dig in the trash and eat right from the waste bins? They are all ill with tuberculosis, they are full of insects, and they never wash themselves," says a participant in Magadan.

Some discussion groups talk about the poorest of the poor with a mix of sympathy and disgust. In Ivanovo people refer to the *bomzh* (homeless) as morally ruined people, without any hope of improving their situation. A group of younger men in Dzerzhinsk suggests that, paradoxically, the homeless might not live so badly after all. "Maybe their life is not that bad because they do not care any longer. So they eat what other people will never eat, and good for them," the men say.

"normal food and decent clothes, but not purchased every month." A group of elderly people says that people in the middle suffer "shy poverty," that is, "not begging, but dying quietly."

Although they may suffer from hunger and perhaps from untreated illnesses, for reasons of pride, few of the people who belong to the middle group want to call themselves poor. With memories of better times still fresh in most people's minds, their recent, deepening poverty has left many feeling humiliated and frustrated. Some see no way out of the crisis. As one participant from Ozerny says, "Sometimes you simply don't feel like living. You think, why don't they just send an armored personnel carrier down and have us all shot dead. Sometimes you don't know what day it is; it doesn't matter. And before, we used to wait for the weekend, getting ready for it."

A participant in Magadan observes, "We seem to forget more and more what wellbeing is." Some in Ivanovo remark that the crisis was manufactured "to enslave us to the West [America]" because "it's easier to rule the people when they are poor."

The "New Russians"

In many of the communities visited in Russia, people report that there is a new elite as well as a large group of newly poor. For study participants, the newly wealthy often include "profiteers" as well as hard-working entrepreneurs who have been able to adjust to the market economy.

In El'mash the attitude toward people who are well off is quite negative. People in this category include government authorities, former party bosses, criminals, and directors and managers of enterprises. All are viewed as dishonest and are described as taking early advantage of their positions during privatization—a period that some refer to as "plunder."

Julia is among the new elite in Ozerny, and she believes that her hard work rather than any special connections contributed to her current success. She has lived in the village since 1952 and is managing reasonably well despite "everything falling apart." Once a deputy director of a trading firm, Julia voluntarily left her job in 1993 when the director was forced to start downsizing. She then began to drink heavily but says she stopped before losing complete control. "I thought, I have a family; I must do something." She managed to find work again in a new bakery and was soon offered a leading position there. Her starting salary was just 150 rubles (US$6) a month, but now she makes 2,000 rubles (US$80), an amount that she says almost no one earns in her village.

Although many would be happy just to be employed in a single job, Julia holds a second job. In addition to working at the bakery, she runs a private sewing business with her husband. They buy cloth from warehouses, hire labor for sewing, and then sell the ready-made items. Julia says she and her husband rise at 5 A.M. every day and regularly work twelve- to fourteen-hour days. They do not take vacations and cannot afford a car, but do not consider the latter so important as they can carry their goods to the market.

Julia tells the researchers that some people are envious of her good fortune, and adds, "They don't care that we get up at five o'clock." She continues,

> It's the old grudge from the Soviet time when my husband was chief engineer at the peat enterprise and I was in trade. Everybody believes that we live as comfortably as we used to. But it was only in town that people could take advantage of their top positions. And we quit our jobs of our own accord.

Study participants across communities acknowledge that some people were quite wealthy under the previous system also, but they claim that inequalities have become much more visible now. European cars, expensive clothing, big houses, good food, and material goods characterize the life of the new elite. When most poor Russians describe a "normal life," a life of wellbeing, however, they do not point to the "luxurious, showy, and conspicuous" new Russians as exemplars of that life. Instead they speak of what they themselves had before communism ended.

Struggling to Hang On

Poor Russians link the deterioration of their wellbeing to the political and economic transition. With the shift to a market economy and privatization of public enterprises, great numbers of industries crumbled. A lack of jobs, wage arrears, and lost or greatly reduced pensions and social assistance benefits are participants' leading concerns and are considered the root of other problems, including crime, alcoholism, and illness. Even those with jobs are described as extremely vulnerable, with wages reported to be as low as 150 to 200 rubles a month (US$6 to $8) in some communities.

Delayed Wages, Vanishing Jobs

Across the communities visited, having a job may not be a ticket out of poverty because there are extensive irregularities in the payment of wages.[5] For many, a reliable income is considered a privilege. Instead of wages, textile factories in Teikovo often offer payment in kind, although such payment is scorned among employees. One worker asks, "Why should I get all that vodka and mayonnaise when I need to buy medicine for my daughter?" Delays in the payment of wages and social benefits are another common problem. "After three months of work this summer, I had to spend another nine months kicking my money out from our administration," explains Alexey, a young man living in Magadan. Fortunately, he has now found a job escorting prisoners, which pays regularly.

There is little recourse for the working poor who want better earnings and wages paid on time. According to one of the Ivanovo participants, any protest or argument with the administration is useless because "you would be fired at once. . . . We are like slaves working for the master." Mine workers in Novy Gorodok explain that they are simply too afraid to protest against persisting wage arrears. "People wouldn't go to the rallies, they are afraid to lose their jobs," observes one miner. Some of his colleagues suggest that their employer deliberately pays them as little as possible. "They keep us at the level of survival so that they prevent any riots," the workers say. Participants in Novy Gorodok mention that sometimes they can make successful appeals to the mine administration in crisis situations. One person recalls, "When my son got ill and I needed a lot of money for treatment, I went to my boss and requested my wage. He gave me part of it."

The delays and in-kind payment of wages also erode worker motivation. "I used to be happy about my work. I knew I would be paid twice a month in due time. Now I don't feel like going to work, as I don't know what I'll be working for," says a participant in El'mash.

In addition to widespread wage problems, study participants also speak forcefully about factory closures and large reductions in the labor force. Older workers seem especially disadvantaged in finding new jobs that match their skills and experience. For instance, after the chemical plant that he used to work for closed, Evgeny, a 39-year-old man living in Dzerzhinsk, discovered that he had the wrong qualifications to find a new job. "Specialists like me," he says, "are not needed by anybody." The Russian military has scaled back its orders from the chemical industry, and Evgeny has little hope of finding new employment in that sector.

Andrey, a former textile worker from Teikovo, shares a similar experience. He was temporarily laid off from a textile factory two years ago, but when the factory reopened, he was not offered employment. "The younger workers were invited; people like us are not needed," he says. People like Andrey, who have spent their entire adult lives working for one employer, feel unprepared and unprotected in the new labor market. "We were not taught to work under the new system," agrees a group of people in Dzerzhinsk. In some communities, working women say they encounter not only age discrimination but also sexual harassment from prospective and current employers.

Large layoffs, wage arrears, and limited employment alternatives also affect agricultural workers. "Our *sovkhoz* [state farm] was flourishing in the Soviet time. We supplied milk and meat to Elista [capital of the Kalmykia region]. There were 36,000 sheep, three milk production farms, and several cattle pens," says a participant from Orgakin. Livestock breeding and agricultural production have since "decayed," and participants attribute the decline to mismanagement and corruption. The local *sovkhoz* directors are outsiders, and poor people believe they have stolen property from the enterprise. "We were the best *sovkhoz* in the district. Everyone had a permanent job and enough money. Water supply and all other supplies were free—the *sovkhoz* paid for them. . . . We had no problems at all," recall poor men and women in a discussion group from the village.

In the late 1980s and early 1990s, the government gave cheap loans to villagers in the farming community of Orgakin to support the transition to privately run farms, but many beginners failed. Now loans are more expensive and usually depend on bribes, villagers say. A few producers, however, were able to succeed in the transition from communism to capitalism. Today, these people run relatively large farms in Orgakin.

Informal Work and Subsistence Agriculture

With jobs in the formal sector scarce, most unemployed people are forced to look for work in the informal sector. The most recent data available show that the informal sector ballooned from 12 percent of Russia's economy in 1989 to 39 percent in 1994.[6] Some people find occasional work in their local communities, whereas others migrate to find seasonal work in agriculture or construction. In Belasovka many men spend their summers building *dachas* (country cottages) for city people, and sometimes they go to Moscow to work one-month shifts in construction. Others in Belasovka have taken up traditional wooden spoon carving because farming no longer provides sufficient income. A 39-year-old divorced woman from Dzerzhinsk says she weaves together whatever odd jobs she can find. Currently, she works as a cook, distributes a free newspaper to people's houses on weekends, and helps a peddler who pays her with a bottle of alcohol that she then sells on the street.

Another way people across Russia attempt to survive is by growing their own food, and one of the leading criteria of wellbeing is whether one owns a plot of land on which to cultivate potatoes, cabbages, and other vegetables. According to a recent poll, three out of every four Russians now grow some or all of their own food, and 55 percent of the population grows half or more of their food on private plots of land.[7] This is striking in a country where some 70 percent of the population is urban; however, widespread reliance on home gardening dates back generations.[8] This is the case both for the poor urban neighborhoods of El'mash and Teikovo as well as a poor village such as Belasovka. In Orgakin the collective farm in the village went bankrupt in 1998, so today most villagers survive by growing their own food and keeping livestock. In Ozerny people of average wellbeing are described as those who can "raise cattle, have a garden, sell potatoes and milk, and have cash, and work for themselves," whereas poor people "live only off their garden and an odd job now and then." Poor people in Magadan cope by fishing and preserving foods.

Men and women say they also cope with poverty by reducing their ambitions and needs.[9] Thus, poor dwellers in the coal-mining town of Magadan, which sits in the harsh northeastern region, have given up hope of moving to a better climate in central Russia. In Ivanovo poor people report that they go without sugar, do not use transport services, and forego all but what is absolutely necessary. A woman there told researchers that she does not eat for several days; she drinks only water and lies in bed to conserve her energy.

Lawlessness and Ineffective Police

In communities where legitimate job opportunities are scarce, theft and organized crime may offer people quick and tempting ways to escape poverty. Many people describe situations where there are very strong temptations to break the law, both out of desperation and as a means to achieve a better life. People repeatedly observe that the police are unable to prevent crime from growing in their community. Some even insist that police exacerbate the lack of security.

Men and women in Belasovka, Novy Gorodok, and Teikovo report a growing problem of theft from vegetable gardens, leaving them vulnerable to hunger. The local militia does what it can to prevent the theft, according to villagers, but their efforts are inefficient, and many people try to guard their own vegetable gardens. "We watched over our potatoes with a gun. People from other towns pretend to come to pick mushrooms. They sprinkle a few mushrooms and some grass over the top of the basket, and underneath they have potatoes," states a group of men and women in Belasovka.

Poor people also describe the strong lure of organized crime. Nikolai, 26, lives in the mining city of Novy Gorodok with his wife and two children. He works at the Belovo automotive plant, but receives his wages irregularly and only in part. Nikolai and his family live in the house of Nikolai's mother-in-law, who also helps them with food, money, and babysitting. At the moment, he is on unpaid leave. Feeling hopeless, he says, "I won't go into criminal structures, but I don't know what to do. I don't know how to start my own business. At the moment we just live from the plot of land."

Although Nikolai chooses not to engage in illegal activity, others in similar situations decide differently. The town's coal industry is in distress, and many miners have already lost their jobs. Theft has increased. "They have nothing to eat, what else can they do?" observes one participant in a group discussion. But most people are not as sympathetic. Ludmilla, a widow and mother of five living in Orgakin, is now heavily disliked by her neighbors because her sons have criminal records. Two of them have recently been arrested for stealing cows. Ludmilla says of one of them, "He had nothing to do. There is no work here for young people." Another one of her sons is in jail for robbing a shop. She explains, "He took just a few cigarette packs and a couple of bottles of wine. I think he did it for his girlfriend. . . . He loves her badly. If I had a cow, I would bribe the judge."

People in several communities agree that it is difficult for entrepreneurs to be successful in business without breaking the law in one way or another. A cabinetmaker in Ivanovo explains openly how it is impossible for him to make a living without stealing. "If I want to make a door or a window, I need to get the material from somewhere," he says. Victor, a successful businessman from Dzerzhinsk, also admits that it is hard to improve one's wellbeing without breaking the law. "Frankly," he says, "it's impossible to do honest business in our time, paying all taxes and observing all rules." In many communities, businessmen like Victor must also deal with powerful networks of organized crime, which often charge "protection money" and control large segments of the economy. Dargoslav, an ice cream trader from Novy Gorodok, reports, "Since the 1998 crisis people don't buy anything; there is no money. The racket understands this, too: before they used to charge me 3,000 rubles, but now they charge only 1,500." Drugs are also a growing problem in Novy Gorodok, which is a station for trade with western Siberia.

Poor people speak of corrupt and ineffective police and of being victims of police harassment. The police force consistently receives negative reviews from participants. Recalling the time his home was robbed, a man from Ozerny says, "When they raided the cellars, nothing was done, no one was found. I was robbed clean. I made a statement. Then I see the policeman drinking with the guy who robbed me." In Magadan people mention rumors of corruption in the police force. "How come a police officer can afford a Jeep?" asks one study participant there. In El'mash people also express distrust of their local police. "It is the kind of police you have no hope of ever reaching. The police are for those at the top," they explain.

Discussion groups from several communities mention that police abuse their position and extort money from citizens for minor offenses. Sometimes police officers use force illegally. An 18-year-old poor man in Dzerzhinsk reports that he was detained several times by the police with false accusations and held in a very cold cell known as "the refrigerator" with other young men simply because police officers needed to fulfill their quota at the end of the month. He reports that false detention is a common practice because young people are easy targets for the police.

Ethnic minorities may also be targets of harassment. A small group of refugees from central Asia have come to Moscow to escape warfare and economic hardship. Many of them stay in Moscow illegally. "Our life is a prison," says one. "We are hiding from the police. They tear up our registration certificates and say that we don't have any rights because we come from a different ethnic group."

Alcoholism

Some people argue that alcohol abuse, like crime, has become more overt and frequent, even among young people and the very poor. Some people also express the opinion that alcoholism is more widespread among women than it was in the past and they consider this very unusual. In Ozerny a group of women asserts, "Already in the daytime there are a lot of drunk people outside the kiosk where they sell booze. They hang around in the streets and may cause trouble."

Julia, the entrepreneur in Ozerny, believes that widespread drinking and alcoholism in the village greatly complicates her role as an employer. She argues,

> If they didn't drink, they would live better. It's a drunken village. Suppose I hire a woman. She works for a while and then she goes back to drinking. I understand it's not easy for her, I sympathize, forgive her once, twice, then I have to talk to her, tell her I was in a similar situation, nearly lost control. But she can't help it and I have to fire her.

In other communities, such as Orgakin, alcoholism is considered to be on the rise, especially among young men, due to the lack of employment. "Young people began to drink more. They have nothing to do, that's why they drink," explains a discussion group participant. Manufacturing alcohol at home is widespread in the region of Novgorod, where rural Belasovka is located, and drinking has increased as a result. Alcohol is brewed for home consumption and for sale and is used as "liquid currency."

Health Risks

Poor people across the communities share worries about rising illnesses due to poverty, and the declining quality and availability of health care services. "Having to pay for health care is a shame," and "If something goes wrong, you have no money, God forbid," exclaim participants in a discussion group in Belasovka.

People in various places note a greater prevalence of illness and link it to economic stress. Mothers in Dzerzhinsk point to consequences of poverty such as bad nutrition and children's hunger-induced dizzy spells at school. In three communities, rising health problems are associated with industrial pollution (box 2).

When sickness strikes, study participants report difficulties obtaining treatment and emphasize the great insecurity this creates in their lives. Residents of Orgakin, for instance, are particularly frustrated that the main medical clinic in the village recently closed down, creating problems especially for the elderly and those with small children. Now only primary medical care is available locally, forcing people with more serious medical conditions to travel thirty kilometers to the district center for treatment.

Poor people in various communities also report that hospitals and clinics often lack medicine, food, blankets, bandages, and other supplies. A person in Ozerny says of the primary health center, "They don't have anything except Furacilin. The situation with medicines is very bad, and there are no dressing materials. The dispensary doesn't provide any treatment, it only writes out an official recommendation to go to a city clinic." In Magadan people observe that their local hospital not only lacks medicine, but also treats patients badly. "The hospital is like a prison. If you want to get medical treatment you ought to go to the large cities further inland, or to the U.S.A.," explains one person.

While Russia has abolished free health care, there are no new systems in place to help cash-strapped people meet their medical needs. "You have to pay the dentist up front, otherwise they just stuff your tooth with sand and it all falls out." A lack of money may lead to terrifying situations for poor people who are ill. A discussion group in Belasovka told a story of a woman who underwent surgery for a fractured leg but couldn't afford anesthesia. A person recalled the woman's screams and said, "I still dread to think of it." In Ozerny, ambulances charge passengers for gasoline before driving them to the hospital. Those who cannot pay cannot ride the ambulance. In Dzerzhinsk and Magadan, however, reports of ambulance services are more favorable.

Decaying Governance

Poor people across the Russian communities visited observe that with the collapse of state institutions and the accumulation of economic and social problems, they have come to rely increasingly on support from social networks of family, neighbors, and friends. In fact, no institution of any nature, whether public, private, nongovernmental, religious, or social, rates nearly as highly among poor people as their personal networks of *blizkie,* "the close ones." The importance of family and neighbors is reflected in figure 1, which summarizes data from discussion groups in the ten study communities.

The findings from the ranking exercise are reaffirmed by data from a separate survey that explored the coping strategies of Russians in response to the severe financial crisis of 1998. In this survey, less than 5 percent of the respondents said that they turned to government agencies for assistance. Whether rich or poor, Russian households were five times more likely to seek help from informal sources such as family, kin, and neighbors than from the government.[10]

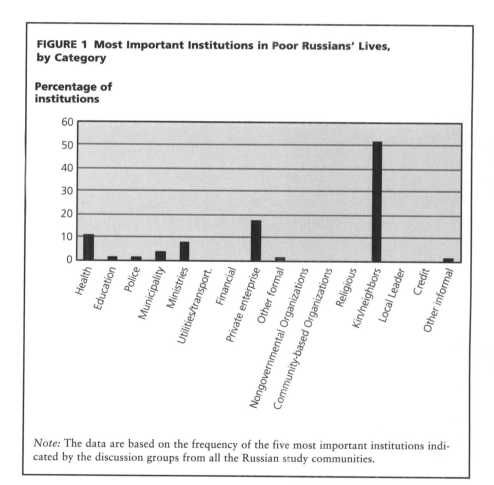

FIGURE 1 Most Important Institutions in Poor Russians' Lives, by Category

Note: The data are based on the frequency of the five most important institutions indicated by the discussion groups from all the Russian study communities.

Bureaucratic Disintegration and Corruption

People frequently associate the crumbling economy and deteriorating institutional fabric of their society with the ruling elite in Moscow. They believe that government performance has been weakened by widespread corruption among government officials who are pursuing their own economic and political interests. Participants in Magadan state, "The ruling elite has destroyed the whole state. The government and the president have robbed us." They also remark, "The fish always rots starting with its head." Others observe that the ruling elite is simply exploiting ordinary people. "Our taxes go to Moscow and only 25 percent comes back," declares a participant from Teikovo.

District and local authorities also receive very low ratings. In Dzerzhinsk, participants claim that "the authorities cheat people." And participants in Magadan say of local authorities, "Our administration consists of thieves who are stealing whatever they can." People in Teikovo report that their local mayor is rude to people who ask him for aid. Occasionally the media can play a powerful role in challenging authorities (box 3).

In Novy Gorodok participants are of the opinion that the local officials do not make any effort to improve the situation in their town. "Why do they get salaries? They just sit in the office and do nothing," says one participant. Some also comment that the town authorities use the local budget for their personal interests. People in Novy Gorodok, however,

---

BOX 3 Local Television Empowers Ordinary People

Faced with problems of bureaucracy and corruption, poor men and women in Novy Gorodok and Magadan have found an ally in the local media. In group discussions, people in Novy Gorodok insist that the local television station has become an important institution in their community because it has helped reveal corruption among local officials and it is sharply critical of the central government in Moscow. The TV station is a key source of information as well as a catalyst for change that can expose problems and force the local authorities to take action. Local TV helps to empower ordinary people, who can contact journalists concerning local issues and draw attention to unaccountability among government officials. Similarly, people in Magadan say that their TV station also is an important ally in their struggle to improve life in their community. "If you call the local TV program *Monitor*, they immediately come to you. And the authorities are afraid of them," observes a woman in Magadan.[11]

---

make a clear distinction between the local mayor, whom they call a thief, and the district governor, whom they credit with securing regular pensions in the region. The governor is a well-known and trusted politician, people explain, because he speaks up to the central government on behalf of ordinary people.

Most politicians, however, are viewed as corrupt, and in some discussions participants remark that they have no confidence that the ballot box is a tool for change. People in Dzerzhinsk, for example, remember that crucial road work began last summer "when the local mayor needed our votes." After the election, all the work stopped. In Teikovo, people claim that the current head of the district administration manipulated the results from the last election to his benefit. Such incidents have also led poor people in El'mash to abstain from voting. "We don't go to the polls, no trust in them," explains one study participant, "The authorities are self-sufficient, and we are too."

People in Orgakin are suffering from severe water shortages but feel largely abandoned by district and local authorities in their struggles to address this urgent problem. In Soviet times, Orgakin's water was supplied through the *sovkhoz* budget. Although their *akhlachi* (local political leader of the community) is the former *sovkhoz* director, he reportedly plays no active role in community life. "He has never tried to get people together. He is afraid of people," villagers observe. Villagers also feel ignored by district officials: "The district authorities do not visit the village for months. When we were rich they came very often. Now they have forgotten about us. They left us."

In addition to problems with basic services, discussion groups state that unemployment benefits and other social assistance programs either do not reach or do not help many poor people. In Teikovo villagers report that the employment office has not been able to pay unemployment benefits for three years. Such benefits are no longer paid in Ozerny, either. People there also indicate that the local labor exchange provides little service. "There's no sense getting registered with the labor exchange. You get neither a job nor a dole. It's far to go there, too," one villager explains. The local employment service in Novy Gorodok offers some training and assistance to people looking for jobs, but study participants there also report that the office lacks adequate resources.

Discussion groups sometimes rank the local welfare agency among the top ten institutions, but nonetheless say that the support it provides is largely insufficient. In Ivanovo a discussion group of men and women rates the social welfare body low because it requires "standing and standing in lines and too many certificates." Recent studies of social assistance spending in Russia find that only 8 percent reaches the poorest tenth of the population, and about one-fifth of poor households receive no benefits at all.[12]

People in Orgakin consider their social protection department an important institution, although they are unhappy with the low level of assistance and the disrespectful treatment they receive from staff there. "I go there and request social benefits for my children. I have to wait for two hours, and then they treat me very badly. If I cry and shout that my child is ill, they'll give me something. But it happens very seldom," says a mother living in Orgakin. A young mother in Ozerny shares a similar experience with her local social security department. "I have four kids and I am a single mother," she explains. "I went there and a staff person looked at me suspiciously because I had a good jacket on. Do I have to wear tatters?" Other women in Ozerny agree that the service at such welfare institutions is indeed biased and unreliable. In Novy Gorodok the local social welfare department arranges charity dinners for poor people, collects secondhand clothing, and seeks ways to help struggling families. People in that town acknowledge that the department does good work, but observe that it lacks the resources it needs to make a stronger positive impact in the community.

The Private Sector

Successful business owners are sometimes well regarded by study participants for helping needy people in their community. People also report—smiling at the irony—that they can turn to members of organized crime networks when in great need. In Ozerny young people explain that they respect a local businessman whom they consider honest. They recall that he used to provide them cheap loans and hard currency until the financial crisis of 1998. In addition, they observe that he provides jobs to the community.

Raiza, a shop owner in Orgakin, enjoys great respect in her village. A group of elderly people ranks her shop as the second most important institution in Orgakin. Only the family is more important, they observe. After Raiza's former employer went bankrupt, she rented a shop building and opened her own business. In her shop, she often helps out her customers by being flexible and letting them pay for their goods later, when they get money. Sometimes she also arranges charity events for poor families. "I only want people to get their salaries. I'd be wealthy then," she says. With persisting wage arrears affecting the community, credit offered at her shop is extremely important for people in Orgakin. Her customers explain that the system is built upon mutual trust, which works well in their small community of 900 people. Raiza explains that her wellbeing has improved since she opened the shop, but emphasizes, "If everybody would get their salary at a proper time, my business would be better and I would feel better myself."

Despite such positive examples, factories and large farms in most communities can offer much less assistance than in the past. Most enterprises no longer provide housing, health care, utilities, day-care centers, and other services.

Civic and Religious Groups

Although several kinds of government services are in decline, few NGOs have stepped in to fill the void. Local NGOs exist only in some of the communities, and international organizations are not well known to many of the participants.

In Belasovka a local veterans' council helps elderly people in various ways, although it does not receive state funding. It continues to exist largely thanks to the enthusiasm of its chairman, who is well respected by the retired people in the village. They say, "You can at least get advice there. Time and again they even help you get some firewood from the collective farm." The work of the Red Cross receives mixed ratings. Only one of eight discussion groups in Orgakin (women ages 25–35) mentions it as an important institution. In Ozerny study participants report that their local Red Cross sells clothes instead of giving them away.

Religious organizations also play only a small role. The Orthodox Church is present in most communities and provides valued spiritual support, but it is generally more important for the elderly than for younger people. "We were all raised to be atheists, and only now did we start getting peace in church," explains a participant in El'mash. A Buddhist temple exists in Orgakin, but it is usually closed. A Buddhist leader used to live in the village until 1997, but since then, there is just a lama who occasionally comes to Orgakin.

Family and Friends

"My parents give one out of their two pensions to our family. I am so grateful to them. If not, we would not survive," says a study participant from Novy Gorodok. The most valued sources of support for nearly every discussion group in the Russian communities consist of parents, the extended family, friends, and neighbors. In all communities visited, people report that they help each other with money, clothes, and food; however, in many discussion groups in urban areas, participants express concern that these ties are thinning under the weight of rising poverty.

In Belasovka, a farming community, people agree that family and friends have become more important now that the state is weaker than it was in the past. They also explain that neighbors in the village help one another stop theft from vegetable gardens. Poor people in Belasovka also explain that they help each other with tasks such as digging a well, repairing the road, building a fence, and installing electrical appliances.

Participants ranked local institutions according to their ability to address key problems and provide support in times of crisis. The results in table 2 are from three of the discussion groups in Orgakin. All the groups rate *blizkie*—the immediate family, kin, neighbors, and friends—as most helpful.

Anna is a young mother living in Orgakin. Like most members of her community, she relies on her family and friends for help with managing daily problems and challenges. Her husband is a plumber at a local school, but his wages haven't been paid in four months. Anna's father has stepped in to support them with goods from his small garden and

TABLE 2 Most Important Institutions, Three Discussion Groups in Orgakin

	Ranking by discussion group		
Institution	Men ages 25–38	Women ages 35–55	Elders
Parents	1	1	—
Extended family	2	2	1
Friends	3	3	4
Neighbors	—	4	3
Local shop	4	—	2
Akhlachi (local political leader)	—	7	6
Social protection department	5	6	—
Khurul (Buddhist temple)	—	5	—
Medical clinic	—	—	5

— Not mentioned.

Note: 1 = Most important (most able to address problems and provide support).

some of his pension. Relatives and neighbors also help. "I often ask for a handful of flour and some salt," Anna explains. She is now able to send her oldest children to school, although she cannot yet afford textbooks for them.

Although social networks are strong in many smaller communities like Orgakin, people in urban areas observe that such ties are not especially firm among those who do not know each other personally. The deepening poverty makes it difficult to keep up relations and reciprocate favors. In El'mash poor women and men point to weak social cohesion and a lack of a feeling of togetherness in their community. "There was an incident when a 35-year-old man felt sick and fainted in the street. No one came up to him. When somebody finally did, it was too late," recalls one resident. People in El'mash still conclude, however, that the most important sources of help in their community are family, friends, and "people you know."

In the textile city of Teikovo, several discussion groups express the notion that the gap between the rich and poor has widened and relations among people are deteriorating: "Before, we all lived alike, now there's a borderline between people." Another participant in Novy Gorodok acknowledges that with a decline in general wellbeing "people have become more spiteful, aggressive, and irritated," and explains, "It's not because of envy; it's because we have impotent anger and nobody to vent it on." Another resident of Novy Gorodok declares, "The New Year is a great holiday but you no longer enjoy it. No hopes for the future. Having guests at home is a burden because there is nothing to put on the table."

Women's Increasing Responsibilities

In addition to poverty's effect on material conditions and social relations, poor Russian households also suffer from increased tension among family members, alcoholism, and divorce. As seen above in the stories of Svetlana and Julia from Ozerny, many women are their family's main breadwinner and, with divorce on the rise, are often the heads of households, too. Because services such as day-care centers and schools are no longer provided by employers, working women, especially single mothers, now suffer an extra burden.

While there are few job opportunities for anyone, women willing to accept low-paying, demeaning, and often risky jobs are more likely to be earning incomes. "Women become more adjusted to the conditions they live in. Today they are ready to fight for their wellbeing not only with the hands and teeth of their husbands but with their own as well," says a participant from El'mash.

Natalia, 38, is one of many mothers who are assuming increased responsibilities. A single mother of a 15-year-old boy, Natalia divorced her husband because he drank too much. Her community, Novy Gorodok, has been hit hard by recent downsizing in the coal industry. She used to have a good job in a boiler house, but she was laid off. "They pay very little here, and not in full," she says about her new job as a floor cleaner. Natalia reports that she and her son are able to survive only because her parents share their pensions both with Natalia and with their other daughter. Her son, who has seen his father only once, is upset that his father does not support them at all. "My son says, 'I will kill him!'" Natalia relates.

In virtually all the communities visited, men and women report that quarrels about money are now more frequent, and the increased stress on couples is contributing to divorce. In Novy Gorodok discussion groups identify "scandals and quarrels in families" and divorce as real consequences of poverty. Similarly, a group of women in Ivanovo observes that a growing number of women in their community divorce husbands who drink or who are unable to provide for their families. "A woman drives her husband out of the house because he doesn't earn money," they say. Some working women remark that living without a husband is an easier way to cope with increased hardships. Women in Teikovo, for instance, maintain that in hard circumstances it is better to get rid of a husband since "he comes and eats up everything including what has been saved by the mother for the children." Another woman with three children decided to leave her alcoholic husband. "I got sick and tired of his boozing," she said. She does not receive any financial support for the children.

When men are embarrassed or frustrated that they are no longer able to carry out their traditional role of providing for the family, there is a greater likelihood of conflict. "Gender relations have become tougher because there are more problems. There can be conflicts in the family because the woman makes more money than the man," a participant from a group in El'mash observes. Also, idle men are more likely to take to drinking, which in turn increases household conflict, the group explains.

In Ozerny, where the local farm cooperative has all but collapsed, some men are taking up home-based sewing work rather than endure joblessness or the temptation to drink. However, doing a job usually reserved for women is a sharp blow to their self-esteem. "Of course I am embarrassed," says Stanis, a middle-aged man who sometimes joins his wife in sewing at home. He normally teaches basic military training at a local school but has found that the 300 rubles he earns from teaching is simply not enough to support his family of four. "What can I do?" he asks, "It is not a man's job, but you want to eat every day."

Conclusion

"Wellbeing is when you have a job, a family, freedom, and a good income to live comfortably and avoid discord in the family," states a participant in El'mash. Poor people across the Russian communities remember the not-too-distant past when, though they were not wealthy, they had secure livelihoods and a sense of wellbeing. Nowadays, many poor Russians dare not even dream about their future. Communities that used to be held together by a few keystone industries or by a large collective farm are now falling apart. In the wake of economic uncertainty, people everywhere speak of alcoholism, crime, poor governance, and family breakups. Social networks of family, friends, and neighbors help with daily survival, especially in rural areas, but nevertheless people feel alone and insecure about the future. "Every day I am afraid of the next," states another poor resident of El'mash.

When asked by the researchers which problems their communities could solve without external help, discussion groups in Russia remained largely silent. Generally, local institutions are weak and poor people look to the government to restore the economy and once again provide a meaningful safety net for those in need. This requires well-governed and accountable public agencies. Poor people in Russia need information about their rights and about how they themselves can mobilize government, private, and civic partnerships to address pressing community needs. People also express a need for greater understanding of how markets work as well as capacity building to support entrepreneurship. Even today, people feel they have been caught unprepared by the rapid transition. For the most vulnerable groups—such as the elderly—more adequate, reliable, and efficient social assistance programs must be developed to help them avoid hunger, treat illnesses, and pay for fuel in the wintertime.

Private businesses of all sizes need a more stable and predictable environment; for workers who do not receive fair wages, recourse must be provided. Many men and women also say that better access to start-up capital that can be obtained "in an honest way" would go far in helping them work their way out of poverty.

Seventeen-year-old Katya lives in a little house outside Teikovo with her mother, who receives a small pension. Katya used to study at a technical school for cooks, but dropped out when she could no longer afford to buy paper to write on. "Anyway, even if I graduate, I would never find a job as a cook," she explains. Now she has no occupation, no plans, and no hopes, as her hometown suffers from mass unemployment. Her mother gave up their old house in town for a smaller village house with a garden. "We will have our own potatoes, so we will not starve to death," says Katya.

TABLE 2 Study Communities in the Russian Federation

RURAL COMMUNITIES

Belasovka, Nizhniy Novgorod region Pop. 1,300	Agricultural production is in crisis, and there are problems of wage arrears and rising prices. Unemployment is growing. A once-successful collective farm now barely functions, and most households tend private plots. Some people carve wooden spoons or brew homemade alcohol to make a living. Others work for public utilities, or on a military base, or in the timber, tourism, or railroad industries.
Orgakin, Kalmykia region Pop. 900	Kalmykia is the only Buddhist nation in Europe. Stalin sent the villagers to Siberia, but they were allowed to come back in 1957. The agricultural sector is collapsing. A collective farm was privatized in the 1990s, but many family farms failed. There are few permanent jobs. Most villagers live by subsistence agriculture and raise sheep, cows, pigs, and poultry.
Ozerny, Ivanovo region Pop. 1,300	In this farming community, a collective farm still exists, but yields are poor and people who work there are no longer paid. A peat enterprise also used to be a major source of employment, but it closed down in 1998, and unemployment is now high. Few services function, and housing is in disrepair.

URBAN COMMUNITIES

Dzerzhinsk, Volga region Pop. 300,000	The town was built in the 1930s. A number of military chemical plants are located within and to the north of the town, which used to be called the "chemical capital of the country." The dilapidated plants have caused extremely high levels of pollution and are in constant danger of technical malfunction and catastrophic explosion. There are high levels of pollution, diseases, and ill health. Workers retire at 45 and have low life expectancy.
El'mash, Ekaterinburg region Pop. 150,000	The community is part of the city of Ekaterinburg, one of the major industrial centers in Russia. Many military plants work at half capacity and have reduced their staff by more than 50 percent. Problems include mass unemployment, high rates of crime, and pollution. Infrastructure is well developed, but there are housing problems for low-income people, especially the young.

Ivanovo, Ivanovo region Pop. 155,000	In this traditional center of the textile industry, a majority of workers are female, and the area is known as "the city of potential brides." Ivanovo received large subsidies during Soviet times, and workers had high wages and benefits, but now industry is in crisis. Many factories have closed, and others are working at minimal capacity. The community faces mass unemployment, wage delays, growing crime, and increasing social inequality.
Magadan, Magadan region Pop. 2,000	This remote gold-mining center in the extreme northeast of Russia is known as "the capital of Gulag." Built by forced labor, the city is now in decline. Tough natural conditions make agriculture nearly impossible, so most goods are brought from thousands of miles away. Wages were very high in the Soviet period, but no longer.
Musorka, Moscow Pop. 80	Most residents are refugees who have fled Central Asia because of financial hardship and war. They live in overcrowded, unsanitary grounds near the Cherkizovsky street market in Moscow, and work as loaders at markets or docks in order to send money to relatives back home. Many lack official status as residents and dare not wander farther than 100 meters from the market for fear of being expelled by police. Many live in old iron cargo containers.
Novy Gorodok, Kemerovo region Pop. 19,700	This small settlement in a coal mining area was built in the 1940s. Men used to work in the mines, and women worked in a knitted goods factory and at an electronics plant, both of which closed in 1992. The coal industry has been in trouble since the 1990s, and there is widespread unemployment.
Teikovo, Teikovo region Pop. 40,000	This mono-industrial textile town suffered the closure of many factories in the 1990s. There is female unemployment and wage arrears. One major textile factory began operating again in 1998, but at only one-fourth of its former capacity. Twenty-five percent of the population consists of retired workers.

Notes

1. The study team was led by Alexey Levinson, Olga Stouchevskaya, Oxana Bocharova, and Anton Lerner, and also included Lyubov Alexandrova, Vera Gromova, and Yulia Koltsova.

2. World Bank, *World Development Indicators 2001* (Report 22099, April 2001), 195. GDP growth resumed after 1998 principally because of rising prices for Russian oil and gas exports, and reached an estimated 7 percent in 2000. Inflation ran at 36.5 percent in 1999 and declined to about 20 percent in 2000. See World Bank, "Memorandum of the President of the International Bank for Reconstruction and Development and the International Finance Corporation to the Executive Directors on a Country Assistance Strategy Progress Report of the World Bank Group for the Russian Federation" (January 11, 2001), 2.

3. World Bank, *World Development Indicators 2001*, 13, 192.

4. The various data sources, methodologies, and estimates of poverty rates in Russia are discussed in World Bank, "Russia: Poverty in 1998" (Human Development and Poverty Reduction and Economic Management, Europe and Central Asia Region, June 2000, draft); and in World Bank, "Making Transition Work for Everyone: Poverty and Inequality in Europe and Central Asia" (Report 20920, August 2000), 38, box 1.2. The official Russian statistical office, Roskomstat, uses income data that have been adjusted to account for informal income sources; the agency reports that poverty grew from 11.7 percent in 1991 to 23.8 percent in 1998. The World Bank poverty assessment, "Russia: Poverty in 1998," compiles poverty rates based on consumption indicators and the same poverty line used by Roskomstat, which is quite high at US$6–$7 per person per day; it reports that 49.1 percent of the population fell below the poverty line in 1998, up from nearly 27 percent in 1992 (p. 4). The 18.8 percent poverty rate is based on consumption data and a poverty line of US$2.15 per day per capita (in 1996 constant dollars), and can also be found in the poverty assessment (p. 9).

5. The problem of wage arrears began to escalate in 1995, peaked in 1998 after the August crisis, and then improved rapidly during 1999 and into 2000. See World Bank, "Russia Labor Market Study: 2001" (Human Development Department, Europe and Central Asia Region, 2001, draft).

6. Daniel Kaufmann and Aleksander Kaliberda, "Integrating the Unofficial Economy into the Dynamics of Post-Socialist Economies: A Framework of Analysis and Evidence" (World Bank Policy Research Working Paper 1691, Europe and Central Asia, 1996), 13.

7. The U.S. Department of Agriculture survey is reported in Alexander L. Norsworthy, ed., *Russian Views of the Transition in the Rural Sector: Structures, Policy Outcomes, and Adaptive Responses* (Washington, D.C.: World Bank, 2000), 10.

8. In the mid-1990s, as a middle class began to emerge in Russia, the dependence on garden plots began to weaken, only to intensify again after the onset of the August 1998 crisis.

9. According to data collected from repeated surveys between March 1993 and September 1996, respondents' average estimate of the minimum income required by an adult Russian decreased by about 1.7 percent each month. See Branko Milanovic and Branko Jovanovic, "Change in the Perception of the Poverty Line during Times of Depression: Russia 1993–96" (World Bank Policy Research Working Paper 2077, Development Research Group, Poverty and Human Resources, March 1999), 2.

10. Michael M. Lokshin and Ruslan Yemtsov, "Household Strategies for Coping with Poverty and Social Exclusion in Post-Crisis Russia" (World Bank Policy Research Working Paper 2556, Development Research Group, Poverty and Human Resources, and Europe and Central Asia Region, Poverty Reduction and Economic Management Sector Unit, February 2001), 5.

11. Since the fieldwork for the study, there has been a government crackdown on the independent media, with journalists who report corruption particularly subject to harassment, prosecution, and physical assaults. In perhaps the most high-profile case, Vladimir Gusinsky, owner of the leading independent media group Media-MOST, was arrested in 2000 on embezzlement charges in connection with a government anticorruption drive.

12. World Bank, "Memorandum of the President of the International Bank for Reconstruction and Development and the International Finance Corporation to the Executive Directors on a Country Assistance Strategy of the World Bank Group for the Russian Federation" (December 1, 1999), 14.

Argentina

Life Used to Be Better

Daniel Cichero, Patricia Feliu, and Mirta Mauro[1]

Daniela, 31, lives with her husband and six children in the same concrete house in La Matanza where she grew up. La Matanza is a satellite city west of Buenos Aires with a population of 1.8 million. Several industries in La Matanza used to manufacture textiles, diesel engines, household appliances, and steel, but they have all shut down. A local Ford plant laid off a thousand workers, and Fiat dismissed another thousand.

In the past, most people in La Matanza earned their living at these factories, but now most of the men work in temporary construction jobs and many of the working women are domestics. Poor people in La Matanza also survive as trash pickers, beggars, thieves, and drug dealers. Some of the areas settled within La Matanza are considered illegal by the municipality and are denied access to all basic services. A group of women from La Matanza rates hunger as the most pressing problem for their community, second only to the lack of work.

Daniela's four boys all attend school, but "they don't have notebooks, pencils, or uniforms." Daniela says that making ends meet has become an endless struggle:

> *I am an only child, I have no relatives. My baby daughter is a year old. My husband juggles temporary jobs. The last time he had work, it lasted three months. He has no contract and there are no sure jobs. I used to work cleaning. It brought some money home, but now with the baby I cannot work, although if something comes up, I can manage. My husband works wherever he can. Last week he was a laborer cutting lawns, which was good as I bought some shoes for the children. I buy whenever he finds some*

*job. . . . I am waiting to be called by the employment agencies. I
have put my name down in all of them. . . . As long as the work
is decent, I have no problem sweeping streets or traveling to the
capital. Perhaps employers would pay for the trip.*

*Another woman in La Matanza, for decades a skilled worker in a tex-
tile mill, has been unemployed since the mill closed. She tells researchers
that a close friend died a few hours after receiving a telegram informing
her she was being laid off. Another woman in the same discussion group
adds, "When it happened to me, I felt like my legs had been cut off."
Elena, a day-care worker, remembers,*

> *In this neighborhood's better days, we had a bishop who support-
> ed us. They say sadness over Menem's policies killed him. . . . They
> found him dead of a heart attack. He was a friend of the workers
> and the unions. . . . When the area's textile plants, which had pro-
> vided jobs for so many, all closed down, he couldn't bear it.*

*In another discussion in the area, men aged 45 to 65 recount their
own stories of downward mobility: "There used to be plenty of jobs at
good pay; you could even land two jobs"; "I worked in the steel industry
as a solderer, and in my spare time I did roofing and construction";
"I worked a backhoe, dug holes for all kinds of underground work, telephone cables, gas lines"; and "I used to make $40 a day at the meat-
packing plant—been out of work since it closed four years ago."[2] In
another group, a young man relates, "In my father's time you were out of
work maybe for a week or so. Nowadays, you're unemployed for years.
The only way out is when you die."*

*The repercussions of the layoffs affect not only individuals, but entire
families and society at large. Poverty is already impairing La Matanza's
younger generations. A mother says, "I'm unemployed, so I can't keep
my kids in school. They have to go to work instead of getting an education." Violence in the home is escalating, as is violence in the streets. Parents fear for more than just their children's education. Women in a
discussion group explain,*

> *The lack of security is tremendous. Anyone can do anything
> to you. There are kidnappings, murders. When we cleaned up
> a vacant field we found all kinds of horrible things—weapons,
> syringes—and we also know that rapes were committed there. . . .*

Riding a bicycle used to be pleasant but I can't ever let my children out; you can't let a child go ride a bike. It's not just that [thugs] will steal the bike, it's that they use knives and guns. . . . It isn't the robberies that scare me so much, it's the rapes. I have teenage daughters and I don't sleep at night because we live in a very unsafe neighborhood. . . . People never used to rob from their own neighbors.

People who want a safer environment for themselves and their families have little recourse in La Matanza. A woman reports, "Within the police department and in my neighborhood there are informants. If we report a criminal we run the risk of being fingered and suffering retribution."

A common theme underlies the sentiments expressed by men and women who participated in the *Voices of the Poor* study in Argentina: the quality of their lives has deteriorated. In urban areas, they attribute the decline mostly to unemployment and crime. From their words, a dramatic picture emerges of the personal and social consequences of market reforms and factory closures. Policy and market changes have also affected the country's agricultural sector; however, poor families in the three rural communities appear to have a better quality of life than those in urban areas on account of their safer, less crowded, and less polluted environments. Still, rural study participants remark that their lives are now more difficult than in the past. According to a villager in Los Juríes, "Before, you could buy everything. It has been years since I bought a chair; I can't buy clothes. There isn't enough money for food. We eat every day, but only at noon, not in the evening."

Argentina suffered a long period of hyperinflation and recession in the 1980s, which lasted well after the nation's transition from military rule to democracy in 1983. In those years, poverty in Buenos Aires skyrocketed from 8 percent of the population in 1980 to 41 percent at the end of the decade.[3] In the 1990s, however, the Argentine economy underwent a massive transformation. Upon taking office in 1991, President Carlos Menem introduced an austerity program and market-oriented policies that initiated a period of unprecedented price stability and high rates of economic growth. The government's reforms included improved fiscal and tax policies, liberalized trade, a large privatization program, the devolution of health and education responsibilities to the states, and changes to the social security system. The second-term Menem administration managed to maintain growth despite the emerging markets crisis of 1997–98, but the economy fell into a severe and prolonged recession in 1999.

Argentina enjoys the highest per capita income in Latin America ($7,550 GNP per capita in 1999)[4] and some of the region's highest social sector spending. However, these averages camouflage large pockets of remaining poverty, a chasm between the incomes of the rich and poor, as well as an inequitable distribution of public resources. Although on the decline, Argentina's poverty rate remained relatively high at 29 percent in 1998.[5] This means about 9 million Argentines live in poverty and about 2 million of these people cannot meet their basic food needs. Urban-rural disparities are also large. While rural poverty statistics are limited, in 1998 poverty rates approached 50 percent in three rural provinces. Further, while Argentina has one of the most advanced education systems in the region and universal primary enrollment, only 24 percent of students among the poorest 20 percent of the population complete secondary school.[6] In addition, poverty-oriented safety net programs are abundant, but 75 percent of poor people do not receive any public assistance.[7] Overall, the gaps in the provision of basic services and infrastructure are far larger than would be expected in view of the country's GNP and the level of public resources devoted to economic and social development.

The key theme that emerges from the study is the impact of the major economic changes and weak social infrastructure on the lives of poor people in Argentina. Researchers met with women, men, elderly people, and youths in five poor urban neighborhoods located in the core and on the outskirts of Buenos Aires, and in three poor rural communities (see table 1, Study Communities in Argentina, at the end of this chapter).

The municipalities and communities in this study were selected according to poverty indicators and geographic distribution. All five urban communities and one of the three villages are from the Province of Buenos Aires, which contains more than 40 percent of the country's population. The remaining two rural communities are located in the northeastern Province of Santiago del Estero, one of the poorest and least populated areas of the country.

Participants were identified with the assistance of municipal authorities and local institutions, including the Cooperativa Unión Campesinos in the case of Los Juríes, school directors in Isla Talavera, and day-care staff in La Matanza. In some communities the institutional linkages were facilitated by the World Bank. A total of seventy-two discussion groups involving 714 men, women, and youths were held, including forty-seven groups in urban areas and twenty-five in rural areas. In addition, sixty-one individual and institutional case studies were conducted, including forty-seven individual case studies with poor women, men, and youths. An independent consultant coordinated the study team, which consisted of nine researchers. The study was carried out in March and April of 1999.

The chapter highlights urban participants' struggles with factory closures and lack of livelihood alternatives. It then reviews the linkages that poor Argentines perceive between downward socioeconomic trends and changes in household relations between women, men, and children. Next, the case study explores rising problems of crime and lack of police protection. It concludes with a discussion of poor people's very mixed reviews of governmental and civic responses to the problems they face.

Lost Livelihoods and the New Labor Markets

Like men and women in La Matanza, people living in the other communities visited in Argentina are concerned first and foremost about unemployment. The economic transformation of the 1990s resulted in a greater reliance on technology and shifted labor demands to skilled workers. This has left many unskilled workers unemployed or earning very low wages in the informal economy. Only 55 percent of Argentina's entire labor force is employed in the formal economy and covered by unemployment insurance, health insurance, and labor legislation protections. The remaining 45 percent are self-employed and informal workers; the latter are more likely to be poor.[8] According to a woman from Florencio Varela, "The job shortage is a neighborhood problem, but it's also a problem for the entire country. There isn't enough work. Men can only get temporary jobs as laborers and sometimes not even that. Often we women have more chance [than men] of finding work, as domestics."

In general, people in many discussion groups attribute deepening poverty and joblessness to extensive governance problems. They also view high levels of inequality as a cause of poverty. A leader of a cooperative in Los Juríes explains,

I believe that this government is not interested in changing things. They want poor people to continue being poor, and if possible to get poorer because that way they have secure votes and no one speaks out, and if someone does challenge them they buy him off with a political job or they find another way to shut him up.

In more than one urban neighborhood, "foreign debt," "inequitable distribution of resources," and "lack of solidarity" are listed as causes of poverty.

A discussion group of young and adult women in Florencio Varela concludes that the five key causes of poverty are: "Companies aren't hiring. They require a high school diploma. Industries have shut down. They hire foreigners over natives. They discriminate on the basis of *buena presencia* [a middle-class appearance]." A list from a group of men in La Matanza underscores the widespread view that poor people are at an increasing disadvantage in finding a job, particularly those who are no longer young: "They ask for a high school diploma, you have to be under 30, and you can't have any kind of health problem or have had an operation. . . . For those who are over 40, no one will hire us. You can look and look, but you'll never find a job." Concerns about age discrimination surface elsewhere. A discussion group of women in Florencio Varela reports that "men, if they are over 35, do not get hired"; and in Villa Atamisqui a woman fears that her husband "will never get hired again because he's in his late forties."

Many poor people also blame mechanization and competition from foreign producers for the unemployment crisis. A group of women in La Matanza observes, "They import junk . . . and you get the fall of Argentine industries like El Hogar Obrero, Textil Oeste. . . . Lots of those plants employed women, too, but they couldn't compete and we've been out of work ever since." A laid-off worker in Dock Sud blames technology: "I believe the more machines you have, the less you're going to need people. Take the loading dock. You used to need 100 or 200 workers to load a ship. Now everything is in huge closed containers and one guy with a crane can load them all. Who needs a work force?" Similarly, people in La Matanza identify "technology versus labor" and "investment in machines rather than workers" as two of the causes of poverty. In Los Juríes people conclude, "Technology generates unemployment because it brings machines."

Other poor people consider technology to be a source of new barriers to employment because higher skills are required to work with new technologies. Participants in a discussion group of young men and women from Barrio Sol y Verde explain,

The machines . . . made the work easy and clear, but now the worker has no job. To run the machines you have to know word processing, and whether you get the job also depends on whether you have buena presencia. *. . . . It isn't enough anymore to have completed primary school. Now you need computer skills to get a job packing vegetables.*

Jobs that require higher skills mean that employers look to hire educated workers. In Isla Talavera, where only a few have an education beyond primary school, young women say, "You need a high school diploma to get a decent job. If not, you'll be exploited by the ones with money." Similarly, a woman in La Matanza comments, "Even to get hired as a servant you need an education."

For those who have jobs, study participants report exploitative pay, abusive treatment, and loss of dignity (box 1). As a man in Sol y Verde describes it, "I work in construction. In the old days, the architects would ask me things. Now I am treated like dirt." Another man from Sol y Verde says, "I used to have a position where I had specific responsibilities. They didn't order me here and there; no, I had my job. Now they make you do every kind of task imaginable and for only $200 a month."

Insecurity and Struggling Families

Barrio Sol y Verde lies in the heart of Buenos Aires. It was a residential neighborhood until the late 1970s, when a military government began bulldozing *villas* in the capital.[9] Since that time, large numbers of poor people from other parts of the city, nation, and continent have ended up in Sol y Verde. A neighborhood activist estimates that 85 percent of the community's men are unemployed. Many households live on what mothers and daughters earn as domestics. Participants in Sol y Verde say that this is a dramatic departure from the past. According to one resident, "Now there are gangs, and since there is no work, they take drugs and drink alcohol."

Just before the researchers visited Sol y Verde, two suicides occurred. The first was a battered wife who poisoned herself. The second was a young pregnant woman who threw herself in front of an oncoming train with two small children in her arms, ending all of their lives.

"I used to get paid $15 an hour, now I get $1.80. At $1.80 an hour, what's left after the bus fare and a sandwich?"

—A poor man, La Matanza

"They expect you to work fifteen-hour days at $1.20 per hour."

—A poor man, Dock Sud

"Now they make you supply your own uniform and tools."

—A poor man, Sol y Verde

"What they want is for us to be some kind of slave."

—A poor man, Los Juríes

"To give you an idea of how things are now, my husband has been working at the service station for sixteen years, and they just informed him they're cutting his salary."

—A poor woman, Moreno

"The law doesn't defend the worker anymore . . . At La Lonja [a dairy plant] they hire people by the month. They make you sign a resignation or a new contract. They can do anything to you; these are ghost contracts."

—A poor woman, Moreno

Attempts to survive poverty—not always successful—often wreak havoc on traditional family roles, and pain caused by these upheavals is borne by women, men, and children. Many participants in urban locations report a dramatic shift of the breadwinner role from men to women. Although women's lives have not drastically improved with employment opportunities, women who enter the work force frequently acknowledge gains in their status, including greater freedom and control over household decisions. A resident of Florencio Varela explains, "Before, when men had jobs, they made most of the decisions. Now that women go out and work more and cover the household expenses, they make a lot more of the decisions. . . . The one who works is the one who makes the decisions."

Unemployment for men, in contrast, has been a blow to their authority and self-esteem. Some men are adapting, particularly those who find new roles helping their families and communities, but many others seem to be withdrawing into antisocial and even abusive behaviors. Children are particularly vulnerable as families struggle with economic hardship and the difficult transition in household gender roles and responsibilities. Trends in gender role reversals are much less prominent in the rural communities visited than in urban settings.

Gender Roles Overturned

In the urban settlements, it is generally agreed that with increased women's employment, men perform more household tasks than they used to. However, men and women disagree about the extent to which men assume responsibility for domestic chores. While men firmly state that they now do some household chores, women say that men cooperate only grudgingly. From a women's group in Florencio Varela, researchers heard: "Now men help more, but this does not represent a significant contribution to household chores," and "Men are more concerned about their own matters." Another woman from Florencio Varela says,

> When I go to community meetings, [my husband] stays home
> and takes care of the kids and sometimes even cooks and does
> the wash. You have to push them to help around the house.
> They know how to do housework, but they wait for the woman
> to do it. . . . They aren't all the same. Some—a few—are different and they take on all the housework.

Sometimes there is a complete reversal of breadwinner and caretaker roles. A man from Moreno reports, "The economic situation changed everything. I feel awful when my wife has to leave for work on Saturdays and doesn't come back until Monday, but she earns $40 per day. I take care of the kids, cook for them; we do okay. I don't hit them and I try not to punish them."

Sudden and extensive gender role reversal has not been easy for men or women. A woman in La Matanza says,

> I watch the unemployed men dropping off their kids at day
> care, which used to be a woman's task. Their heads are low; I
> think they feel humiliated. Now that the woman is working, the
> man feels very impotent and sad. One man in our neighborhood
> left his family just so he wouldn't be a burden anymore. He

could no longer help support them because he couldn't find
work. He was just one more mouth to feed.

A woman from Sol y Verde says, "You can't do anything right for a man stuck at home. He criticizes everything; he's always in a bad mood." The emotional toll that unemployment takes on men affects the whole family. "Since he's been out of work, my husband has little interest in life. He doesn't know what to do with himself," says a woman from Moreno. "He paces; it scares me sometimes. Lately he's been helping around the house a lot, even though he doesn't like it, but I'm worried about him." A woman from Dock Sud observes, "Men are more difficult now. . . . They won't discuss things; they're more impatient. They get angry a lot easier. When they're jobless they're anxious and they take it out on you."

Almost universally, discussion groups of men speak of the frustration, anger, and humiliation that stem from a diminished traditional male role and the misery of joblessness. "As the father of the family, it troubles me that my wife has to travel to another city and work. Being out of work makes you anxious and puts you in a very bad way. It is the worst thing that can happen to you," says a man from Florencio Varela. Men also state that joblessness is undermining their effectiveness as fathers and husbands, which in turn they relate to problems with children and to domestic strife. A man from Sol y Verde notes, "When I was young we showed more respect for our parents. I used to call my father 'Sir.' Now, my kids say to me, 'What the hell do you want?'" According to a group of men from Moreno, "There is no place for the man anymore, no role. Men used to be closer to their children."

In the three rural communities visited for the study, gender roles are reported to have changed little in the past decade, largely because men and women have traditionally shared demanding household and agricultural tasks. Also, rural areas are typically more cut off than urban areas from broader forces that shape social change. In Los Juríes men report,

The man's activities haven't changed, they're the same as they've
always been because we are the ones who bring home the bread.
. . . We've always gone to work in the fields to plant the cotton,
harvest the cotton. . . . We don't have much time to concern
ourselves with housework, but we tend the garden and the ani-
mals, which the women also do. We also haul water and bring
firewood. But it hasn't changed much. We've always done that.
Our other occupation is to raise our children, to educate them.

Similarly, people in Villa Atamisqui indicate that men's household activities have remained relatively constant over the past decade. When they return from their temporary work in other provinces, men "split wood, make repairs to home and fence, talk with children cook, clean house, and tend the goats and chickens." In Isla Talavera women fish from canoes, hunt, raise poultry, and till the soil as they have always done. Marveling at their strength, the director of the local elementary school describes mothers in Isla Talavera who manage to send as many as ten children to school every day with clean uniforms, which were washed in the river, scrubbed against rocks.

Some rural people perceive that women are gaining more authority in the household despite few changes in responsibilities. A young man in Villa Atamisqui says, "Men used to come back from working several harvests and be able to say, 'Here is the money I've earned.' Now, if they're lucky, they work one harvest, but the rest of the year they have no income. So women now have more say over household expenditures."

Abuse at Home

Domestic abuse of women is present in all eight of the study communities, according to discussion groups. They associate it with social norms that sanction violence, as well as with rising poverty and alcohol abuse. While people acknowledge that problems of domestic violence are now dealt with more openly, they say that it remains a widespread problem.

In the rural settlement of Villa Atamisqui, women trace domestic abuse to long-standing social norms. "Sons beat their mothers" and husbands "teach their sons to beat women up," these women say. Participants in urban areas also recall when abuse of women was widely accepted. According to a woman from La Matanza, "Women used to put up with everything: infidelity, mistreatment, and sexual relations out of obligation instead of love. The union was maintained for the sake of appearances. There was more abuse and one stayed quiet." Similarly, a woman from Florencio Varela reports, "In the old days, the man was boss and lord . . . not so much as lifting a finger around the house. Before, people didn't talk much about wife battering. Women kept quiet and didn't even ask for help. Perhaps there was more violence then, but women put up with it."

Other discussions associate domestic abuse against women with women's employment and men's frustration with unemployment. A young woman in Sol y Verde observes, "When my father was out of work he felt really bad. He was home all day doing nothing and got worse and worse. My brothers and sisters went to school, my mother went to work, I already had a job, but he had nothing to do but take it out on us. That's why families break up."

Alcohol consumption is also widely associated with violence against women. "The woman works, brings in the money. The man asks for money to buy a beer, and she doesn't want to give it to him. That's when the hitting starts," explains a young man from Florencio Varela. Many beatings are linked to drunkenness, as well. Women in Villa Atamisqui note, "Drunkards have a tendency to batter."

Some women, such as Luisa, a 43-year-old public health promoter in Sol y Verde and a mother of seven, find the resources to leave violent homes. Luisa's husband became increasingly violent after he lost steady work doing maintenance for a garbage collection business:

> *In my house it was all fighting; I had to put up with a lot. I tried to be patient, to wait until he realized, to not give it too much importance, but always the fighting. . . . Everything was an excuse for a beating. When I answered it was because I answered, when I didn't answer it was because I didn't answer. I got angry and didn't speak. He would come close and be all nice and then again the fight. I didn't have any friends—I couldn't have any friends. He threatened me. He even threatened me in front of the children.*
>
> *I left home with my children; I couldn't stand it anymore. I managed to get a small house and I left. I withdrew. The children see their father very little. He still lives close by in Sol y Verde, but they rarely see him, only when I take them, and I have to stay with them.*

Effects on the Next Generation

The daily struggle to survive has negative impacts not only on women and men but also on children, as frequently both parents must be absent from the home. In cities, both men and women speak of a crisis in day care. A discussion group of men and women from Moreno reports,

> *There are small children in the street. They have homes, but their parents are working and they're out in the street all day without supervision except for maybe a sibling who's*

only a year or two older. Some older street children are
fending for themselves. They get tired of having no food
at home and go off on their own. Many disappear. Some
return, others don't.

In part because schools occupy and care for students during the workday, study participants in almost every community rank their schools very high. The residents of Florencio Varela explain, "The school is good for learning because the children get fed and because it allows us to go to work." In Sol y Verde people also appreciate the school "not so much for the learning, but because the children are safe and well cared for and the teachers are kind to the children." Though a primary education is practically universal in the urban locations, sending children to school is a hardship for parents. Says a parent in La Matanza, which has the largest elementary school in the nation (2,200 pupils), "You might have to make your child go without supper for a month in order to have enough to buy him his school uniform." Only the people of Moreno rank their schools relatively low; they say they lack teachers, discipline is weak, children are mistreated, and the facilities are dirty.

While people recognize the importance of a secondary (and university) education for obtaining many jobs, the need to begin working causes many poor youths to drop out. According to recent statistics, 37 percent of youths between the ages of 14 and 18 in the lowest consumption quintile do not attend school.[10]

Absence of adults at home, according to discussion groups, is linked to increases in juvenile delinquency, abandonment, and incest. Many people also describe an increase in teen pregnancies. "Nowadays you see 14-year-old mothers. Girls aren't being educated and protected anymore. Maybe it's because their mothers have to work and aren't around to educate them better," says Claudia, a woman from Dock Sud. A parent from Sol y Verde reports, "In my son's class today there are several pregnant 11-year-olds. It's not only accepted, it's common." Sexual abuse is also becoming commonplace. Dock Sud study participants mention the case of a 7-year-old hospitalized with infections after sexual abuse by her caretakers—her grandfather and stepbrother. In Sol y Verde participants tell of a couple whose urgent concern, upon learning that their daughter had been raped by her babysitter/cousin, was that they no longer had anyone to watch the girl and her many siblings while they worked.

When speaking of the dangers that children face, however, participants are especially concerned about street crime. Substance abuse is often mentioned as a closely related problem. See box 2 for comments from various discussion groups.

Parents in the study also raise questions about modern cultural forces that reinforce consumer values and violence. "What you're worth is measured by what you have," asserts a 46-year-old man from La Matanza. "My kids come home from school saying, 'I have to have this brand of sneaker, that brand of clothes.' It's the culture of consumption; it happens to children; it's instilled in them very young. If you could hear my 7-year-old daughter . . ." A group of men from Moreno say that in the past "there wasn't so much violence and sex on TV . . . one grew up in a

---

BOX 2 Crime and Drugs Fill the Gap

"The oldest is supposed to look after the younger children, but the siblings don't obey. They skip school, get into trouble."

—A woman, Sol y Verde

"There aren't many job opportunities for young people. This leads to drugs, drinking, and robberies."

—Discussion group of men, women, and girls, Sol y Verde

"Teenagers say, 'Why should I bother to study if it won't get me a decent job?' They see that the ones who get ahead have chosen the path of crime."

—A man, La Matanza

"Here in Isla Maciel, we young people hang out all day with nothing to do, so what do you expect? When you need money, you have to get it somehow."

—A young man, Dock Sud

"We believe the violence comes mostly from the drug problem. What we are working for is the regeneration of employment. The drug issue is closely tied to joblessness."

—A neighborhood organizer, Dock Sud

"I keep wondering what will become of the guys I used to hang out with, since you need an eighth-grade education to be a manual laborer in construction. Can you believe it? To haul concrete! And people ask why there's so much crime and drugs."

—A male teenager in Dock Sud who landed a construction job after a two-year search

---

healthier environment." A man from a discussion group in La Matanza states, "The reality is we don't have enough to eat anymore, but they bring color TV and Adidas in here. Young people aspire to have them— things their fathers can't provide—and that's where the delinquency comes in."

Pervasive Crime

In all of the urban neighborhoods visited, people make frequent references to crime and violence in their lives and indicate that it is increasing. An older resident of Moreno reports, "Ten years ago this was a tranquil place. There were about 100,000 people. Now there are over 500,000. Everything is totally messed up." Carmen, 66 years old and also from Moreno, lives with crime and drugs literally at her doorstep:

> I live across the street from a house where they sell drugs. [Buyers] come in cars; they get the wrong place a lot and come bursting into my house. They insult me, they shout, "Where is so-and-so!" One time they grabbed me. You don't know how terrifying it is . . . I'm so afraid that someday they'll do something to my son.

Carmen tells the researchers, "I went to the police but they don't do anything."

Participants in other urban areas experience the same kind of fear and anxiety. "The violence is bad here ... You can get robbed at any hour and often [attackers] are armed. For no reason they'll wound you or kill you," reports a study participant from Sol y Verde. In Florencio Varela women say: "You can't hang clothes to dry because they'll steal them off the clothesline"; "What kills you is they'll steal your TV set and immediately sell it for $5 to buy drugs, while you'll be paying for the thing for years"; "Every night around nine, we start to hear gunfire."

Poor people assert that fear of crime and lack of police protection have also eroded community ties. "Nowadays when a child is being abused, the neighbors don't get involved. In the old days they would intervene and defend the child," says a woman from La Matanza. According to Claudia, a woman from Dock Sud, "It's every man for himself. People will watch you getting killed and say to themselves, 'I'd better stay out of it.'"

Police Brutality

Across urban communities, many discussion groups single out the police force as one of the worst institutions both in their daily lives and during a crisis. They indicate that the local police are not only ineffective but also corrupt and sometimes repressive. In Moreno a participant says, "You have to pay them to come, and even then they don't do anything. The muggers will rob you whether there's a cop nearby or not." A discussion group of men and women from Dock Sud reports:

> Far from defending us, the police mistreat us; they come in and rough up teenagers and don't do anything to the real criminals. . . . The gangs pay them off. . . . They'll round up a bunch of people and beat them up, but not the thieves. . . . The police are just another gang. . . . The police chase criminals into here, shooting the whole time when there are children playing in the street. When we protest, they shove us around and say we are defending the criminals. . . . They insult us and threaten us.

In Sol y Verde a young man asserts, "We're more afraid of the police than of the thieves. They grab street criminals and throw them in front of oncoming trains." Claudia, of Dock Sud, reports, "Now, the police steal from you, and when you go to [the police station] to report a crime, you come out raped."

In contrast to the treatment poor people receive, discussion groups say that the police cater to the wealthy and powerful. In Florencio Varela participants say, "The reason we don't have any protection in our neighborhood is because [the police] are all over at the weekend houses, protecting them because those people bribe them"; and "Here security is like everything else: the only ones who have it are the ones who pay for it." In Los Juríes, a woman notes,

> It's clear that when the [agribusiness] firm files a claim against us peasants, the police take it, but when we go into the police station to make a report on what the company's agents have done to us, the police don't let us file a complaint. They tell us the boss isn't in, come back at six; or you go and they're

*out of forms—they give you a thousand excuses. But the
company can go there at any time it pleases, and the police
will take their claim.*

Safer Places in the Countryside

Poor people in rural areas report a very different crime situation. In Isla
Talavera people say, "It's peaceful here. You don't need to lock your
doors." Residents of Villa Atamisqui state, "None of [what happens in
cities] happens here." Participants of Los Juríes remark, "Our community is very tranquil. There is no violence. We heard once that the drug
problem had reached Santiago [the capital of the province], but we don't
have it here. The violence here is poverty.'

Community bonds also appear much stronger in rural areas. In Los
Juríes poor people explain, "Around here we help each other out. We
all get together and make empanadas to raise money for the community
center, or if I'm out of sugar my neighbor will give me some." In Isla Talavera men in a discussion group say, "Living in poverty isn't pretty, but
to be a poor person is nice because we help one another," and "We of the
island have fewer problems: we are poor, but happy."

There are numerous indications that life in rural Argentina is changing, particularly in places such as Isla Talavera, an island in the delta
north of Buenos Aires. There the number of tourists, the price of property, and the cost of living have already begun to soar. In places such as Los
Juríes, much of the land is owned by large conglomerates. Due to new
laws that encourage landowners and corporations to reclaim abandoned
lands, poor people say, it is only a matter of time before development
destroys the livelihoods of the 90 percent of people in the area who have
occupied and farmed the land for decades.

Limited Community and Governmental Responses to Poverty

In addition to joblessness, hunger, and crime, people in all of the
communities visited lack or have inadequate access to most basic
services. Polluted drinking water, substandard housing, and nonexistent
or inadequate transportation, electricity sanitation, and communication services are widely reported. A number of poor people in the communities, and poor women in particular, have mobilized organizations

and resources to provide needed services. In addition, there are a striking number of government assistance programs for poor people in Argentina. While extremely important in terms of daily survival, few of these programs seem to result in greater economic opportunities or better provision of basic services to poor communities.

A new study on social capital in Argentina finds that rates of civic participation in organizations and groups are very low relative to those in other countries. Within the country, the level is lowest in the greater metropolitan region of Buenos Aires, where several of the study communities are located. The survey also reveals that very poor people are more likely to participate than middle-income groups, but not as likely as the significantly better-off groups, which suggests that "the very poor participate as part of a coping strategy, while the less poor find the opportunity cost too high or the experience too unrewarding." More women participate than men, although leaders of organizations are more likely to be male. Poor people's organizations also tend to consist of other poor people with similar backgrounds, and "serve mainly for self-help and 'getting by' rather than for leveraging new resources, transforming situations, and 'getting ahead.'"[11] These patterns are mirrored in the communities visited for this study, and raise important challenges for building more inclusive and empowered communities that can bring meaningful change.

Community-Based Actions and Partnerships

Men and women in the five urban communities say their community-based organizations provide important services but are not as effective as they could be. In rural areas, few local organizations are even acknowledged in discussions about institutions that help poor people in their daily lives. In explaining the relatively limited effectiveness of local organizations, a participant in Moreno states, "There is a lack of unity and support, there is always a 'but.' . . . In the neighborhoods there are always disputes among different groups; if one wins, the others try to bring them down, and vice versa." In Florencio Varela a resident says, "The cooperative society doesn't do anything. We don't even know where it is located. They all function the same way. You ask them for something and they ignore you." In Dock Sud a villager reports, "Here we have a housing cooperative, but apart from that, for everything else, everyone fends for themselves."

Against this backdrop of weak local institutions, however, stories emerge in several communities of civic activism to address hunger and other pressing needs. Moreno, on the western outskirts of Buenos Aires, is one such place. Moreno residents used to hunt duck and squab and work in the cattle industry. There were three large meatpacking plants, some employing more than 5,000 workers. Residents also found employment at textile plants and a tile factory. Moreno now has a number of gated communities, one of which employs over a thousand people as domestics, groundskeepers, and pool cleaners.

Nowadays, hunger is a pressing problem. Women in various Moreno neighborhoods have organized soup kitchens for residents. These initiatives rely on local leadership and support, and many also turn to public, private, and civic partners outside the community. As a group of participants explains, "Several women in the neighborhood have run a soup kitchen for four years now. They go out and ask for donations from supermarkets and department stores. The women who are a little better off chip in a few pesos, a poultry plant donates some chickens." The group also explains that "for ideological reasons" this particular soup kitchen does not receive help from the municipality.

Women from another part of Moreno describe extensive partnerships between a neighborhood group and the municipality for the delivery of food in their neighborhood:

> We started our soup kitchen three years ago . . . in my home.
> The municipality provides food and assistance through Plan
> Trabajar. . . . We serve fifty children and ten senior citizens. At
> first it was small, but we've been expanding. The municipality
> gave us carpeting. The fathers of the children [who eat there]
> helped with the construction.

A third group of women focuses on hunger relief for older people: "We serve meals to the elderly three times a week. The municipality gives us starches and grains. The rest we provide ourselves, but often there simply isn't enough food. Neighbors contribute some, but there are grandparents here who have to go without."

In yet another neighborhood in Moreno, women who run the local soup kitchen needed a proper place to prepare the meals and serve them. Under the tutelage of an elderly bricklayer, these women mixed and poured the concrete and raised the community building. It is also used for community events, birthdays, wakes, and other milestones, and several *Voices of the Poor* group discussions were held there.

In the other four urban neighborhoods there are also soup kitchens, day-care centers, and a variety of other neighborhood organizations. With little police protection is available, some of the urban communities in the study have tried to reduce crime on their own. Women in one neighborhood installed and pay for local streetlights. In several urban neighborhoods, women activists use a "buddy system" to avoid having to walk alone. People in La Matanza who founded a settlement on a dump-site proudly recount their neighborhood crime-watch successes. They banished a young, violent criminal from the area and only allowed him to return after many months, reformed and repentant. They threatened a neighbor who was dealing drugs from his home with arson, thereby convincing him to desist.

Community-based initiatives can be found in rural areas as well, and many of the most highly regarded ones benefit from government support. A good example is the Farmers Union Cooperative, which a group of men in Los Juríes ranked the second most important institution in their community. They proudly claim that it was created "by us, ourselves." "Through it," they explain, "we manage credits that come from external sources, we distribute them to people who need them and to our members." Also through the cooperative, "we receive information from other institutions and we solve problems. For instance, in this lot we had planted seeds, but we couldn't enclose it with a wire fence. Through the cooperative we obtained credit to fence and enclose all lots of land." The men indicate that the cooperative serves as the contact point for all the government programs in Los Juríes, "and through this channel, these programs are more effective." They say, "The cooperative is like the central rural commission."

In Isla Talavera the local school functions as the point of delivery for a range of government services, including transportation, employment, food, education, birth control information, and vocational training. The school provides uniforms and shoes to all children, as well as breakfast, lunch, and a snack every day. Local men are employed at the school in repairs, maintenance, and vegetable gardening. The "school bus" is actually a ferry, and it serves other members of the community as well. Carrying adults and children each day, it is the only means of transportation many residents have to leave the island. Also, whenever there is a flood, the municipal government dispenses mattresses, blankets, food, and drinking water at the school.

The Isla Talavera school houses a women's workshop funded by a provincial government program called Manos Bonarenses, which provides sewing machines, fabric, and a trainer. Local women started by making sheets and became quite proficient. They now embroider shawls and pillow shams, and quilt baby blankets, bibs, and other items. The province pays cash by the unit for their handiwork. In the words of one beneficiary, "At the school they taught us to sew. They give us the fabric and we sew at home or at the school. Some of us earned enough at it to buy sewing machines and work at home." Some people speak of matters that cannot be quantified. A 53-year-old woman says, "Five years ago I started coming to the school. It changed my life. I used to be holed up in my house. Now I have work and I have friends. They took away all my shame here. There is great camaraderie." The women of Isla Talavera have heard that elsewhere the province supplies a layette to new mothers, and they are working toward obtaining that benefit, too.

Government Helps Poor People Survive

Poor people express appreciation for a large number of government assistance programs, many of which build on and support strong community-based associations and leadership. Manos Bonarenses, discussed above, is but one of the government programs that participants mention favorably. They also give high marks to Plan Trabajar, a municipal jobs program that employs 30 percent of all men and 20 percent of all women in La Matanza, and to Barrios Bonarenses, a provincial government work program to improve neighborhoods in Sol y Verde. Another valued program is Plan Vica, a provincial government plan that distributes a weekly ration of milk, eggs, cereal, and rice to pregnant women and children through the age of 6. Beneficiaries also receive information on nutrition and child development from a *comadre*, a locally trained, female outreach worker. Other programs mentioned include Plan PAIS, a national employment program, and Plan Asoma, a national program to alleviate hunger among the elderly (Dock Sud). Los Juríes receives assistance from additional government programs: INTA, Prohuerta, Programa Social Agropecuario, Plan Surco, and Plan de Fortalecimiento de la Sociedad Civil.

Despite the plethora of programs specifically targeted to poor people, however, coverage is limited. As mentioned above, only one-quarter of poor Argentines receive any public assistance. Forty-four percent of children from birth to 2 years in the lowest consumption quintile—one of the groups most vulnerable to long-term harm from malnutrition—receive benefits from public nutrition programs.[12] There are significant regional disparities in public spending, with rural and indigenous areas often left out of government social programs. People living in squatter settlements, such as the members of one group in La Matanza, cannot receive many benefits because their settlements are illegal. In addition, many poor people are undocumented aliens and thus cannot use services such as health clinics.

Participants in the study express deep concerns about how social programs are implemented and whether they actually reach the intended beneficiaries. Political interference is identified as a problem in some discussion groups. In general, people do not feel they can participate in improving the programs intended to help them. For instance, although Plan Trabajar is appreciated by most study participants, a day-care director in La Matanza indicates that many of the beneficiaries appear to be selected arbitrarily, and adds, "We have practically no access to Plan Trabajar; it is politically organized around fifteen neighborhoods. We managed to work for six months, but after that they pulled the plug."

"What will become of us when the program ends?" poor people ask. Indeed, the residents of Los Juríes describe hardships resulting from the elimination of a monthly subsidy that used to be paid to small landholders (of ten hectares or less). Similarly, people in La Matanza are feeling the cuts to several assistance programs: "The hospitals used to be free and they gave you the prescriptions. Now for them to see you, you have to be dying. It never used to be like that. They would always attend to you the same day"; "Now they charge $5 any time you go to the clinic"; "Ten years ago we had the FONAVI housing program."

Participants also sometimes express mixed emotions about the effectiveness of social assistance in providing a path out of poverty. In Florencio Varela *manzaneras* (neighborhood activists) observe, "Plan Vida relieves the problems, but it doesn't resolve them. The same can be said of the housing program. Sure, we all need housing, but first we need jobs because I for one would like to be able to pay for my house and call it my own." In Villa Atamisqui a similar line of reasoning is heard: "People go to the municipality to receive handouts of medicine and food. It's no good—it would be better to give them jobs." Finally, a young man in Dock Sud points out that "when they give you a box of groceries they're also taming your dignity."

Problems beyond Poor Communities

The many social assistance programs notwithstanding, poor people voice strong disapproval of the government itself, and especially of politicians. People in Villa Atamisqui identify the failure of government institutions as their primary problem, and rank political parties among the lowest of all institutions. In many cases, their anger toward the government is palpable, with critiques including gross economic mismanagement, large-scale corruption, and a total lack of accountability. A discussion group participant in La Matanza charges, "The policies of the national government put us out of work." Men and women in a discussion group in rural Los Juríes express their frustrations with the government:

> Ever since Menem took power we are worse off in the countryside. . . . If we don't get a change of government things are going to get even worse. . . . The municipal government only remembers us when it's time to vote. . . . They have what they have thanks to our sweat. . . . In election years, the municipal candidates come here for a day, they pat you on the back and give you a kilo of sugar. . . . They deceive you, they lie to you, they toy with the misery of the people. They promise, "When we win we'll build roads. Whenever you need something, the doors of the municipal government will be open. We'll be there to help you." These are false promises—how many years have they been promising such things and the roads are still the same? . . . We go in to see them and are told, "They just stepped out," or "He's in the capital, come back another time."

Poor men and women in the study also reveal a fair amount of resentment toward the upper classes. At more than one location, participants use derogatory terms (*ricachones, cogotudos*) for people with money and note "excessive accumulation of wealth" by a few in the nation. One man adds, "They're going to keep squeezing us. . . . Next they'll be putting little stamps on our foreheads that say 'Slave So-and-So.'" A young man in Dock Sud notes that the political beliefs held by neighborhood residents are a source of stigma: "One of our problems is that the Anglo [his neighborhood] got labeled as a 'red' zone. If you say you're from here, you won't get a job." In fact, the neighborhood was the site of intense repression under the military dictatorship. Some community activism still faces resistance—at times brutal—from public authorities (box 3).

Conclusion

Argentines who shared their perspectives and experiences do not speak entirely with one voice, but they do converge on four issues. First, their lives used to be better, both materially and otherwise. Second, unemployment is destroying their families and communities. Third, crime has become an inescapable fact of life for poor people in urban areas. And fourth, neither elected officials nor the police are much help, but a range of civic and government initiatives do play important roles in their lives. Soup kitchens, food programs for pregnant women and young children, vocational training, and other initiatives are valued, even if they are not catalysts for broader social change. Access to these resources, however, is very uneven.

Labor markets are shifting dramatically and poor people are finding it difficult to cope. With 89 percent of the country urbanized and extensive poverty affecting the cities, job creation is critical. Small entrepreneurs and informal workers need supportive regulations. In addition, poor people want better access to training and skills development programs, as well as financial services to help them generate incomes and develop the economy in their communities. Poor neighborhoods desperately need infrastructure improvements. Study participants also clearly called out for major police reform.

Argentina needs to protect a larger share of its poor population with effective safety nets. This will require expanded efforts to reach the most vulnerable as well as greater use of temporary programs that can be mobilized when the economy is in crisis. The study highlights some successful community-government partnerships in the delivery of social programs, and these efforts should be increased. People say they rely on these supports, and express concern over benefits that do not arrive as promised and that leave them dependent or without resources when the program ends. There are no channels for their participation in the design or delivery of government services. More transparent and accountable processes would help to reduce uncertainties, political interference, and corruption, improve the coverage and targeting of programs, and raise low levels of civic engagement among poor people.

Some participants in the study acknowledge that government–civic partnerships for community development require a two-way commitment. As a participant in Sol y Verde explains, "In the neighborhood there isn't as much progress as we would like. It's the fault of the municipality, but it is also our fault because we neighbors cannot seem to get together and agree on many things, including cleaning the streets and cutting the grass." In addition to more and better public support for basic services, community improvements will require building local capacities for organizing and problem solving. Measures that support successful civic groups include providing more information to community organizations on government programs and on their rights, and supporting broad-based community involvement in setting priorities and overseeing implementation. Local groups can also be valuable partners in monitoring the use and impact of the programs designed to benefit them. Other supportive actions include an improved legal environment for community activism as well as direct legal aid to poor men and women.

With the exception of some male community activists, poor men in Argentina are having trouble coping with the changes forced upon them. Male teens are at severe risk of taking up criminal activity and drug abuse, and female teens are becoming single mothers at a startling rate.

Old people in these communities live in fear and suffer from hunger. In the midst of all this, many adult women in Argentina are responding with ingenuity and collective action, and even humor. So, despite the grim circumstances of life in Florencio Varela, a woman can look at a stinking mound of garbage and say, "It's been here for about two years and it's starting to seem like it belongs. Pretty soon we'll be celebrating its anniversary." Perhaps quite different landmarks could be celebrated if greater numbers of communities had more dynamic local economies and the organizational strength and resources to resolve their pressing needs.

TABLE 1 Study Communities in Argentina

arrio Sol y Verde, Buenos Aires Province Pop. 9,500	An inner-city area of Buenos Aires, the settlement is located in the municipality of José C. Paz (population 205,000). Ninety-five percent of the dwellings have electricity; 90 percent of adults are literate, and only 8 percent of household heads did not complete primary school. The main concerns in the municipality are related to unemployment and to problems with relief assistance and food provision.
Dock Sud, Buenos Aires Province Pop. 1,200	The settlement is located in the municipality of Avellaneda (population 350,000). From the turn of the century to the late 1970s it was one of the main industrial sectors in Buenos Aires, with huge meatpacking plants and a soap factory. Dock Sud today is an abandoned shell; only an oil refinery and a shipping container firm remain in operation. Mail carriers, taxis, and ambulance drivers refuse to enter Dock Sud, saying it is too dangerous. Residents come and go via a footbridge or by boat. Either way, they are prey to armed youths. The area is awash with industrial runoff and raw sewage when it rains.
La Matanza, Buenos Aires Province Pop. 1.2 million	La Matanza's dwellings include Ciudad Evita, a complex of high-rises built by the government in the 1950s, *villas*, and the El Tambo, San Pedro, José L. Cabezas, and González Catán settlements. The José L. Cabezas settlement was established by 170 local residents who invaded a landfill and built regular houses on a traditional street grid, with a plaza. They have not obtained basic services yet and as far as the municipality is concerned, their community is illegal.
Florencio Varela, Buenos Aires Province Pop. 260,000	One of the poorest communities visited, Florencio Varela is located on the southern outskirts of Buenos Aires, where many settlements have been established on public and private lands. Roads are not paved, and there are no sewers, telephones, or gas lines. Electricity is obtained via illegal connections. To enter and exit, residents must use a single narrow path that leads to the paved road and young toughs charge them a "toll" for their passage.

URBAN AREAS (continued)

Moreno, Buenos Aires Province Pop. 370,000	On the western outskirts of Buenos Aires, which used to be mostly country estates, Moreno is now plagued by unemployment, high crime rates, a serious drug problem, AIDS, polluted water, and mounds of trash. In recent years it has undergone a large demographic expansion.

RURAL AREAS

Villa Atamisqui, Santiago del Estero Province Pop. 9,300	Mud-brick huts are found throughout the area, and most homes lack water and electricity. Primary education is not universal and many people are illiterate. Chagas' disease, a debilitating blood infection caused by an insect that nests in the mat roofs of poorly built houses, is widespread. In the town, juvenile delinquency and drug abuse are problems.
Los Juríes, Santiago del Estero Province Pop. 30,000	Most men work on cattle ranches and cotton plantations and most women work in some form of agriculture as well. Travel is by horse and mule. Residents have occupied area settlements for more than three decades. Some of the settlements visited have long-standing activist, peasant cooperatives.
Isla Talavera, Buenos Aires Province Pop. 500	The village is located in the municipality of Campana (population 71,500). Cyclical flooding is a major problem. A significant number of people live in yellow two-bedroom houses that the government provides to flood victims. People increasingly work for the owners of weekend homes. A large percentage of the population of Isla Talavera receives some form of public assistance. The main problems are unemployment and lack of transport and communications.

Notes

1. The study team was led by Daniel Cichero, Patricia Feliu, and Mirta Mauro, and also included Silvia Fuentes, Hernán Nazer, Blanca Irene García Prado, Héctor Salamanca, Mariano Salzman, and Norberto Vázquez.

2. Throughout this chapter, $ refers to Argentine pesos. The peso has been at parity with the U.S. dollar since 1991.

3. World Bank, "Argentina: Poor People in a Rich Country," vol. 1, "A Poverty Report for Argentina" (Poverty Reduction and Economic Management, Latin America and Caribbean Region, Report 19992-AR, 2000), 3–4.

4. World Bank, *World Development Indicators 2001* (Report 22099, April 2001), 12.

5. World Bank, "Argentina: Poor People in a Rich Country," 3–4.

6. Ibid., 108.

7. The other two components of the safety net are social insurance (57 percent), a contributory program that doesn't reach the many poor people who work in the informal sector; and education and health (36 percent). World Bank, "Memorandum from the President of the International Bank for Reconstruction and Development to the Executive Directors on a Country Assistance Strategy of the World Bank Group for the Argentine Republic" (September 2000), 9.

8. World Bank, "Argentina: Poor People in a Rich Country," 8.

9. The urban poor in Argentina live in three kinds of housing: *barrios, villas,* and settlements. *Barrios* are generally older neighborhoods with paved streets, concrete construction, and basic services. *Villas* are shantytowns with precariously constructed housing and chaotic layouts, usually lacking basic services. Settlements are planned, organized seizures of public or private property in which lot size and shape are regular and streets are designed on grids. Settlement residents work collectively to "normalize" the legal status of their community and obtain services.

10. World Bank, "Argentina: Poor People in a Rich Country," 31–32.

11. World Bank, "Together We Stand, Divided We Fall: Levels and Determinants of Social Capital in Argentina" (Latin America and Caribbean Region, April 2001, draft).

12. World Bank, "Argentina: Poor People in a Rich Country," 30.

Brazil

Gains and Losses in the *Favelas*

Marcus Melo[1]

Forty-five-year-old Maria Vargas migrated many years ago from rural Alagoas to Sacadura Cabral to escape poverty. Upon arriving in the city, Maria worked as a domestic. In time her brother helped her find a better-paying job in a textile factory. After a year, she left the factory job to marry and begin a family. After seven years of marriage, her husband died, and Maria returned to domestic work because its relative flexibility allowed her to maintain her own household. Then one day while working, Maria fell from the second story of her employer's home. The fall disabled her, and for the past twelve years Maria has had to rely on sewing to support her seven children.

Located near São Paulo, Brazil's largest and most industrial city, Sacadura Cabral is a densely crowded home to 3,000 people. Sacadura Cabral is a favela, an urban slum where many homes lack legal tenure. According to a resident of Sacadura Cabral, "In the past, everybody worked in the factories and the wages were good." Heavy industry used to thrive in the area, but today the men often work at jobs with less security as car washers, janitors, night watchmen, construction workers, or tradesmen. Most women clean houses or offices or wash laundry in addition to their responsibilities as housewives. Some people still work in factories, and both men and women are petty traders and vendors. Peddling illegal drugs is not an uncommon activity, especially among young men. "Before, everybody had jobs at the mills at good wages. Now whoever has a job has a low income," says a participant from Sacadura Cabral.

Maria has had to face other severe tragedies, notably the rape and murder of her 4-year-old daughter:

If she were alive she would be 18 and beautiful. I suffered a lot with this; the whole family suffered. My eldest son withdrew from school for some time. The teachers kept calling me about it. He was the one who found her in that condition. I was not at home when she disappeared. I spent six days looking for her.

Of her life now, Maria says,

I have a partner, but he lives with his mother and I live with my children alone. This is because I want to avoid problems between him and the children. That is why I never lived with anyone else. I see my friends who live with men at home. Sometimes the men want to beat the children, rape them.

Surrounded by poverty and violence, Maria clings to her accomplishments. She is proud that she never allowed her sons to quit school even though they had to repeat grades, and now all of them are studying to attend university. Her sons also work, and "they already have managed to buy their cars," she says. One of her sons declined a position as manager in a butcher shop so that he could continue his studies. "I raised all my children amid drugs, robbery, cocaine, marijuana, and crack, but thanks to God none of them ever got involved with these things," says Maria. "For a poor mother living in a favela with many sons, it is a victory."

Fernando, Maria's 21-year-old son, holds great hope that he can help make life better in Sacadura. He started working at age 8 in the textile factory where his mother returned to work, but dreams of being a judge someday. Fernando aspires to study law because, in his view, education and awareness of rights are vital to the future of the favela. *He says, "In a favela people have no idea of their rights. We have police discrimination, the politicians abuse us, and others use their knowledge to take advantage of us. So I want to know all about rights and obligations."*

Maria's hardships—and hopes—are typical of those faced by many poor people who participated in the *Voices of the Poor* study in Brazil. Like Maria, many women have become their household's sole or primary breadwinner. Many people encounter violence firsthand, and they despair as it tears apart their families and communities. Many also express deep appreciation for the local public services and social programs that somewhat ease their struggles. Education in particular is seen as a path out of poverty.

Brazil's transition to democracy in 1935 coincided with a period of economic instability, recession, and high inflation that lasted until the mid-1990s, despite high-profile, aggressive initiatives to turn the economy around. In 1993, however, Brazil began to make significant economic and social gains, and by 1998 poverty had fallen by more than a third (to 22 percent of the population) in this five-year period. In 1998 Fernando Cardoso became the first president in Brazil to be elected to a second term, and much of his popularity rested on his success in controlling inflation. Other major reforms of his administration include better banking policies, a privatization program, and a major drive to improve education. Poverty continues to fall in Brazil, although at a slower rate on account of a recession and currency devaluation triggered by the emerging markets crisis in 1997 and 1998.

Poverty and inequality remain Brazil's most important challenge. The extent and severity of poverty remain high for a country whose GNP per capita was US$4,350 in 1999.[2] Almost 35 million Brazilians, or more than one-fifth of the population, live in households with per capita incomes of less than 65 reais per month (about US$36 in February 2000). There are also significant regional inequalities. More than 60 percent of Brazil's poor people are concentrated in the country's northeast region. Slightly over half the population below the poverty line lives in urban areas, but the most extreme poverty is in the countryside. Additionally, poverty rates are higher in small and medium-sized cities than in large cities.[3] This chapter focuses solely on urban areas.

As study participants' views and experiences reveal, income data alone do not adequately convey what it is like to be poor in urban Brazil. While men and women in poor urban areas may have higher earnings than their rural counterparts, they face other disadvantages that interlock to greatly diminish their quality of life. These deprivations relate to living in crowded and polluted communities beset by crime and violence.

Brazilian researchers visited ten poor neighborhoods located in the cities of São Paulo, Recife, and Itabuna (see table 2, Study Communities in Brazil, at the end of this chapter). São Paulo has a population of 16 million. Recife is Brazil's fourth largest city and one of the urban centers for the country's most impoverished and drought-stricken region, the northeast.

Itabuna, a remote, medium-sized city in the northeast, was selected to provide an urban setting somewhat smaller than the two megacities. All communities discussed in this chapter are, or until recently were, *favelas*. Brazil is the only country in the study where only urban communities were visited so as to inform the development of an urban strategy. Geographic diversity, unemployment, poverty levels, and the degree of community organization are factors that guided community selection within the cities.

Participants for discussion groups were identified following an initial visit to community leaders, associations, or other informal groups, such as *grupos de mães* (groups of mothers) in the communities. Individuals selected for case studies were either participants in discussion groups or were individually identified by leaders or other participants.

A total of eighty discussion groups were held, twenty each with men, women, male youth, and female youth. A total of fifty-one individual and institutional case studies were also completed, including thirty-one with poor people and the remaining twenty with people who used to be poor but had moved out of poverty.

The Fundaçao de Apoio ao Desenvolvimento da Universidade Federal de Pernambuco (known locally as the University Foundation at the Federal University of Pernambuco), a development foundation based in Recife, Brazil, coordinated the study. Fieldwork was conducted during March and April 1999.

This chapter explores two urgent issues that emerged in all ten of the study communities: the shortage and low quality of employment, and the extremely high prevalence of violence and crime that affects the daily lives of those who live in the *favelas*. People also spoke extensively about the effects that class barriers and power relations have on their lives. The chapter then turns to infrastructure improvements and poor people's appreciation of the benefits that these government services have brought to their communities. The chapter closes with a look at important institutions in the lives of *favelados*, including their own local activist groups, which have won new services for their communities.

Joblessness, Underemployment, and Workplace Abuses

Official unemployment for Brazil's six largest metropolitan areas in 1998 was between 7 and 8 percent. In the *favelas*, however, residents report far higher levels of joblessness. Many poor people also stress that the work available to them is of very inferior quality. Few have formal jobs, and many with temporary or informal work consider themselves underemployed. "Here in Sacadura there are a lot of former metalworkers looking for jobs, and they will take anything," says Mário, 48, himself a former metalworker. "Today, Santo André and the greater metropolitan area is becoming a commercial center instead of the industrial center it used to be. . . . Commerce creates many jobs, but the income is much lower." Men and women from the communities visited in Itabuna and Santo André ranked unemployment as the single most pressing problem facing their communities.[4]

The poor women and men who participated in the Brazil study emphasize the difference between informal work—which they sometimes refer to as "subemployment"—and employment in the formal sector. Among Brazil's poor population, 22 percent are employed without a formal labor contract, 37 percent are self-employed, and 15 percent are inactive. Only 15 percent of poor people have jobs in the formal sector.[5] Work in the informal sector is legally unregulated, leaving employees and small entrepreneurs vulnerable to abuses and without legal recourse. Informal workers do not have access to social insurance and other government social programs tied to the workplace. They also find it much more difficult to obtain credit, business leases, and other market opportunities. Many people with informal jobs mention such problems as working irregularly and being paid unfairly or not at all. A man from Sacadura Cabral says, "I worked six years in a company that did not pay me correctly. So I sued them and they threatened to kill me. I had to go into hiding."

For some, however, self-employment in the informal sector can provide a path out of poverty. Box 1 describes one man who has been able to make a better living through entrepreneurship, although he considers his livelihood precarious.

Despite opportunities in the informal sector, people frequently express a strong preference for a formal job. According to a discussion group of men and women in Vila Junqueira, a job in the formal sector "allows you to feed your family, have your children in school, and maintain a harmonious household." Most of the Brazilian communities visited have experienced sharp declines in the number of local jobs in the formal sector. A participant in Bode explains, "Here in the community there are no jobs, but there is work." A group of young women in Borborema says that in the past people had options for employment and very often found work they enjoyed, but "today when you have a job offer, you have to accept promptly, otherwise another comes and takes your place."

BOX 1 Climbing Up in Sacadura Cabral: The Story of Valdeci

"I came to São Paulo in 1980 [from Paraíba] to work in the mills, and I stayed for seven years and one month," reports Valdeci of his first venture to the city in search of work. Metalworking paid very well, he says, but he returned to his village after he lost his job in 1987. Back home, Valdeci couldn't make ends meet and he returned again to São Paulo to take a difficult job for a transport company that went out of business after four years. Valdeci then spent a year unemployed before deciding to open a business selling cigarettes, sweets, and other goods he imported from Paraguay. He says, "I made about fifteen trips there; I liked it, it was nice. But when you got there things were hectic. You arrived at 10 A.M., and had to do the shopping quickly in order to travel again at 6 P.M."

"My life started improving about four years ago. . . . My kids have a medical plan, my wife also. The eldest daughter is at school." Valdeci indicates that before he had his own grocery store, he and his wife scraped by on wages they earned from their jobs. "With our wages we could eat only beans," he says. "Today we can afford to buy some furniture for the house." Valdeci stresses that his good fortune has not come easily. "I work a lot. I wake up very early and go to sleep very late. I close at eleven, and at half past four I am already waiting for the bread at the grocery."

Valdeci also reports that he is insecure about the future. There are plans to build apartments in Sacadura, which could destroy his home and business. "If I am unable to continue my business, I will leave. I will not be able to continue if they build these apartments."

Several study participants insist that even steady employment with the government or in a factory may not be enough to escape poverty. According to a group of men and women in Sacadura Cabral, many new jobs created in the formal sector are unskilled and low paid. While workers laid off from the manufacturing and financial sectors find these jobs preferable to those in the informal sector, these new positions do not provide an income level that allows workers to adequately support their families. The discussion group explains, "Now even people with jobs have a low income."

Poor men and women frequently state that education can provide them with the skills to obtain secure, better-paying positions, but the need to maintain an income prevents them from obtaining more education. A young man in Morro da Conceição says, "You have to choose between working or studying because you can't do both. And if you choose to study, what are you going to eat?" Similarly, Lúcia, a 17-year-old girl in Nova Califórnia, believes that the long-term wellbeing of the community depends on creating opportunities for people to get an education while they work: "Without that, the children of those poorer and in more need will not be able to rise in life because without education and a job we will have nothing."

Life amid Violence

People living in Brazil's *favelas* report an extraordinary prevalence of violence and crime in their everyday lives. They say they must cope constantly with crime in their streets, and the police offer little protection. They also indicate that the extent of physical abuse of women and children in the home is greater than it used to be.

Fear in the Streets

Brazilians in the communities visited say they contend daily with theft, vandalism, muggings, rapes, gang fights, murders, and organized crime. In Bode, where people seldom report crimes for fear of reprisal, a young mother declares, "People can't leave their houses and children can't play outside because there are so many muggings and shootings, day and night." Similarly, teenagers in Nova Califórnia say, "People are very hostile here. They even have knife fights over soccer." Young people in Vila Junqueira report, "People get killed at parties and on their way to and from parties." Residents of Novo Horizonte warn, "You can be walking along when a shootout starts, get hit by a stray bullet, and never even know what happened." Poor people emphasize that when they go to work, what few belongings they own are vulnerable to thieves because they live in shacks that cannot be secured.

Crime is particularly bad in the Vila União *favela* of Recife. Vila União was founded in the 1980s, when 200 families organized a struggle to live there. The municipality removed the families after a year, but the struggle continued for two more years and in 1990 the municipality authorized the building of the community's first legal homes. Today 450 families live in Vila União, which is adjacent to the *favelas* Barbalho and Airton Senna.

Paula, 48, lives in Vila União and recounts being held hostage for five hours when the shop where she worked was robbed. She says, "I almost died and was so traumatized I could never work there again." Shopkeepers are afraid of people from the *favelas* and put bars on their shops to prevent people from entering. A woman explains, "We can actually enter only a few shops here. At the others, you have to say what you are going to buy, the owner fetches it, and then hands it to you through the bars—only after you've paid for it."

While the level of crime in Vila União is particularly high, none of the settlements visited for the study is spared. In Morro da Conceição participants say, "When we go out we don't know if we'll come back alive." Entra a Pulso residents state, "Around here we're used to living with thieves, drug dealers, and rapists." People in Sacadura Cabral report, "We even had a rape-murder of a man. But the rapist bragged and got killed, too."

Almost unanimously, participants name the Brazilian police force as the worst institution in their communities. Police are described as absent, ineffective, rude, brutal, and corrupt. "When the police finally get here the cadaver's been on the ground a long while," reports a young woman in Borborema. Young women in Nova Califórnia say, "The police come to this community very rarely. When they do, they come hitting, disrespecting people, and beating up the younger street children. We go and complain and they insult us. There's no security here." Likewise, a young woman in Padre Jordano says, "I'm tired of seeing violent muggings at bus stops. And when we go to the police station to complain they laugh in our faces." People in Vila União fear the revenge of criminals and insist that organized crime bosses continue their operations from jail.

Young people in Entra a Pulso claim that the police used to kill three people a day in their community. They also charge, "When the police come here, it is to rob. They order everyone to the ground and humiliate us," and "The policemen bring arms in here and exchange them for drugs." Rather than viewing the police as a source of help to the community, Sacadura Cabral residents say they frequently add to the lack of security:

> When the police come here, we cannot so much as look at them. They storm our homes. One time they marked people's front doors with an "x" to keep track of where they'd been. They come up to you and tell you to raise your arms and spread your legs. Then they hit your legs. Then they call you a bum and demand to see your papers. But they hardly look at the documents. . . . The criminals have public safety here, we do not.

Severe corruption in the police department leads a young man in Nova Califórnia to ask, "Why would we want a police station in our community?"

Still, many poor people in the study identify better security as an urgent priority, and single out the police as the institution in greatest need of reform. A men's group in Novo Horizonte suggests that to reduce crime, a police officer should be assigned to the community and should respond when problems arise. The men remark that if there were a policeman posted locally, he would know the residents and not arrest or harass people at random as currently happens. In Vila União a 51-year-old woman says she is afraid to leave her house because "we do not have police patrols."

Residents of Bode tried unsuccessfully to remedy their policing problem:

> In November 1992 we built a police station with our own hands and money to curb the violence. The police agreed to come here after lots of pressure. They abandoned the station in February 1993 after criminals destroyed it in a shoot-out. Then for about five years addicts and prostitutes used it. Finally we got fed up and tore it down with sledgehammers. What's needed is a purging of the police force and a whole new start. Around here, what's needed is a civilian police force, because the problems are grave.

Fear in the Home

In recent years women have gained increasing authority over decisions in their households, most study participants say. Others maintain that social norms underpinning the higher status of men have changed little. While shifts toward more equitable gender relations might suggest greater harmony among couples, participants in nearly all discussion groups instead report extensive turmoil. Wife battering in particular is said to be widespread. Several women in the study mention that they have chosen to run households on their own rather than expose themselves and their children to potential abuse.

Traditional Gender Roles

Some women and men see few changes in gender relations. A man in Novo Horizonte says, "When a woman marries, she can only go out to parties if the husband approves." A man from Nova Califórnia says, "If I make a rule at home, she must follow it because I know better." Another man there says, "To work outside the home a woman must have her husband's approval." Many women in Novo Horizonte concur, saying: "Men do not allow their wives to work and forbid them to go out. It only happens because as he works, he wants to be the big boss and think that the woman is his property"; "There are men who say, 'If you go to your mother's house, you'd better not come back anymore'"; and "There are women who only do what a man says, who stay under men's feet."

However, most study participants believe that women are shedding traditional roles and gaining more control of their lives on many fronts. Young women in a discussion group in Nova Califórnia, for instance, identify numerous activities that take women outside the home and sometimes into leadership roles, such as working, joining community campaigns, attending university classes, and going to parties. "Today," they say, "there are even women mayors." The women insist, "This shows that things have changed a lot; today women have more power than before."

Women in Nova Califórnia and elsewhere associate women's increasing power in the home with their growing earning capacity. A group of women in Entra a Pulso tells researchers,

> *Before, women had no say in how the money was spent even if they worked. Now things are different. Women figure out the budget with the men, contributing their share, but also keeping some money for their own choices. Today, when the woman earns more, the man has to lower his head to her and accept. He cannot complain about the type of work she does because her earnings are what supports the family.*

A discussion group of men and women in Entra a Pulso agrees that "whoever has the money controls the situation. Whenever the issue is about cost, the last word goes to the one with the money."

While the status of women may be rising in general, poor people generally conclude that women are still less powerful than men. "Women today say, 'You're okay, but I earn more than you,' thinking they could be superior to you—a *man!*" exclaims a man from Novo Horizonte. And in response to an assertion by male participants that women have acquired more power than they had in the past, members of the women's discussion group in Novo Horizonte agree, but clarify that men still have more power than women do. "Women are fighting to end discrimination and they will keep on doing so," asserts a woman from the group.

Study participants provide numerous illustrations of the work that remains in creating more equitable and harmonious gender relations, and they draw particular attention to men who behave irresponsibly. A community activist and cleaning woman in Padre Jordano says, "Here there are men who help and men who exploit their wives. She goes to work and he goes to a bar, leaving the kids with others. That happens a lot." A woman in a discussion group in Borborema says, "In this community you find . . . lazy men who are always drunk, rude men. Near here there's a guy who does nothing while his wife works hauling cement, and on top of it all she does all the housework." Rita, 33, of Novo Horizonte states, "There are many men who exploit their wives, expecting them to do all the housework even though the woman has a job outside the home." A woman in Nova Califórnia adds that some women comply with their domination. "A woman's power depends on her. If she lowers her head before the husband, she can lose power," she says.

Physical Violence against Women

Domestic abuse of women is said to be very common, and discussion groups from more than half the communities visited indicate that the level of violence against women is worse than ever. Suzana, 16, from Novo Horizonte says, "The women here do not live well. Their lives are full of fights with their husbands, beatings by them. Sometimes the police are called in and the husband goes to jail. Other times they let him be." According to a woman in Borborema, "We have a neighbor who calls his wife a whore and beats her up if she doesn't have his clothes ready on time. She cries quietly, but everybody knows. He has total control and beats her over any little thing."

Various explanations for male violence are given. A woman in Entra a Pulso says, "Sometimes women are hit because lunch isn't ready when the man gets home from work.' A man in Nova Califórnia says, "Discord in the home is caused by wives complaining when the men go to a bar and drink." A community leader and nurse's aide in Nova Califórnia says, "The main consequence of poverty is violence, particularly in the home. If a man is out of work, he doesn't help around the house, but he does get in the way more than ever. He's drinking and squabbling, blaming things on his wife." She says women in the *favela* endure rape, assaults, and even murder in their homes, and drugs and drinking are almost always involved.

A number of participants describe cases of domestic conflict that result in murder. Geraldo, a 27-year-old community activist in Borborema, recounts how his father used to come home drunk at dawn and beat his mother. The family had to go on the run when his father, caught in a romantic triangle, killed a neighbor. Carla, 33, of Bode says her father was an alcoholic and a philanderer. "He used to come home and beat my mother for any stupid thing," she says. "Others would come to break up the fights and end up getting hit themselves. . . . Then one day she shot and killed him while he slept."

A relatively recent and important source of support to women are the *delegacias da mulher*, police stations in Brazil that are staffed by women who raise awareness about domestic violence and who provide guidance and support to battered women who file court complaints. These stations, however, do not appear to be widely available and are specifically mentioned only in Morro da Conceição. According to one woman there, the stations mean that now women's "rights are more equal." Beyond this community, however, women do report that they have better access to justice. As a woman from Nova Califórnia mentions,

> *Women can now go to the police for any little thing and the police take their side. The men go to jail, things actually happen. Before when a woman was hit, that was that, women kept living with them.*

Likewise, a man from Sacadura Cabral acknowledges, "In the past the courts did not take the women's word. Now it is different."

This rising consciousness about women's rights emerges in many discussions in Brazil, and provides hope that levels of violence will decline in the future. In Vila Junqueira, the one *favela* in the study where participants conclude that domestic abuse is declining, a women's discussion group explains that women are fighting for and attaining more equitable relationships: "Women are asserting themselves, valuing themselves, and respecting themselves. They also demand respect. They used to be very passive and forgot about themselves." A woman in the group says, "Women had to obey men. Now there is no obedience, now we have agreement. You discuss whatever you want with your husband."

Rather than endure violence, some women in Brazil are choosing to leave abusive relationships and take the difficult step of managing poor households on their own. Marilene, a poor woman, explains,

> *My life improved in every way when I left my husband and came to Sacadura. When I was with my husband, I used to live*

in hospitals. . . . My parents used to cry; I was just a bag of
bones because of my suffering. I had to sue him to get him to
pay child support, but he does not. I have to return to the
lawyer, but I do not have time. He calls saying that this month
he cannot afford it. Today I want to live by myself. I have a
boyfriend, he calls me, we go out and it is okay. But I don't
want him in my house telling me what to do, dividing my
things. I have five children; they used to say that I am their
father and mother.

Recent surveys indicate that female-headed households are in fact slightly better off economically in Brazil than male-headed households.[6] A group of young women in Vila Junqueira reports that today many women take care of the house entirely: ' Women want to work to build their lives; they do not marry. They want to leave their parents' home and live by themselves."

Violence, Substance Abuse, and Children

As the most powerless of all, it is perhaps Brazilian children who suffer most from the violence that permeates their homes and streets. Many parents express fear for their children's safety and frustration that they cannot shelter them from physical and sexual abuse in their homes, and from violence and drugs in their communities.

"Here there is battering all over the place. Women hit men, men hit women, and both hit children," says 16-year-old Suzana of Novo Horizonte. A young man in Vila União says,

I've always done everything at home—wash the clothes, mop
the floor, sweep the yard, fix things when they break—and still I
must endure my father's insults and beatings whenever he comes
home drunk. . . . I remember my father beating up my mother
when he came home in a bad mood or when she'd done some-
thing wrong. Then later everything would be fine again and
they'd have sex. I used to see all of it.

Young people in Sacadura Cabral relate stories of fathers coming home drunk or drugged to beat or rape them.

Parents aren't the only ones who commit violence. A girl in Padre Jordano says, "There are brothers who batter their sisters. My brother is like that." According to an older woman in Morro da Conceição, "Today there are sons who batter their mothers. This didn't exist before, but today it is common." Older women in Vila União relate cases of children killing parents and parents killing children.

For many children in Brazil, there are few places to turn for protection, support, or guidance. "In the past, if a father raped his daughter he was condemned by everyone. Now nobody cares," argues a young woman in a discussion group from Vila Junqueira. Unsafe at home, many children turn to the street. A woman in Borborema explains, "Many children run away because they can't stand to watch the fighting. It frightens them to see the father beating the mother or the mother cheating on the father. They fall from life."

The Streets

Outside the home, children have little choice but to navigate through violence and crime. Marluce, a 48-year-old mother in Vila União, desperately hopes to move out of the neighborhood so that her sons will be able to avoid violence and pursue their careers. "The violence and drug problems are getting worse," she says. "The teenagers in this community seem more rebellious than they used to be." A group of women in Bode recounts the following story:

> [A boy in the neighborhood] rode a bike mugging people, starting when he was 8. At age 12 he was shot nine times and left in the dump. We found him alive. Now at 17, he receives a disability pension. They say he uses it to buy marijuana because he doesn't have anything in his life. He's an addict.

According to Brazilian discussion groups, drug abuse is pervasive and growing worse. A man comments in Vila União, "Drugs are commonplace around here. Right in this room are two youths who sell and use them." The drugs used by poor Brazilian children reflect their low status. An Entra a Pulso discussion group points out, "They have to use cheap chemicals like industrial glue." Participants in Borborema also attest that many children in their community sniff glue.

An educator from Bode laments, "When I see a 12-year-old child sniffing glue, who went through day care, it seems like the time that she spent there didn't help at all. . . . She still ended up as a *marginal* [someone on the margins of society; see box 2]. I myself couldn't do anything. . . . I left her there. . . . I don't know what is in her head."

Poverty and the lack of employment opportunities for youth drive many young people to sell as well as use drugs. A group of men from Bode reports,

A child turns to drugs out of need to help the family. There's a boy here who deals drugs on the sidewalk. He's the teco-teco, who passes the drugs. The older ones are called airplanes. They take the drugs outside the favela to rich buyers. They earn 50 reais easily, and their mothers think it's okay because it guarantees the next meal.

A young person in Vila Junqueira notes that people can't get hired without first having work experience, so many youths find jobs in the drug trade and treat it as an occupation: "Some people deal drugs to support their families but don't touch the stuff themselves." A group of adults in Bode concludes, "Parents talking to their children [about the dangers of dealing drugs] accomplishes little since . . . drugs provide income." However, a resident of Entra a Pulso warns: "Youths start out selling drugs to help their parents support the family. Then they start using. They're curious about what rich people see in it. Before the parents realize it, the kid is trafficking or dead."

In Padre Jordano both men's and women's groups view drugs and violence as a single problem. "Here we have some boys who, when they are on drugs, make a lot of noise, get into fights, and do not respect the residents. . . . It is like hell . . . and it looks as if this problem will not stop because they are addicts who induce others to begin using." In Borborema women state, "There is no violence when there are no drugs. . . . Drugs lead to violence and to death."

Poverty, Power, and Social Class

Brazil has the highest level of income inequality in Latin America, a region well known for its sharp inequalities and slow progress in narrowing the gaps.[7] In vivid terms, poor Brazilians across the study communities convey how underlying power relations greatly constrain their access to opportunities for a better and more secure life. Even within urban areas, inequality is very high, with startling contrasts between a densely populated *favela* and a better-off neighborhood or commercial center. It is against this backdrop that participants frequently say they are exploited, demeaned, and discriminated against in their contacts with public and private authorities.

The reasons for mistreatment and exclusion are multiple, and can include a person's social class, race, or place of residence. Women and men in Vila Junqueira say, "If you wear a suit you are treated as 'sir,' but if you are wearing sandals they send you away." In Sacadura Cabral women say, "There are people who won't even sit next to someone from here." A group of young men in Nova Califórnia say, "The bus driver, just because he has his job, treats us as if we aren't human." And in Novo Horizonte a group of men and women say, "In that rich district they won't so much as look at a poor person."

Some in the study speak of racial discrimination. A woman in Sacadura Cabral says, "They insult you because you're black," and teenage girls in Nova Califórnia say, "Many people despise you because of your color."

Though poor people face exclusion and rudeness on a daily basis, most of the people who joined the discussion groups do not see themselves on society's lowest rung. In fact, they take pains to distinguish themselves from os marginais, those on the margin (box 2). As a woman in Vila União says, "There are many people living in absolute misery here. You can see them on the streets. It is pitiful, but I do not know any of them."

Residents of favelas also widely report that they are stigmatized in job markets simply because of where they live: "If I say I am from Novo Horizonte, they'll retract the job offer because they think we are all criminals here," says a teenager in Novo Horizonte. A domestic worker in Borborema says, "If we want to get a job we can't let on that we live in Borborema because that is a grave strike against you." An electrician in Bode remarks, "One day a company called me for a job, but when they realized I lived in Bode they changed their minds, thinking that I was one of those marginais they couldn't trust."

In Entra a Pulso a gate locked from 10 P.M. to 10 A.M. prohibits residents from entering a shopping mall adjacent to the neighborhood. People there say, "It was easier to bring down the Berlin Wall than this one."

Some people in the study describe a variety of contexts where they feel demeaned. In a discussion group in Padre Jordano, researchers heard the following:

When we go to the hospital we expect to have to wait longer than scheduled. Someone higher than us will come along and cut in front without a second thought. Retail establishments discriminate against us, too. When we shop, we see the guards on their walkie-talkies. Once I got mad and asked a guard, "Why are we persecuted and followed when we shop? You ought to know a poor person's money is cleaner than a rich person's—we got it from hard work instead of corruption."

In Borborema a poor person said, "The rich are those who always win and who rule over the lives of the poor."

Poor Brazilians' Interactions with Institutions

Struggling against glaring inequities, *favela* neighborhood associations have a long history of successfully tapping into public and private resources and securing a range of legal victories and infrastructure

---

BOX 2 *Os marginais*—the Poorest of the Poor

As described by Brazilians in the study, the *marginais* are people who live under bridges or on the street, eat garbage, collect junk and cardboard, beg, depend on charity for food and clothes, and never send their children to school. They may use a piece of cardboard as a mattress and tin cans for cooking, and their shelter may be nothing more than a plastic bag. They are viewed as "not wanting anything more from life" but also as "needing everything." People point out, "They are the most abused by the police," but in some communities the *marginais* are portrayed as having "no scruples," as being "thieves, murderers, and drug addicts," and as "trying for the easy life by harming others." One can infer that in these communities there are both street people who commit crimes and those who do not.

While some participants deny the presence of *marginais* in their area, in five communities people identify a specific portion of their population as being on the margins: in Sacadura Cabral the estimate is between 12 and 42 percent, depending on the discussion group; in Bode, 12 percent; in Novo Horizonte, 12 percent; in Vila União, 1 percent; and in Entra a Pulso, 15 percent.

People in Padre Jordano report that in the past, 50 percent of the community could have been categorized as *marginais*, but nowadays that number is down to zero because people have either improved their circumstances or have been squeezed out. They assert, "Our reality is like this. We must not be passive. We must always strive for a better life. But at least we have our little shacks to sleep in, our TV sets to watch, and our daily meals. We are neither beggars nor *marginais*."

improvements for their residents. Poor men and women of Brazil largely credit their community-based organizations with achieving these gains. With the exception of the Catholic church, other public, private, and civic organizations that operate in poor communities receive a mixed review.

Many study participants view elected officials, civil servants, employers, and vendors as largely serving the interests of the rich. While individual public services and certain elected officials receive favorable comments in some discussion groups, the government in general draws sharply critical remarks. Entra a Pulso residents believe, "The rich only come here every four years looking for votes so they can become even richer." Young men and women in Borborema state, "The blame for poverty lies with the government."

In Morro da Conceição, where the *favela* association is very strong and has a long track record of pressing for basic services, comments from a group of men and women include:

▸ "This government . . . harms the country by allowing a poor distribution of income, concentrating wealth on the rich."
▸ "The rich in this country have become richer."
▸ "The number of people living in extreme misery is increasing."
▸ "Until a few years ago we didn't have hunger in this community, but today we do."
▸ "The government is ruining everything so that it can pay loan sharks."
▸ "Government is not fulfilling its role in solving social problems."

At the same time, residents of this *favela* see themselves as partly responsible for shortfalls in government performance. A group of men and women in Morro da Conceição say: "We vote wrong"; "We don't monitor our elected officials"; "We don't demand our rights"; and "People are badly informed."

In the other *favelas* visited as well, poor people speak forcefully about the need for an informed and engaged civil society, and about the pivotal role this has played in the development of their communities. The importance of community-based organizations in the *favelas* is reflected in figure 1, which summarizes data from discussion groups in the ten Brazilian study communities. Each group was asked to identify and rank the most important institutions in their daily lives. Although a wide range of institutions may be considered important, poor people often rate them poorly in terms of their effectiveness.

What Works and What Doesn't in Novo Horizonte

The *favela* of Novo Horizonte is about a decade old and used to be one of the poorest communities on the outskirts of Itabuna. Its 4,000 residents are mostly underemployed and working in the informal sector. The

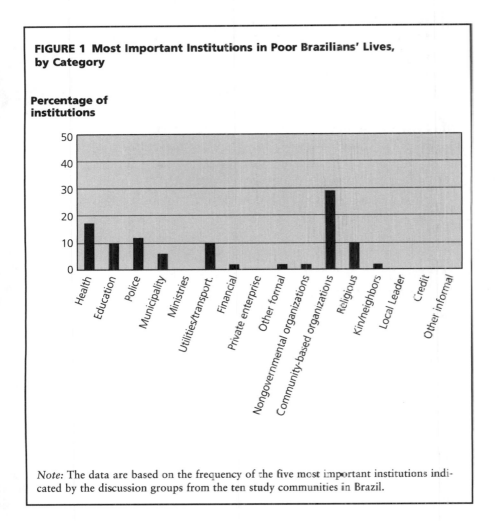

FIGURE 1 Most Important Institutions in Poor Brazilians' Lives, by Category

Note: The data are based on the frequency of the five most important institutions indicated by the discussion groups from the ten study communities in Brazil.

area used to be among the most violent in Itabuna, and it lacked virtually all basic infrastructure and services. Today, there is a local school
and a health clinic, and violence is reported to be declining, although it
remains very high. Housing is still precarious, and sewage and garbage
fill the streets.

Poor women and men from Novo Horizonte worked in small groups
to identify and then rank the institutions that are important in their daily
lives and in crises. Table 1 lists the top five institutions mentioned by a
group of young women and a group of adult men and shows the order in
which they are ranked.[8] Both groups note that some of these institutions
still need improvement, but they rate them highly because they provide
much-needed services, have a presence in the community, and are responsive when problems arise. By contrast, institutions such as the police
and the municipality may be very important, but they receive low ratings
because the groups consider them to be uninterested in helping to solve
local problems.

The school is ranked highly by both women and men not only
because education is a top priority, but also because the school is local.
Men say that the school "serves the needs of the community," and keeps
children off the streets. Women say they put school at the top of their list
because "nobody could learn without the school here, and if it is located
in the community it makes things easy, doesn't it?"

For the discussion group of men, the most important institution is
CONAB, which is the local distributor of the *cesta básica*, a national food

**TABLE 1 Most Important Institutions, Two Discussion
Groups in Novo Horizonte**

	Ranking by discussion group	
Institution	Young women	Men
School	1	2
CONAB (food assistance)	—	1
Friends	2	—
EMBASA (water supply and sewerage)	3	4
President of community	—	3
TELEBAHIA (telephones)	4	5
Health clinic	5	—

— Not mentioned.
Note: 1 = Most important.

program that provides staple goods on a regular basis.[9] Men indicate that the program is critical because "the community has 70 to 75 percent of its underemployed people who depend on this *cesta básica* to live."

Despite problems with reliable service, men in Novo Horizonte still rate the water company, EMBASA, very well because it gives out containers to people who cannot afford service so they can at least collect water. By contrast, the men's group is very critical of the local electric company for its aggressive efforts to cut the power lines to poor homes that have illegal connections. They report that the inspectors come every two weeks and "it is negatively affecting this community." They also lack trust in this agency because since privatization, it frequently changes its policies, has many cumbersome procedures, and provides little service.

Poor men and women in Novo Horizonte indicate that they care a great deal about how they are treated when asking for services. In fact, the most important evaluation criterion for the women's group is that an institution "provide courteous service." The men also value institutions "that give attention and listen to people." According to a member of the men's group, "I feel insulted when they tell me to come back some other time. . . . We are there feeling weak from hunger, thirsty. And then the guy there, hidden, tells us 'come back tomorrow,' not willing to attend to us."

With a ranking of eleven, the public hospital is rated as among the worst institutions by the women's group. The women report, "It is very common to see people in long rows . . . and the hospital is not able to attend to all the people who need it . . . doctors see only five to ten people per day." People can also turn to private hospitals and clinics, but their high fees present a severe obstacle. Even during emergencies, "the private hospital only helps us if we pay. . . . If you have to die, you will die."

Progress in the *Favelas*

Even amid exclusion, joblessness, and violence, study participants from the other *favelas* also say that they are better off in general than they were in the past. Many, such as Maria (whose story opens this chapter), ventured to the cities from destitute and remote places in the northeast, and they cite tangible improvements in their lives. Almost all participants in the study have witnessed significant advances in their community's infrastructure over the last decade. Practically all households in the *favelas* now have electricity and easy access to telephones, most have health clinics and a hospital nearby, and housing and sanitation have gotten better in many communities. A group of men in Nova Califórnia says,

> Ten years ago this community had nothing. There was no water, electricity, public telephones, garbage collection, nothing. Life was much, much worse. Today is great. . . . Before, we had to carry water from the cistern and use candles. At one in the morning we'd go line up for a can of water and there'd already be twenty or thirty people waiting in line. . . . In comparison to the past, we live in heaven.

Similarly, men and women in Vila Junqueira say, "Here we had a smelly river; it was a big *favela*. We don't live in wooden shacks anymore, we have water, electricity. . . ." In the same community, 16-year-old Tiago concurs, "Life has improved for my family and for everyone here. Today people have a car, TV, VCR, a good refrigerator, and a good stove." A group of men and women in Entra a Pulso affirms, "In the past it was a lot worse. There was no health clinic, no waste collection, and no Catholic Church." The changes have had a dramatic impact on the lives of individuals. In box 3, other Brazilians describe substantial change for the better.

Though grateful for what they have, study participants also hope for and expect further advances. Many communities still lack infrastructure for disposal of raw sewage and solid waste, and reliable water service is a problem for nearly all communities. A man in Nova Califórnia reports, "The sewage running in front of the houses causes disease and no one can stand the smell. When it rains, it comes in the front door and one has to take everything up off the floor." According to a discussion group of women in Vila União, "In the winter the sewers overflow and the streets flood, to say nothing of the mosquito invasion. And here in the *favela* some houses do not have toilets so people use the street." Men and women in Morro da Conceição say that garbage causes children to get sick and creates "a terrible smell." Elsewhere, people indicate that the filth causes animal and insect infestations. A young woman in Borborema quips, "Borborema without open sewers just wouldn't be Borborema."

In eight of the *favelas* visited, irregular water service emerges as an important problem. Participants in Nova Califórnia say, "We have it only once a week." Women in Morro da Conceição note that "without water you can't do anything—no cooking, no washing." Not surprising-

"When we arrive, the doctors show us how to take care of our children, how to give medicine at home. . . . If you arrive without eating, you get lunch, dinner, they really help out. Now, I think that they have to improve their service only a little. . . . They have to respect the line, and skip people who try to be seen before us."

—A discussion group of women in Bode speaking of the Instituto Materno Infantil de Pernambuco, a well-known center for maternal and child health and HIV infection in children

"If someone cannot be helped there . . . they take them to the hospital. . . . They give preference to seniors. . . . It is very good for the community."

—A discussion group of Nova Califórnia men and women speaking of Health in the Home, a highly rated city initiative that provides dentists, doctors, and psychologists in mobile offices

"Transportation is excellent, we have buses all the time and they never come late. And when they are late, it is very often acceptable. There are reasons for the delay."

—A discussion group of men, Vila Junqueira

"CELPE serves us well, they quickly fix the street lighting. . . . We don't have to wait ages."

—A discussion group of men and women, Vila União

"Despite living in a *favela,* my life has improved. I have my house, my six children have a good education, and thanks to God, we do not want for food or work. Sometimes I feel inferior when those high society ladies pass by clutching their bags as if we were thieves, but I'm proud to be here and to have obtained my plot of land."

—A man from Entra a Pulso

"I was a seamstress and my husband was a farmworker. When the plantations failed we came here with six children. He worked in a factory and was able to buy me a sewing machine, but no one would rent to us with so many kids. Then a woman told me to come to this place [as squatters] where no one would bother us. A woman told me, 'Don't leave. Stay here and educate your children because that's why you came.' I've lived twenty-two years in this shack we built. The *favela* has improved a lot in the last eight years. The mayor started projects and the community provided the labor. Everybody helped, and thank God now we have a proper neighborhood."

—A woman from Vila Junqueira

ly, four communities rate the water company very low. A discussion group of men and women from Nova Califórnia reports: "The water comes every fifteen days, when we phone them"; "The telephone rings and rings, and no one answers"; and "When they come to turn on the water they come with hostility."

Self-Help in Brazilian *Favelas*

The communities visited in Brazil display a strong capacity for mobilizing collective action and bringing improvements to their communities in the face of many barriers. Six of the ten *favelas* possess very active community organizations. The Catholic church is another local institution that receives high praise for its contributions to community organizing and development. People in many of the communities have worked collectively—often successfully—to resist eviction, win infrastructure improvements, create local institutions, and secure land rights. These community struggles often predate Brazil's return to democracy in 1985.

Local Leaders Making Connections

In Vila União 21-year-old Paolo wrote to a company in Rio Grande do Sul that makes dairy products and cakes, and he convinced them to offer a culinary training course to young people in his community. Paolo has brought other training workshops to Vila União, and he obtains donations from hotels and churches for a local food pantry. He was recently elected a community leader and is currently trying to obtain a building to house vocational programs for the community. As a child, Paolo engaged in hard labor, received constant beatings, and was cruelly exploited by his father, who later abandoned the family. Paolo believes that his participation in a victorious squatter resistance was a turning point in his life. He says the memories of that community struggle fuel his current activism.

Geraldo, a 27-year-old Borborema resident, worked in a sugar mill before he was 10. As a child he witnessed his father regularly beat his mother, and he was forced on the run with his family after his father killed a neighbor. Today, Geraldo is also a community activist. He says,

> *I have my own house where I live with my wife and three children. My wife works as a maid. Our relationship is a good one. Though we have our troubles, she is an understanding person. Today, thanks to the grace of God, I am a community leader, a representative. At least I am something in this life. I intend to be a politician in order to build a better life for the community,*

as well as for my own family. I do not want my children to go through what I did. That is everything I desire.

Dona Ana, 56, is another Borborema resident who finds deep satisfaction in community work. She lost her father at age 7, began working in the fields at age 9, and lost her mother before she was 15. Several of her brothers are deceased and her husband died when she was 46. Her daughters are domestic workers. Dona Ana, who volunteers in a soup kitchen supported by the Catholic Church, says,

> *I adore my job. I know I don't earn anything but I feel happy, important. I'm helping children to feel a sense of togetherness, to learn how to share. . . . I believe the person who helps others does not want for things. It is really good to be able to give hope, happiness. What a joy to see people happy—I feel at peace. When someone asks, 'Is there any soup left, Dona Ana?' and I reply that there is, I feel content. In my soup recipe I put in a bit of kindness, a little love.*

Neighborhood Associations

The Padre Jordano settlement sits on land that belongs to the Brazilian navy. Though the community was founded forty years ago, its tenure remains insecure. Repeated attempts to forcibly remove the residents have so far failed because the community has been staunchly united in its resolve to resist eviction. A neighborhood association founded in 1988 obtained street lighting, sanitation, and water supply. Residents are now anxious to build a day-care center. They say, "We only need the government or some other institution to donate the material. We'll take it from there and raise the building."

Discussion groups in the Brazilian *favelas* invariably express strong support for their neighborhood associations. Residents of Vila Junqueira rated their neighborhood association, headed by Mr. Durvalino, as the second-best institution in their community. They say: "It is the only institution that really strives to solve the problems, that tells the truth and operates at any hour"; "The community helped me build my house"; "Here people care without wanting anything back"; and "We have been able to achieve many things thanks to Mr. Durvalino. We are very inspired by him; he is a fighter, a warrior. All that we have came through his action: the water, the pavement, the church. If we had three of him things would be even better here."

Similarly, people in Nova Califórnia strongly endorse their local neighborhood association, which was created by the Citizenship Committee of Banco do Brasil. Participants in discussion groups there say:

▸ "We go to the Citizenship Committee whenever we need help. They've helped us in many different ways over the last few years."
▸ "I went to [the committee president] when my daughter was sick. She took us to the doctor and found money for the medicine."
▸ "They'll give you wood, roofing, and everything to build a shack. They've given sewing machines, refrigerators."
▸ "The school problem was solved because the president of the neighborhood went and talked to the mayor. He sent her around with a notebook. Whoever wasn't studying gave their name. My daughter wasn't studying, now she is. Now anyone who wants to study is in school."
▸ "The neighborhood association has done the maximum possible to serve the community. What it doesn't do is because circumstances don't allow. For our part, we do whatever we can to strengthen the association. The better the association is, the better for the community."

The Church

Another highly valued local institution is the Catholic Church. With the exception of Sacadura Cabral, where half the residents are evangelical Protestants, the communities visited in Brazil are predominantly Catholic. In many communities the local church serves as a community center and a meeting place for local organizing. Bode residents, for example, are pleased with the church for its role in mediating conflicts, providing a soup kitchen, and encouraging community organization. In Vila Junqueira, the church distributes *cestas básicas* for the people in the community, and is rated the most important institution. A group of men and women there says, "The church helps the community in material and spiritual ways. Saturday afternoon, everyone goes to attend the church." Similarly, in Vila União, the church is seen as a "shelter for the poorest."

In the city of Recife, Father Marcos oversees a large parish and is hailed for his community work in two of the *favelas* in the study. People in Borborema credit him with reducing violent crime, saying,

"Before Father Marcos came to work here, it was a slaughterhouse. Every morning there'd be three corpses in the street." Similarly, in Entra a Pulso, where the church emerges as the community's most important institution, residents say, "Only the Catholic church and Father Marcos help us in any situation. Others help, but sometimes their doors are not open."

Conclusion

The squatter settlements visited in Brazil have existed for decades. In recent years, a combination of local activism and government action has brought marked improvements to their physical infrastructures. In Padre Jordano, for example, residents built a water tank and paved a pathway with building materials supplied by a local councilor. In Sacadura and Vila Junqueira people participated actively in housing schemes implemented by the local government. Participants deeply appreciate basic services that are accessible and well run—particularly the local public hospitals, clinics, and mobile health care units in several of the study communities.

Despite deep and complex problems facing the *favelados*, poor communities in Brazil unquestionably demonstrate a strong capacity to mobilize and to form partnerships with government agencies, elected officials, and private sector leaders to attract the various resources required to address pressing infrastructure needs. Skilled activist leaders and supportive government policies can also help communities unite to address other local needs: just policing and safety from crime, responsive local governments and equity in accessing services, the creation of decent jobs, greater dignity and respect among family members. Innovation is needed in policies and programs that support poor people's entrepreneurship and that open up training opportunities for working people to improve their skills. Although Brazil has universal free health care, social insurance policies for Brazil's large pool of informal workers also need attention, as many social programs and safety net schemes are tied to formal employment or unemployment and have only limited reach among poor people.

Many people have found that banding together allows them to win improvements incrementally, which keeps them motivated and hopeful. Residents in Bode, for example, endured intense pressure to evict them until 1981, when they obtained official legitimacy as a community.

Women say, "What were our weapons? Pots and spoons. But we still won." Bode residents remember this victory fondly and the community has continued to fight for and win improvements, including construction of brick houses and a clinic, and paved streets. Marcos, a 47-year-old community leader in Bode, believes that developing "soft variables"— those aspects of life beyond the mere subsistence necessities, such as education, health, culture, and better family relations—is now as essential to the development of the community as was building infrastructure. He says, "One has to fight a lot. One has to be persistent. The problems here are numerous."

TABLE 2 Study Communities in Brazil

Bode Pop. 70,000	This densely populated community was settled spontaneously in the 1920s after a bridge was built linking the center of Recife, currently a city of 3.3 million, to the islands of Pina. In the 1970s a second bridge was built and the settlement received legal status in 1981. The main sources of livelihood for men are fishing, petty trading, bricklaying, mechanics, woodworking, and plumbing. Women work as laundresses, domestics, housewives, and prostitutes. This community has main infrastructure services, including schools and two primary health centers. The vast majority of the residents are Afro-Brazilian.
Borborema Pop. 24,000	This community was formed by squatters in the 1970s after a channel was dredged, creating an embankment near the Borborema bus station. The inhabitants of Borborema have no security of tenure; however, the municipality has never taken legal action to evict the squatters. Men work primarily as masons, doormen, petty merchants, electricians, and carpenters. Women work as laundresses, domestics, cleaners, and dressmakers. There is a primary health center in the community, as well as schools. Sanitation is very poor due in large part to flooding.
Entra a Pulso Pop. 5,000	This settlement, created in the 1950s, was the result of a planned invasion next to the city's largest shopping mall. The settlers are in the process of securing legal status. Men work as bricklayers, electricians, handymen, metalworkers, painters, janitors, and night watchmen. Women work as domestics, laundresses, janitors, and seamstresses. The *favela* has most core infrastructure services, including a primary health center and schools, but sewage problems are frequent and sanitation is poor.
Morro da Conceição Pop. 9,000	Morro da Conceição is one of the oldest squatted areas in Recife, created around the 1930s. It is also one of the most politicized communities, having a highly active neighborhood association and a church with a long-standing, highly politicized activist priest, as well as several NGOs and institutions. The main sources of livelihood for men and women are commerce and informal activities. The chief problems facing the residents are landslides and water shortages. Also, many houses are on steep slopes and are not easily accessible. The settlement has schools and a health clinic, but no waste disposal.

RECIFE (continued)

Padre Jordano
Pop. 2,500

This settlement, only 500 meters from the beach, is surrounded by tall buildings and shops, which make it practically invisible. The terrain belonged to the Brazilian navy in 1959, when the land occupations began, and various initiatives to remove the residents have so far been unsuccessful. Men work as night-watchmen, janitors, plumbers, painters, bricklayers, and petty traders on the beach. Women mostly work as domestics and as petty traders on the beach. There is no health center, and until the mid-1990s the slum had no street lighting, sanitation, or water supply.

Vila União
Pop. 2,300

This *favela* is the result of an organized struggle by 200 families in 1988. In the early 1990s, pressure on the municipality resulted in the land being donated to residents. Men mostly work in the informal sector as masons, mechanics, metal-workers, and painters. Women work as domestics and house-wives. All houses have electricity but there is no sewage collection. There are five schools and a health clinic. Seventy percent of the residents are Afro-Brazilian.

ITABUNA

Nova Califórnia
Pop. 2,500

Cocoa plantations in Nova Califórnia have been in decline for at least a decade because of pests. Most residents are unemployed or agricultural laborers who depend on informal activities to survive. There are also small tradesmen and owners of grocery shops, bars, and bakeries. There are limited public services such as water, lighting, telephone, and regular waste collection, although most houses receive electricity. The only transportation is provided by a private bus company. The community has a post office, but no health center.

Novo Horizonte
Pop. 4,000

This community, created in 1989, was considered one of the most violent in Itabuna, but today the level of violence has diminished somewhat. Most people are underemployed or work in the informal sector. Men look for work as masons, carpenters, and merchants; women work as domestics. There is a school and nearly all the homes have access to electricity, but there is no garbage collection. Lack of sanitation is often cited as a priority problem.

Sacadura Cabral
Pop. 3,000

The community of Sacadura Cabral, settled in 1966, is close to the main commercial center of Santo André. Once a center of heavy industry and union activity, it has suffered severe job losses in the last decade. Most of the population consists of migrants from the north of Brazil, and their children. Economically active men are employed in the manufacturing industry, in services, and in informal occupations such as car washing. Women work as domestics or shop attendants. The streets are not paved and are commonly flooded with rainwater and sewage. The community has a primary health clinic and a primary school.

Vila Junqueira
Pop. 834

The first residents occupied the area about 1966. In 1987 the residents organized and petitioned the municipal government for ownership of the land. As a result, the area was subdivided into lots, some of which are located on the hillside, exposing homes to the risk of landslides. Men work as masons, electricians, mechanics, carpenters, and plumbers. Women work as domestics and janitors. Residents say their main priorities are getting a health clinic, street lighting, electricity, and a primary school.

Notes

1. The study team was led by Marcus Melo and also included Denilson Bandeira, Josineide Menezes, Mirna Pimentel, Flávio Rezende, Rosane Salles, Ana Flávia Novaes Viana, and Ruben Vergara.

2. World Bank, *World Development Indicators 2001* (Report 22099, April 2001), 12.

3. Poverty data and analysis from World Bank, "Attacking Brazil's Poverty: A Report with a Focus on Urban Poverty Reduction Policies," vol. 1, "Summary Report" (Report 20475-BR, Brazil Country Management Unit, PREM Sector Management Unit, Latin American and the Caribbean Region, 2001), 2–5.

4. In Recife other problems came to the fore, including violence and lack of policing, urgent water shortages, and lack of other basic services.

5. World Bank, "Attacking Brazil's Poverty," 6.

6. World Bank, "Attacking Brazil's Poverty," 16.

7. Quentin T. Wodon, "Poverty and Policy in Latin America and the Caribbean" (World Bank Technical Paper 467, Latin America and the Caribbean Regional Studies Program, June 2000), 4.

8. The groups' completed lists each contained a dozen public, private, and civic organizations. Other important local institutions that received lower ratings and do not appear on the chart include the Protestant school, banks, the supermarket, and Health in the Home. Among the worst institutions noted by women are the public hospital and the president of the community.

9. CONAB is the Companhia Nacional de Abastecimento (National Food Supply Company). Elsewhere, other organizations, including the Catholic Church, distribute the *cesta básica*.

Ecuador

The Perils of Poverty

Alexandra Martínez Flores[1]

Esteban, a 49-year-old farmworker, lives on the outskirts of Paján, a town named for the abundance of straw in the area. Finding work for a decent wage was easier for Esteban when the Ecuadorian sucre was worth more and the local economy could count on coffee production and processing. That was before the 1997–98 El Niño weather disaster devastated the town's crops, homes, and infrastructure.[2] Since El Niño, many Paján farmers have stopped growing coffee because new plants require two to three years to bear fruit, and such long-term investments are no longer affordable. Some are switching to less profitable crops such as corn and rice; others simply do not have the means to farm their lands or rebuild their homes, and they have not returned to the countryside that surrounds Paján.

El Niño was followed by a national economic crisis that intensified in early 1999, the time of this study.[3] "Most people are not in a good situation," says Esteban. "The two previous weeks have been the worst. . . . We are desperate. . . . As the saying goes, 'If you have enough for rice, there isn't enough for butter.' It's been a while since I last bought meat. I can't afford it anymore."

Esteban is separated from his wife and four children and lives with another couple in an invasión, an illegal squatter settlement, founded seven years ago on the edge of town. He says, "We share food ... in order to manage better." Esteban feels that it is getting harder to live in his neighborhood. Petty theft is on the rise, "but there is no major crime such as murder or rape ... I sometimes have to intervene to calm down other people who are fighting ... Sometimes they fight out of jealousy. But they don't get into fistfights, they use machetes." Esteban also mentions children in one family who get into fights because they are on drugs: "They go mad . . . They don't care who they hit."

Life is easier in the center of Paján than in the settlements and small villages that surround it. The only permanent asphalt road passes through the town, while the roads outside become impassable in the winter months when rivers overflow and floodwaters and mud take over. Just about everyone in the city has electricity, though 60 percent of households in the surrounding area do not. Sewerage exists only in town. Since El Niño, however, even people in town have had to scramble to get water. Sediment from the flooding damaged the dam that supplied the town's drinking water, so now people can get water only two or three times a week from five recently dug wells. When asked about the work of local authorities to ensure safety, restore infrastructure, and improve the difficult conditions in the community, Esteban responds, "Up to now, no one has done anything for us. I don't know what either the mayor or the council member is doing. They ignore us. . . . I've been here for three years and nothing has changed. It has worsened."

Undertaken in the midst of the 1999 banking crisis, this study reveals poor Ecuadorians' anxiety over their daily survival and uncertain futures. Fueling their fears are not only the sudden bank closures but also weather disasters, the country's extended struggles with political and economic instability, and people's own persistent battles with hunger, unemployment, farming hardships, violence and crime, discrimination, lack of basic services, and environmental threats.

Since democracy was restored in 1979, weak political parties, strong regional interests, high-level corruption, and cronyism have repeatedly undermined government initiatives to tackle Ecuador's pressing economic and social problems. Moreover, the 1999 banking crisis set in motion a deepening recession and increased political unrest. After a year of no growth in 1998, real GDP plummeted more than 7 percent in 1999 and inflation reached 60 percent. Per capita incomes averaged US$1,360 that year.[4] In January 2000, President Jamil Mahuad was forced from office amid an attempted coup, large demonstrations by indigenous organizations, and widespread discontent regarding economic policy and corruption.[5]

Ecuador has some of the highest levels of poverty and inequality in Latin America. According to consumption-based statistics, 46 percent of the population, or 5.1 million people, fell below the poverty line in 1998; and nearly 2 million of these people could not meet their basic food needs. This is a striking increase in poverty since 1995, when 3.7 million people qualified as poor.[6] The largest increases took place in rural areas and along the coast, where El Niño disrupted economic activity. Indeed, rural poverty is much higher than urban poverty, and in communities with a majority indigenous or black population, 85 percent of the population falls below the poverty line.[7] A recent survey reveals that the poorest tenth of the population receives just 1 percent of national income. Similarly stark inequities exist in the provision of basic social services.

Researchers traveled in March 1999 to five rural and four urban communities (see table 2, Study Communities in Ecuador, at the end of this chapter). The communities were selected on the basis of data provided by the United Nations in *The Geography of Poverty in Ecuador,* which charts poverty according to the purchasing power of community members.[8] In addition, communities were selected to ensure regional, geographic, and ethnic diversity. A total of 646 people participated in discussion groups, including 592 poor people (92 percent) and 54 "not so poor" people (8 percent). Among the poor participants, 148 were men (25 percent), 268 were women (45 percent), and 176 were youths (30 percent). A total of 56 individual case studies were conducted, 28 each in the rural and urban communities. Among this number, 45 case studies were of poor people and 11 of people whose situations are somewhat better. The fieldwork was conducted by the Centro de Planificación y Estudios Sociales (CEPLAES), an Ecuadorian NGO, which hired a study team of four women and five men who were either anthropologists or sociologists.

This chapter opens by exploring the principal needs of poor people in the nine communities visited for the study. It documents the effects of the banking crisis as well as long-term problems with hunger, inadequate livelihoods, migration, violence, discrimination, environmental risks, and education. Following this, poor people relate their experiences with government and civic institutions, revealing the many weaknesses of these important supports in the fight against hunger and poverty. The chapter concludes with a look at the intersection of gender roles and violence in the family.

Problems and Priorities

The torrential rains and flooding brought by El Niño in 1997 and 1998 and the ensuing years of recession affected everyone in the country, but some groups were hit harder than others. The wellbeing of people in poor rural communities on the coast has been severely affected by El Niño and the economic crisis, but in other rural areas visited poor people appear to be less disadvantaged by the shocks, most likely because these communities have never had much access to markets, jobs, or public services. The urban poor also report very steep drops in their welfare in recent years due to joblessness, inflation, and declining access to basic services.

Wellbeing requires more than secure livelihoods and public services. Across the study communities, wellbeing has been diminished by crime (including racially motivated violence) and the separation of families by migration. The threat of losing one's home or farmland to environmental shocks or legal action compounds poor people's vulnerability. Education is highly valued by study participants, but school fees present a formidable obstacle. Exploring the leading problems experienced by poor people conveys a fuller sense of their predicament.

Hunger

Poor people in many communities report that in difficult times such as these, their households have to reduce the quality and quantity of food consumed. The most vulnerable households are those headed by single women or elderly people; such households are increasingly common as more and more young people and men migrate in search of incomes.

Across the country, children, especially those under 6 years of age, are the ones most at risk from poverty and hunger. In 1998, 39 percent of children in Ecuador in the lowest consumption quintile had stunted growth, and 14 percent had severely stunted growth.[9] For them, poverty may result in permanent harm to their physical and mental capacities. Programs that provide nutritional supplements to children and pregnant women exist in Ecuador, but coverage is limited and relatively few study participants even mention them as important.

Hunger is reported to be a major cause of illbeing in the urban areas and the highland town of La Calera. Women in Nuevas Brisas del Mar and Isla Trinitaria say, "If you eat breakfast, you'll have to skip lunch." In urban Paján, where day laborers lament that their employers no longer provide them with a meal, there is a saying: "If there's enough for rice, there's not enough for shortening; if you buy sugar, there's no money for anything else." One man in Atucucho explains that he was forced to sell his working tools in order to get money to feed his family.

In rural areas, where subsistence farming is the primary means of livelihood, people suffer less from outright hunger; however, many note a decline in the quality of their food. As greater quantities of agro-chemicals are needed to grow food in poor soil, the food produced is described as less tasty and nutritious. In Caguanapamba and El Juncal, both men and women say, "Before, the food was better because we did not consume chemicals." Similar remarks are heard in the Tumbatú and Tablas watersheds.

Urban and rural participants also indicate that hunger is rising because of the degradation of common property resources. In the Amazon settlements, poor people report that they eat far less fish, game, and wild fruits and nuts than they used to because those resources are now scarce. They attribute the depletion to the fact that the forest has receded and the rivers have become increasingly polluted since the arrival of roads, the oil industry, and large numbers of non-indigenous colonists. Similarly, in coastal cities, people report eating less fish and shellfish because their local sources are overfished and polluted. In the sludge-filled mangroves of Isla Trinitaria, women recall a time now past when they were able to gather enough shellfish to feed their families. In Nuevas Brisas men say that their boats are too small to go out to sea where a good catch can still be had.

Livelihood and Property Insecurity

Hunger stems directly from poor people's precarious livelihoods. In rural areas visited for the study, land shortages particularly constrain opportunities for young adults. In addition to the shocks affecting the overall economy, other problems that rural participants mention frequently are depleted soils, the inability to purchase agricultural inputs, inaccessible markets, and lack of wage labor opportunities. Urban participants focus largely on unemployment and underemployment.

Rural Concerns

People considered to be better off usually possess tools for earning income, such as land for growing cash crops, livestock, dirt bikes, chain saws, or motor boats. In nearly all the rural communities visited, land belongs to fathers, who founded the settlements and who may allow their sons to live on the land and cultivate produce. Many young people possess no land at all in Asociación 10 de Agosto, Voluntad de Dios, La Calera, and Tumbatú and Tablas. A group of elderly men in Tumbatú explains, "There isn't enough land for all our children since we ourselves have small lots, and besides, if you don't take good care of the land it doesn't produce as it should. . . . Some of us have legal properties, some of us don't." In Tablas, Miguel Salgado, a 37-year-old laborer, says, "Few people have land, and most don't have any. What you see there is my house. I must admit that I live on my parents' land, and I know sooner or later they will throw me out because perhaps they will want to sell some of it." A group of men and women in Caguanapamba and El Juncal says that a majority of the young people in their village migrate because "the young ones don't have land to cultivate."

Farmers of all ages report that soils are exhausted, causing an increasing need for fertilizers and pesticides, the costs of which are out of reach for poor people. A woman in Tumbatú says, "There are people who can't work their land because they don't have the resources [to treat their crops with agrochemicals]." In 10 de Agosto and Paján, people say they are selling their cattle because it is becoming unaffordable to maintain the herds. In all five rural localities people point to the low prices paid for agricultural products and the lack of access to credit needed to purchase agricultural supplies as major causes of poverty. "If we had loans to buy agrochemicals and seeds we would improve our circumstances," states a woman in Tumbatú.

Inaccessible markets are another problem for poor people in rural settlements. "There are no good roads," says a man in 10 de Agosto. "To get produce off the farm you have to use horses." In describing pressing community needs, women farmers in El Juncal similarly assert, "Transportation and roads should be ranked first because we have no means for getting our produce to market." Women from Tumbatú and Tablas concur: "We have no way to get our produce out, it spoils. . . . We need a proper bridge."

Urban Concerns

Many urban study participants say the 1990s brought deep declines in their wellbeing, and they express little support for the economic reforms made by the government. Poor people indicate that the job market offers far fewer jobs, and those available are much more precarious than jobs in the past.

In several communities, residents consider the country's economic crisis to be a key cause of poverty. Discussion group participants from Isla Trinitaria state that before the mid-1990s there was more work, more food, and cheaper fuel. Now they report that many goods have become unaffordable, with one woman predicting that prices would rise further in a month. Others from the same neighborhood say that "the government has ruined us." Wage arrears are also reported. A man from Isla Trinitaria says, "The reality is that this country is messed up. I have stable work, but I have not been paid for a month." In Paján a participant states that the local bank used to provide good loans but now "the bank is not efficient. There are no loans because of the economic crisis."

In Atucucho the effects of the economic crisis are large and diverse. Local vendors report dramatic declines in sales, and other self-employed workers report steep drops in their workload. Permanent workers indicate that wages have been reduced, while other workers have been fired or simply are not paid. Temporary jobs are fewer and are available for shorter periods of time. Women working as domestics say they are paid less for more hours, and many have been fired.[10] For those still working, transportation costs can consume almost all of a domestic's meager wages. A woman in Atucucho says, "There are mothers and housewives who work as domestics and make 250,000 sucres a month [US$21]. And you know how expensive bus tickets are. They can hardly pay for anything else."

These trends are mirrored in the other urban neighborhoods. In the town of Paján, discussion groups explain that middle-class townspeople are teachers, professionals, merchants, and public employees, whereas poor people can find work only as journeymen or day laborers. In such a difficult environment, entrepreneurship does not necessarily increase wellbeing. "Selling needles is not a business. A business is a pharmacy or a pool hall, something you can live off," explains a man in Isla Trinitaria. In Nuevas Brisas del Mar poor people, notably men, have to content themselves with fishing and loading goods for the market, neither of which pays well. A man from Isla Trinitaria who works as a banana loader says, "I earn nothing." Many report that they cannot find a stable job.

Many urban households lack secure property rights, which greatly constrains livelihood opportunities. As squatters or renters, people can be evicted by city officials or private property owners at a moment's notice. In Isla Trinitaria one man intent on having his own business "even stopped eating and dressing properly" so that he could put his resources into building a small shellfish business. But after he built his business, he learned that the mayor had other plans for the land:

> *[The mayor] wants to move us at gunpoint some fifty meters away. All that sacrifice and effort for nothing. We wanted papers that would give us some [property] rights, but at the time they said there were none. . . . The mayor [now] says that those with papers can see how much they will be compensated for their property. I have no papers. I have no money because I risked everything on this. . . . How will my family eat if there is no income? There is no work. The mayor or whoever evicts us will put us onto the streets.*

For urban study participants, unemployment is viewed as the source of most other problems. "There is no work. . . . We get sick and we don't have the money to get cured," explains a discussion group of adult women in El Juncal. Men in Atucucho say, "Lack of jobs drives people to crime, limits the educational prospects of children, and denies us proper care at the hospital." "People lose their motivation and get drunk. People here drink a lot . . . too much," says a man in La Calera.

Migration

The voices of poor people in Ecuador are voices of people on the move, traveling to new places in hope of improving their circumstances. The agricultural settlements of 10 de Agosto, Tumbatú and Tablas, and Voluntad de Dios, and the urban settlements of Atucucho, Nuevas Brisas, Paján, and Isla Trinitaria were founded less than twenty years ago. In all the communities visited, it is common for men and women to spend months or years away from their families working in distant factories or on farms, in other people's homes as domestics, or selling handicrafts abroad. Heavy migration contributes to overcrowding, hunger, and pressure on scarce urban services. One woman in Isla Trinitaria reports six families living in the same house, each with four or five children.

Marta Guevara is a 38-year-old married woman with eight children who has lived in the highland town of La Calera for many years. She reports that many men in her community migrate, while "people left behind live off what they receive, what those who are abroad send them. Those who work outside the province usually come back every other week."

The women and elderly people left behind to maintain households and farms carry a heavy work burden. "Women like me have to get up at five in the morning, especially those of us with little kids, and we work until nine or ten at night," says Marta. A man in Caguanapamba says, "It is true that we men abandon the home. Because of migration, we don't return for three months. Women have to take charge of everything. They pay heavily and endure this life." Likewise, a man in Voluntad de Dios confides, "Without my wife I couldn't have accomplished all that I have. She always helped me and supported me in everything. She works and cares for the farm, the children. . . . I feel bad leaving her with so much work." Children are also working to help their families cope. Youths fortunate enough to be sent to schools in the cities often live apart from their parents and siblings. And the children who remain in the countryside, according to Marta from La Calera, are vulnerable to malnutrition and delinquency because their fathers are absent and their mothers too busy and poor to provide adequate care.

Violence and Race

Poor people in Ecuador face an array of physical dangers. In all three urban settlements visited, there were extensive discussions of gang fights, muggings, robberies, rapes, and murders. In both the urban and rural communities visited, there were also many reports of ethnically and racially motivated violence.

Young people are the most likely to be assaulted, caught in crossfire, or picked up by the police. Sometimes youths are perpetrators. Stories such as the following told by a woman in Nuevas Brisas are not uncommon:

> During Christmas a girl went out with her girlfriends. It was about three in the morning when the girl was heard screaming. We got up. She was holding onto the window of Julia's sister's house. A [gang member] said, "She's my wife." Julia's sister answered, "You don't have a wife." She let the girl in and locked the door behind her. On the street corner there were five boys waiting to rape that girl.

Many poor people in Ecuador consider the insecurity and violence in their lives—both physical and psychological—to be the result of racial discrimination. In Caguanapamba and El Juncal indigenous peasants fear being attacked when they go into town, and they say the authorities tend to dismiss their legal complaints against mestizos.[11] Residents of La Calera report that until recently, indigenous people, especially the elderly, were not allowed on buses. "[People] said they stink," explains a group of men and women there. Residents of La Calera also describe verbal abuse from the mestizos for whom they labor, and they say they used to be forced to call landowners "master." The indigenous people in Amazon settlements speak of physical attacks by mestizo colonists—both random crimes, such as muggings and rapes, and also organized attempts to usurp indigenous lands. Indigenous farmers also report being cheated by mestizo middlemen who purchase their produce.

There is a saying in the urban settlements of Nuevas Brisas and Isla Trinitaria, "When you see a black man running, you are looking at a thief." A young Nuevas Brisas man reports, "People from other parts believe we are all gang members, drug addicts, and robbers. . . . I know some people have thought this about me." In Isla Trinitaria study participants use disparaging terms to describe the black people who live at the "far end" of the dock, which is also the area most affected by flooding, crime, and pollution (box 1). The lone black participant in one of the discussion sessions felt so uncomfortable that she walked out.

Black Ecuadorians in coastal communities say they are persecuted not only because of their skin color but also because they live in poor neighborhoods. A Nuevas Brisas woman says she lost a job washing clothes when her prospective employer learned where she lives. In neighborhoods where gangs are a problem, people believe that the police not only do not help, but actually make things worse by harassing, blackmailing, and arbitrarily jailing youths. "If you go downtown for work, the police think you're there looking for someone to rob. . . . If they see you they take you in . . . there's no one to say otherwise," says a young man in Nuevas Brisas.

Interlocking Environmental Risks

People in the poor communities visited in Ecuador face a myriad of environmental risks to their health and safety. Chief among these is poor water quality, but they also include intense storms and resulting floods and mudslides, the presence of untreated human wastes, and industrial pollution. Sometimes these hazards combine to pose severe threats, especially because so many of the poor communities have unfavorable geography and lack basic infrastructure. Study participants repeatedly emphasize that the many disadvantages of their physical environment make it extremely difficult for them to escape poverty.

Not one of the nine locations visited in Ecuador has reliable access to potable water, and all the communities include the lack of clean water on their list of priority problems. National-level data reveal that three-quarters of the people in the country's lowest consumption quintile do not have access to piped water, compared with about 12 percent without piped water in the richest quintile. According to a participant in a discussion group of women and men in Caguanapamba and El Juncal, "There is no drinking water in the community. . . . There are water tanks but they are not enough." Dirty water is an insidious and pervasive threat, and participants consistently report regular bouts with intestinal maladies. In Isla Trinitaria young men and women say, "The water we get is dirty, sometimes it has larvae." In Paján villagers note that "the water stinks." In Caguanapamba and El Juncal, women explain that the lack of safe water puts children at risk because "sometimes they are home alone and don't take precautions; they drink the water out of the faucet without boiling it."

None of the communities has a proper waste management system, but the problem of raw sewage is most acute in the four urban locations. People have to live along "black waters" filled not just with excrement, but also with the untreated effluents from the larger metropolitan area. The worst case is in Isla Trinitaria, where shacks are perched on an

---

BOX 1 Racism in Isla Trinitaria

Alejandra, 52, lives in a house with twenty-one other people, eighteen of whom are her children. Her family is one of two that live on the embankment, considered by the rest of the settlement to be the worst place to live. Her house is built over brackish water, has no patio and no septic tank, and is at constant risk from floods. Alejandra says, "The people here are racist. If you're black, they exclude you." Two of her children were killed in street assaults. When neighbors pass by, "sometimes they don't greet us. They whisper, 'That black family lives there.' They think because they're white they're worth more. They disregard us, as if we were worthless beings. [Other people] don't feel the same pain we do and they think such things will never happen to them. I am referring to the death of my sons."

Her husband works, but "sometimes . . . does not get paid his salary; sometimes we have to sell our personal belongings. The children are always hungry." Alejandra asserts that blacks have scant access to community resources. "If a *cholo*[12] has bad luck, [social services] come help; but they ask me to pawn or sell something."

embankment in a filled mangrove swamp, surrounded by stinking, stagnant waters containing wastes, garbage, dead animals, even human corpses. Mothers hope that small children will not lose their footing and slip into the lethal pools.

Women in several discussion groups, and mothers in particular, also worry a great deal about water and food safety because of the use of agricultural or industrial chemicals and other pollutants. In fact, two communities visited are located in places that bear a disproportionate share of the environmental costs of the larger society's activities, and study participants report many different forms of pollution. In Voluntad de Dios an oil company drilled four oil wells, which residents say has poisoned their crops and water sources, decimated local wildlife, and caused respiratory illnesses in their children. Francisco, the president of the community council, says that about fifteen years ago the residents were happy to see a road being built by the oil company because they thought it would bring them development and progress, but now they see it as a source of problems. Instead of improvement, roads brought oil exploration and pollution. According to a group of women in the community,

> The oil wells suck the earth's vitamins, coffee bushes don't grow beans anymore, the yucca plant dries up, the noise scares birds and animals away, and they die. The oil wells contaminate the ground, make the children ill with cough, catarrh, eczema, constant flu. This is because of the smoke from the wells and from the pollution in the water that we drink.

In Caguanapamba and El Juncal, people report that a dairy factory is polluting the local river.

In addition to being exposed to pollution disproportionately, poor people are frequently forced to live in geographically risky places: in barren earthquake- and volcano-prone areas, on riverbanks, at the base of denuded slopes, or in mucky tidal zones. The Tumbatú and Tablas watershed is prone to both mudslides and floods. In Atucucho, just days before researchers arrived, mudslides had killed two children and a mother of seven. The people of Nuevas Brisas have repeatedly lost lives, homes, and livelihoods to flooding. A man in Pajàn recounts, "Since the El Niño phenomenon, well, all that I had achieved has failed . . . everything I worked for . . . lost. My house turned upside down and filled with water. Others robbed me of my land. . . . Now I'm here . . . living in the dirt."

The lack of sewage infrastructure, moreover, deepens the hazards of poor communities' geography. In Paján coffee farmers displaced by El Niño now live in hillside shantytowns, where the threat of mudslides is constant. A man there reports, "When it rains the water is waist-high . . . the pestilence is bad . . . a channel brings the sewage water right in here." Trading one risky place for another, these farmers appear to be even more disadvantaged in their new location.

Striving for Education

Poor people widely consider education to be of utmost importance. "Ten years ago we were not very worried about education. We were more pre-occupied with surviving and getting food. Now we are more concerned about education," says a participant in El Juncal. In every locality visited for the study, the cost of educating children is cited as a difficulty. Researchers note that indigenous people view education as one of the few means available to their children to escape poverty; however, unafford-able school fees and the need to work keep many from completing their education.

For poor children, the pressures to leave school entirely for work are intense, and dropout rates are exceptionally high. Only 12 percent of children in the bottom consumption quintile complete lower-sec-ondary schooling. Nationwide, indigenous children average only 2.5 years of schooling.[14] Educational expenditures reveal the stark inequal-ities in opportunities for higher education. The lowest consumption quintile receives only 4 percent of public and private dollars spent on education, while the richest 20 percent receives 57 percent of total ed-ucation spending.[15]

A teacher in Nuevas Brisas says, "Families lack the economic means. Many [children] have to shine shoes for a living. . . . We started out [this year] with thirty students and finished with twenty." In La Calera, a young man says, "I couldn't go on to university because I couldn't afford it. My brothers and sisters were getting older and I had to see that they were educated, too, and I was afraid that if I flunked out the money would have been wasted." These reports from poor people are consistent with a 1998 survey that found cost to be the single most important fac-tor explaining why so few Ecuadorian children complete school.[16]

Nonetheless, as education is so highly valued, often scarce family resources will go first to children's schooling. "I've been working but I haven't managed to acquire anything, except partial education for my kids," says a woman in Nuevas Brisas. In Atucucho a woman says, "Almost every family has a child in high school, some have one at the university. . . . Parents find a way to educate their kids. Education is a way to get out of poverty."

Many indigenous study participants emphasize the importance of literacy as well as the need for vocational training, business skills, and savvy in dealing with the mestizo world. "We need to study. There are no training courses," says a woman in Voluntad de Dios, and in Caguanapamba women say, "We want vocational training." There is some vocational training available in Atucucho, and women there say, "We must find ways to make money. In the neighborhood they gave two courses, one on hydroponics and the other on raising poultry."

Encounters with Institutions

Men and women in this study voice little confidence in government institutions. Reports of local government activities, however, are somewhat more favorable than ratings of central authorities and elected officials. In general, there is a pervasive sense among study participants that they have been abandoned by their government.

Poor people also paint a mixed picture of the support provided by many nongovernmental and community groups. While most people come into contact with a range of institutions, many of their services, study participants report, are unreliable or simply fail to reach them. Few speak of any channels for accountability. In Isla Trinitaria, for example, poor men and women identify no less than forty-six public, private, and civic entities that have played some role in the community, but many in the study had only vague information on the names and functions of the various institutions. In a few areas, such as Atucucho and La Calera, organizations are visible and in general participants are able to talk about most of these organizations at length, explaining in detail why particular institutions are beneficial to the community or not.

Government Services

The government and elected officials in particular are often viewed with disdain by study participants, who speak of widespread corruption and lack of accountability. A group of young people in El Juncal, for instance, argues: "The government does not really govern, the rich are the ones who govern"; "Getting to be the leader is not a matter of merit; they are unprofessional"; and "Each government has a different program that cheats the people."

Study participants were especially angry over the government's management of the economy, and many expressed the view that the government—and not the pressures of global markets—is responsible for setting high prices and creating so many hardships for poor people. Residents of Isla Trinitaria directly blame the government for the bank crisis, high prices, and unemployment. In Tablas a young woman reports, "The government raised the price of gasoline," and in El Juncal, women propose, "The government should reconsider and not raise the prices of basic goods so much. . . . The government should have compassion and not raise the price of electricity."

In addition to economic concerns, participants suggest that there are widespread problems with corruption. They indicate that they must often pay bribes to get their needs addressed. A group of young women in Tumbatú asserts, "The government should make sure the congressmen do not steal." Similarly, men and women in Caguanapamba and El Juncal report:

> *A lot of money intended for the people comes from abroad, but instead of using it to make improvements, they steal everything. . . . One government is out, and the next one asks for money abroad. They beg for money, in the name of small farmers, in the name of education . . . but nothing ever comes to us. All these well-known projects, but the country's debt keeps on growing.*

In some rural communities, discussion groups indicate that local government is more important and effective than the national government agencies for the local provision of basic infrastructure and services. In Tumbatú a young man reports that "the municipality helps us by providing machines and petrol to construct the sewage system, along with the FISE [Ecuadorian Social Investment Fund]." A young woman from the same community suggests, "The municipality should help out more, but at least it helps with the machinery; it provided us with recreational facilities and created a park." In La Calera a participant says, "The Ministry of Agriculture, no, they haven't done anything; they don't even come . . . near us, they don't know about our community. They only come if diseases show up in the animals." In rural Paján, most villagers are unaware of the work of government institutions in the area.

In dealing with local governments, poor people appear to have very limited bargaining power to get pressing community needs addressed or even to prevent harm to their community. For example, people in La Calera agreed to let municipal authorities locate a regional dump in their community in return for building a sports field for their children. As a result of the dump, roaming packs of feral dogs and plagues of flies have become major problems that the municipality has not effectively addressed. At the time of this research, the sports field was only half completed.

The urban communities had very little positive to say about municipal services. In Nuevas Brisas del Mar discussion groups consider their municipality useless because it does not provide garbage collection. Much of the trash ends up in an open sewage canal, which carries disease and gives off nauseating odors. The Nuevas Brisas settlement is not officially recognized as a unit by local municipal authorities, creating great difficulties for obtaining basic services. The settlement now gets its electricity from wires that hang from poles. There is no potable water, and residents must purchase costly bottled water for drinking and cooking. Nor does the settlement have a police station, a fire station, or public transport stops. A discussion group of men and women from Nuevas Brisas says that the municipality "only serves those in high society. Here they don't provide anything; they say it's because of the gangs." Some observe that local officials are often not paid their salaries, which also negatively affects their performance.

Reports of ill treatment by civil servants are common. Women and men in a discussion group in Nuevas Brisas told researchers, "It's awful. . . . They are abusive. . . . They treat one almost like a dog. . . . The mayor even slapped a woman who asked for help." According to a poor man in Paján,

Sometimes they'll serve you, sometimes not. First they look at you and decide whether . . . they like you. If you don't have

money to bribe them, then they don't help. It's always been like this. . . . A poor person can't go and get assistance because they are not going to serve him.

As illustrated in table 1, poor people frequently indicate in their evaluations of institutions that they highly value being treated fairly and with respect. A discussion group of women and men in Nuevas Brisas identified and ranked various criteria that they consider important for evaluating institutions that operate in the community. They thought it especially important that an institution be responsible, and defined responsible as following through a project until its completion. The discussion group also singled out criteria related to behaviors, attitudes, and skills. According to this group, an institution should not discriminate against poor people in the services it provides, should treat people well, and should have trained staff and good management. Against these standards, many institutions in the lives of poor men and women in Nuevas Brisas fare very poorly, even though the services they provide are considered important.

When reports are positive, they usually refer not to local government as a whole, but to remarkable individuals within an overall failing system. Some poor people in Paján place their hope in a new mayor who has built roads, a bridge, and a distance-learning school, and has reduced corruption. Similarly, in Nuevas Brisas people speak very highly of their parliamentarian, Homero López, who is responsible for draining the terrain on which most of the settlement is now constructed.

The need for improved health care emerges as important in many of the communities. Less than 60 percent of the poorest consumption

TABLE 1 Evaluating Institutions, Discussion Group of Men and Women in Nuevas Brisas

Criterion	Order of importance
Responsible	1
Has the necessary resources	2
Does not discriminate	3
Provides good and respectful service	4
Professional staff	4
Caring director	4

quintile use public health facilities, instead relying on home treatment or private services.[17] In rural areas, poor people say they have difficulty accessing health care due to bad roads and lack of transportation. In urban areas health care is more accessible, although problems with rude and discriminatory treatment by health staff are very frequently reported. For example, although discussion groups in Nuevas Brisas consider the hospital to be very important, a poor man says, "They shout at us, and treat us badly." A woman adds, "How they serve you depends on who you are: if poor, let 'em bleed, if rich, treat 'em well." Men and women in Isla Trinitaria say of Guayaquil hospital, "The treatment is good, but not right now because the doctors are having trouble getting paid." In Paján men and women report, "If you're not a friend of the doctor or the nurse, they won't see you promptly"; and "[At the local health center] they make you wait from eight in the morning until one in the afternoon."

NGOs and Churches

Although government institutions seem best positioned to address the complex, underlying causes of poverty among citizens, the fact that they rarely do so means that poor Ecuadorians rely upon assistance from other sectors to survive. While a few NGOs are identified as doing some good in poor communities, many people say that they have very little information about what help is available to them through these institutions. Others remark that assistance comes with undesirable strings attached or stops before communities have the capacity to sustain projects.

"Only the NGO projects have helped us," says a woman in 10 de Agosto. People in Paján, a neglected disaster area, are enthusiastic about any source of assistance they receive. The residents of Nuevas Brisas are grateful to Fundación Natura for filing a legal claim on their behalf after a massive oil refinery spill caused their local river to burst into flames. Doctors without Borders and a group that established a furniture co-op are highly appreciated in La Calera. Plan International is remembered by the residents of Caguanapamba and El Juncal for having brought latrines, vegetable gardens, and electricity. In many communities, the individual beneficiaries of training programs directly attribute the improvements in their wellbeing to the intervention of outsiders.

Yet poor people have plenty of criticism of foreign and national NGOs, as well. Men and women in Isla Trinitaria say there is "little publicity" on the activities and programs that NGOs implement within the community. They believe NGOs would be more successful if they did more outreach: "When they come here, people think they are politicians. They need to do more publicity." A man in Atucucho says of an international children's aid organization, "For what they do for children, they merit a 'ten,' but for them to sponsor a child we have to advertise our poverty. Institutions shouldn't use human beings. And they keep part of the money they get."

People in the Tumbatú and Tablas basin believe that outside agencies have sowed divisions within their communities. The researchers add that several appropriate technology projects brought to Tumbatú and Tablas by NGOs sit unused and in disrepair for lack of local know-how. The people of Voluntad de Dios and other indigenous communities are suspicious of researchers and students, whom they believe have used them and have come only to "suck the blood out of the community." Nevertheless, because the needs of poor Ecuadorians are so severe, something often said of NGOs is "We wish they would come back."

The Catholic Church is widely appreciated in poor communities in Ecuador for helping people meet urgent material as well as spiritual needs. Various missions and orders are credited with providing disaster assistance, low-cost housing, day care, and social and educational services. In Nuevas Brisas people credit the bishop with helping to reduce gang activity. In Isla Trinitaria a priest provided emergency loans and grants, medicines, clothes, and food to community members. He organized women into health brigades, provided a link to other organizations, arranged vocational workshops, and led the building of a school. Similarly, in Atucucho, a section of Quito, the capital, the previous local priest was able to draw on Quito's former mayor, Rodrigo Paz, in order to bring many facilities to the community. The priest was highly praised by a poor man as "a pillar for the development of the community. . . . He got us electricity and water . . . a health post . . . garbage collection. He was a man of action."

Community Action

Given the limited support of state and civic institutions, poor people often turn to their own organizations. Overall, the indigenous communities in Ecuador are well organized with representation at the grassroots, regional, and national levels. There are also vibrant urban neighborhood groups. Most of the communities visited for this study, however, showed signs of weak local institutions, and study participants expressed frustration over the difficulties of local organizing and the barriers to obtaining needed services and infrastructure. Men and women state that rising economic and social pressures are creating both greater hardships and some new opportunities for community activism, particularly among poor women. Many indigenous men and women also report that their traditions are fading and that they feel more insecure.

Struggling Community Groups and Eroding Traditions

Poor people in Ecuador have a strong tradition of local organizing. Many of the informal community institutions mentioned in discussions were forged based on ethnic and cultural bonds, on the common experience of having cleared and settled on frontier lands, or on the collective memory of participating in an organized seizure of urban terrain.[18] *Minga*, or collective work, is used and valued in all the communities. The communal house is an important place in communities that have one, and obtaining one is a goal for others. The people of Voluntad de Dios built their own pharmacy and collectively procured a refrigerator and radio.

Indigenous community organizations and federations have a long track record in Ecuador. There are about 2,300 grassroots indigenous organizations, which in turn have about 180 second-tier organizations that are identified as associations, unions, or federations, and are frequently affiliated with provincial, regional, and national organizations. The indigenous communities of La Calera and Voluntad de Dios both participate in a larger political organization of indigenous groups, though the people of Voluntad de Dios say they prefer their local organization to the regional one.

While study participants generally rate their neighborhood or village organizations very highly, they nevertheless raise many concerns about their lack of effectiveness and express a clear need for stronger local institutions so their communities can advance. A man in Paján says, "Our problem is that we are not united." A group of young men in Tumbatú and Tablas indicates, "Lack of unity is a cause of poverty." "Another problem affecting the community is that some residents don't want to participate in making the community better. They don't collaborate," says a man in El Juncal. In Isla Trinitaria a group of men and women declares, "We have to get organized as a committee in order to protest, but this means money and time, and we don't have this. There are too many problems." People in La Calera rank social organization as their community's greatest need; people in El Juncal rank it second. In addition to lack of unity, resources, time, and energy, poor leadership is also said to present a formidable barrier to organizing in poor communities.

In the four indigenous communities visited, many groups report that traditional practices are falling away, although Quichua is still spoken.[19] A man in La Calera says, "We have let traditional health practices disappear. Now, everything costs money. If a poor indigenous person gets sick, into the hole he goes. . . . He dies, no less." Similarly, men and women in Caguanapamba and El Juncal say, "There is a problem with culture. Young people migrate and forget who they are." The media also bear some responsibility. According to a man in La Calera, "TV is teaching bad things, now kids and women watch soap operas." Similarly, a group of women in Caguanapamba says, "The media creates new needs and we forget our ways."

People in indigenous communities take a historical view of their ethnicity. As a man in La Calera asserts. "The causes of poverty started about 500 years ago. We have been exploited . . . since the arrival of the Spanish." In Caguanapamba and El Juncal, indigenous men and women say, "When they play the national anthem, it means nothing to us." Cultural decline is also perceived to be eroding indigenous organizations. A group of men and women from Caguanapamba and El Juncal indicates, "There was no corruption before. We are also learning the bad [embezzlement] practices of the state."

In the few places in the study where community groups are especially active, their work is greatly appreciated. For instance, discussion groups in La Calera, a Quichua community, rank the village *cabildo* (council) as one of their most important institutions. According to a group of men and women, "The *cabildo* is in the center of our community life because it coordinates with different NGOs." Nevertheless, the current council president points out its limitations: "It is not an organization, but the community needs a speaker, so they elect one and if there is any problem, the NGOs talk to the council. So the council needs to be present to solve any problem."

The more cohesive and organized communities in the study are also often more able to marshal external partnerships and resources. For example, 10 de Agosto's health dispensary, community meeting house, elementary school, high school, and chapel are the products of the collective labor of the people of 10 de Agosto, with contributions from the region-al indigenous organization (FOIN), the municipality, and the Swiss Red Cross. "Before, we didn't have any medicines and we couldn't see any patients. Now thanks to the help of FOIN and the Swiss Red Cross we have managed to overcome this problem and people have improved their health," states a health promoter from 10 de Agosto.

Women Active in Community Affairs
Men in La Calera describe some of their "community" activities as: "play football [soccer]," "talk with friends," and "drink." If men appear to be somewhat distant from community development activities, women are participating in greater numbers. In almost every locality, people say the participation of women at community meetings—both in numbers and in influence—has increased, and women are assuming leadership roles. Male migration from rural areas is a commonly cited reason. A woman in Caguanapamba explains,

> My husband works far away, so I make the decisions. . . . Ten years ago it was different; we'd wait for the husband to return and decide. . . . Now all the women in the community make the decisions at home and in the minga. The men are rarely here. . . . We've formed groups and named leaders.

Women from Isla Trinitaria say they have always participated in com-munity activities and assert, "Women are always ready to work in the community." But over the past ten years women are increasingly working on community development through their own institutions and work-shops. Women have generally been the instigators in demanding water, sewers, and health facilities. Fighting against crime is also one of their main concerns.

There is disagreement among women regarding their influence over community affairs. In some communities, men still generally retain au-thority over major decisions. For instance, when asked about whether women make any decisions regarding credit or water management, Cristi-na Rodríguez, a woman in Caguanapamba, says, "No, I don't decide about that. My husband as the man goes to the meetings and he agrees with other men to work on these things." And a group of women in Nuevas Brisas says, "There are few women who decide on anything, ex-cept for the neighborhood association president. She makes decisions in the community."

Gender Dynamics in the Family

As at the community level, women's roles in the domestic sphere are changing in Ecuador, although the pace of change is uneven. In rural communities, traditional gender roles and inequities remain strong even though women may be the de facto heads of households as they manage homes and farms for extended periods while men are away working. In communities such as Asociación 10 de Agosto, moreover, women don't have the right to inherit land from their fathers; only sons may inherit land. In urban Ecuador, where many women work outside the home, they seem to have gained more decision-making power at the household level in recent years. With these shifts, study participants largely report that domestic abuse is on the decline. Nonetheless, physical violence against women appears to remain quite widespread in the communities visited.

Two discussion groups in the squatter settlement of Isla Trinitaria, a group of women and a group of men, held intense debates over changes in gender relations in the household. Both discussion groups agree that relatively little has changed regarding domestic gender roles: women largely take care of children, household chores, and meals, while men provide the money and make the decisions. As one woman succinctly says, "The man decides, the woman executes." Another woman concurs, "The man makes the decisions because he is the one who provides." Similarly, the men's discussion group is unanimous that "the woman leaves it to you to decide" and that "one has to decide for the women."

Both groups in Isla Trinitaria conclude, however, that women's authority over household decisions is growing, especially in homes where women are earning incomes. Although it is very difficult to find work, women typically hold jobs as cooks, domestics, and traditional healers. Some differences of opinion regarding women's decision-making roles appear to be generational. An old man who has been married for a long time asserts that he "decides about everything." But one of the younger men in the discussion group says that women also make household decisions nowadays. Younger women remark that the traditional distribution of power in households is shifting, especially if the woman works outside the house. As one woman notes, "If a woman makes money, she can make decisions as well."

One indicator of continuing gender inequalities is the widespread domestic abuse of women that is reported. When discussing trends in gender violence, discussion groups indicate that women are verbally and physically abused and that this is frequently associated with economic stress, alcohol consumption, and long-standing social norms that seem to sanction violence against women. Although abuse is still very much present in the lives of poor women, in all but two of the communities visited, Asociación 10 de Agosto and Isla Trinitaria, study participants hold that gender violence is declining.

A woman in Isla Trinitaria, where domestic violence is not declining, says,

> *Some men mistreat their families physically, verbally, and psychologically to the point of sending the family member to the hospital, and [even causing] death. [Men] . . . who have experienced violence in their childhood . . . think they have to deal with things in a similar way in their homes; therefore, the violence never ends.*

Alejandra, also from Isla Trinitaria (see box 1), recalls, "One time I came [to the community hall] and my husband threw me out of the house; he treated me badly and humiliated me with his words, but I stay because I have nowhere to go. I wish men wouldn't hit their wives and insult them."

The discussions on gender roles and trends in domestic violence in Isla Trinitaria and other areas tended to elicit angry responses on the part of the female participants, and at times, empathetic reactions from male participants. When asked, men also say they experience violence. To the question, "What forms of abuse do you experience at home?" men in Isla Trinitaria respond: "I get home and she isn't there"; "The food isn't ready on time"; "There are no clean clothes to put on in the morning"; "They cook foods that you don't like"; and "My wife keeps me waiting." In more than one community, there are men who say that hitting their wives is an acceptable method for obtaining the wives' compliance in such matters. (Indeed, as seen in box 2, this same reasoning is used to justify adult abuse of children.)

Other men in the study view domestic violence as a social problem. A man in La Calera reports,

> *Yes, there are abuses. I have seen friends lose their heads. They become like drugged. With alcohol . . . we think we are the kings of everything. These are very grave problems. This has to do with poverty and unemployment. People don't have work to do so they drink.*

Box 2 Child Abuse and the Vulnerability of Girls

Poor people, when discussing domestic violence, also raise the issue of physical punishment of children. Girls appear to be particularly vulnerable to abuse and sexual assault.

"I once saw a boy who had been burned in the mouth with a hot tablespoon by his own mother because he ate something he shouldn't have," recounts a woman in an Isla Trinitaria discussion group. Child battery and corporal punishment by parents are frequently justified as a way to make children behave. Another woman responded to the above story with, "Abuse is meant to get them to do something good in life. I do whip them so that they will shower or do their chores." Another Isla Trinitaria woman says, "There are children who don't get the affection they need from their parents. You can see sadness from the lack of love in their little faces. Instead they get beatings and verbal abuse."

Girl children have heavier burdens of household labor, and they are often kept from attending school so they can care for younger siblings. In several communities visited, including La Calera, Pajan, and Isla Trinitaria, participants remark that girl children are especially likely to suffer abuse, often sexual. A woman in Isla Trinitaria observes, "In some families you can see there is sexual abuse against the girls; they are beaten, marked, many times burned. I think those things are the result of frustrations."

Similarly, Miguel Salgado, a laborer from Tablas, believes that "the economic crisis brings about a certain disunity. That's why when we did the discussion groups this morning, we men said that poverty brings about distrust, misunderstanding, and if we don't control that and think about it, even homes will break up."

In the several places where violence against women is reported to be declining, many women attribute the reduction to women's increasing decision-making power, both in the home and in the community. In Caguanapamba and El Juncal, for instance, some women say there was more domestic violence ten years ago than there is now. Male migration, which may keep men out of the home for many months at a time, is also a factor. In urban neighborhoods such as Atucucho, Nuevas Brisas, and Pajan, the decrease in domestic violence against women is also attributed to the establishment of police stations for women known as *comisarías de la mujer*. Of the *comisarías*, the men of Isla Trinitaria say, "They're useful for having husbands thrown out of the house." Women say, "It's important. They give shelter and protection. They need to do more outreach."

In all the communities, widows and single mothers, considered the poorest of the poor, are subject to the greatest disrespect and violence.

"I am afraid of men, they are so mean," says a 48-year-old widow and mother of nine in 10 de Agosto. "Some treat me badly. They don't respect me because I don't have a man. They speak to me as they wish." Without a husband to provide protection, she says, she cannot walk alone in peace.

Conclusion

Researchers visited with poor women and men of Ecuador on the heels of the El Niño disaster and amid a national banking crisis. Poor people shared the hardships of coping with these shocks as well as many other severe and persisting risks. Being poor in Ecuador means facing hunger, joblessness, poor farming conditions, violence and crime, ethnic discrimination, polluted or inaccessible drinking water, and profoundly unsafe environments. Many of the urban squatters, migrant laborers, rainforest colonists, and highland farmers feel deeply insecure and believe that they are forced to eke out a living in dangerous places because they are exploited, mistreated, and forgotten. Most people in the study perceive that these problems are deepening, and they are not hopeful that better times lie ahead.

Poor people across most of the study communities have been greatly harmed by the unstable economy, lack of jobs, and rising prices for basic goods. They also indicate that they are not served by existing safety net programs. These initiatives appear to be poorly managed and far too limited, given the duration and intensity of the recession and the extent of hunger in the country. A more effective government response to the economic contraction is urgently needed.

Many participants in the Ecuador study acknowledge intense feelings of abandonment and disadvantage, feelings that seem to long predate the current set of crises. In Voluntad de Dios a woman says, "We suffer in the countryside because we never receive any help from whatever government is in power." According to a woman in Tumbatú, "We are a community abandoned by governmental authorities. . . . We seem not to exist." The indigenous and black communities visited for this study are the most disadvantaged, with participants from these areas repeatedly describing experiences of being excluded from economic opportunities, targeted for abuse and violence, bypassed by public services, and harassed by the police.

In addition to economic recovery, poor men and women repeatedly draw attention to three improvements that would help them make great strides toward healthier and more productive lives: (a) agricultural supports for small producers, (b) improved access to education and vocational training for adults and children, and (c) clean drinking water. Secure land tenure and affordable health care also emerge as important needs in both urban and rural contexts. In Atucucho a group of men says, "Due to the illegal status of our settlement, we miss out on many opportunities for help from some organizations, since they are afraid to invest in these illegal areas." In the urban settlements there is also a pressing need for greater safety from crime and violence.

Poor people suggest that the public and private institutions working in their communities could make vast improvements in their lives if they would simply carry out their responsibilities. In the face of political favoritism, neglect, and shabby treatment from local officials, poor people in urban Paján identify three criteria for a good institution: "provide help regardless of one's affiliation to any party or to any group . . . be kind and professional . . . and hire local people rather than bringing in people from other areas."

TABLE 2 Study Communities in Ecuador

RURAL COMMUNITIES

Asociación 10 de Agosto, Municipality of Archidona, Napo Province Pop. 552	This Amazon village, located in the Napo-Galerías National Park, is bilingual and bicultural (Spanish and Quichua). Men earn their living from subsistence farming, hunting, fishing, and small agricultural production of *naranjilla* (a fruit). Women help out in the fields and collect wood, in addition to being in charge of all the household chores. There is a community center, a church, a health center, a primary school, and a secondary technical school focused on eco-tourism. The village has no running water, no sewerage, and no electricity. Among its many problems are encroachment by colonists, distant markets, and depleted soils.
Caguanapamba and El Juncal, Municipality of El Cañar, Cañar Province Pop. 2,000	These two communities, combined for purposes of fieldwork and reporting, are located in the highlands near the archeological ruins of Ingapirca. They are bilingual and bicultural Quichua communities, although residents say that traditions are being lost. Men make a living by subsistence and small farming, and some are also artisans. The communities have no sewerage, no potable water, no electricity, and no health center, although a nurse visits daily. The villagers also lack schools and roads. Their lives are complicated by male out-migration, depleted soils, and deforestation.
La Calera, Imbabura Province Pop. 1,000	This highland town, hit by an earthquake in 1986, is a bilingual, bicultural Quichua community. Men's livelihoods consist of subsistence farming along with agricultural labor in neighboring areas. Women typically work at home. La Calera has some basic services including electricity and running water (albeit not potable water); the sewage system is incomplete. There are schools, recreational fields, some telephones, and a speaker system through which messages are relayed to residents. The main problems for the community are lack of access to markets, deforestation, land conflicts, and the fact that men must migrate to find work.

Tumbatú and Tablas, Municipality of Bolívar, Carchi Province Pop. 500	These two communities, combined for purposes of fieldwork and reporting, are located in the basin of the River Chota-Mira. The villagers are mostly black. Men work as subsistence farmers and wage laborers. Tumbatú has a church, a community center, a school, a recreational field, and a health center (a doctor visits every eight days), but there is no potable water and no sewage system in either community. Residents consider the lack of a paved road and bridge to the nearest city to be one of their main problems.
Voluntad de Dios, Municipality of Lago Agrio, Sucumbios Province Pop. 3,265	This Quichua- and Spanish-speaking community in the Amazon was settled forty years ago, but the legalization of the properties came only in 1975. The community is surrounded by colonist settlements and is an area of oil exploitation. Men's livelihoods come from subsistence farming and small agricultural production of yucca, banana, corn, cocoa, coffee, and rice. The community lacks basic services such as water, electricity, and sewerage. It has a community center, a recreational field, a school, and a basic health post. The main problems are pollution from oil wells and encroachment by colonists.

URBAN COMMUNITIES

Atucucho, Metropolitan District of Quito, Pichincha Province Pop. 84,000	This urban settlement is located in northwest Quito, on the slopes of the Pichincha volcano. Its population is largely mestizo. Most men make a living as construction workers, carpenters, plumbers, street vendors, and masons. Women work as domestics and informal vendors, and recently many of them have emigrated to Europe. Only the main street of the settlement is paved. There is electricity but no potable water or sewerage, and only a few homes have telephones. The main problems are violent crime and gangs, mudslides and floods, and the presence of raw sewage.

URBAN COMMUNITIES

Isla Trinitaria
(Andrés Quiñónez),
City of Guayaquil,
Guayas Province
Pop. 1,600

Andrés Quiñónez is an Isla Trinitaria neighborhood in the process of acquiring legal status as a cooperative. Residents are immigrants from the coast, and about 25 percent are black. Men work as mechanics, construction workers, street vendors, longshoremen, and guards; women work as cooks, domestics, and traditional healers. The majority of homes are located on sand and gravel landfill, but some rest on stilts over water. This poses problems for the legalization of property ownership, and many residents worry about the threat of eviction. There is no sewage system and no potable water, and only four homes have telephones. There is a day-care center in the settlement, and a school in a nearby cooperative.

Nuevas
Brisas del Mar,
City of
Esmeraldas,
Esmeraldas
Province
Pop. 1,100

This settlement is not recognized by local municipal authorities. Most houses are built on a sand landfill, but some are on stilts over water. The settlers include black Ecuadorians and some displaced Colombians. Men work as fishermen and street vendors, women as washers and domestics. There is no health center in the settlement, although there is one nearby. There is also no police station, no fire station, and no public transport. There is a neighborhood association, a day-care center, a school run by the Catholic Church, and a few other NGOs working in the area. An open sewage canal traverses the settlement. When the tide is very high, flood waters spill garbage and sewage throughout the neighborhood.

URBAN AND RURAL AREA

Paján,
Manabí Province
Pop. 6,731 (town),
38,791 (rural area)

Urban and rural areas of Paján were combined for reporting purposes. This coastal community was declared a disaster area in 1997–98 due to El Niño. Its population is largely mestizo. Although the region used to produce coffee, Paján's working population now makes a living out of small agricultural production and odd jobs. Most women work at home or as vendors and seamstresses. In the surrounding villages, women also work as agricultural laborers and as domestics. All the town homes have electricity, but only about 40 percent of rural homes have it. There is a health clinic in the town. The rural communities have no permanent roads to the urban area, and dirt roads often become impassable in the winter. There is no potable water, and only the urban area has sewerage. The main problems in the area are homelessness, hunger, unemployment, and mudslides.

Notes

1. The study team was led by Alexandra Martínez Flores and also included Milena Almeida, Elizabeth Araúz, Santiago Baca, Pablo Cousín, Nicolás Cuvi, Oswaldo Merino, Eduardo Morcillo, María Moreno, and Edith Segarra.

2. El Niño is a disruption of the ocean-atmosphere system in the tropical Pacific having important consequences for weather around the globe. In 1997 and 1998, the El Niño phenomenon produced devastating effects in Ecuador. Flooding and landslides caused extensive damage to infrastructure, creating large economic losses. At least 386 people were killed and an estimated 30,000 lost their homes; about a quarter of the population was at risk from the spread of infectious diseases, resulting in part from reduced access to drinking water and sewerage.

3. When the researchers arrived in Paján, the government had just issued decrees freezing all checking and savings accounts, and all financial activity in the country was paralyzed. The day before banks were set to reopen, researchers found a line of about a hundred people who had spent the night there. Many of these people were very poor and anxious to cash their government social assistance checks, which had been provided since the 1998 El Niño crisis.

4. According to a World Bank Group report on Ecuador, "A combination of factors precipitated the 1998–1999 recession: natural disasters occurred in 1997–1998; world oil prices collapsed in 1998; and the international financial situation was chaotic in 1997–1998. Long-standing structural rigidities, poor policy response, and political gridlock exacerbated these problems and handicapped the administration's ability to respond rapidly to the deteriorating economic and social conditions." See World Bank and International Finance Corporation, "Republic of Ecuador: Joint IBRD/IFC Country Assistance Strategy Progress Report" (Report 20444, June 1, 2000), i. See also World Bank, *World Development Indicators 2001* (Report 22099, April 2001), 12.

5. The new president, Gustavo Noboa, set in motion further economic reforms and dollarization of the currency, which succeeded in reducing inflation and unemployment and promoting economic recovery. Ecuador became the fastest growing economy in Latin America in 2001. Social and political unrest has also calmed down. Whether dollarization was the right policy for Ecuador, however, remains a topic of local debate.

6. World Bank, *Ecuador: Crisis, Poverty and Social Services* (Latin America and Caribbean Region, Human Development Department, 2000), vol. 1, vii–ix and 1–6. The 1998 poverty line was 126,535 sucres per person every two weeks. A household was classified as being extremely poor if its total consumption expenditure was below the food poverty line (which is lower than the poverty line and is based on the cost of

a basket of basic food items that would provide an average of 2,237 calories per person per day).

7. About 10 percent of the Ecuadorian population is black. Estimates vary widely on the size of the indigenous population, from a low of 10 percent to a high of 40 percent (the latter according to indigenous organizations). There are thirteen officially designated non-Hispanic ethnic groups in Ecuador, each speaking its own language. The largest (90 percent) are the highland Quichua-speakers, also known as Runa. Quichua, spoken in Ecuador and northern Peru, is a distinctive form of Quechua, the language of the former Inca empire and the principal indigenous tongue of the Andean region today. Several dialects of Quichua are spoken in Ecuador. See Martin van Nieuwkoop and Jorge E. Uquillas, "Defining Ethnodevelopment in Operations Terms: Lessons from the Ecuador Indigenous and Afro-Ecuadoran Peoples Development Project" (Sustainable Development Working Paper 6, World Bank, Latin America and Caribbean Regional Office, Environmentally and Socially Sustainable Development SMU, January 2000).

8. United Nations Development Programme, *The Geography of Poverty in Ecuador* (New York: UNDP, 1996).

9. World Bank, *Ecuador: Crisis, Poverty and Social Services,* vol. 1, 34. Growth is defined as stunted when the height-for-age ratio is two or more standard deviations below the WHO/NCHS/CDC reference median. At 39 percent, Ecuador's rate of stunting is considerably higher than corresponding rates in many countries of the region, but it represents a significant decline from the 49.4 percent of the country's young children who suffered from stunted growth in 1986.

10. CEPLAES, "Estudio Cualitativo del Impacto Social de la Crisis en Comunidades y Barrios del Ecuador" (Quito, 1999).

11. Mestizos are people of mixed European and indigenous ancestry who speak Spanish and consider themselves part of the dominant Hispanic culture.

12. *Cholo* is a pejorative term used to describe a mestizo or an acculturated indigenous person.

13. World Bank, *Ecuador: Crisis, Poverty and Social Services,* vol. 1, 7.

14. Kristine M. Ivarsdotter, "Annex 8: Indigenous Education in Ecuador," in World Bank, *Ecuador: Crisis, Poverty and Social Services,* vol. 2, 3.

15. World Bank, *Ecuador: Crisis, Poverty and Social Services,* vol. 1, 40.

16. Ibid., 36. Cost was mentioned by 35 percent of the respondents, while other explanations include lack of interest (19 percent), the need to work (16 percent), and lack of access (10 percent).

17. Ibid., 31. Surveys reveal that the poorest income groups spend more on private health care than they receive in public health care expenditures. Overall, the poorest quintile receives 7.6 percent of public health care spending, while the richest

quintile receives 38.1 percent. Poor people are also more likely to use health clinics and centers, which are less equipped than hospitals to deal with serious or complex problems.

18. There are many forms of social organization at the local level, including formal parish boards (*juntas parroquiales*) and more informal neighborhood improvement committees (*comités pro-mejoras*) in urban areas. In rural areas, organizations are also very diverse, but the most common is a commune (*comuna*) whose government is called a *cabildo*. In Tumbatú and Tablas and La Calera the local group is referred to as a *cabildo*. In other communities people mention *directivas de la comunidad* (Asociación 10 Agosto), *comité pro-mejoras* (Atucucho), and *comité barrial* (Nuevas Brisas).

19. Beyond the small sample for this study, there are areas in the country where cultural traditions and local indigenous activism are in fact gaining strength. Institutional efforts to promote indigenous rights, cultures, and languages have received some government support. For instance, recent legislation provides for indigenous land rights and public support for bilingual schools, which are managed autonomously by indigenous organizations. The government has also provided legal recognition and training to indigenous organizations. See Nieuwkoop and Uquillas, "Defining Ethnodevelopment," 6.

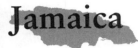

Jamaica

Island in a
Turbulent World

S. Jacqueline Grant and Toby Shillito[1]

Leroy Henry is a 33-year-old man who lives in Duckensfield. He has eleven siblings. His parents worked in the canefields to support their children, but often they didn't earn enough to regularly feed the family. Leroy's education was sporadic and brief, and he stopped attending school altogether when he was 9 years old. "Sometimes I did child labor for little or nothing at all," he recalls.[2] Leroy now works as a laborer for the Tropicana Sugar Company. He feels fortunate to be employed, as half of the villagers are not.

Leroy has seven children by three women, a not uncommon situation for Jamaican men. He says of his children,

> *Two of them go to Happy Grove High School and four of them go to Stokes Hall Technical. Because of the work I do, I can't [afford to] send them to school on a regular basis, but I send them as regularly as I can. I still don't have a proper dwelling. I have two rooms; the children live in one and my wife and I live in the next. I have an outside kitchen and pit toilet. I use most of my pay to school the children, so I can't build a good house. It makes me uncomfortable in more ways than one, especially the bathroom situation.*

Leroy's community, Duckensfield, is home to 375 families. The area's large agricultural estates have attracted a good deal of development.

Duckensfield has electricity and telephone service, but 40 percent of the households must fetch water from public pipes rather than pipes in their yards. Local health care services are inadequate, and poor people face costly transportation expenses if they need a doctor.

Hoping for a better life, Leroy says, "I would like to see for the twenty-first century a comfortable home for my family and more pay than what I am getting now." For his community, he wishes for skills training opportunities such as in woodworking, arts and crafts, and dressmaking "so that my children and other young people who are leaving school without a profession, at least they could get something to do."

Young people in Duckensfield also express fervent hopes for better educational and training opportunities because if they had more skills they could leave Duckensfield in search of better jobs elsewhere. Locally, the only work they can find is street vending, day labor on agricultural estates, or small-scale fishing, all of which offer meager returns. They express frustration that "many young people have to depend on their parents, relatives, and friends for food, clothing, and shelter."

Leroy is one of the more fortunate among poor Jamaicans. Communities across the island are attempting to deal as well as they can with global forces that affect their daily lives: factory closures and the loss of agricultural jobs, destructive weather, the effects of the international drug trade, and the push and pull toward a better life in Jamaican cities and off the island.

Despite slow economic growth over the last thirty years, poverty has declined in Jamaica. In 1999 some 473,000 people, or 16.9 percent of the population, lived in poverty, down from 26.1 percent in 1996 and 28.4 percent in 1990.[3] In the 1990s, the economy barely grew, averaging 0.3 percent growth between 1990 and 1998 and −0.4 percent in 1999, the year of the fieldwork for this study.

Jamaica's steady progress in reducing poverty in part reflects strong public investment in education and health, and, to a much lesser degree, in safety net programs.[4] The country has near-universal school enrollment through age 14, and enrollment at higher levels continued to increase in the 1990s. In addition, there is a well-established health care system, and life expectancy is 69 and 72 for males and females, respectively.[5] Jamaica has very strong social networks among family, friends, and neighbors, and these informal ties have provided an invaluable coping mechanism for poor people during periods of economic turmoil and recession. These positive trends notwithstanding, significant inequities persist in the country. Poverty is much higher in rural areas than in cities; in 1999, the poverty rate in the Kingston metropolitan area was 10.6 percent compared with 22 percent in rural areas.[6] There are also sizable gaps in both the coverage and quality of many economic and social programs aimed at reducing poverty.

Despite the country's poor economic performance, in 1997 the People's National Party (PNP) became the first political party to win a third consecutive term since the country gained independence and launched democratic rule in 1962. When Prime Minister P. J. Patterson took office in 1989, his administration intensified its predecessor's program of structural adjustment and market liberalization in a concerted effort to control very high levels of inflation, modernize the economy, and improve international competitiveness. The policies included exchange rate liberalization, privatization, reduction of public sector employment, removal of price controls, and tax and financial sector reforms. By the mid-1990s the economy showed signs of recovery and low levels of inflation; however, this proved to be temporary. Triggered by a crisis in the banking sector as well as external shocks, another long period of recession set in during 1996.

Researchers visited nine communities—five rural and four urban—that were selected on the basis of geographic diversity, levels of poverty, and, where possible, linkages with ongoing projects and research to ensure follow-up activities (see table 2, Study Communities in Jamaica, at the end of chapter). Communities selected also represent a diversity of context-specific poverty problems, such as land tenure, housing, isolation, and unemployment. Research in Railway Lane, one of the most deprived inner-city areas in the country, had to be discontinued because the community relations needed to visit this community safely at night could not be established in the short time available for fieldwork.

Facilitators used creative methods to identify individuals and groups for participation in the study. Some discussion group participants were selected because they had special needs or a particular experience of interest to researchers. Other participants were selected as researchers encountered them in their neighborhoods, such as when waiting at a clinic or a bus stop. In order to crosscheck the information gathered, additional individuals were randomly interviewed at the start and end of fieldwork in each community. In addition, facilitators presented their findings to community members before departing, an event that often turned into a celebration of community expression.

A total of 1,265 people participated in forty-two discussion groups in the nine communities. In addition, 165 case studies were completed. This figure includes thirty-five case studies of poor women, men, and youth, nine case studies with people who were poor and are now better-off, and 121 institutional case studies.

The UK-based OneWorld Development Network conducted the study during May and June 1999 using local facilitators with previous training in participatory appraisal methods.

When asked to speak about their lives, poor people in Jamaica remark upon the pressures they feel from global forces as they try to escape poverty. While many have been able to improve their circumstances, this study focuses on those who are still poor. The chapter opens with a discussion of these global forces and then reviews poor Jamaicans' strategies for climbing out of poverty. This is followed by poor people's evaluations of local institutions, cultural traditions, and social ties that provide vital support in their lives. It concludes with a discussion of women's growing economic independence and the turmoil this is creating in gender relations in poor households.

Buffeted by Global Forces

Jamaicans are not isolated from the rest of the world. On the contrary, competitive markets, austerity policies, tourism, harsh weather and hurricanes, labor migration, and the drug trade all play major roles in shaping their lives on the island. In the following sections, poor people describe the tremendous power these forces have over their communities and their prospects of escaping poverty.

Scarce Livelihoods

Discussion groups across the study communities unanimously agree that economic opportunities have declined over the last twenty years and especially over the last decade. Unemployment is widely viewed as the leading cause of poverty and the most pressing problem for rural and urban communities alike. People point to the unfavorable conditions of the economy, the lack of government leadership in turning the economy around, and problems of increased foreign competition. In urban areas, people speak repeatedly of factory closings and layoffs, and in rural areas they indicate that large plantations and processing plants used to offer many more jobs. For small farmers, increased competition and fluctuating farm prices, lack of credit, and difficulties accessing markets greatly constrain rural livelihoods.

Factory Closings and Increased Competition

The village of Freeman's Hall has suffered from the decline of one export crop after another. Sugarcane was the dominant crop from the 1700s until the 1960s, when it was replaced by bananas, which were viewed as more profitable. People in Freeman's Hall remember the 1960s and 1970s as the good times, when residents worked largely in the banana and coffee industries. Although local farmers were unable to effectively market their produce, they enjoyed government supports that allowed them to sell their produce to a central factory or a commodity board. In addition, residents of Freeman's Hall supplemented their farm income by working for the parish council (local government body) and the public works department. Men from each district did road maintenance and weeding, and some helped to build roads and a large—now abandoned—reservoir. Then in 1988 Hurricane Gilbert wiped out their crops and destroyed both the banana boxing plant and the coffee plant, which never reopened. In the wake of Gilbert, residents of Freeman's Hall lost not only their jobs but their opportunities for supplemental income as well, as the public works projects were also terminated for financial reasons.

Study participants in Freeman's Hall view the hurricane and the closure of the local banana boxing plant and coffee farm to be at the root of their poverty. Similarly, a discussion group of older women from Duckensfield ranks unemployment as their major problem. They say simply, "We cannot find anything to do." When all of Duckensfield's factories were in operation, there was hope of a job. With only two factories currently operating (Tropicana Sugar Estates and Eastern Banana Company), chances of employment are slim. Factory closings are considered a major cause of poverty in Bowerbank and Thompson Pen, as well.

Small and Remote Farmers in Competitive Markets

Replacing sugar and bananas, yams are now the cash crop in Freeman's Hall. Yam prices fluctuate, and farmers often harvest their crops prematurely to take advantage of a better price. But yams picked early perish faster, and the result is fewer marketable yams. Another common problem facing farmers is lack of credit to purchase yam tubers and fertilizer; thus, a farmer may plant only 100 rows of yam when he or she has the productive capacity to farm 1,000 rows. People in Freeman's Hall explain that they lack "backative," the capital to finance rational agricultural production.

The pressures of global competition and difficulties accessing markets are other issues cited as contributing to farmers' hardships. A woman explains, "I have 150 chickens eight weeks old, but people would rather buy those foreign chicken parts. If I lower my price, I'll be selling at a loss." Farmers in Millbank report that from 1997 to 1999 the price of the local crop, dasheen (a starchy root also known as taro), fell 25 percent. If their highly perishable crop is not sold locally, farmers have to choose between throwing it out or paying to transport it to Kingston. The transport is very expensive because the only way out of Millbank is around a landslide and over a decrepit bridge. As one farmer laments,

> Oftentimes our produce rots in the fields even though people are starving here in Jamaica and around the world. One of the reasons we can't sell our produce locally is because foreign produce floods the market with too much of the same type of stuff. Because of the bad road, no outside buyers come here. I borrow money and plant the ground and can't sell because of this.

Poor access to markets also forces farmers in Accompong to give their produce away or let it rot. In Little Bay, it is not only farmers who are disadvantaged by the rough state of the roads; local fishermen also have difficulty reaching buyers before their products spoil.

Tourism Out of Reach
One in four jobs in Jamaica depends on tourism. More than 80,000 people are employed directly in the sector, and another 170,000 engage in related activities. Tourism is also Jamaica's main source of foreign exchange and accounts for more than a fifth of its GNP. Though poor people note that increased tourism often means increased prostitution and drug trafficking activity, many rural Jamaicans are keen to attract

tourism and hope for the infrastructure improvements that would make it possible.

Most discussion groups in rural communities report that fishing, farming, and tourism are their primary sources of income, and that these all require, at minimum, adequate roads and other infrastructure. Poor roads are viewed as the biggest constraint. The bad condition of the roads in Accompong, for instance, makes it difficult for tourists to reach the community. As a result, a group of young men says, the rich heritage and culture of the Jamaican Maroons—descendents of Africans who resisted slavery and founded free communities—do not receive the exposure and recognition they deserve. Potential earnings from tourism that could employ young men as guides and in other service areas are lost. Similarly, a young man in Freeman's Hall suggests that one solution for unemployment in his town would be to develop eco-tourism: the Quashie River flows along the eastern boundary of the village and is flanked by steep hills and valleys, representing an ideal ecotourism attraction.

Errol Campbell, a 35-year-old man in Little Bay, explains how policies to develop tourism can bypass poor people:

> Right now tourism is taking root all along the sea coast, but the people who live here can't access money for the development of their properties to help them earn tourist dollars. The government puts up institutions such as Self Start Fund and RADA [Rural Agricultural Development Authority], but you have to have enough collateral before you get their loans. The system is in place but not for poor people. All we can do is block roads and sometimes people get arrested and go to jail when they protest, so nothing good comes of it.

Not all study participants, however, are enthusiastic about opening their communities to tourism, and some express concerns about the rising crime and environmental damage associated with the industry. In Little Bay, Tanisha Patterson, a teacher, weighs the pros and cons of promoting tourism:

> In terms of development, tourism is already spreading from Negril to Little Bay, and I have no doubt that the tourists will come to the village to enjoy what is here. I think we are going

to have an influx of commercial business paving the way for
population growth, employment. However, on the negative side,
this will create environmental problems.

A project to build a road between Portland and St. Thomas stood to
dramatically increase access to Millbank, but Millbank residents in this
study viewed the proposed road as imposed by the government and also
as a potential thoroughfare for gunmen. They concluded that it would
offer few benefits to their community. With such feelings widespread in
Millbank, many "accidents" occurred in which equipment fell down hills.
The government eventually abandoned the project.

Extreme Weather and Environmental Change

A woman in Cassava Piece says, "It's nasty when a storm comes. If we
start fortifying structures, landowners come see what we're doing. We
can't do anything to make the houses more secure because they don't
want any concrete structures upon their land, not even a bathroom."

Periodic intense rains are the norm for tropical Jamaica. When fierce
storms and hurricanes hit, recovery can take years and, for people with
precarious housing and scarce assets to begin with, sometimes generations. Some communities must dig out from flooding and mudslides over
and over again.

Hurricane Gilbert devastated Jamaica in 1988, and residents in most
of the communities visited report that housing problems have been
constant ever since. In Duckensfield and Millbank, Gilbert blew down
houses or tore away rooftops. Joselyn Harris, a 76-year-old Millbank
woman, recalls Gilbert as the most shocking event of her life. She says,
"All we found after Gilbert was a wooden chair." Gilbert destroyed 80
percent of the homes in Freeman's Hall. Although some families received
assistance, by 1999 many homes still had not been repaired. Little Bay
lost most of its housing and subsistence crops in the hurricane. Eleven
years later, some families had not yet recovered from the physical, financial, and social trauma.

Of the nine communities visited, only Accompong and Thompson
Pen were spared direct devastation by Hurricane Gilbert, and a large
number of Gilbert victims went to those communities seeking housing
and jobs. Bowerbank also received an influx of Gilbert victims. The
failure to replace housing destroyed in the disaster, combined with the

increase in demand from new residents, has condemned Bowerbank to an acute housing crisis that has lasted over a decade.

Gilbert destroyed not only homes, but livelihoods. As mentioned above, local banana crops, the banana boxing plant, and a post office were destroyed and never rebuilt. Young women in Little Bay calculate that Gilbert increased local poverty by a factor of six. To make matters worse, Little Bay's fishermen suffered deep losses once again when Hurricane Mitch struck in 1998.

Hurricanes are just one of many environmental disasters facing communities in Jamaica. In 1992 a dam broke in Thompson Pen and a river burst over its banks, flooding much of the community. Millbank also faces potential disaster every May and October, when the village is prone to flooding and landslides. The most recent major flood occurred in 1990, and the last big landslide was in 1998. Study participants in Millbank fear that local deforestation and development may intensify storm damage, but there seem to be few options for slowing these trends. "The government doesn't provide alternative work for men who cut down trees, and they have to live, so they cut down the trees," explains a group of elderly Millbank women.

The Local and Global Drug Trade

With opportunities for legal and secure livelihoods in Jamaica on the wane, illicit employment, especially growing ganja (marijuana) and selling drugs, is viewed by many as the only dependable source of income. In some communities, ganja cultivation is the primary source of livelihood. Many poor people also see the robust global market for drugs as an opportunity, and they may work in the drug trade outside Jamaica for several years trying to get ahead financially. Those who fail are arrested, imprisoned, or deported. Meanwhile, back home, the quality of life in poor Jamaican communities declines as the sale and use of drugs rises and healthy young men succumb to the hazards of the trade.

Rural discussion groups see ganja farming as an important source of income, without which many people could not survive. A group of women in one study community acknowledges that residents "mostly fish and grow ganja here." Farmers point out that ganja sells for double the price of dasheen, and unlike the root crop, it is not perishable. In three rural communities visited, groups readily identify growing and selling drugs as a means of social and economic mobility.

Several Jamaicans say that family members have traveled abroad and been arrested, most often because of involvement in the drug trade. A 44-year-old mother of eight in an urban community says,

My children's father went to the U.S. to try to make life better and send a little money. He sent us clothes, money, and food. My kids could go to school and they were eating well. In 1988, the Thursday after Hurricane Gilbert, a man came. He told me my babies' father had gone to jail in the U.S., along with three of his brothers, his cousin, and his sister's boyfriend. All of them went to prison in America. Some say they got twelve years, some say they got fifteen. No one will tell me exactly. Once in a while I get a letter from him, or he phones if he needs a birth certificate or wants a picture of the family.

Poor communities in Jamaica are not immune to drug use among their members. Young people in one settlement indicate that crack and cocaine use is common in their community. People in a rural area express fear of local "cokeheads" and consider drug use to be a community problem. A recent murder committed by a drug user involved with the trade has left them shaken. They see drug trading and use, especially of cocaine, as one of the impacts of poverty and contend that the drugs come from outside their community. However, in poor neighborhoods ganja smoking appears to be more widespread and accepted than use of hard drugs. The research team noted much ganja smoking in one urban community, and points out that young men in a certain rural community oppose street lighting for no reason other than that they want to be able to smoke ganja in peace.

Finally, Jamaicans living in poverty are affected by anti-narcotics activities. A man in another village recounts a terrifying event in the late 1980s:

The government sent helicopters to destroy ganja. The wings of the helicopter blew down all the food crops and killed the tied-up animals. When we tried to get compensated for our losses, nobody would help us. My family suffered terribly. It takes years to recover from something like that.

The Struggle for a Better Life

To find better opportunities, many poor Jamaicans migrate, start small businesses, and do whatever it takes to invest in education. Many parents still value schooling and provide it to their children at great sacrifice, although education doesn't hold the promise it once did. Nowadays, many people in the study observe, even educated people cannot find jobs locally.

Going Away to Get By

Study participants frequently name migration—to Jamaican cities and beyond—as a key strategy for getting out of poverty. "Jamaicans don't feel like this is their home. Ask anybody. If they get a visa, they're gone," says an unemployed man in Cassava Piece. Heavy migration among young men and women of working age often deepens poverty in the places they leave behind, as poor youths and the elderly are left to fend for themselves.

Discussion groups in Bowerbank and Cassava Piece say that a visa is a ticket out of poverty. In Duckensfield men obtain U.S. and Canadian farmwork contracts, which range from six weeks to six months. Many other Jamaicans migrate without a contract in the expectation that they will find opportunities abroad. A man in Little Bay explains, "As long as I can remember we have had a plague on us. The basic living conditions are so bad that most people must leave the community. For the people who can't leave, they just have to sit and cope with the bad." A woman in Freeman's Hall speculates, "We figure that the criminals—just like everybody else—leave here for where there's more opportunity."

Migration, though it may be seen as the best way to lift a family out of poverty, also brings emotional and practical hardships to spouses, parents, and children left behind. Many women see their mate only once every few years, says a discussion group of women in Freeman's Hall. Older people in Accompong discuss the sorrow of missing distant family members who do not keep in touch. For those who stay behind in Jamaica, remittances from family members overseas can be a vital source of income. Relatives abroad are expected to send money and goods back home, and those who cannot may be shunned for failing to do so. A man from Bowerbank reports,

When I came back from America I found I had lost my whole family. When I got shot [in America] I couldn't hustle anything to send back, so they all turned their backs on me. Many nights I don't eat. I sell cakes for a guy once in a while and I pray and give thanks for that. Sometimes my son's girl cooks for me. My children's mother doesn't want me anymore because I don't have anything to give her. She cooks for me sometimes, but I often go to bed hungry. Sometimes I cry.

Local Entrepreneurship

Although many Jamaicans go abroad to improve their lot and that of their families, a few men and women have managed to come out of poverty through entrepreneurship in their communities.

Alvin McKenzie, of Millbank, was born in 1950 and has five siblings. His family of eight lived in a two-room house. His parents were too poor to send the children to school, so most of them are illiterate. When Alvin got older, he says, he began to farm dasheen, bananas, and plantains, sometimes selling to large exporters such as the Agricultural Marketing Corporation. He continues,

Then I became an expert on the Giant Swallowtail butterfly and linked up with Dr. Beckford Grant from the University [of the West Indies] and I learned a lot from him. I also work as a trail guide for an NGO called Valley Hikes. All of that helps to move me out of poverty. I hope to see a better life for the future. . . . I would like to see improvement in the community, especially towards the young people coming up, in terms of skills training. If the infrastructure is put in place I will help to motivate the youths in my community so they can have a better lifestyle like myself.

Carol Wright, a 42-year-old woman from Thompson Pen, improved her life after she set up her own day-care center at home. To support herself and her two children, Carol used to work in a factory, but she quit because a manager mistreated her. She next got a job cleaning airplanes, but that money turned out to be insufficient after she had another child with a man who wasn't working regularly and her grand-mother grew more ill. Remembering that her grandmother used to care for community children, Carol decided to go into business for herself:

> *A sign was placed on the gate saying I am taking in children to provide day care. I started with four children, and that's where it all started for me. I got so many children I could not keep the young babies due to lack of space. Members of my family helped me to care for them. I made enough money to send my daughter to high school, and my 10-year-old son goes to Spanish Town Primary. My eldest daughter is now in Teachers College.*

Carol plans to expand the day-care center with the help of her sister Phyllis. Both Carol and Phyllis believe that the secret of their success is hard work, dedication, determination, education, and working together as a family.

Although poor communities have several needs that entrepreneurs could hypothetically fill, many businesses in these communities fail. A 78-year-old Accompong man traveled to England when he was 30 and stayed for three decades. He found work as a cab driver and eventually became one of the cab company's managers. Fulfilling his lifelong dream, he returned to Accompong with enough money to open a grocery store. Nevertheless, his business failed in the 1980s when no one had much money for purchases. He is now destitute.

Education Loses Its Appeal

Public support for education is particularly high in Jamaica, accounting for 7 percent of the GDP and 63 percent of social spending in fiscal 1998/99. School enrollment is nearly universal (95 percent) in primary and lower secondary school. The uneven quality of schools remains an important challenge, however. Some 30 percent of sixth-grade students are functionally illiterate, and educational outcomes are lower in inner-city and rural schools, where poverty is most heavily concentrated.[7]

In Cassava Piece two discussion groups of women report that the high cost of keeping a child in school is a leading factor in the low levels of education. Even in primary school, families must pay for school supplies and other necessities, and fees are required once students reach secondary school. Jamaicans explain that in hard times, children may attend on a rotating basis with siblings or they may be withdrawn from school entirely. The low quality of education is also a major concern. In Little Bay, the researchers note, "Many stressed that the low level of children graduating from the local all-age school was due to an inadequate curriculum and poor teaching standards." Some study participants say that apathetic faculty and staff are another problem. "If a child stops going to school for a long time, neither the teacher or the principal try to find out what happened—they don't care," observes a poor man from Thompson Pen.

Nonetheless, individuals who have benefited directly from the sacrifices they made to educate their children give education unqualified endorsement. Joselyn Harris, an elderly poor woman in Millbank, says, "We sent all the children to school. Education is the best thing. By 1988 all our kids had finished school and found good jobs. Now it is our children who support us."

Other parents aren't so lucky. In Freeman's Hall parents spoke of having sold off livestock to finance the education of their children. Despite having some children who clearly excelled at school, however, their families gained absolutely no economic advantage.

Although some still tout the value of education, study participants very frequently point out that education can no longer be counted on to lift people out of poverty. "It is a murderous act that children who passed their exams have to go weed banana crops down on the Bellinfanti property," says an older man in a discussion group in Freeman's Hall. Likewise, people in Accompong express disgust that young residents who succeed academically cannot find suitable work in their own community. A 60-year-old woman in Duckensfield says,

> For years I did domestic work and my husband cut cane. . . .
> We made huge sacrifices to send our children to school on our
> very small wages. My husband and I spent all our earnings on
> their schooling, yet today two of them can't even find work,
> much less support us now that we are old.

As young men in Bowerbank explain, "Without a godfather [a mentor and advocate] or some kind of contacts you can't get anywhere. I know plenty of people who went to high school who can't find work." A man in Cassava Piece concludes, "Education doesn't make you rich. I know a guy who passed eight [high school] subjects and is unemployed like the rest of us." His perception is that skilled workers are in the same predicament: "There are plenty of men here with job skills, but we still can't get work."

Poor People and Public Services

Poor Jamaicans have sharply negative assessments of their elected officials and give low ratings to many government programs that operate in their communities. In addition to the problems with education mentioned above, health care services and social assistance programs appear to be very weak as well.

Government and "Politricks"

According to a young man in Thompson Pen, "It's the government that causes jobs to be lost, schools to be inadequate, and factories to be closed and downsized." Another says, "We have never been represented by anyone. Nobody will have anything to do with us." A mother of two who lives in the same community likewise concludes, "The government always lets us down: too many promises, never fulfilling them."

Discussion groups in all nine communities rate politicians very negatively. Men in Bowerbank say specifically of their parliamentarian, "When he did want the vote, we did see him, but since we have already given him the vote, we have never seen him again." They also say politicians "make enough promises to fill the Mona dam," and identify political deception—"politricks"—as a major cause of poverty. Others in Bowerbank agree with the men's discussion group and view the parliamentarian as a "jacket-and-tie thief" and a "criminal." Men in Duckensfield associate politics with bloodshed, and say politicians "carry a bag of empty promises and violence." An older man in Cassava Piece says, "I've never seen a politician do anything good for Cassava Piece. Never voted in my life because it only divides people." The kindest words heard about elected officials are from a man in Little Bay who quips, "When the politicians go abroad and use poor people's name to beg for money, they should at least give us some of it when they return."

Social assistance programs also receive relatively low ratings from study participants. Resources devoted to such programs in Jamaica amount to 0.6 percent of the GDP, far below the level in most other countries in Latin America and the Caribbean. The government devotes substantially larger resources to programs involving microenterprise development, training, community development, low-income housing, and public works, which may have contributed to the reduction of poverty in an environment of slow economic growth. In their existing form, however, many of these programs do not seem to be serving many of those who are currently poor.

The food stamp program is mentioned by study participants in five of the communities visited but receives generally poor reviews because of the very small size of the benefit and difficulties in obtaining it. In Millbank food stamps are described as a "government handout of approximately US$4 per fortnight to the most needy in the community." And in Little Bay, a remote community isolated by bad roads, an elderly woman reports, "When I go to get the food stamp, it costs me J$200 [US$5] in carfare to go and collect it; so, for J$240 in stamps, it doesn't make much sense."

People also say little about the contribution of public works or housing programs. In Freeman's Hall a discussion group of men recalled that back in the 1970s they could find temporary jobs with the public works department in building and maintaining roads. However, these opportunities disappeared in the 1980s with the change in government and the introduction of sweeping austerity policies. Bowerbank is the only community where residents mention the National Housing Trust (NHT), and according to a discussion group of men there, "You can't trust a person in the NHT. They come and register people, but nothing ever happens."

In several communities participants acknowledge that opportunities for training have increased in recent years; however, the fees and distance to the training locations keep many of them from taking advantage of the courses. In Cassava Piece women in a discussion group say that income is lost during the training period, yet "there are families to be cared for." Discussion groups from six communities made specific references to the training provided by the local Social Development Commission. In Accompong study participants credit the commission with helping the community to develop tourism; however, in other communities its contributions appear more limited and some of its programs appear to have ended for lack of participation.

Valued Institutions in Little Bay

Poor women and men from the community of Little Bay worked in small groups to identify and rank the institutions that are important in their daily lives. Table 1 lists the top eight institutions mentioned by a group of women and a group of men, all over 30 years old, and shows the order in which each group ranked them.

Participants in Little Bay describe several qualities that they value in institutions. They want institutions to provide support in times of need, to be reliable, and "to do what they are supposed to do, all the time." They trust an institution when "we can depend on them whenever we need help." In addition, they value timeliness: "When we have a serious problem, they come quickly on their own and help to ease the pressure." Institutions are also highly regarded if they build unity and collective pride, include people in decision making, and come "into our community and ask for our opinions and ideas."

By contrast, institutions that "have the power to help yet refuse to help, and those that are lazy and never come into the community at all" rate badly. "They have no business with us," remarks a participant. On this basis, the lowest-ranking institutions are the member of Parliament and the country's prime minister. The parliamentarian scores low for not

TABLE 1 Most Important Institutions, Two Discussion Groups in Little Bay

	Ranking by discussion group	
Institution	Women	Men
School	1	1
Negril Area Environmental Protection Trust	2	4
Negril Coral Reef Preservation Society	3	4
Shops	4	3
Church	5	2
National Water Commission	6	8
Member of Parliament	7	6
Prime minister	8	7

Note: 1 = Most important. The women's group ranked both environmental NGOs in fourth place.

investing resources in the community despite promises of support before elections. Generally, people feel rejected by him.

The National Water Commission receives low ratings because it has never served the community in any way, although it has a specific mandate to help. Poor people remark that "the water commission should run pipe in the community and meter it and charge us; we are willing to pay." Another Little Bay participant adds, "They say that their motto is 'water is life,' so it looks like they want us dead."

Institutions that score well include the school, two environmental NGOs, local shops, and the church. Despite worries about the low quality of the education provided, people value the school because it continues to operate despite difficult conditions in the community. Women in particular express concern that without some form of education, children will not learn to read and write at even a basic level. The school also serves as a central meeting place and as the only source of shelter for the community during natural disasters.

The Negril Area Environmental Protection Trust is well regarded because of its efforts to protect the sea and local environment, and because it helps to provide some members of the community with jobs.[8] The Negril Coral Reef Preservation Society is valued for helping to clean up the community—especially the beaches—which in turn helps protect the coral reef where fish breed. The women appreciate the preservation society for helping community members take pride in their community.

Shops are seen as important for the food and other goods they provide, as otherwise villagers would have to travel far to make purchases. The church also scores well because it offers spiritual support and material assistance in times of need, and strengthens communication between the various groups in the community. Women in particular rank the church highly, as they perceive it to be an institution that helps to instill discipline.

A Caring Culture under Strain

All the discussion groups in Jamaica describe helpful neighbors and supportive communities, and it is these resources that poor people say provide them with the greatest support in their daily lives and in crises (box 1). There is a strong tradition of women looking after children and less fortunate members of the community, and of men

When listing possible means of economic betterment, discussion groups in Thompson Pen, Millbank, and Freeman's Hall often mention an informal savings institution they call "pardner." Pardner participants are almost always women who pool money through regular payments to a common fund over a specific period. Participants take turns drawing out the total sum, which is typically used for major expenses such as a house, a car, or school fees.[9]

One woman who has improved her life by "throwing pardner" is Murtle Stanley, a 42-year-old mother of two in Freeman's Hall known as Miss Rose. An employee of the local coffee farm for twenty years, Miss Rose was recently promoted to supervisor. In addition to that job, she has farmed a small yam crop and worked as a higgler (vendor), selling snacks. The father of her children worked many years as a farm laborer in the United States. Pardner helped her accumulate savings from her earnings and his remittances until they were able to build a house, which they constructed over a nine-year period and recently completed. They plan to celebrate their long-time relationship by marrying.

reaching out to help youths and prevent discord. Many communities report that residents work together to deter crime. Although even today the impulse to help others is strong, poor people in various communities express deep concerns that economic strains combined with encroaching foreign cultures and values are eroding many of the vital bonds that enrich and bring security to their lives.

Helping the Young and Less Fortunate

Miss Lynnie, an elderly woman in Little Bay, tells researchers that in 1997 her house burned to the ground, killing her great-grandson. She was able to recover from the tragedy because her church provided material assistance and her neighbors came together to build her a new house and assist with the burial. Similarly, a group of adult men in Bowerbank reports, "We look out for each other here." A group of young women explains, "If a person has no dinner, we share," and "We live in glass houses and we can't afford war." They say that when "some people get and some don't," discord and violence can result. Residents of Millbank say simply, "Maroons look after their own, even the sick and the mad."

Men and women in Little Bay identify the community role of women as ensuring that all children are well cared for. In Freeman's Hall women give meals and lunch money to children whose parents cannot afford to. One woman there describes her role in the community as cooking dinner every Sunday for an elderly man who is sick and lives alone. Women in Millbank report that part of their weekly routine is to help elderly people by bathing them, cooking for them, taking them to the health clinic, giving them clothing, or running their errands. Millbank women also regularly care for other people's children when their parents go to market or are away for other reasons. Elsewhere, women explain that part of their role in the community is to give advice and comfort to the mothers of small children.

Complementing the Jamaican woman's role as nurturer is the man's traditional role as provider, protector, and peacemaker. Men's obligations extend beyond blood ties; a discussion group participant in Cassava Piece specifies the obligation to "take care of the youth, even when they're not yours." One role model in Thompson Pen is Lloyd Jameson, an 87-year-old former taxi driver who spends his time and money providing clothing to needy children and mentoring youths in his community.

In relating local efforts to solve community problems and cope with crises, poor Jamaicans describe countless examples of collective action and ritual. When researchers for this study visited Bowerbank, many residents were painting and repairing the local school and constructing a fence of salvaged wood around it. In Millbank, where traditional Maroon holidays are still observed, local farmers report that they are carrying out a collective decision to protect their economic interests by not selling dasheen to farmers from outside the area who will then compete with them for sales. In Freeman's Hall most of the women go down to the Quashie River together each day to wash clothes and bathe small children. The men take turns digging furrows in each other's fields, a practice referred to as "a day for a day." At night they play dominoes. When someone dies in Freeman's Hall, people do "nine nights up," a wake in which the entire community visits the family of the dead person, sings hymns, and shares food and liquor.

Resisting Crime and Conflict

With the exception of Duckensfield, all communities in the study report that the only local crime is petty theft from fields or clotheslines. Urban and some rural communities visited acknowledge that there used to be extensive violence, and indicate that much of it was politically motivated. However, they report that this has now disappeared. These reports are not consistent with recent qualitative research in five other poor urban communities in Jamaica, which found that violence is a pressing problem, especially gang violence related to "unemployment, lack of work and opportunities, and hopelessness."[10]

Women in a discussion group in Cassava Piece, a residential area near Kingston, assert, "You can sleep with your door open," and "We have good neighbors; it's comfortable and safe any time of night, unlike some areas where gunmen are running through." A new resident affirms this by saying, "I come from Rema, where there's lots of gunfire. Been here two years and I haven't heard a single shot."

Similarly, in Bowerbank, one man says, "This is a ghetto community but we don't have any violence." Despite their squalid, overcrowded surroundings, a young man insists, "This is the best community in Kingston." Another man says, "You can leave your keys on top of your taxicab, come back and find them untouched," and a young women says, "You can walk through this place with your eyes closed without anybody troubling you." One man who can afford to leave Bowerbank told researchers that he prefers to wait for new housing to be completed rather than leave the peace and security of his neighborhood.

In rural areas where police and legal institutions are largely lacking, participants report taking an active role in ensuring public safety. Accompong residents say that when a crime is committed, the community is always able to identify the perpetrator because there are few places to hide in their small and isolated territory. People in Millbank cite a recent case in which members of the community ensured that a local man who poisoned a river in order to catch crawfish was charged with the crime. Similarly, participants in Little Bay say, "When the bad men come into this area, we take care of them and hand them over to the police." There is no police station in Little Bay, and the residents see no need for one.

People in many of the communities refer to a time when things were not peaceful due to the political violence that surrounded national elections and the change of government in 1980. A Bowerbank resident born in 1971 recalls,

We could play anywhere without fear in 1975. My mother
and father had jobs so we had some money and clothes.
The frightening time was in 1981 with the political violence.
Lots of gunfire. One night my mother had to put me in
a dresser drawer. I spent a whole night and a day in that

drawer. Then she took me out and brought me to her friend's in Doncaster.

A young woman of Bowerbank also recalls, "One year people started quarreling, throwing stones, and wielding machetes. It was so bad the police put the curfew on right through the morning. They would take the men out of their beds no matter what they were wearing."

Residents of Freeman's Hall acknowledge that their community has a reputation for being violent but only because "political bad men came here to hide out in the early 1980s." An old man recounts, "Those criminals died out. The police killed them all off. Now you can walk at night and nobody will molest you." Thompson Pen shares a similar reputation. A woman there says, "People think it's unsafe because back in the early 1980s the men used to run through here with their political warring. But that's all over now as most of those men are either dead or in prison." Finally, people interviewed in Duckensfield believe that because their community actively excludes political types, the gun violence and arson common in the 1980s have not recurred.

Maroon Traditions under Stress

Despite the fact that many communities still work together to preserve safety, some participants caution that local traditions and community supports are breaking down. Opinions about the causes and effects of social changes vary, with important differences emerging along generational and gender lines in several communities. Different social groups often express distinct and sometimes conflicting views about changing cultural traditions, material prosperity, and gender roles and responsibilities. The Maroon communities visited show many signs of stress.

The first Maroons were slaves of the Spanish who escaped into the mountains of Jamaica in the late 1600s. Isolated in their hidden settlements, the Maroons preserved many traditions based on their African heritage. After Jamaica came under British control, organized Maroon insurgents waged guerrilla warfare against the slaveholders, finally signing a peace treaty with the British government in 1739. Under the terms of the accord, the Maroons received land, freedom from taxation, and a measure of self-government.

Today Jamaica has several communities of Maroon descendents, and two, Accompong and Millbank, were visited for the study. In Accompong the older men express a passion for their culture and heritage and feel closely connected to the oral history and traditions passed on to them by elders. These men rank erosion of Maroon culture as the most pressing problem facing Accompong. Younger men and women from the village, however, say their primary problems are unemployment and lack of roads that would enable them to earn incomes instead of struggling with subsistence agriculture and a "hand-to-mouth existence."

Generational differences also emerged in Accompong when discussion groups were asked to stratify the community according to different levels of wellbeing. The older men do not define wellbeing in terms of economic criteria, but rather in terms of community respect and social prominence based on social achievements. Younger men, however, use economic indicators in determining those who are better and worse off.

In Millbank, though use of the Maroon language died out in the 1960s, traditional biodiverse farming methods are maintained, including the cultivation of "food forests" that combine herbaceous crops, root crops, fruit trees, and native tree species. Older Maroons in the village report that young men show little interest in farming nowadays. Many younger men there say they resent Maroon law because it does not allow them to own property. Lacking land titles, which the outside world requires as collateral for credit, they perceive Maroon law as a barrier to their economic advancement.

Young Maroon women also challenge traditions. Many young women in the two Maroon communities seek more modern lifestyles but lack the means to pursue their aspirations. In Accompong young women agree that they are the group most likely to watch TV and to desire consumer goods, and many choose to migrate because they have little hope of finding jobs and meeting their material goals locally.

Nevertheless, older women from Accompong state, "Younger women are not competitive in many ways, they sit back waiting on their partners to finance their daily needs. The young women are not motivated and in these days the family cannot afford housewives in the community." Various discussion group participants in Accompong express concern that young women are increasingly unwilling to farm. Older women worry that these young women are consequently more dependent on men. They also fear that younger women will not do their duty in passing Maroon traditions along to their children.

Many of the young men, meanwhile, feel exploited by women who don't work hard, and say: "When a man's on the fork, the woman should be on the hoe"; "One hand can't clap"; "Take up a woman you take on a burden"; and "We are fed up of coming home from a hard day's work to see the women in yard clothes [smartly dressed] every day."

Some study participants are also concerned about teenage pregnancy and increasingly unstable partnerships between young men and women. Pamela Griffith, a poor young woman from Millbank, says,

I am 20 years old and I am the mother of four children, two girls and two boys aged between 6 and one and a half. I had my first child when I was 14 years old. The reason I entered into a relationship was for financial stability. The monetary benefits stopped as soon as I had the baby. I entered into another relationship almost immediately. This resulted in two more children. This relationship ended shortly after the birth of the second child. The financial support in this relationship stopped after my children's father took up drinking and gambling.

When asked about her hopes for the future, Pamela relates, "I want to learn to read and write and get a good job so that I can send my children to a good school so that they will not have to farm but will be able to get good work."

Women Reach for Independence and Security

In every Jamaican community visited, there is agreement that a woman's primary role is to care for the children and the home. Sharp rises in male unemployment, however, have driven large numbers of women out of the home and into the workplace to support their families. These changes in breadwinner roles are providing increased authority for women, but often at a price. There are widespread reports of greater conflict and instability in gender relations.

Poor men and women both indicate that women are more likely than men to be employed because they have more education and are more willing to take on work that men refuse to do. According to a woman in Cassava Piece, "We women will work for what no man would work for. Women will come down to get better or to keep the home going, but the man stands on his pride." In Bowerbank a poor man shares his frustration that "the woman finds a job easier than the man nowadays." Poor women's job opportunities, however, are mainly in the informal economy, where pay can be very low. In the formal economy, women's unemployment rate is 23 percent, compared with 9 9 percent for men.[11]

A woman in Bowerbank speaks for many others when she explains that a woman must have her own economic means so that "she doesn't feel helpless." Indeed, many women across the communities acknowledge their drive for financial independence and express appreciation for the greater freedom that having an income brings to women. "With your own money, you can buy your own things and not depend on anybody," says a woman in rural Millbank. Other women advise, "Have your own shelter and finances so you don't have to stay in an abusive relationship." In discussing the impact of changing gender roles on households, a woman in Cassava Piece remarks, "More women work now, so they don't have to put up with men's foolishness." In some urban communities women mention greater freedom to choose family planning methods.

Women's earning responsibilities have expanded in rural areas, as well. In Little Bay more women than men are now employed, in part because women have capitalized on a boom in the fishing industry over the last decade. Women are now actively selling at local markets and do more extensive farming as well. In Millbank participants indicate that ten years ago women were only sellers at the market, whereas now they buy, sell, and participate more fully in farming activities. Rural women, however, have not increased their control and authority over household decisions to the same extent as their urban counterparts, both because men are still generally perceived to be the main providers for the family and because there are fewer economic opportunities for women's advancement in the countryside. Participants also point out that in those households where men remain the sole breadwinners, little has changed in terms of women's responsibilities or power.

In Jamaica the benchmark of manhood is to provide material support for children and send them to school. "Any man that doesn't take care of his young, I won't have anything to do with," says a man in Bowerbank. Others point out that a father's responsibility is replicated, not reduced, if he has children with more than one woman. Another poor man in Bowerbank explains that if you have J$100 and babies by four mothers, then "the money must be shared by four."

Men in discussion groups express intense frustration with being unable to find stable and gainful employment, and say they are abandoned by women when jobless. To highlight their frustrations, men from Bowerbank say: "Lose the job outside, you lose the job at home"; "When you have no work the woman just switches on you and she's gone"; "A man must get a job to get a woman"; and "Men stick with women when they lose their jobs, but women leave men who lose theirs." In Bowerbank young men grumble that women have the upper hand in many areas: "It's the woman who picks the man now, not the other way around." One man went so far to say, "If I come home and find a man in my bed, and the woman says to me, 'That man is the one providing the food,' all I can say is, 'Cover him up better,' because he is providing the food." A young woman in Bowerbank states that "men have to work with woman's independence or leave it."

In some communities, female-headed households are perceived to be the best off in the community. Participants in a discussion group of women in Bowerbank express the view that "a man in the house makes you worse off," and "I get more than I need when a man's not in the house."

Some men suffer intense poverty-related stress. Franklin Stockton, a 23-year-old Thompson Pen resident, helps support his mother (a single parent) and his siblings (one of whom is a single mother). He says the stress caused by poverty can make him both violent and ill:

> *I live in a big yard with lots of households. I notice that the older heads [of households] handle the lack of funds better in that they can face the facts without quarreling. The question is, how are we going to make money? Are we going to borrow, or what? When there's no money it tends to cause a lot of stress and then it can get physical. . . . On what I earn, I can't even take care of my own needs consistently. I can't keep up with the bills when my mother or my sister's baby gets sick. I get so stressed out from the responsibility that I get sick, too.*

Greater economic independence appears to have given many poor women a larger measure of protection from domestic abuse. There is general agreement across the communities that domestic violence is on the decline. Most reasons given for this decline relate to joblessness among men and women's increased economic roles. A young woman from Bowerbank says, "Men know that we can survive without them, so they will treat us better; men are no longer 'lord and savior.'" In urban areas, women perceive that their ability to afford separate homes also contributes to the decline in violence.

Another factor mentioned in the decline of violence is women's improved access to legal and other assistance, such as the Women's Bureau, which links women to services such as medical care and agricultural extension and also provides legal aid and contacts with victim support groups.

Even though physical violence against women is widely perceived to be declining or rare, there are references that it occurs in most communities, and quarreling, particularly over money and adultery, is said to be common. In Duckensfield some women in a discussion group explain that it is not uncommon for men to have two women, one at home and one outside, and one woman quips, "The woman at home gets the beating and the woman outside beats the man." A discussion group of young men from Freeman's Hall concurs that infidelity is a common reason for violence: "If the woman is giving him bun [cheating on him] then he would have to beat her."

Conclusion

When Jamaican farms and industries faced increased competition in global markets during the 1990s, many formal work opportunities for poor men and women disappeared. Although jobs are tighter, poor Jamaicans engage in trades, run small shops, higgle (sell) on the streets, work as domestics, drive taxis, take factory and daily farm wage jobs, fish, and migrate in large numbers to other areas of the island and overseas in search of more opportunity. Some resort to work in the drug market and risk arrest both at home and abroad. Women in many communities have shed their traditional role and strive for their own economic security, which increases their work burdens yet affords them greater independence.

Despite slow economic growth, Jamaica has reduced poverty. The strong public commitment to more equitable development in Jamaica is matched by numerous government initiatives aimed at reducing poverty. Many of these programs, however, will need to be reoriented and strengthened if poor people are to receive more meaningful benefits from them. Substantial public spending is devoted to education, for example, but many families still struggle to keep their children in school, particularly at the secondary level. In addition, participants point out problems with the quality of education and report that today's youth are ill prepared to get ahead in the harsh labor market. Many no longer view education as a gateway to greater opportunity.

Poor people want help rooting economic development in their local communities, yet the government's numerous community development initiatives seem to keep passing them by. A beekeeper from Little Bay is frustrated that he lacks sufficient collateral for a local loan program. "What I want," he says, "is the government to support what the poor people are doing." Many farmers express hope that the Rural Agricultural Development Authority will provide a more efficient extension service for advice and support on marketing, distribution, and processing. For remote communities, roads and transport are greatly needed to get produce to markets. In urban areas, most people hope that new factories and service industries will be established, which could provide stable and adequate livelihoods. Many poor people want training and skills development that can help them succeed in the changing economy, although such investments are often out of their reach.

Poor Jamaicans demonstrate tremendous resilience in the face of the recent economic changes, environmental shocks, and other risks in their lives. At times of adversity, poor men and women say social ties provide invaluable support, as do cultural traditions that bring people together and foster a culture of caring, sharing, and helping one another in crises. A woman in Thompson Pen recalls that after Hurricane Gilbert, "I never even had to ask my neighbors for help—they just did." At the same time, older people express concern about where their society is headed. Young people in Jamaica have lived in a global market all their lives and expect to be able to compete in it and benefit from it. Many youths, especially women, say they want the comforts to be had in other parts of the world. Yet, "the more modern we get, the less we care," notes a poor man in Duckensfield. "We're following the ways of foreigners."

TABLE 2 Study Communities in Jamaica

URBAN COMMUNITIES

Bowerbank,
outheast Kingston
Pop. 1,000

In the late 1980s, in what was supposed to be a temporary measure, the government resettled people in a series of long, barrack-style buildings in a section of Kingston. Those relocated were mostly refugees of Hurricane Gilbert or people displaced from McGregor Gully, a squatter settlement plagued with heavy political violence in that period. The number of people living in Bowerbank now grossly exceeds its capacity. Entire families live in one-bedroom board units and use communal bathrooms and kitchens. In the cramped outdoor areas, wet laundry hangs and sewage runoff festers. Employed men generally work as vendors, security guards, construction workers, taxi drivers, and mechanics. Employed women tend to be dressmakers, higglers, domestics, and factory workers.

Cassava Piece,
north Kingston
Pop. 2,500

This community is located near Kingston, encircled by more affluent residential areas and adjacent to a shopping center and golf course. Landlord-tenant relations dominate life in Cassava Piece, although many landowners live in the community and materially are not much better off than their tenants. As many as forty families use a single pit latrine. Seventy percent of the men work as caddies, gardeners, and construction or repair workers. Fifty percent of the women are domestics and 40 percent are higglers. Many residents either work at the golf course or obtain informal jobs through family contacts there.

Railway Lane,
Montego Bay
Pop. 2,000

Known locally as Railway Gardens, this squatter settlement is located near Montego Bay's popular open market. It is surrounded by other squatter communities such as Canterbury, Norwood, and Flankers, but has the worst housing shortages and sanitary problems of any of them. Thirty percent of men and women within the settlement rely on informal vending opportunities associated with the tourist trade, while 40 percent beg or steal. In recent years prostitution and gun and drug crimes (20 percent of inhabitants sell drugs to survive) have become common in this area as exclusion of poor locals from the tourist zones in Montego Bay has increased.

Thompson Pen,
Spanish Town
Pop. 3,990

The community is a section of Spanish Town, Jamaica's second largest city. It lies parallel to the polluted Rio Cobre, which floods often, most recently in 1992. In the 1950s and 1960s, Thompson Pen was a prosperous area dominated by sugar and rice production, but these industries have since declined or folded. Fifty-four percent of households in Thompson Pen are headed by women, and unemployment is 70 percent. Some workers commute to Kingston, and some are employed in the remnants of the sugar industry or in cattle raising or small factories. Among employed women, 50 percent are factory workers, 30 percent are higglers, and 20 percent are domestics. In the case of men, 20 percent work in local factories while the other 80 percent are artisans or laborers.

RURAL COMMUNITIES

Accompong Town,
Maroon state
Pop. 800–1,000

This is one of several Maroon territories located in the mountains of St. Elizabeth. It is adjacent to Cockpit Country, a large wilderness area with unique "eggshell" topography, rain forests, and hundreds of species, including a rare Giant Swallowtail butterfly. The town center boasts a monument to Cudjoe, the eighteenth-century Maroon warrior and leader. By virtue of the Treaty of 1739, Accompong residents have sovereign collective rights of territory and local governance. Ninety percent of the men are farmers and 80 percent of the women are occupied exclusively in household tasks.

Duckensfield,
St. Thomas Parish
Pop. 1,350

.

This community consists of flat, flood-prone terrain in a river basin about thirty kilometers from St. Thomas. Residents consider crocodiles, protected by the government, a threat to their wellbeing. Duckensfield has electricity, telephone and water service, a health clinic, and a post office. Most homes have sanitary facilities, but half of these are pit latrines. Half the households are headed by women and half of workers are unemployed. Most men work for agribusiness (sugar and bananas), and most of the women are higglers. People in Duckensfield report they are worse off since the agricultural estates stopped allowing them to cultivate small plots on their property. Residents include Jamaicans of Asian descent.

Freeman's Hall, outheast Trelawny Pop. 1,255–2,000	The area used to consist of sugar plantations that relied on slave labor. Today people farm tiny hillside plots while the fertile flatlands are still owned by a half-dozen families in holdings of several hundred acres. Landowners do not reside in the area. There is no running water, and many homes do not even have pit latrines. For every two women living in Freeman's Hall there is only one man, but 70 percent of households are headed by men, most of whom are grandfathers. A local high school graduate estimates that only 10 percent of the men and 35 percent of the women are literate. Ninety percent of the men are farmers, and most women are engaged in household tasks.
Little Bay, Westmoreland Pop. 300	This series of fishing hamlets in eastern Negril lies south of a mangrove forest called the Great Morass, which is also Jamaica's second largest watershed. The U.S. Agency for International Development has a coastal resources project in the area to address the problems of reef destruction, dwindling fish stocks, and coastal pollution. The local sugar industry is a major contributor to effluents. Thirty percent of the men fish and 50 percent are in agriculture; 15 percent of the women are in agriculture and 50 percent are domestic workers. Literacy is 30 percent for men and 60 percent for women. Little Bay is without water and sanitation services.
Millbank, Portland Pop. 800	Located in an isolated valley in northeastern Jamaica near the John Crow and Blue Mountain National Park, this is one of the wettest places on earth, and landslides and floods are common. Millbank is fourteen kilometers from the nearest permanent road, and only 20 percent of the homes there have electricity. Millbank has no health clinic or post office, but it does have a traditional Maroon governance structure, which consists of a colonel, major, captain, secretary, treasurer, and chairman, and three ambassadors. There are eight Maroon settlements in the area and two-thirds of Millbank residents are of Maroon descent. The community retains its identity through oral history and defends its autonomous status and collective right to 500 acres of land from a 1739 treaty. Seventy-five percent of both men and women are farmers. Literacy is roughly 10 percent for men and 15 percent for women.

Notes

1. The study team was led by S. Jacqueline Grant and Toby Shillito and also included Hugh Dixon, Paulette Griffiths-Jude, Ivelyn Harris, Glenroy Lattery, Cecilia Logan, Genevieve McDaniel, Oswald Morgan, Steadman Noble, Michelle Peters, Vivienne Scott, and Karen Simms.

2. Study participants in Jamaica held their discussions in patois, an English-based creole language spoken widely in Jamaica. The comments were translated into standard English for the purposes of reporting.

3. *Jamaica Survey of Living Conditions 1999* (Kingston: Planning Institute and Statistical Institute of Jamaica, 2000), 24.

4. Declining poverty very rarely accompanies a declining economy. One hypothesis is that real wages have been increasing as inflation eases. Although more analysis is needed, other observers suspect that the income data may be understating the significant contributions of informal sector activities and overseas remittances, both of which were emphasized by participants during the *Voices* study. See World Bank, "Memorandum of the President of the International Bank for Reconstruction and Development to the Executive Directors on a Country Assistance Strategy of the World Bank Group for Jamaica" (Caribbean Country Management Unit, Latin America and the Caribbean Region, November 2, 2000), 5, box 1.

5. Ibid., 4, 6.

6. *Jamaica Survey of Living Conditions*, 24.

7. Only 14 percent of public spending on secondary education benefits students from the poorest 20 percent of the population. World Bank internal memorandum, March 2000.

8. In 1994 sixteen organizations joined forces to launch the trust in order to protect the conservation area. Its responsibilities include managing the marine park, ecological reserves, and reservation areas; raising funds for local environmental projects; and raising awareness in the community about sustainable development and tourism.

9. Daily pardner is also very common, particularly in urban areas, and is chiefly used by street vendors and higglers, who find it useful as a form of saving for purchasing their stock.

10. The study also reports that politically motivated and drug-related violence poses important threats as well. See Caroline Moser and Jeremy Holland, *Urban Poverty and Violence in Jamaica* (Washington, D.C.: World Bank, 1997), 16.

11. World Bank, *World Development Indicators 2001* (Report 22099, April 2001), 57.

Conclusion

An Empowering Approach to Poverty Reduction

Deepa Narayan and Patti Petesch

The poverty problem is immense, whether seen through the eyes of one poor woman struggling to feed her family, or seen through aggregate poverty statistics: 2.8 billion people living on less than two dollars a day. Much has been learned over the last century about how to reduce poverty, yet it persists. We could assume that no fundamental change is needed in the development approach to poverty reduction—only more money. Or we could pause to reflect upon what should be done differently to respond to the voices of the poor. Indeed, our overarching conclusion is that poverty can be reduced only if we build strategies around what we have learned from poor people, from their realities as they experience them.

In this final chapter we focus on four common themes that emerged from the fourteen case studies in this book, which are representative of the diverse country studies conducted for the Voices of the Poor initiative:

- ▶ the importance of an array of assets and capabilities in poor people's lives;
- ▶ the often adverse impacts of economy-wide shocks and policy changes on poor people and their communities;
- ▶ the culture of inequality and exclusion in mediating institutions; and
- ▶ widespread gender inequity and vulnerability of children.

Drawing on these findings, we conclude by urging an empowering approach to development that views poor people as resources, as partners in poverty reduction.

Poor People's Assets and Capabilities

Development ultimately should increase people's freedom to live the lives they value. Poor people's options are sharply constrained by a dearth of assets and capabilities. In many countries, moreover, poor people feel that inequality in the distribution of assets is increasing, that the gap between rich and poor is widening. In Bosnia, Bulgaria, the Kyrgyz Republic, and the Russian Federation, poor people reported that the middle class is disappearing. In Mbwadzulu, Malawi, a man said, "Only God knows the future, but I think the poor will continue to get poorer while the rich will continue to get richer. Because they have money they will continue doing business. The poor will keep facing problems."

Poor people described several dimensions of deprivation and inequality and a correspondingly wide range of assets and capabilities they need to increase their freedom of choice and improve their lives. Ten assets and capabilities that emerged as important in poor people's daily experiences are categorized and described in Table 1, and they are discussed individually in the sections that follow. The need for some of these assets and capabilities, such as material goods and education, is obvious, while others are frequently overlooked.

Material Assets

> *In order to feed two children, I sold all the valuable things I had in the house. . . . Now we are at the bottom of society. What is my future and that of my children? What prospects do we have? Sometimes I ask myself why I live at all.*
> —A war widow in Tisca, Bosnia and Herzegovina

Without the protection of material assets, the slide into poverty is quick. In every country poor people noted the central role of material assets in preventing them from falling to the "bottom of society." In country after country, poor people said that once they lose their property—through natural disasters as in Bangladesh, through war as in Bosnia and Herzegovina, through paying dowry as in India, or through selling off property to pay debts and feed families in all parts of the world—they give up

Table 1 Assets and Capabilities of Poor People

Asset or capability	*Examples mentioned by poor people*
Material assets	Employment; ownership of productive assets; land; house; boat; savings; jewelry
Bodily health	Freedom from hunger and disease; strong, healthy-looking bodies
Bodily integrity[1]	Freedom from violence and abuse; sexual and reproductive choice; freedom of physical movement
Emotional integrity	Freedom from fear and anxiety; love
Respect and dignity	Self-respect; self-confidence; dignity
Social belonging	Belonging to a collective; honor, respect, and trust within and across social groups
Cultural identity	Living in accordance with one's values; participation in rituals that give meaning; sense of cultural continuity
Imagination, information, and education	Inventiveness; informed and educated decision making; literacy; entrepreneurship; problem solving capacity; expressive arts
Organizational capacity	Ability to organize and mobilize; participation in representative organizations
Political representation and accountability	Ability to influence those in power; accountability of those in power

hope of ever climbing out of poverty. Temirbek, a man from Tash-Bulak, Kyrgyz Republic, who sold off his sheep one by one until there were none left, cried, "One can patch torn clothes, but how can one patch an empty stomach?"

Lack of clear property rights, and in rural areas, declining access to common property resources compound poor people's insecurity and keep them trapped in low-paying formal jobs or on the lower rungs of the informal economy. People with few assets have extremely limited bargaining power to negotiate a fair deal for jobs, wages, or other contractual arrangements. In order to lease a boat in Ampenan Utara, Indonesia, poor fishermen must promise half their catch to rich boat owners and cover their own operating expenses as well. The fishermen noted, "This is a very unfair arrangement because up to nine fishermen have to share one boat. The catch after a four-day trip might be worth 1 million rupiahs. After deducting operating costs and fuel, each man would get only 20,000 rupiahs [approximately US$3]."

Some people who managed to climb out of poverty named migration and entrepreneurial activities as key livelihood strategies. Yet for those with few assets, the type of entrepreneurship within reach, such as petty vending, does not necessarily increase wellbeing. A poor man in Isla Trinitaria, Ecuador, explained, "Selling sewing needles is not a business. A business is a pharmacy or a pool hall, something you can live off."

Bodily Health

You have to pay the dentist up front, otherwise they just stuff your tooth with sand and it all falls out.
                                    —A discussion group participant in Russia

The relationship between income and health emerged in every country.[2] Every community in Malawi reported that hunger is its most critical problem. Poor agricultural workers in Bangladesh described a vicious cycle in which inadequate food leads to weakness and reduced energy to work, which in turn leads to lower income and less food for the household, which leads to worsening weakness and illness.

For poor women in Fadli Pur, Bangladesh, wellbeing requires a "physically fit husband, and a son for every mother." In La Matanza, Argentina, a group of men assessing their chances of getting work said that in addition to needing an education, "you can't have any kind of health problem or have had an operation. . . . For those over 40, no one will hire us. You can look and look, but you'll never find a job." Lacking property and bargaining power, poor people in all the communities visited emphasized the importance of their only asset—their bodies—and their ability to do hard labor even on empty stomachs.

Living in unsanitary, dangerous, crowded, and poorly serviced urban areas increases poor people's exposures to health risks. When poor men and women get sick, their illness may lead to destitution or death. Yet they have no way to safeguard the good health they need to work and survive. Health services are nonexistent or substandard, and people typically must pay for transport, consultations, medicine, and bribes to receive even so-called "free services."

Bodily Integrity

"Here there is battering all over the place. Women hit men, men hit women, and both hit children,"
                                    —A 16-year old girl in Novo Horizonte, Brazil

Bodily integrity—freedom from physical violation and freedom of movement—is a fundamental human right. But poor people, particularly women, live in fear of bodily harm and often feel helpless to protect themselves and their daughters from abuse by men inside and outside the home. Young women in Bangladesh said they cannot move about freely because they encounter teasing, harassment, and abuse, and even fear having acid thrown in their faces. In Ghana women talked about being forced into sex within marriage and unwanted pregnancies, and they fear being infected with HIV/AIDS by husbands who refuse to use condoms.

Many poor neighborhoods in urban communities are especially unsafe, with high levels of crime, drugs, gang warfare, muggings, and murders. Young men are particularly susceptible to abuse by police and are the most likely to be assaulted, caught in crossfire, or thrown in jail. Discussion groups in Morro da Conceição, Brazil, told researchers, "When we go out we don't know if we'll come back alive." A woman in La Matanza, Argentina, said, "It isn't the robberies that scare me so much, it's the rapes. I have teenage daughters and I don't sleep at night because we live in a very unsafe neighborhood."

Emotional Integrity

I don't know when I will see the light of happiness. I have to give three daughters in marriage but I do not have any assets to do so. I cannot give them clothes. I don't know how to secure respect for them in society.

—A poor man, Khaliajuri, Bangladesh

Love and freedom from constant fear and anxiety are essential for well-being. Poor women and men, on the brink of disaster, suffer the anxiety that naturally accompanies the multiple threats they face from war, physical danger, hunger, unemployment, delayed pensions, and debt. Poor people also worry about the loss of family and friends and about not being able to care for their families, help their neighbors, or participate in cultural rituals.

Although most hold on to some hope, many poor people verge on hopelessness, particularly in Eastern Europe and Central Asia and in urban areas in Latin America. Some turn to alcohol and drug abuse, and some commit suicide. A young man in La Matanza, Argentina, remarked, "Nowadays you are unemployed for years. The only way out is when you die."

In Bosnia the scars of war run deep. An older woman in Tombak, Bosnia, said, "I am burned out because of fears and worries for my family in the war. I had to send a husband and two sons to the front lines and wait for them to return—or not. . . . You can never recover from spiritual impoverishment." An older man in Glogova, Bosnia, said, "I can hardly breathe; nerves are suffocating me. The doctor told me that my life hangs from a thread and that I am not allowed to get stressed—but how?" Having lost everything, including her house, an internally displaced woman in Vares, Bosnia, cried, "Our souls, our psyches, are dead."

Respect and Dignity

When they give you a box of groceries, they're also taming your dignity.

—A young man, Dock Sud, Argentina

Over and over again, poor people asserted that handouts, humiliation, and shaming hurt even when they are in tatters and starving with nowhere to go. Poor men and women know that if they stop believing in themselves, their lives will become even more unbearable. A 52-year-old Ghanaian woman who sells yams and salt in Asukawkaw said, "A woman can move out of poverty by having faith in herself and the determination to make do with the little she has."

Self-respect and self-confidence are closely tied to the ability to earn a living and belong to society. Poor men who have lost their capacity to take care of their families said they have lost self-respect and are ashamed to face their neighbors, wives, and hungry children. In Bulgaria people often described the alienation and demoralization they feel in the face of massive unemployment. Students in Dimitrovgrad, Bulgaria, described people without jobs as "lifeless faces without self-esteem." The shame that arises from poverty and having to wear secondhand clothes often keeps children from attending school.

Women's sense of self-respect and dignity is frequently threatened by physical violence. In one community in Brazil where physical abuse is declining as a result of consciousness raising, women in a discussion group said, "Women are asserting themselves, valuing themselves, and respecting themselves. They also demand respect. They used to be very passive and forgot about themselves."

Social Belonging

Living in poverty isn't pretty, but to be a poor person is nice because we help one another.
—A discussion group of men in Isla Talavera, Argentina

Poor people, like all people, experience a deep longing to belong, to care and be cared for, to be honored, and to experience the bonds of solidarity. A sense of belonging not only affirms one's humanity but also creates bonds of trust and reciprocity, the give and take that is part of being human. In Jamaica poor people said that social ties provide invaluable support in times of adversity. A woman in Thompson Pen recalled that after Hurricane Gilbert, "I never even had to ask my neighbors for help—they just did." Proverbs in the Kyrgyz Republic capture the importance of social bonds: "It is better to have a hundred friends than a hundred rubles"; "Don't look for a good house, look for a good neighbor." In India both men's and women's groups said that influence, honor, and respect in society are important indicators of wellbeing. Women in Netarhat described "people with voice in the community" as happy. In Konada those "whose word has no importance" were considered to be the poorest of the poor.

But economic deprivation has placed these social ties and mutual obligations under great stress. Many poor people in Russia said that their circle of support has shrunk to the family. In Bulgaria and the Kyrgyz Republic, poor people spoke about the importance of being able to offer a cookie to a guest or to meet friends at a coffee shop, and the increased social isolation and depression that results when they cannot afford to do so.

There are important gender differences in social belonging, and these are cast in sharp relief when a man abandons his wife or dies. In many countries, when a husband dies, his widow is thrown out of the home by the husband's family. In some places, as in Bangladesh, poor women sometimes find new strength to start over by joining women's groups.

Cultural Identity

Respect to the mosque is respect to the tradition, you know, when you feel your identity, have that sense of belonging to the Muslim world. . . . Women don't enter the mosque, and yet the mosque is a sacred place for me.
—A woman from Kok Yangak, Kyrgyz Republic

Social, cultural, and religious rituals and practices affirm cultural identities. People have multiple cultural identities as mothers, workers, members of particular class, ethnic, and religious groups of particular countries. Cultural identities are not static, and everywhere there is evidence of change. Poor people talked about the importance of gifts, gestures of hospitality, entertainment, religious rituals, and celebrations that affirm that they are part of society, despite the pain of poverty.

In India rituals and worship are a part of daily life. Rituals involving sacred trees, for example, are so important that in some communities they emerged very high on the list of institutions important in poor people's lives. In Indonesia people talked about the role of traditional rituals and ceremonies in their lives. Jamaicans in rural areas described several examples of collective ritual. In Cassava Piece the extension of men's obligations beyond blood ties was expressed as the obligation to "take care of the youth, even when they're not your own." In Freeman's Hall men take turns digging furrows in each other's fields, a practice referred to as "a day for a day," and at night they play dominoes. When someone dies in Freeman's Hall, people do "nine nights up," a wake in which the entire community visits the family of the dead person, sings hymns, and shares food and liquor.

In Latin America and Africa, poor people often talked about the importance of churches and mosques in affirming their faith and providing solace.

Cultural practices, however, can also be exclusionary. In Nigeria the poorest of the poor are excluded from social events and ceremonies. In India women are excluded from many community and religious rituals conducted by men. In Ughoton, Nigeria, it is taboo for women to enter the Court Hall because it is regarded a sacred place. Women may sit outside, where they can only listen while important decisions are made. In Adaboya, Ghana, the churches are perceived to sow seeds of disunity by engaging in competition between denominations.

Cultures are dynamic and changing. But rapid change can leave people disoriented and searching for meaning. Poor people in some indigenous communities spoke about the erosion of traditional practices, which leaves people feeling adrift. A group of women in Caguanapamba, Ecuador, said, "The media creates new needs and we forget our ways." Lost traditions are not adequately replaced by national symbols. In both Caguanapamba and El Juncal, Ecuador, indigenous men and women said, "When they play the national anthem, it means nothing to us." Indigenous groups also remarked on negative changes in their community ways: "There was no corruption before. We are also learning the bad embezzlement practices of the state."

Imagination, Information, and Education

I became an expert on the Giant Swallowtail butterfly and
linked up with Dr. Beckford Grant from the University of West
Indies, and I learned a lot from him.
> —A self-educated man in Millbank, Jamaica

Women and men living in poverty exercise imagination, creativity, and inventiveness, and are the repositories of local knowledge. Poor people all over the world weave, sew, embroider, create art and crafts, do metalwork, construct buildings, create household artifacts, fish, harvest grain and vegetables, gather forest products, and raise livestock. They also establish institutions, build schools for their children, and organize security patrols to protect themselves. Some of these ideas are inspired by the need to do a lot with little, to solve their own problems as others pass them by. Some ideas are marketed, others bring simply the joy of creation and perhaps honor and recognition from others. Oral traditions remain strong, particularly in rural areas, and people with these skills are valued.

Poor men and women talked about the need for information and about the importance of education. An indigenous man in Ecuador said that "men and women without education cannot get good jobs" and are "easy targets" for fraud. In Isla Talavera, Argentina, sewing schools have transformed many poor women's lives. A 58-year-old woman said, "Five years ago I started coming to school. It changed my life. I used to be holed up in my house. Now I have work and I have friends. They took away all my shame here. There is great camaraderie."

Organizational Capacity

[The Farmers Union Cooperative was created] by us, ourselves.
Through it we manage credits that come from external sources,
we distribute them to people who need them and to our mem-
bers. . . . We receive information from other institutions and
we solve problems. . . . The cooperative is like the central
commission.
> —A group of men, Los Juríes, Argentina

Finding themselves excluded from many formal institutions of the state, society, and markets, many poor people consolidate their resources to undertake collective action. Sometimes these organizations grow, achieve formal recognition, and form coalitions with other organizations in powerful movements to claim rights and justice.

In Latin America, neighborhood and community organizations have emerged after decades of organizing and mobilizing. Some women in Argentina have started soup kitchens to end hunger in their neighborhoods, a movement that eventually attracted municipal government as well private sector support. In one neighborhood in Moreno, women who run a local soup kitchen built a community center under the tutelage of an elderly bricklayer. The women serve meals in the building, which is also used for community events, birthdays, wakes, and other milestones. A strong tradition of local organizing is present in Ecuador, as well. In one village, Voluntad de Dios, people built their own pharmacy and collectively procured a refrigerator and radio.

In India many local organizations are caste-based. In recent years, a large number of interest-based and self-help groups have emerged in Andhra Pradesh. In Bangladesh NGOs have been particularly effective in organizing women's credit groups. And in Indonesia, local initiatives that were suppressed by the imposition of government-created organizations have recently begun to reemerge.

Women's support of other women has been a potent force in enabling some to break out of cycles of domestic violence and abuse. In Battala, Bangladesh, training, literacy, and widening social networks have helped women learn their rights and increased their confidence to resist abuse. Women said they join forces and protect one another if any woman in the community is beaten by her husband.

Political Representation and Accountability

There has never been anyone who represented us in any of the different governments.

—A woman, Thompson Pen, Jamaica

All people hope to live in societies where they are protected from criminals and violence, represented and served by accountable public officials, and treated fairly by employers and the state. For poor people, these ideals are seldom realized. Even in countries with formal democracies, poor people feel neglected, abused, and exploited by state officials.

Cynicism and anger over this abandonment are evident everywhere but are especially prominent in countries of the former Soviet Union, where people once experienced effective delivery of basic services and now face both high state capture and widespread corruption.

In country after country, poor people rated politicians and police as among the worst institutions. Attention from politicians is viewed as seasonal. "When he wanted our vote, we saw him," said a resident of Bowerbank, Jamaica, "but once he got our vote, we never saw him again." Politicians are said to make enough promises "to fill a large dam." Poor Jamaicans identify political deception, or "politricks," as a major cause of poverty.

In dealing with local governments, with the exception of some well-organized communities in Brazil, poor people feel they have very little access and no bargaining power to get pressing community needs addressed or to prevent harm from coming to their communities.

Poor people regard the police as agents of oppression, not protection. Over and over again poor people said that justice and police protection are only for rich businesses, rich people, and those with connections. In Dock Sud, Argentina, a group of men and women said,

> *Far from defending us, the police mistreat us; they come in and rough up teenagers and don't do anything to the real criminals. . . . The gangs pay them off. . . . They'll round up a bunch of people and beat them up, but not the thieves. . . . The police are just another gang.*

Impact of Economic Turmoil and Policy Changes

Poor people from several countries expressed deep concern over the economic upheavals and policy changes that are buffeting their lives. This study, however, was not designed to disentangle and evaluate the effects of specific economic policies or trends on the lives of poor people. Instead, we present the analyses of those who are currently poor, who recount the negative impact that certain economic policies and market changes have had on them and on their households and communities. Depending on the country, poor people mentioned privatization, factory closures, the opening of domestic markets, currency devaluation, inflation, reductions in social services, and other related changes as having depleted their assets and increased their insecurity. Table 2 summarizes the most common economic policy and market shifts mentioned by study participants.

Poor people adopt a wide range of coping strategies that help in the short term but lead to increased vulnerability and a depleted asset base.[3] Mothers serve fewer meals, women accept demeaning and very low paid work, men migrate, children are withdrawn from school, health care is deferred, housing crumbles, and old people stay in bed to conserve energy. When crises are prolonged, people deplete their savings, sell their property, and assume more and more debt. People also said they lose sleep, become less social, and sometimes turn to activities outside the law.

Economy-wide Stresses, Deteriorating Livelihoods and Incomes

Several countries included in the study went through difficult economic times for some or much of the 1990s. With factory and farm closures, many participants from these countries faced the loss of "regular" or "normal" jobs. In addition, many poor people who work in the informal sector reported that their livelihoods have been greatly harmed by market downturns and policy shifts. Yet, in all the countries, some poor people in selected communities identified rising opportunities for themselves. Participants stressed that entrepreneurship in particular provides an important path for some out of poverty, but it is mostly the better-off groups that can break into new ventures.

In the wake of the transition to market economies in the four countries visited in Eastern Europe and Central Asia, people reported steep drops in living standards. Especially hard hit were the "one-company towns" and villages that once revolved around large state farms. Participants from across the region repeatedly remarked that they feel unprepared for work in a market economy, which they find fraught with uncertainty. Temirbek, a poor farmer from Tash-Bulak, Kyrgyz Republic, voiced the sentiments of many participants from the region when he said,

> *When collective farms were disbanded, we thought everything would be fine. We could be masters of our own land and would enjoy good profits and become rich. It turned out to be the other way round. We were used to having problems solved for us. When we faced problems, we realized that we were*

not prepared for the new way of life. Formerly, jobs, salaries, and prices were stable. Everything was available in the stores. When the so-called "market" economy came down, it ruined everything old. This has resulted in poverty.

In all countries visited in this region, poor people connected extensive unemployment and underemployment to the dismantling of the state before functioning markets were in place. Those lucky enough to still have jobs said they receive wages late or in-kind, if at all, and unions have lost their clout. Many have resorted to petty trade and informal wage jobs in agriculture or construction, but even these are precarious and disappear in the long winter months. Most people reported that it is simply too risky to start a business in the current environment; they cited such factors as the unpredictability of markets, lack of start-up money or collateral for credit, difficulties obtaining inputs, and crumbling transport.

Table 2 Adverse Economic Changes and Their Impacts on Livelihoods, Consumption, and Public Services, by Country

Economic effects of market and policy changes	*Country where mentioned*
Deteriorating livelihoods and income	
Increased unemployment; decline in availability of "regular" or "normal" work	Ghana, Malawi, Nigeria, Indonesia, India, Bosnia, Bulgaria, Russia, Kyrgyz, Argentina, Brazil, Ecuador, Jamaica
Closure of private and public enterprises	Ghana, Nigeria, Malawi, Indonesia, Bosnia, Bulgaria, Kyrgyz, Russia, Argentina, Brazil, Ecuador, Jamaica
Liberalization of the agriculture sector and/or privatization of farm cooperatives	Malawi, Jamaica, Kyrgyz, Bulgaria, Russia
Increased reliance on the informal economy	Ghana, Nigeria, Indonesia, Bosnia, Bulgaria, Russia, Kyrgyz, Argentina, Brazil, Ecuador, Jamaica
Rising prices	
Inflation; rising prices for basic goods	Ecuador, Bosnia, Bulgaria, Indonesia, Kyrgyz, Malawi, Nigeria, Russia
Crumbling public services	
New or increased fees for health care	Bosnia, Bulgaria, Kyrgyz, Russia
Erosion or delays of pension benefits	Bosnia, Bulgaria, Kyrgyz, Russia

In all four countries of Latin America and the Caribbean, people described the economic and social devastation of their communities in the wake of macroeconomic crises and policy reforms. They felt directly harmed by numerous plant closures, the shift to a service economy, and the rise of the informal sector. According to a poor woman in Florencio Varela, Argentina, "The job shortage is a neighborhood problem, but it's also a problem for the entire country. There isn't enough work. Men can only get temporary jobs as laborers and sometimes not even that."

The Indonesian case study explores the widespread insecurity triggered by the 1997 financial crisis. The most damaging effects were felt in communities in Java's urban centers and in rural areas with strong urban ties, although even some remote communities in the outer islands were touched. Massive layoffs in the formal sector and the collapse of credit sources sent people scrambling into the informal sector to survive. Petty trade on the streets became much more precarious as the numbers of sellers rose but market demand dropped. Rural participants in Java described being deeply disadvantaged by the tough competition from migrant workers for the already scarce wage labor jobs on area farms and plantations. Home-based workers, such as artisans making leather bags, purses, and shoes in Galih Pakuwon, went bankrupt after the prices of their raw materials increased, credit became tighter, and market demand dropped. Those dependant on subsistence farming were less affected.

Market liberalization can have adverse effects on poor agricultural producers. In Malawi policies to promote trade and open the agricultural sector led to sharp increases in the price of fertilizer, which is largely imported. Most poor households survive by cultivating small plots of maize, and the policies increased their hardship in nearly every community visited. "The main problems we are facing now are diseases and hunger. Hunger is brought on by the increase in the price of fertilizer. We work as hard as possible, but we don't harvest much due to inadequate fertilizer," explained a woman in Chitambi, Malawi. Despite rising hunger, some participants acknowledged benefits from economic reforms and the recent transition to a more open political system, which has brought increased freedom to engage in business or grow cash crops, higher prices for agricultural products, and free primary schooling.

Study participants in other countries also reported that some economic changes have had favorable effects. India and Bangladesh experienced steady economic growth in the 1990s, and people in selected communities described new agricultural and enterprise development. In

Jaggaram, India, there is a thriving new cashew trade, but poor people without land in the area said they have been unable to participate. Also, wages have not improved. For people living near the Zavar export processing zone in rural Dhamrai, Bangladesh, daily wages for agricultural as well as factory work were reported to be far higher than in other areas of the country. Yet, workers there said that there is little job security, and they often must combine several income-earning activities to support their families. Poor Bangladeshis living in slums of Dhaka and Chittagong likewise reported better job opportunities, although they said the steady flow of migrants greatly reduces job security and keeps wages very low.

Participants from most countries often qualified their reports of new economic openings by mentioning that they don't have the wherewithal to take advantage of the changes. They said their leading obstacles to opportunity include barriers to financial services, lack of special connections, difficulties accessing markets (due to inadequate transport, long distances, weather, and such), and lack of skills. For instance, a poor Jamaican farmer from Millbank explained,

> One of the reasons we can't sell our produce locally is because foreign produce floods the market with too much of the same type of stuff. Because of the bad road, no outside buyers come here. I borrow money and plant the ground and can't sell because of this.

Many poor people do break out of poverty, of course. Researchers specifically sought out and conducted interviews with men and women in every community who had managed to escape poverty. As reported in *Crying Out for Change*, self-employment or entrepreneurship is the most frequent path out of poverty mentioned by these participants.[4]

Rising Prices

In all regions, poor people expressed concerns about the cost of food and frequently described spikes in food prices due to specific policy crises. They said they cope by cutting back on the number of meals and forgoing costlier, often more nutritious items, such as meat or fish. In many cases, women, children, and the elderly eat little so the household's main breadwinners have enough energy to work.

In Russia participants frequently mentioned August 17, 1998, when a currency devaluation set off an "uncontrollable surge in prices." In urban and rural communities in Bulgaria, Kyrgyz, and Russia, poor people described living off the food they grow and preserve themselves because store-bought goods have become unaffordable. In Ecuador people reported that many basic goods have become unaffordable in the wake of El Niño and financial crises that followed. Ecuadorian participants also noted that the government's approval of higher fuel and electricity prices has pushed up prices of other goods.

Neneng, a mother in Indonesia, said that since the economic crisis she serves one meal a day instead of three. Similarly, an elderly man from Pegambiran, Indonesia, said that he could no longer eat sufficiently when rice jumped from Rp. 500 per kilogram to Rp. 2,500 in the wake of the economic crisis. In Bangladesh slum dwellers said food prices rise during large strikes against the government. Higher food costs were also reported in Malawi and Nigeria.

In all regions, street vendors and shop owners said their livelihoods are hampered by poor people's lack of purchasing power. In Ghana people expressed fewer concerns about inflation but simply said no one has any money. "Now, customers don't buy my yams," said a woman from Babatokuma, Ghana, "not because people are no longer hungry or because they don't eat yams anymore, but because they don't have the money."

Crumbling Public Services

Poor men and women in the four European and Central Asian countries described the wrenching effects created by the elimination of free medical services. Participants related frightening experiences of going without needed medical services and medications and of receiving surgery without anesthesia.

Elderly participants from the region also reported extensive suffering as they struggle to cope on their meager pensions, which do not cover rent, heating, or medical expenses. A pensioner in Sofia, Bulgaria, stated that there has been "a true genocide of pensioners." "If you don't grow something, you're dead," said a pensioner from Kalofer, Bulgaria. In Kyrgyz elderly participants reported delayed or erratic pension payments, and benefits paid in the form of vegetable oil instead of cash. Moreover, many elderly participants said that they share their meager pensions with their unemployed adult children.

The Culture of Mediating Institutions: State, Market, and Civic

Policies clearly matter. The impact of policies on poor people depends greatly on how these policies are implemented by society's institutions. Poor people engage daily with a range of state, market, and civic institutions. While each is governed by explicit formal rules and regulations often reinforced by the legal system, these formal rules may be displaced by informal rules and expectations that support an institutional culture of exclusion and inequality.

Poor people's relationships with institutions reflect their powerlessness in society. They often experience institutions as corrupt, lawless, and discriminatory, and as functioning on the basis of clientelism and patronage. Not surprisingly, poor people have little trust in and low expectations of the institutions that are supposed to help them. There is little evidence that institutions treat poor women and men as citizens with rights, including the right to be treated with respect and dignity.

Corruption

There is enough money to go around the country and make life worth living, but corrupt practices would not allow us to share in the national wealth.
　　　　—Discussion group, Umuoba Road–Aba Waterside, Nigeria

Poor people often described the state as self-serving. Corruption was seen to be pervasive at both national and local levels. In Nurali Pur, Bangladesh, people said local officials are corrupt, unaccountable for their "dishonest acts," and show respect only to the rich. In Magadan, Russia, a discussion group said, "Our administration consists of thieves who are stealing whatever they can," and, "The ruling elite has destroyed the whole state." Poor people in Caguanapamba and El Juncal, Ecuador, concluded, "A lot of money intended for the people comes from abroad, but instead of using it to make improvements, [government officials] steal everything." In Bosnia and Herzegovina people spoke bitterly about being impoverished by war while many others, including politicians, became rich as a result of the war. A participant in Glogova said, "Before the war it was absurd that a politician or functionary owned a gas station, restaurant, casino, building material yard or such. Now this is completely normal."

Innumerable examples of administrative corruption permeate all the country studies and indict many government agencies that deliver basic services and government support to poor people.

Clientelism and Patronage

There is no state; there are only individuals who are using the chance to get rich in the name of the state.
—A young man, Capljina, Bosnia and Herzegovina

A participant in Kalaidzhi, Bulgaria, put it simply: "You have to be on good terms with those in power, otherwise you are lost." The state has become a private dispenser of favors. All over the world poor people talked about the importance of having connections and having patrons in order to access government services. Elderly people in At Bashi, Kyrgyz Republic, reported, "If you have no relatives among high government officials, people treat you as second-rate." In Zenica, Bosnia, participants said, "Everything here is done through contacts." They said services are available "only if you have someone of your own . . . a cousin, uncle, close friend . . . and money plays a big part."

Poor people in rural Indonesia fear speaking out because they know that if they displease village authorities, they have nowhere to turn, although there is some indication that this is changing. In almost every country, poor vendors mentioned the necessity of giving bribes and other offerings to police and hoodlums to protect themselves from harassment and eviction. Poor people concluded that only those with high social status, official positions, or wealth have any influence.

Lawlessness, Crime, and Conflict

Now everyone steals everything. In the past, government officials who stole or embezzled public property were prosecuted and imprisoned. Now they only indict petty criminals, but those who steal millions escape with impunity.
—A man in Tash-Bulak, Kyrgyz Republic

Despite formal rules meant to protect them, poor people have extensive experience with the illegal behavior of agents of the state and private sector. State capture by the ruling elite is mentioned particularly in the former Soviet Union countries. A Roma man in Razgrad, Bulgaria, noted,

"There is no mercy for you if you have stolen a chicken. There is no prison for you if you have stolen a million."

Poor people feel the most exposed to crime and lawlessness. The police in many communities are viewed as agents of repression and extortion rather than as agents that uphold the laws of the country. In Argentina poor people said, "When we go into the police station to make a report . . . the police don't let us file a complaint." In El'mash, Russia, people stated, "It is the kind of police that you have no hope of ever reaching; the police are for those at the top"; and in the slum of Battala, Bangladesh, they said, "The police arrest the innocent; without bribes nothing happens."

Discriminatory Behavior

A woman always gets 50 percent less than a man on the excuse that a woman cannot work as hard as a man.
—A poor woman in Nurali Pur, Bangladesh

Despite official rules that make discrimination illegal, behavior by state, market, and civic institutions reflects prejudice against poor people, women, and excluded social groups. Discrimination is not only demoralizing but robs poor people of opportunities and access to services and resources that are rightfully theirs. Excluded social groups include the Roma in Bulgaria, the low castes and untouchables in India, "the hated poor" in Bangladesh, indigenous and Afro-American groups in Latin America, and slum dwellers everywhere.

In many communities, for example in Indonesia, women are not included in any decision making. A man in Renggarasi, Indonesia, noted, "When women are involved in the meeting, they are only given the task of preparing and serving refreshments."

Poor people reported that government service providers invariably reach the rich over the bodies of the poor. In India the rich get to the front of the line for services even when poor people have been waiting for hours. In several places people said that service providers first look at their face, name, or address and then decide whether they deserve any attention.

Poor people also experience discriminatory behavior from members of society at large. In Novo Horizonte, Brazil, a group of young men said, "The bus driver, just because he has a job, treats us as if we aren't human." In Ecuador both indigenous groups and Afro-Ecuadorian groups experience racial discrimination. Discrimination against blacks is so widespread that it is captured in a common saying: "When you see a black man running, you are looking at a thief."

Alienation and Hopelessness

For eight years now my ties have hung on the door; for eight years I have not gone to work. This is killing me. I feel useless to myself and my family.
—A displaced man in Tombak, Bosnia and Herzegovina

Poor women and men experience deep feelings of alienation and hopelessness in their encounters with state and private sector institutions. They have low expectations and little hope that things will change with new governments.

Old and young alike feel abandoned by their governments. In Teshie, Ghana, a man said, "What have we done? When development starts at Accra, it ends at La. When it starts at Tema, it ends at Nungua. We are always left stuck in between." In Voluntad de Dios, Ecuador, poor people said, "We suffer in the countryside because we never receive any help from whatever government is in power." In Ozerny, Russia, a participant remarked, "Sometimes you simply don't feel like living. You think, why don't they just send an armored personnel carrier down and have us all shot dead here. Sometimes you don't know what day it is; it doesn't matter."

Households under Stress

Women have more responsibilities because they have dual functions, managing the household and also generating income. Besides, women must obey their husbands as well.
—A poor woman from the remote Indonesian island
of Nusa Tenggara Timur

From the intimate, emotion-filled, often tense conversations with poor women and men about household trends, two patterns emerged. First, despite some changes, gender inequity within households and in society remains deeply ingrained and results in women's heightened insecurity. Second, when poor households are in stress, children are extremely vulnerable.

The Persistent Insecurity of Women

He has total control . . .
>   —A poor woman, Borborema, Brazil

According to men and women across the study communities, inequities in gender relations remain entrenched:

- Women are working outside the home in much larger numbers, but they often have fewer livelihood opportunities and earn less than men for the same work.
- Women shoulder the vast majority of household and child-care responsibilities in addition to their economic roles.
- Women must often cover household and education expenses with their earnings.
- Women rarely own property in their own names, and what little they do own can be taken from them.
- Domestic abuse against women is prevalent.
- Women face destitution and social ostracism in the event of separation, divorce, or their husband's death.
- Women endure extreme insecurity in areas where dowry and polygamy are practiced.

The changing economy and increased breadwinner responsibilities for women, poor people said, have created enormous strains on households. With men out of work or underemployed, the financial contributions of women are critical to household survival. Yet both men and women reported that men feel inadequate and powerless in the wake of market changes and greater unemployment. Underemployed men or those without jobs were widely said to be resorting to antisocial and "irresponsible" behaviors. Participants from all regions pointed out that it is humiliating for men to accept work that is extremely low paid and demeaning, to count on a wife's earnings, and to do household chores. "Being out of work makes you anxious and puts you in a very bad way. It is the worst thing that can happen to you," said a man from Florencio Varela, Argentina.

Poor people frequently identified economic stress, women's changing roles, and the strains these place on gender relations as important causes of domestic violence against women. In Hyderabad, India, a woman offered this rationale: "The husband is not ready to accept the increasing awareness, exposure, and participation of the wife in spheres outside the household, and as a result beats the wife to demonstrate his supremacy." Similarly, a community leader and nurse's aid in Nova Califórnia, Brazil, explained, "The main consequence of poverty is violence, particularly in the home. If a man is out of work, he doesn't help around the house, but he does get in the way more than ever. He's drinking and squabbling, blaming things on his wife."

Although levels of physical violence against women were reported to be declining in some communities in countries as different as Ecuador, India, Indonesia, Jamaica, and Nigeria, women widely cautioned and men readily admitted that physical violence is still very common. In the nine other countries visited, trends reported in physical violence against women are not encouraging. Women in Brazil, for instance, acknowledged the work of churches, the police, community groups, and neighbors to increase awareness and provide shelter for women who are beaten in their homes, but they said rising unemployment and drug abuse among men overwhelm these efforts. In most other countries, kin and neighbors often turn a blind eye, and help from the authorities was reported to be very difficult to obtain. Typically, police and prosecutors are loath to interfere in "family affairs." An older woman in Dimitrovgrad, Bulgaria, explained, "As you can see, women are harassed in all sorts of ways; wife-battering is quite common, too. . . . There's no one to advise them, no one to turn to if they're abused. The police won't even show up if you report a husband beating his wife."

Some women confront these circumstances by deciding to live alone and raise their children singlehandedly, despite the fact that it leaves them open to ridicule, public shame, and harassment by men on the street. The chapters on Argentina, Brazil, Jamaica, Russia, and Bulgaria mention women who have consciously chosen to live independently from men. A discussion group of women in Jamaica advised, "Have your own shelter and finances so you don't have to stay in an abusive relationship."

Women also risk profound insecurity should they lose their partner. There are now formal laws in all countries that, to varying degrees, legally safeguard women's interests when their husbands die or abandon them. In practice, however, there are many pressures on women to disregard their rights and follow customary practices, which do not recognize women's claims on family property or to child support. People in several countries reported that in-laws confiscate the property of widows. In Kyrgyz Republic, for instance, women said that making any legal claims is considered shameful because it violates local customs that give full property rights to men and their families. In Nigeria as well as parts of Ghana and Malawi, widows often lose their husbands' property to in-laws in accordance with traditional family rules, despite national laws that are supposed to protect women upon a husband's death. In Bulgaria, where divorce is reported to have surged in the past decade, a participant from Dmitrovgrad said, "There's no law to oblige men to pay [child] support money, and it's practically impossible to sue them for more money. It's up to you to track him down—meanwhile, he's changed his residence five times."

The vulnerability of poor women to being overworked, poorly paid, abused, and stripped of their property merely deepens their powerlessness and voicelessness in the family. Along with the many other disadvantages of living in poverty, these processes undermine a household's ability to safeguard all its members and give everyone, particularly children, a chance for a better life.

"Let the Children Be All Right"

There are small children in the street. They have homes but their parents are working and they're out in the street all day without supervision, except for maybe a sibling who is only a year or two older. Some older street children are fending for themselves. They get tired of having no food at home and go off on their own. Many disappear. Some return, others don't.
                              —A discussion group of men and women
                                        from Moreno, Argentina

Children bear the brunt of their family's poverty and insecurity. Without the means to provide for their children, parents face agonizing choices over using extremely limited resources to somehow make life better for their children. Despite their efforts, many poor parents are unable to protect their children from the dangers that surround them in their communities, on the streets, and also in their homes.

Poor parents in every country expressed a range of worries and aspirations on behalf of their children. In Russia, where poverty is considered shameful, parents make tremendous sacrifices to give their children acceptable clothes and some spending money so they will not be ashamed in the company of friends. A woman from Ozerny, Russia, said, "Our only concern is for the kids to make it in life." A young person in Vares, Bosnia and Herzegovina, said, "We have no entertainment because we have no money. It is very sad that our parents don't have money to give us. It makes them sad and they say they would gladly give us money if they had any. I am afraid to have any hope."

"Even Children Sleep on Empty Stomachs on Most Days"

In every region of the world, children born to poor families get off to a rough start. A mother of seven in Nampeya, Malawi stated, "Whenever I have a child, the child is found to be malnourished. Some of my children suffer from malnutrition due to lack of food, as you can see. . . . He has many diseases because he lacks food." In Ecuador preschool children are at the highest risk of inadequate food consumption, with one-quarter of Ecuadorian children in this age group found to have stunted growth in 1998.

Hunger was reported to be relatively new to children in the countries of Eastern Europe and Central Asia. A former miner from Kok Yangak, Kyrgyz Republic, explained, "I've been working in this mine for twenty-seven years, and I had some property but sold it all when they stopped paying us. All we have in our house now are two beds with mattresses. My wife and son are hungry all the time." In Sarajevo, Bosnia and Herzegovina, a participant said, "Children are hungry, so they start to cry. They ask for food from their mother and their mother doesn't have it." In Bulgaria the Roma also said that their children are hungry.

With hunger and poverty comes illness. Mothers in Dzerzhinsk, Russia, said that poorly nourished children have suffered dizzy spells at school. Water pollution endangers children's health in very many communities visited for the study.

Poor Children's Poor Options

Poor parents believe that education can benefit their children, but they face many obstacles to sending and keeping children in school. In many instances, schools are of low quality or too distant to reach. A man from Achy, Kyrgyz Republic, said, "We have only a primary school. After the fourth grade, our children have to go to other schools. The schools are far away and there is no bus service, so the kids have to walk, and it's very difficult for them, especially in the winter, because it's cold."

Many families reported that school fees are unaffordable. Even in countries where primary education is free, there are still the costs of school clothes, supplies, and other expenses. "You might have to make your child go without supper for a month in order to have enough to buy him his school uniform," said a parent in La Matanza, Argentina.

Without education, poor villagers in Phwetekere, Malawi, fear being "condemned to poverty indefinitely." But there are many immediate pressures on poor parents to keep children out of school and put them to productive work for the household.

When money is scarce, girls in several countries are much less likely to receive schooling than boys. "The river must flow backwards before [girls] can go to school," is a common saying in Kawangu, Indonesia, although some girls in the village now attend school. In Africa and Asia, educated girls were said to be harder to marry. A women's group from Phwetekere in Malawi observed, "Free primary education in itself is not enough. The constraints for girls to persist in school are quite insurmountable." Poor girls in all regions face the added dangers of harassment and assaults on the streets.

In some cases, children work hard to pay for their own, often intermittent, education. In Elieke Rumuokoro, Nigeria, a 15-year-old girl had to drop out of school last year because her parents had difficulty paying her school fees and buying the recommended texts. She hawked oranges and performed other jobs to earn money to pay the fees in order to be readmitted this year. Similarly, many poor children in Nuevas Brisas, Ecuador, shine shoes for a living to pay for their education. A young man from Brazil commented on the tradeoff many children and young adults face: "You have to choose between working or studying because you can't do both. And if you choose to study, what are you going to eat?"

Child labor is common in almost every country. Children tend family plots and livestock and engage in petty trade, selling family crops and other products. Participants from several countries described children 7 and 8 years old who help their families survive by selling rice, salt, or ice water, or even by begging. In rural areas, children are involved in fishing, collecting cow dung, chipping bricks, and gathering twigs for fuel. Children work for others in factories or mines, in homes and on farms, earning very small wages or simply daily food rations. In Nurali Pur, Bangladesh, about half of the children 8 to 12 years old were reported to work for food as day laborers for wealthy families in nearby villages.

Drugs offer some children an enticing escape from their harsh daily realities. Drug abuse is recognized as a problem among some urban youth in Argentina, Brazil, Bulgaria, Ecuador, Jamaica, Malawi, Nigeria, and Russia. In Brazil poor children "use cheap chemicals like industrial glue" to get high. Participants frequently said that youths turn to gambling and crime as well as drugs because they are idle and don't have anything else to do. Dealing drugs is a lucrative way for poor children to earn money for themselves and their families, but the risks are high. In Entra a Pulso, Brazil, a participant said, "Youths start out selling drugs to help their parents support the family. Then they start using. They're curious about what rich people see in it. Before the parents realize it, the kid is trafficking or dead."

Dangers within the Family

Violence in the home was reported to be part of life, particularly in some of the urban communities of South America. Speaking of her children, a woman from Isla Trinitaria, Ecuador, said matter-of-factly, "Abuse is meant to get them to do something good in life. I do whip them so that they will shower or do their chores." Unfortunately, violence toward children in the home can go far beyond well-meaning reprimands.

Violence between adult partners also affects children. "Many children run away because they can't stand to watch the fighting. It frightens them to see the father beating the mother or the mother cheating on the father. They fall from life," said a woman from Borborema, Brazil. A woman in Malawi said she left home when she was 13 years old "to run away from the troubles I was facing." A large group of homeless children live in Bulgaria's Sofia railway station, and they told researchers that they fled their homes after their parents' divorce or abuse, often in the wake of unemployment. "It's my parents' fault—they're poor, too, and they abandoned me," said one youth. The Sofia street children said now they are attacked by skinheads and beaten up, or forced into prostitution by organized crime thugs.

Girls are particularly vulnerable to rape. "In some families you can see there is sexual abuse against the girls; they are beaten, marked, many times burned," said a woman from Isla Trinitaria, Ecuador. Many girls are forced to marry their attackers, as reported in Ghana and Bangladesh. Sometimes girls are held back from school "for their own safety." A man in Kawangu, Indonesia, explained, "We keep girls from school to protect them from being kidnapped by outsiders, as that will mean the family will lose the bride price the girl would have brought them."

Childhoods lived struggling against the pain of hunger, humiliation, and violence often turn into adulthoods spent in similar patterns of survival. Poor people understand how poverty conspires to trap their children. A mother in the village of At Bashi, Kyrgyz Republic, warned, "The children of the rich are going to be rich, too, and have good education, and the children of the poor will stay poor." In Vares, Bosnia, an adult stated, "Young people cannot survive here, not psychologically nor materially. This society kills you."

Addressing State Failure: An Empowering Approach to Development

In closing the final volume in the *Voices of the Poor* series, we want to focus on state failure to reduce poverty and human suffering in this age of plenty and of technological marvels. In this context, we define state failure as a failure to serve poor people. We focus on states rather than other development actors because governments set the essential policy environment that affects the speed and quality of development. Government policy shapes the actions of poor people, the private sector, NGOs, and donors.

A difficult lesson of development has been that it matters not only what actions are taken to reduce poverty, but also how these development decisions are made, acted upon, and evaluated. Therefore, the recommendations include some of the many measures available for promoting equal and effective relationships between poor people and the state. Fostering such partnership processes requires a dual focus on actions that, on the one hand, improve state capacity to grasp poor people's needs and the poverty impacts of public policies, and on the other hand, strengthen poor people's capacity to mobilize, articulate and defend their interests, and hold governments accountable.

The problem is poverty, not poor people. Those who care most about reducing poverty are poor people themselves. Hence, effective poverty reduction must tap into the motivation, desire, determination, imagination, knowledge, networks, and organizations of poor women, men, and children. Given the scale of the problem, any poverty reduction strategy must mobilize the energy of poor people to take effective action and make them essential partners in development.

The findings suggest five actions to reorient states to become more effective agents of poverty reduction:

1. promote pro-poor economic policies,
2. invest in poor people's assets and capabilities,

3. support partnerships with poor people,
4. address gender inequity and children's vulnerability, and
5. protect poor people's rights.

1. Promote Pro-poor Economic Policies

Economy-wide policies and market downturns can have sharply adverse effects on poor people's livelihoods, ability to purchase food, and access to basic services. In some places, the opening of domestic markets to international competition has forced small producers to compete with lower-priced foreign goods or has made key imported inputs unaffordable. In other places, people have found themselves pushed into the low end of the informal sector as policy and market changes have led to factory closures and the collapse of large farms and agro-industries.

Policy reform (including macroeconomic, trade, and regulatory policy) should be designed taking into account their expected impacts on different economic and social groups. It will also be important to monitor actual impacts of policy changes to inform the policy design process. Various tools, ranging from quantitative macro-micro–simulation models to qualitative and participatory approaches, can be used to analyze the poverty and social impacts of reform, depending on the circumstances. Moreover, initiatives to catalyze faster economic growth will likely be better crafted and enjoy wider support if they emerge from broad-based debate and reflection on economy-wide policy choices and constraints.

At the local level, poor people need greater livelihood opportunities and security so they can build their asset base and protect themselves from shocks. While improving agricultural productivity is key to faster rural development in some areas, agriculture alone will not provide sustainable livelihoods for all. Promoting economic policies that create urban and rural jobs for large numbers of poor people, most of whom have low levels of education, is a critical policy challenge. Investing in education and skills is obviously an important long-term strategy.

Policy decisions that support the domestic business environment for micro-, small, and medium enterprises should become a central focus of poverty reduction strategies. Millions of poor families depend upon self-employment and entrepreneurship. Yet creating a supportive environment for microbusiness—through actions affecting property rights, access to loans, requirements to register a business, information about markets, or technical improvements—is not yet a part of policy thinking in most places. Private sector development policies should be informed by firm surveys that cover micro- and small enterprises. In addition, building the capacity of producers organizations, such as farmers groups and street vendor associations, and the development of business clusters for small enterprises, should be explored and supported where appropriate.

As poor households diversify risk, one or more family members often move to urban areas or even overseas, and cycle in and out of their villages. This creates rural-urban linkages and networks not yet systematically considered in policy thinking. These rural-urban ties have the potential to create urban demand for goods produced at lower prices in rural areas. In rural areas, better links can help to diversify livelihoods, increase local purchasing power, and generate savings for investment back into agriculture. Infrastructure development should complement business development of local economies and urban-rural linkages to provide synergies for local area development.

2. Invest in Poor People's Assets and Capabilities

In addition to actions described above that help poor people accumulate material assets, measures are needed to give people some protection over the assets they already have, as well as to enhance their nonmaterial assets, which are less familiar in the development discourse. These nonmaterial assets are critical for increasing access to opportunities as well as for societal wellbeing. They give meaning to people's actions and lives.

Although every country in the study has some type of social assistance program to ease poor people's hardships, the coverage and quality of this assistance are problematic almost everywhere. Property rights and social protection measures that help poor people hang on to their assets, especially when crises strike, remain an urgent development challenge.

Poor people also need ways to protect their physical and mental health, such as through microinsurance schemes. Ensuring their physical safety at work and in their communities is also essential, and though poor people attempt to address some safety issues themselves, their calls for major police reform are widespread.

Economic growth depends on the productive actions of million of people. Frightened or alienated people do not contribute to economic prosperity or peaceful societies. In some contexts, social, ethnic, religious, and cultural barriers also pose important risks to communities. To build trust and social belonging in ways that are meaningful to excluded people, *how* development is managed is equally as important as *what* development occurs. Politicians, community leaders, teachers, and local officials are often on the frontlines of local discord or unrest, and need incentives, training, and resources to support social inclusion and respect for diversity.

Given that even most formal democratic systems do not represent poor people's interests, it is essential to deepen democracy through investment at the local level, particularly in poor people's organizations. Grassroots capacity to mobilize and take collective action is a critical asset in poor people's struggles to fight poverty. Organizations of poor people and civil society intermediaries that are accountable to poor people are essential for effective participation in local governance structures.

3. Support Partnerships with Poor People

There is increasing evidence that whether the issue is forestry, irrigation, rural roads, urban toilets, sewage, credit, or drinking water, poor people have proven themselves able partners who make wise decisions, and they protect their communal and private investments with care and vigilance that far surpasses that of any government agency.

The development challenge therefore is to ensure that actions to reduce poverty fully integrate processes that help poor people both assert and defend their interests. This often entails support for knowledgeable intermediaries to work with poor people and their organizations to mobilize and develop capacity for identifying and taking action on shared goals. These intermediaries can also help local groups network, negotiate, and influence events that affect their lives. Planners and implementation agencies should ensure poor people's access to information about their rights and new opportunities. Partner agencies also need to develop rules, incentives, and channels for working directly with local communities and their representatives. This usually includes investing in trained facilitators who are accountable to poor people.

There are no easy solutions for identifying local partnerships that do not reinforce existing hierarchies but rather build on the strength of local cultures to foster more inclusive development processes. Participatory processes can offer a way forward for navigating complex and changing local institutional landscapes, but even these tools will fail if vulnerable groups lack effective means to channel their aspirations and provide quick feedback when actions go awry. Rapid qualitative studies grounded in participatory techniques can foster shared learning among local people and agencies about leading risks and opportunities. They can also reveal the most trusted and effective local institutions for reducing these risks and helping poor people protect their assets and access new opportunities. In addition, traditional monitoring and evaluation systems to assess policy effects need to be complemented by site surveillance systems that provide governments prompt feedback from stakeholders. Poor people's feedback on government performance through participatory techniques and citizen report cards should be routinely collected and made available in the public domain. User assessments of the coverage and quality of their services can provide useful feedback to refine strategies.

Development interventions are especially unlikely to benefit poor and excluded groups in areas beset by deep social barriers and conflict, but these are often the poorest areas of a country and in greatest need of support. In these contexts, medium-term investments in networks across social divides and in conflict resolution and reconciliation are critical elements of an overall approach to development.

4. Address Gender Inequity and Children's Vulnerability

Gender-based barriers affect all aspects of poor women's lives and undermine their ability to improve their own and their families' wellbeing. The silence that surrounds domestic violence against women is not a private affair, but a matter of public policy. Victims need direct support and legal aid to protect them. State institutions need to formulate policies and investment decisions based on sound gender analysis. In almost every instance, there are important reasons to gather, analyze, and present both quantitative and qualitative poverty data disaggregated by gender.

Gender inequities take different forms across countries and across urban and rural regions within countries. Tailor-made strategies are needed to address the gender-based barriers confronted by poor women in their households, in the workplace, and in public affairs. Measures are also needed to reduce women's very heavy work burden and to help men and women adjust to changing roles as breadwinners and caretakers.

There is also an urgent agenda for reducing the extreme vulnerability of poor children. Inadequate supervision, street crime, drugs, and pollution pose widespread dangers for children and youths in urban areas. Perhaps the single most important public action in this respect is devising means for providing child and youth care and nutrition programs for poor families. In addition, poor households need scholarships to make it possible for poor girls and boys to stay in school rather than leave in order to contribute to family income.

5. Protect Poor People's Rights

Poor people are often acutely aware of their rights and violations of their rights concerning wages, jobs, contracts, firings, and benefits. In other areas, though, poor people often lack information about their rights. Even when they have this information, poor people know that, given their dependence on those with money and assets and their lack of access to justice, demanding rights will mark them as troublemakers and can even endanger their lives and the lives of their families. Lack of options and lack of organization render poor people powerless.

The importance of a culture of rights and obligations was expressed well by 21-year-old Fernando, who grew up in the *favela* of Sacadura Cabral in Brazil surrounded by crime, drugs, and abuse of power. His sister was raped and killed when she was four, and his mother lives alone in order to protect herself and her remaining children from potential harm at the hands of boyfriends. Fernando dreams of becoming a judge someday. He aspires to study law in order to empower himself and raise consciousness throughout his community. In his view, education and awareness of rights are vital to the future of the *favela*. He said, "In a *favela* people have no idea of their rights. We have police discrimination; the policemen abuse us, and others use their knowledge to take advantage of us. So I want to know all about rights and obligations."

Many, like Fernando, remain hopeful; they have not given up the will to live, to try one more time. Others express resentment, alienation, and anger. Inequalities matter greatly: the wider the gap, the harder it is to hold on to hope. In Teikovo, Russia, people said, "Before we all lived alike, now there's a borderline between people." In Novy Gorodok people acknowledged that with the decline in general wellbeing, "people have become more spiteful, aggressive, and irritated. It's not because of envy; it's because we have impotent anger and nobody to vent it on." Those who have been plunged into poverty overnight because of the dismantling of political and economic systems experience the most acute hopelessness, even years later. It is when people give up hope that there can be no turning around. It is when the young give up hope that there is no future. A young girl in Bosnia cried, *Hope dies last, but for me, even hope has died.*

State action largely determines whether poor people in a country feel hope or feel abandoned. State policies determine the role that poor people and their organizations, the private sector, and NGOs can play in poverty reduction. Poor people's voices and experiences point out some clear directions and strategies. However, solutions have to be locally owned and adapted. The question raised by the voices of poor women, men, and children is the central question facing us all: How can societies be transformed so poor people feel empowered to create lives of dignity, security, and wellbeing?

Notes

1. "Bodily integrity" is a term used by Martha Nussbaum. See "Capabilities, Human Rights, and the Universal Declaration," in Weston and Marks, *The Future of International Human Rights*, Transnational Publishers, 1999.

2. The relationship between healthy bodies and wellbeing emerges with such frequency that we have prepared a policy note with the World Health Organization, titled *Dying for Change*, to be published in early 2002.

3. Increased vulnerability may not be captured by consumption expenditure surveys until it drops below the set poverty line. However, it is documented in studies using other measures of wellbeing, including nutritional status and school attendance.

4. This finding is based on a content analysis of 147 life stories documented during the fieldwork. See pages 64 to 68 of *Crying Out for Change* for a review of the many other factors that poor people indicated as contributing to their upward mobility.

Appendix 1

Development Indicators for Fourteen Country Case Studies

Growth, Poverty, and Inequality

Country	Gross domestic product (average annual % growth)[1]		Average annual population growth rate (%)[1]	Population (millions)[1]	Population below the national poverty line[2,a]				Inequality: Gini index[1,b,c]	
	1980-89	1990-99	1980-99	1999	Survey year	%	Survey year	%	Survey year	%
Ghana	3.0	4.3	2.9	19	1991-92	51.7	1998	39.5	1998	39.6
Malawi	2.5	3.6	2.9	11	..	..	1998	65.3	1998	40.1[2]
Nigeria	1.6	2.4	2.9	124	1985	46.3	1996	65.6	1996	50.6
Bangladesh	4.3	4.7	2.0	128	1988-89	57.1	1995-96	53.1	1995-96	33.6
India	5.8	6.0	2.0	998	1987-88	38.9	1993-94	36.1	1993-94	31.5[3]
Indonesia	6.1	4.7	1.8	207	1995	11.4	1999	27.1	1999	31.7
Bosnia and Herzegovina	..	..	-0.3	4	..	..	..	..	..	..
Bulgaria	3.4	-2.7	-0.4	8	..	..	1995	18.2[d]	1995	27.0[2]
Kyrgyz Republic	..	-5.4	1.5	5	1996	43.5	1999	53.3	1999	37.2[2]
Russian Federation	..	-6.1	0.3	146	1991	11.7	1998	23.8	1998	48.7
Argentina[e]	-0.7	4.9	1.4	37	1990	41.4	1998	29.4	1998	49.0[2]
Brazil	2.7	3.0	1.7	168	1993	34.2	1998	22.0	1998	58.4[4]
Ecuador	2.0	2.2	2.3	12	1995	34.0	1998	46.0	1998	58.0[2]
Jamaica	2.0	0.3	1.0	3	1990	28.4	1999	16.9	1999	37.9[2]

Sources: [1] World Bank, *World Development Indicators 2001* (unless otherwise indicated) table 4.1, 194–196; table 2.1, 44–46; table 2.8, 70–72.

[2] Argentina: "Poor People in a Rich Country," vol. 1 (World Bank, Poverty Reduction and Economic Management, Latin America and Caribbean Region, Report 19992–AR, 2000), 3; Bangladesh: "Bangladesh: From Counting the Poor to Making the Poor Count," vol. 1 (World Bank, Poverty Reduction and Economic Management, South Asia Region, Report 17534–BD, 1998), 6; Bulgaria: *Making Transition Work for Everyone: Poverty and Inequality in Europe and Central Asia*, (World Bank, 2000), 35; Brazil: "Attacking Brazil's Poverty," vol. 1 Summary Report (World Bank, Brazil Country Management Unit, Poverty Reduction and Economic Management, Latin America and the Caribbean Region, Report 20475–BR, 2001), 3; Ecuador: "Ecuador: Crisis, Poverty and Social Services" (World Bank, Human Development Department, Latin America and the Caribbean Region, Report 19920–EC, 2000), 5; Ghana: "Poverty Trends in Ghana in the 1990s" (Ghana Statistical Office, October 2000), 8; India: Government of India estimate; Indonesia: "Poverty Reduction in Indonesia: Constructing a New Strategy" (World Bank, Environment and Social Development Sector Unit, East Asia and Pacific Region, Report 23028–IND, 2001), 6; Jamaica: "Jamaica Survey of Living Conditions 1999" (The Planning Institute and the Statistical Institute of Jamaica, August 2000), 5; Kyrgyz Republic: "The Kyrgyz Republic Interim National Strategy for Poverty Reduction 2001–2003 and Joint IDA/IMF Staff Assessment" (World Bank, Central Asia Country Unit, Europe and Central Asia Region, Report 22327, 2001), 5; Malawi: "Profile of Poverty in Malawi; 1998" (National Economic Council, Government of Malawi, November 2000, revised), 43; Nigeria: "Nigeria's Poverty: Past, Present and Future" (World Bank, Nigeria Country Department, 2000), 3; Russia: Roskomstat official poverty incidence in *Making Transition Work for Everyone: Poverty and Inequality in Europe and Central Asia* (World Bank, 2000), 38.

[3] "Global Poverty Monitoring, India," www.worldbank.org/research/povmonitor/countrydetails/India.htm (2001).

[4] Brazilian Institute of Geography and Statistics (IBGE), http://www.ibge.gov.br/english/estatistica/populacao/trabalhoerendimento/pnad99/sintese/tab7_1_11.shtm (2001)

Note: ".." means that data are not available or that aggregates cannot be calculated because of missing data in the years shown.

[a] These figures cannot be used to make comparisons between countries, as different countries have different definitions of poverty.

[b] The Gini index measures the extent to which distribution of income (or consumption expenditure) among households within an economy deviates from a perfectly equal distribution. A Gini index of zero represents perfect equality, while an index of 100 implies perfect inequality (one person having all the income). Because the underlying household surveys differ in method and the type of data collected, Gini indexes are not strictly comparable across countries.

[c] Refers to expenditure shares by percentile of population, unless otherwise noted.

[d] Poverty headcount based on the international poverty line of $4.30 per person per day. The population living below the international poverty line of $2.15/day was 3.1 percent in 1995.

[e] Population below the poverty line and Gini index refer to urban areas only.

[f] Refers to income shares by percentile of population.

Trends in Social Indicators

Country	Life expectancy at birth, total (years)		Infant mortality (per 1,000 live births)		Illiteracy rate, female youth (% of females ages 15–24)		Illiteracy rate, male youth (% of males ages 15–24)	
	1980	*1999*	*1980*	*1999*	*1980*	*1999*	*1980*	*1999*
Ghana	53	58	94	57	46	13	21	7
Malawi	44	39	169	132	60	40	29	20
Nigeria	46	47	99	83	58	18	32	11
Sub-Saharan Africa	**48**	**47**	**114**	**92**	**56**	**27**	**34**	**18**
Bangladesh	48	61	132	61	74	61	52	40
India	54	63	115	71	58	36	33	21
South Asia	**54**	**63**	**119**	**74**	**62**	**41**	**36**	**23**
Indonesia	55	66	90	42	15	3	7	2
East Asia & Pacific	**65**	**69**	**55**	**35**	**15**	**4**	**5**	**2**
Bosnia and Herzegovina	70	73	31	13	..	..	..	..
Bulgaria	71	71	20	14	1	1	1	0
Kyrgyz Republic	65	67	43	26	..	..	..	..
Russian Federation	67	66	22	16	0	0	0	0
Europe & Central Asia	**68**	**69**	**41**	**21**	**4**	**2**	**1**	**1**
Argentina	70	74	35	18	3	1	3	2
Brazil	63	67	70	32	12	6	14	10
Ecuador	63	69	74	28	9	4	6	3
Jamaica	71	75	33	20	8	3	17	10
Latin America & Caribbean	**65**	**70**	**61**	**30**	**11**	**6**	**10**	**6**

Low & middle income[a]	60	64	86	59	31	19	17	11
High income[b]	74	78	12	6	..	..	..	..

Note: ".." means that data are not available or that aggregates cannot be calculated because of missing data in the years shown.

[a]Low-income economies are those with a GNI per capita of $755 or less in 1999. Middle-income economies are those with a GNI per capita of more than $755 but less than $9,266. All the countries presented in this table are classified as either low or middle-income economies.

[b]High-income economies are those with a GNI per capita of $9,266 or more in 1999.

Source: World Bank, *World Development Indicators 2001.*

Appendix 2

Country Currencies and the 1999 Exchange Rate

Country	Currency	Exchange rate to USD in 1999
Argentina	Argentinian Peso	1.000
Bangladesh	Taka	49.09
Bosnia and Herzegovina	Convertible Mark	1.83
Brazil	Brazilian Real	1.81
Bulgaria	Lev	1.836
Ecuador	Sucre	11,786.8
Ghana	Cedi	2,647.3
India	Indian Rupee	43.06
Indonesia	Rupiah	7,855.2
Jamaica	Jamaican Dollar	39.04
Kyrgyz Republic	Kyrgyzstani Som	39.0
Malawi	Malawian Kwacha	44.09
Nigeria	Naira	92.34
Russia	Ruble	24.62

Source: The Economist Intelligence Unit

Appendix 3

Overview of Study Themes and Methods

The study is organized around four primary themes: wellbeing, problems and priorities, institutional analysis, and gender relations. A brief explanation of each theme is followed by fieldwork methods and a checklist of study issues to be explored. This overview is based on the *Methodology Guide* used by local researchers. The full document is available on the *Voices of the Poor* Web site at http://www.world-bank.org/poverty/voices.

1.   Exploring Wellbeing

Methods: small group discussions, ranking, scoring, cause-impact analysis, trend analysis, and in-depth interviews with individuals or households.

1.1 How do people define wellbeing, or good quality of life, and illbeing, or bad quality of life?
Checklist of issues to be explored:

- Discuss local definitions of wellbeing, deprivation, illbeing, vulnerability, and poverty. Since these terms do not always translate easily in local languages, it is better to start by asking the local people for their own terminology and definitions that explain quality of life. *Local terminology and definitions must be included in the analysis.* Different groups within the same community could be using different terms or phrases for the same subject. All of these need to be recorded.

- Develop a list of criteria on the basis of which households or individuals are differentiated and categorized.
- Identify different wellbeing categories of households or individuals, as identified by the local people. Allow the community to come up with their own categories. Do not impose ideas. There is no fixed number of categories that a community can come up with. Usually these vary from three to six categories, but there could be more. Characteristics (or criteria) of households or individuals in each of these categories should be clearly recorded.
- Calculate the number or percentage of households or individuals in each category of wellbeing or illbeing. This could be presented in terms of exact numbers or indicative scores. This will give an idea about the problem of poor or deprived people in a community.

1.2 How do people perceive security, risk, vulnerability, opportunities, social exclusion, and crime and conflict? How have these changed over time?

After discussing people's definition of wellbeing and poverty/illbeing, explore the following themes:

Risk, security and vulnerability
- Does security or insecurity figure in people's definitions of wellbeing?
- How do people define security?
- Are some households secure and others insecure? How do people differentiate between the two?
- What makes households insecure or at greater risk?
- Has insecurity increased or decreased over a given period of time? Why?
- What are the main kinds of shocks that people have faced?
- Are some individuals/households more insecure than others in the same community?
- Are some people better able to cope with sudden shocks to their sources of livelihood? Why and how?

Opportunities, social and economic mobility

- Do people feel that opportunities for economic and social mobility have increased? Decreased? Why and for whom?
- What are the consequences of these changes?
- Who or which group(s) has benefited the most? Which groups have been unable to take advantage of opportunities or have been negatively affected? Why?
- Is it possible for people to move out of poverty?
- What is needed to enable people to move out of poverty?
- What needs to change for the poor to have greater economic and social opportunities? Is this likely?

Social exclusion

- Are some people or groups *left out* of society, looked down upon, or excluded from active participation in community life or decision making?
- Who gets left out, and on what basis? Why?
- What is the impact of such exclusion or being left out?
- Is it possible for those excluded to ever become included?
- What determines the likelihood of this change?
- What are the differences in power between those included and excluded?
- What makes some people powerful and others not?

Social cohesion, crime, conflict

- How do people define social cohesion?
- Is there more or less social unity and sense of belonging than before? Why?
- Is there more or less crime and conflict than in the past, or has it stayed the same? Why?
- Are there conflicts between groups in the community? Which groups? Why?
- Have intergroup conflicts increased or decreased? Why? How?
- Does anyone benefit from the increased violence? Can the situation be changed? How?

1.3 How do households and individuals cope with decline in wellbeing and how do these coping strategies in turn affect their lives?

Researchers should explore the following questions:

- Have there been any changes in the number and types of wellbeing categories, and has the proportion of people/households in each category increased or decreased over the last ten years?
- Have the criteria for determining the categories changed over the years?
- What has changed? What caused the changes? How are these changes reflected in the lives of the people? Have people become better or worse off? Is there a "typology of deprivation"—sudden, seasonal, structural, cyclic, chronic?
- How have people coped with these changes?
- Are there any foreseeable changes in the future? What and how?

1.4 Individual case studies.

Researchers should conduct in-depth discussions/interviews with:

- A poor woman
- A poor man
- A woman or man who has fallen into poverty
- A woman or man who used to be poor but has moved out of poverty

2. Problems and Priorities

Methods: small group discussions, ranking, scoring, listing, trend analysis.

2.1 List the problems faced by different groups within the community and rank them in terms of priority.

2.2 Are there differences in the problems and priorities experienced by different groups of people within the community (according to age, gender, social hierarchy, and economic wellbeing)? Identify the problems faced by poor people.

2.3 Have these problems changed over the years or have they remained the same? What are poor people's hopes and fears (visions) for the future?

2.4 Which of these problems do poor people think they can solve themselves and which will require external support?

3. Institutional Analysis

Methods: small group discussions, listing, scoring, ranking, and two mini-institutional profiles.

3.1 Which institutions are important in poor people's lives?

- What are the most important formal, informal, government, nongovernment, and market institutions within or outside the community that affect poor people's lives positively or negatively? Why are these judged to be important? Are there any gender differences in the lists of important institutions?
- Which government institutions and NGOs have the most positive or negative impacts on men and women? Why? Give examples of poor people's experiences. Are there any gender differences?

3.2 How do people rate these institutions?

- How do poor people rate these institutions in terms of the trust and confidence that they place in them? Why? Give examples of why people rate particular institutions high or low, and discuss any gender differences in the ratings.
- How do poor people rate the effectiveness of these institutions? What factors do they consider in judging effectiveness? Give examples of these factors, and explain any gender differences in the ratings.

3.3 Do poor people feel that they have any control or influence over these institutions?

- Which institutions do poor people think they have some influence over?
- Which institutions would they like to have more control and influence over?
- Do some people/groups have some influence over these institutions while others are left out? Who is left out?
- Profile two institutions in depth.

3.4 How do poor people cope with crisis? What formal and informal safety nets are available?

- How do poor people cope during financial/economic crises (due to, for example, loss of property, jobs, or livelihood; crop failure; environmental crisis; or poor health or death)? In what specific ways do these crises affect their lives?
- What institutions, formal or informal, do poor people turn to in times of financial crisis?
- Do they mention any government programs? Give details.
- Are government programs reaching them?
- What are their recommendations for change, improvements, or for new programs if none exist?
- What features should new programs have?
- Do poor people mention any NGO programs?
- Do they mention any informal social networks?

- Are there any gender differences in coping methods and recommendations for change?
- If the community as a whole is affected by some event (such as flood, drought, or earthquake), how does it cope?

4. Gender Relations

Methods: small group discussions, scoring, and trend analysis.

4.1 Are poor women better off today as compared to the past?

- Are there any changes in the following areas? If so, why?
  – Women's and men's responsibilities within the household
  – Women's and men's responsibilities in the community
  – Women's and men's roles in the decision-making process within the household
  – Women's and men's roles in the decision-making process in the community
  – Violence against women within the household
  – Violence against women within the community
- Do women feel they have more or less power today (however they define it)? Why or why not?

4.2 Are there differences in gender relations among different groups within the community?

- Are some women better off (however they define it) than other women in the same community?
- Are changes in gender relations experienced differently by different groups of women in the community?